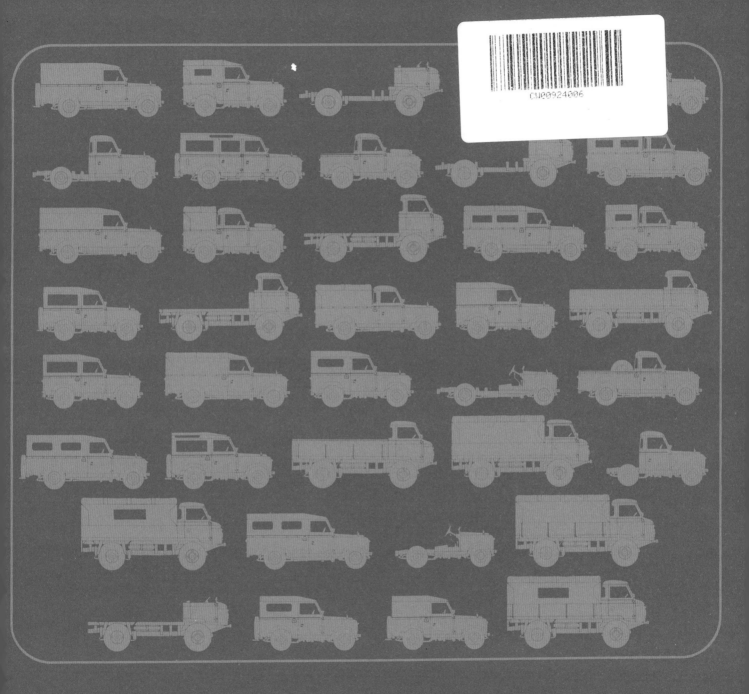

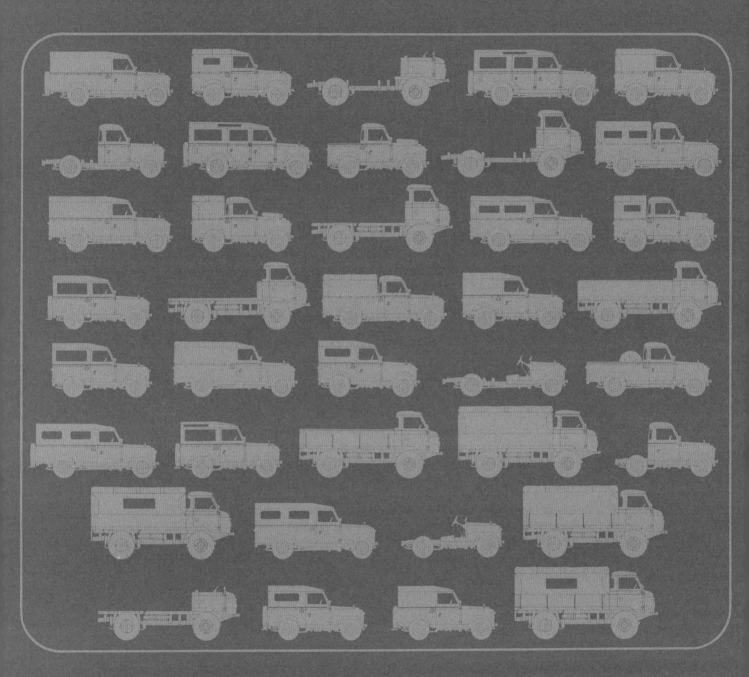

The Land Rover File

An Eric Dymock Motor Book

The Land Rover File

All Models Since 1947

An Eric Dymock Motor Book

Dove Publishing Ltd

First published in Great Britain in 2006 by
DOVE PUBLISHING LTD
31 Argyle Terrace, Rothesay, Isle of Bute, PA20 OBD

Text copyright © Dove Publishing Ltd 2006

Designed by Janet McCallum

British Library Cataloguing-in-Publication Data
A catalogue record for this book is available from the British Library

ISBN 0-9534142-8-0

Printed in China by 1010 Printing International Limited

Contents

Foreword

A line in the sand on an Anglesey beach began the design phase of the first Land Rover. Technical director Maurice Wilks had been so impressed with a utilitarian ex-military 4x4 used at his holiday home that he decided Rover Cars should make one of its own. We break new ground with the seventh in the series of Dove Publishing's File Books. The format is bigger; there is more text, and a longer history section than other File Books as well as a comprehensive and independent report of the company's past and current activities.

Editorial Director Eric Dymock was delighted to accept the challenge of charting all Land Rovers from 1947 in one volume. We have almost lost count of the books that have been published on Land Rover in 60 years, but none has attempted to detail all five separate strands of Land Rover, year by year with specifications and photographs, in one comprehensive work. Here is a guide to special-purpose Land Rovers, Land Rovers built overseas, and every production model. Information has been accessed from museums and collections, the publisher's own sources, and from Land Rover's archives. Many of the photographs have not been seen before in what we hope will be the definitive guidebook to Land Rover's heritage.

Mike Roberts
Publishing Director, Dove Publishing Ltd

History of a Legend

Rover technical director Maurice
Wilks tested early Land Rovers at his
Anglesey holiday home. Legend has
it that he designed the first Land
Rover by sketching the outline in the
sand on this beach. Picture taken
from holiday film footage, probably
shot around 1948.

1936–1939 Manufacturer since 1904 of One of Britain's Fine Cars, Rover together with other Midlands motor manufacturers with the exception for a time of Nuffield, became involved with what was known as the shadow factory scheme. Britain was rearming, creating factories not only widely dispersed in case of air attack, but also capable of dealing with sudden demands of the military in the event of war. Shadow factories were not secret. The government expected them to have a deterrent effect on aggressors. Unfortunately they did not, the Munich Crisis of 1938 came and went, buying the country a little more time to make ready, and on 27 April 1939 the Rover board minuted: "Mr Wilks (the managing director) reported that discussions had taken place with leading officials of the Air Ministry, and suggestions made by the Ministry that we should undertake the erection, equipment, and management of a factory for the manufacture of aeroplane engines. He pointed out that in the event of war this scheme would mean the stoppage of manufacture of motor cars by us." Rover had plants round Coventry and Birmingham, and the Air Ministry wanted it to run a new one at nearby Acocks Green. Rover was not to risk capital; the government was erecting the factory, equipping it, stocking it, and even providing the workforce. In July 1937 Rover began making aero engine components, then on the brink of war it was asked to manage a second, much bigger site at Lode Lane, on the northern edge of the Urban

The Lode Lane site as it was in 1940. Built just outside Solihull, it was one of the Government's shadow factories, designed to deter German aggression.

History of a Legend

District of Solihull, south west of Elmdon Airport. A few miles from Acocks Green and three times the size, employing 7,000, it was to build Bristol Hercules 14-cylinder air-cooled sleeve valve radial engines for the Royal Air Force's new heavy bomber. Four of the 1700bhp (1267.7kW) 2360cu in (38.68litre) engines were to be used in the Short Stirling, prototypes of which were flying in May 1939 and which was to be assembled at the Austin works in Longbridge. Hercules engines were made in association with the Rootes Group at Ryton-on-Dunsmore, in a factory that had machine shops, assembly lines and test houses. Building work started in June 1939 and was completed by September 1940. Rover wisely bought up 200 acres of surrounding agricultural land.

1940 The first Solihull-built production Hercules engines were tested in October, and other Rover plants also produced Bristol aero engine components. On the night of 14 November, apparently in response to an RAF raid on Munich, the German Luftwaffe attacked Coventry. Radio guidance systems provided the bombers with unusual accuracy, and most of the city centre was destroyed, including the Rover car works in Helen Street. The board was told: "Our Coventry works have been severely damaged. It has been necessary to transfer the offices, and these are now being located in that portion of the Chesford Grange Hotel, which is available."

Detailed model built by Rover of the Lode Lane site, in full wartime camouflage. It housed 7,000 workers employed initially to produce engines for the RAF's heavy bombers.

1941–1945 Rover worked with Frank (later Sir Frank) Whittle's Lutterworth Power Jets company, in the development and production of jet gas turbine aircraft engines. Power Jets' production facility at Whetstone was small, so Rover was commissioned to develop the Whittle engine for production, and manufacture. The plan was for Gloster Aircraft, with whom Rover was already working on Armstrong-Whitworth Albemarle (another Bristol Hercules aircraft) airframes, to build the aircraft. Whittle proved problematical but Rover's role was momentous, engaging its engineers in advanced technology, which they were able to exploit long after direct connections with aircraft had ceased. The principles of gas turbines were well known, but because of the extreme temperatures and pressures they created, manufacture was regarded as almost impossible. Their attraction lay in the limitations of propeller-driven aircraft above 450mph (722.4kph). Whittle formed Power Jets Ltd in 1936, tried to interest Armstrong-Siddeley but met with scepticism, and it was not until BTH (British Thomson-Houston) agreed to produce his drawings for the Whittle Unit (WU) 1, that he made progress. The resulting experimental power unit still made formidable demands on the available metallurgy. Heat and stress in the combustion chambers were twenty-five times what existing materials could cope with, yet an engine was built, and ran on 12 April 1937.

Despite his first engine running out of control and threatening to blow the test house to pieces, Whittle persevered, and in December 1940 the Air Ministry paid for an improved W.1X. This was followed by a contract for a practical flight engine, the W.1, which first ran in April 1941, and flew in the Gloster E28/39 aircraft from Cranwell on 15 May, with 850lb (385.6kg) of thrust at 16,500rpm.

The engine weighed 623lb (282.6kg), and the aircraft's maximum speed was about 338mph (543kph) in level flight. Demand for production remained urgent, and led to Rover making some of the world's first aircraft jet engines. By late 1941 Rover, BTH, and Power Jets were building versions of the W.2 Mark 4 and the W.2B. A second Gloster aircraft, with a production Rover W.2B, inadvertently exceeded maximum revs, and attained an astonishing 466mph (748.1kph) probably the fastest speed of any aircraft up to that time. Had it not been for the war a Rover engine might have gained the world's absolute speed record.

Complications with Whittle continued. The Wilks brothers and Rover engineer Adrian Lombard, later Rolls-Royce aero engines' director of engineering, contributed more to the development of the engine than Whittle gave them credit for. However the brittle relationship ruined any hope of Rover manufacturing jet engines. The inventor blamed Rover for delays, claiming it had failed to keep to its agreement not to re-design anything. Rover asserted that Whittle was obstructive, and promptly re-designed the W.2B into the W.2B/26, with straight through instead of reversed combustion chambers. The leading Rover engineers on the project were sworn to secrecy, literally over a Bible, and segregated in a private area converted from the directors' dining room at the old Helen Street factory. A guard was posted on the door, and only people directly connected were allowed in, even though most of the engineering work on the turbines continued at Lode Lane.

Matters came to a head in November 1942, when Rolls-Royce engineer SG Hooker persuaded Lord Hives to intervene. Rolls-Royce was concerned at the difficulties between Whittle and Rover, which threatened to keep British jet aircraft out of the war. It was worried about equipping the

Royal Air Force with the best aircraft, although it was certainly eager not to be left out of new aero engine development. Rolls-Royce was committed to piston engines. Its work on turbo fans and turbo props in its Derby experimental shops had been disappointing.

Hives was keen to gain a share of the jet work, and set up a staff at Derby to build a W.1. Rolls-Royce got on better with Whittle, and when Hives and Hooker met managing director Spencer Wilks, for a wartime dinner at the Swan & Royal in Clitheroe, Hives suggested that jet engines were not in Rover's line. Wilks agreed that he would be relieved to be rid of them. Hives' response was, "You give us this jet job and I'll give you our tank engine factory in Nottingham."

From 1 January 1943, Hooker became chief engineer at the former cotton mill at Barnoldswick near Skipton, where Rolls-Royce planned W.2B production, and henceforth it became Rolls-Royce's jet engine development centre. The pace quickened and jets went into service with the Royal Air Force. A Rolls-Royce B.23 engine flew in the F9/40 Meteor on 12 June 1943, and a batch of 100 engines was delivered as the Welland 1, going into action against V1 flying bombs in August 1944.

Accordingly Rover's place in the development of one of the Twentieth Century's most demanding technologies was established, although it never again involved itself with aircraft jet engines. The tank engine, a version of the V12 Merlin was made at Solihull, and it was called the Meteor in honour of a name associated with Rover since 1888, when the Starley and Sutton tricycle was made at the Meteor Works in West Orchard Street. Rover's dalliance with the gas turbine engine continued with experimental gas turbine cars in the 1950s, and later Rover managing director William Martin-Hurst revived interest with the gas turbine Rover-BRM

racing at Le Mans in 1963 and 1965. A gas turbine Land Rover was built, and when Rover merged with truck maker Leyland, the technology was applied to a heavy prime mover. Rover-designed gas turbines were used as auxiliary power units (APUs) in Nimrod maritime reconnaissance aircraft and Vulcan bombers but so far as passenger cars were concerned gas turbines remained uncompetitive.

Heavily engaged in war production, by 1944 Rover had 24,000 employees in 18 factories, including an underground machining facility at Drakelow near Kidderminster. By 1945 it had made some 57,400 Hercules engines.

Rover's managing director Spencer Wilks. In 1941 he extricated Rover from its troubled partnership with Sir Frank Whittle.

Spencer's brother Maurice Wilks was Rover's technical director. He was so impressed by an ex-US Army Jeep that he created the Land Rover.

1945-1946 As soon as the war was over, Rover turned the Solihull shadow factory over to car production. The first post-war saloons came off the production line in December 1946 but to repay war debts, the government imposed strict controls on manufacturing. These included rationing steel according to success in export markets, particularly North America. Rover's first post-war new car project was the M-type or M1, a small 2-seat coupe powered by a 57mm x 68.5mm 4-cylinder 699cc 28bhp (21kW) engine with overhead inlet and side exhaust valves. Spencer Wilks, managing director since 1933, "strongly advised" the board in January 1945, "that we should aim to expand our output, and that to achieve this we should not look primarily to our pre-war models, but that we should add to our range by the introduction of a 6HP model." One anomaly of the scarcity in materials and resources was that although steel was in short supply, aluminium remained relatively plentiful, so when the M1 design was begun, using lots of aluminium seemed a good idea. It was thought that Solihull might make 15,000 full-sized cars and a further 5,000 M-types, so work began on an aluminium chassis with a strong box-shaped scuttle, for a car with a 77in (195.6cm) wheelbase and only 160in (406.4cm) long. Three prototypes were built, and ran before the end of 1946, well-proportioned coupes with a distinctive Rover style. By 1947, when changes in car taxation and government pressure to adopt a one-model policy conspired against it, the M-type seemed unlikely to be sold in sufficient numbers to fill the vast factory space acquired during the war. When it was abandoned, it left a gap in Rover's future model strategy.

The first peacetime project for Rover was the Fiat 500 inspired M-Type or M1. Envisaged as a small family car with a 699cc engine, aluminium was used for the chassis because of steel shortages, and three prototypes were built in 1946 before the project was finally abandoned.

1947 Rover technical director Maurice Fernand Carey Wilks, Spencer's younger brother, was impressed by a war-surplus Jeep he used at his holiday cottage in Anglesey, and for ground clearance at his home Blackdown Manor near Leamington Spa. A notable vehicle of the Second World War, the Jeep had been the result of United States Army Quartermaster Corps General EB Gregory's specification for a quarter-ton combat truck, with four wheel drive capable of carrying three men and a .30 calibre machine gun. It had to bear a 600lb (272kg) payload and weigh no more than 1300lb (590kg). All but a handful of the 135 American car manufacturers approached decided it was impossible. The

deadline was critical. It left no time for elaborate engineering, only two of them had any hope of meeting it, the near bankrupt American Bantam Company of Butler, Pa. that had made Austin Sevens under licence, and Willys-Overland of Toledo, Ohio.

Over three days in July 1940 engineer Karl Probst, who owing to Bantam's precarious finances did not know if he would be paid for the work, designed a light truck with a wheelbase of 80in (203.2cm), a track of 47in (119.4cm), and light enough to be manhandled. The specification stipulated an incline approach angle (the slope it could climb without fouling) of 45 degrees, and a departure angle (a bank it could descend) of 35 degrees, together with the ability to wade

The ex-US Army Jeep that Maurice Wilks used as a family runaround. It was only when it finally wore out that, convinced there would be a demand for a four wheel drive agricultural truck in the export market, he convinced the board to agree to research the project.

through water 18in (45.7cm) deep. A prototype had to be available in 49 days. Bantam managed it and Willys did not, but the small Bantam firm did not have the production capacity the army needed, so Willys was instructed to get on with development.

Bantam's engine had been rather feeble, and one reason Willys received the go-ahead was its engine, based on a 1927 Overland-Whippet side-valve 4-cylinder that had provided a meek 30bhp (22.4kW). It had been developed by Delmar G "Barney" Roos, who raised the compression ratio from 5.7 to 6.48:1, fitted aluminium pistons instead of cast iron, Cleveland graphite bearings and manganese valve springs, and a counterweighted crankshaft. This raised the power to 60bhp (44.7kW) @ 4000rpm and torque to 100lbft (134Nm) @ 2000rpm. To demonstrate the reliability of his amended engine Roos ran test examples flat out at 4400rpm

A Willys Quad – only two prototypes were built. It was the Willys design proposal for the Jeep, and lost out to Bantam's design, which Willys built.

continuously for 100 hours, proudly calling it the Go-Devil. The resulting Willys Model MB went into production, served on every battlefront with almost every Allied army; even the Wehrmacht cherished captured Jeeps. The lusty Go-Devil 2.2-litre produced sufficient power for nearly 60mph (96.3kph), and provided vigorous performance across rough country. Willys made 362,841 of them, and Ford joined in the programme to make another 281,446 calling it the GPW, identical save for the front chassis cross-member being an inverted U-section, not tubular. The Jeep was the archetype for millions of 4x4 utility and sports utility vehicles (SUVs) for the leisure and recreation markets that were to follow in the years to come.

Maurice Wilks in post war Britain meantime detected a strong demand for ex-army Jeeps. He was also aware of the success Standard Motor Company of Banner Lane, Coventry, was achieving with Ferguson lightweight tractors in export markets. Astute following a lifetime's experience in the motor industry he felt sure a small agricultural truck had potential. When his Jeep wore out, and with no replacement available, Maurice with the approval of his brother, conceived something that would not only provide transport, but also do jobs on the farm like hauling logs, pulling a plough, and acting as a power source for machinery. Together they decided Rover should make a Jeep-style vehicle as a temporary measure to augment car production. The company had official licence under government rationing to make no more than 1100 cars, so once the M-type proved a non-starter something else had to be found to keep the factory going. They examined the possibilities of an ex-WD half-track Ford, with a big side-valve V8, but decided against it.

In September 1947: "The board considered the position, and also the numerous product lines which had been under discussion, since car manufacturing had recommenced. Mr Wilks said that he was of the opinion that an all-purpose vehicle on the lines of the Willys-Overland Jeep was the most desirable. Considerable research had been carried out on this vehicle by our development department." It was agreed that this should be sanctioned; Maurice Wilks set up a design team, one of whom, Gordon Bashford was sent off to an ex-WD surplus vehicle dump in the Cotswolds to buy two Jeeps.

The first prototype was built before a Rover-made chassis was available, so it used one of the Jeep frames with a Rover rear axle and springs, and a rather timid 48bhp (35.8kW)

1,389cc Rover 10 engine. The production run was to be short, so the design had to be plain, and next to nothing was to be spent on tooling. The effect of the truncated design phase, as with the US Jeep, was to impose utter simplicity. The Land-Rover, as Wilks began calling it with a hyphen, had to be simple in plan and simple to make. In the event it was also simple to service, simple to repair, and strong. Its straight body panels were made from locally supplied aluminium under the trade name Birmabright, with gussets and brackets of galvanised steel. A chassis fabricated from off-cuts avoided using rationed steel sheet, and there was no need for expensive press tools. The Land-Rover hyphen continued in use up to 1978, was gone by 1980, and Land Rover prospered without it.

The designers employed a production saloon gearbox, even the steering wheel was a standard Rover spring-spoke, and almost the only new item was a transfer box to take the drive

Early Land Rover prototype fitted with centre-steer, showing its agricultural abilities on farmland, probably near the Lode Lane factory. Agricultural vehicles were exempt from purchase tax.

The centre-steer prototype under
construction in the Lode Lane jig
shop in 1947.

to the front wheels. Both axles were broadly similar which was a useful economy. The transfer box had two ranges, allowing the driver to select four high gears for driving on main roads, and four low ones for haulage off-road. The simple body was not only easy to make, but also easy to repair in the rough and tumble conditions Land Rovers were expected to endure. The first prototype had no doors, once again in the style of the Jeep, and a drop-down tailgate provided access to the load space behind the driving seat. Once Rover's own chassis was ready, for the sake of simplicity it too had a wheelbase of 80in, much the same ground clearance as a Jeep, and similar approach and departure angles. Gestation occupied barely a year. Spencer Wilks ordered a pre-production run of 25 pilot vehicles, later enlarged to 50, which were completed in 1948. He expected to make about fifty or so a week for a year or two. The aim was to keep the price below £450 and the hood, the spare wheel carrier, the starting handle, and even the doors and passenger seat were optional extras. In the event they were all included in the price. It was ready for launch in April 1948 and in production by July.

One prototype had the driving seat in the middle, ostensibly because a farmer might want to use it instead of a tractor. Early internal pictures showed one pulling a plough but a more credible explanation was the endeavour to persuade the authorities that it was essentially an agricultural vehicle, and not subject to purchase tax. Prototypes were tried out on neighbouring farms pulling an 8ft tandem-disc harrow, carrying livestock, running power benches and threshing machines. When Tom Barton, one of the design team, was working on the transmission, he had to include power take-offs and winches for driving a tree-root and chaff cutter. There was further wrangling with the tax authorities over the Land Rover's agricultural designation, and whether it was eligible to use unrationed red-dyed commercial petrol that was restricted to agricultural and commercial users. It took until 1956 to decide the issue.

1948 The first short wheelbase 80in Land Rover was launched at the Amsterdam Motor Show alongside the two-month-old 75 saloon in April, and proved an immediate success. Orders began to flow in, and also from exhibiting at the Bath and West Show of May 1948. The first production version had permanent four wheel drive, with a freewheel device to disengage the front wheels, and a 50bhp (37kW), 1595cc engine derived from the Rover P3 60 car. Within a year the stopgap proved capable of outselling Rover cars, and by the end of it, met government obligations by exporting to nearly 70 countries. Fulfilling expectations of seeing farmers and small businesses through the aftermath of the war, the first year's production was only 3048 but 8000 were made of the 1949 model, which doubled to 16,000 in 1950. Rover was soon making 1,000 a week, and their earnings reached over £2.5 million a year in foreign currency. *The Autocar* called it "A practical road and cross country vehicle built to high standards." Harold Hastings, the Midlands editor of *The Motor* was more cautious. "It is a vehicle intended to bash over fields in far-flung parts of the empire on unmetalled tracks. So why should it be built with the same care as a Rover 60? Surely something more agricultural would be better and cheaper." In October a Tickford-bodied Station Wagon was introduced to try and broaden the Land Rover's appeal and in December Rover chairman E Ransom Harrison told shareholders that judging from the volume of enquiries and orders, "…this vehicle will be something very much more than an additional source of production. It may yet equal, or even exceed our car output."

1949 The first Land Rovers were exported to the USA with modifications to comply with local regulations. One of the virtues of simple design proved to be its adaptable nature. Once again the American civilian Jeep CJ2A was a role model with Power Take-Off (PTO) attachments. A shaft was added to the transfer gearbox for operating a winch, a small electrical generator, or a belt-drive for farming machinery. The Land Rover Mobile Welder of 1949 (£825) was one of the first attempts to sell a specialist model, and although sales were slow, it showed the way for a succession of Land Rover fire engines, camper vans, snowploughs, police and military vehicles, small armoured cars, ambulances, riot control vehicles, overhead cable repair platforms, pick-up trucks, mobile workshops, and personnel carriers. There was a Land Rover with an air compressor selling at £996 and in October 1948 a Station Wagon but it was not a success. An excursion into the leisure market, it was assembled by Tickford, and had a body made of aluminium panels on a coachbuilt wood frame. The well-proportioned seven-seater had a metal cover over the bonnet-mounted spare wheel, but sales proved disappointing and only 641 were made. As a passenger car it attracted purchase tax, making it twice the price of an ordinary open-bodied Land Rover. Yet it was not forgotten. The market may not have been ready for it in 1948, but Rover remained convinced that a well-equipped, and even luxurious all-purpose vehicle would be made in due course. Production in 1948-49 was 5,709 Rover cars and 8,000 Land Rovers.

1950 Changes to Land Rover were kept to the minimum but some evolution proved necessary for the revised 80-inch. Larger more powerful headlamps were needed, and now shone through apertures in the grille, rather than the protective mesh. A hard top was optional. A minor change to the

Press reaction to the Land Rover was enthusiastic. This 1949 story in *The Commercial Motor* was reprinted in advertisements.

gearbox brought it into line with the Rover P4 saloon, and the four wheel drive system was changed to a selectable type, using a simple dog clutch in the transfer gearbox. Drive to the front axle in high range was engaged by pressing down on a lever topped by a yellow knob, low range selected by pulling another red-topped lever rearwards. Selecting low range automatically engaged four wheel drive. The first 40,000 production examples of 1948-1950 had four wheel drive without a central differential, and with commendable resource Rover fell back on another item in its inventory, and put a freewheel in the front drive to get rid of tyre scrub. So although four wheel drive was permanent in the sense that it was permanently engaged, it was temporary in suffering the front wheels to run at a different speed when necessary. The freewheel allowed them to run faster than the rears on corners. The disadvantage was that four wheel drive needed to be as effective coming down hills as going up, so engine braking on early Land Rovers was transmitted through the rear wheels only.

1951 Using a Rover luxury car engine with overhead inlet valves and side exhausts, something it had in common with

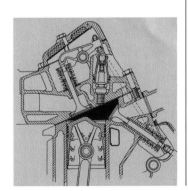

Cutaway drawing of the overhead inlet, side exhaust Rover engine. In 1951 the 2-litre engine replaced the original 1.6-litre in the Land Rover.

contemporary Rolls-Royces and Bentleys, had been part of the stop-gap programme of the early days. The nature of the design and the production process made it necessary to use existing components, and it seemed pointless to introduce a new engine for something of which only a few hundred might be sold. Now that the Land Rover had taken on a life of its own a larger-bore 1997cc replaced the 1595cc engine. Power increased by only 2bhp (1.5kW), but torque went up to 101lbft (136Nm) developed at only 1500 rpm, against 80lbft (108Nm) at 2000 rpm of the earlier one.

1952 The success of the Land Rover led Minerva SA of Mortsel Antwerp, makers of armoured cars since 1914 and high quality touring cars in the 1920s, to take out a licence for its production. A second overseas manufacturing contract was signed with German manufacturer Tempo, to make Land Rovers with a locally manufactured steel body and a revised chassis, for the West German Border Police. Rover had to acknowledge that it now owed its survival as a manufacturer to the remarkable vehicle, which saw service not only on the quiet farms for which it had been intended, but also in every desert, jungle, swamp, mountain and trouble spot throughout the civilised and uncivilised world. The failure of the 1949 Station Wagon, as a result of the purchase tax regulations despite an encouraging reception by the press and dealers, brought a new resolve to look at the market again, and a programme was put in hand for what was tentatively called the Road Rover, a large estate car with rear wheel drive only. Various proposals reached running prototype stage but none achieved production because they were bulky, heavy, and grew unwieldy during development. Nevertheless the following autumn would see the introduction of the 86in wheelbase so-called utility Station Wagon.

1953 In April the board was told: "After discussion it was agreed that Mr Wilks' proposal that the Road Rover be put into production be approved." Development work continued. A large estate car on a P4 passenger car chassis, the first versions had a Rover car-like grille, and later ones a chunky appearance heavily influenced by a contemporary Chevrolet with a deeply curved windscreen. None of the Road Rovers produced over the years had any of the subtle touches Rover designer David Bache was applying to mainstream car models. One prototype was referred to unflatteringly, as The Greenhouse. To improve the load space area, the first series Land Rover's wheelbase was extended to 86in although the payload was unchanged. The first long wheelbase Land Rover,

with a 107in (271cm) wheelbase was introduced with a 6ft (182.9cm) load bed with a truck cab and was known as the Pick Up. On October 1, Minerva began manufacture of 10,000 Land Rovers for the Belgian military, using components shipped from Solihull, and a local steel body with distinctive sloping front wings. Belgian police, army, navy and air forces hoarded them, sometimes for years, before using them.

1954 Land Rovers could now be bought in other than green. The first ones wore the light green used on Rover cars, but as part of a new strategy for 1954 customers were able to choose grey or blue. On 3 December 1953, three days after his 80th

Sir Winston Churchill's 80th birthday present was an 86in Land Rover, delivered to Chartwell in Kent.

History of a Legend

In 1953 Land Rover built a special review vehicle based on the 86inch for the Queen's Royal Tour.

birthday, an 86in Land Rover UKE 80 was registered in the name of Sir Winston Spencer Churchill KG, OM, CH, MP, and delivered to Chartwell.

1955 Somewhat confusingly a new engine in production for Rover cars was adapted for Land Rovers. It had separate rather than siamesed bores to improve cooling, and retained the previous engine's 1997cc capacity. Land Rovers were now popular for use on many expeditions overseas, and six undergraduates from Oxford and Cambridge travelled from London to Singapore in two short wheelbase Station Wagons. After crossing the English Channel in Bristol Freighter aircraft, the trip was entirely overland, with the exception of a ferry across the Bosporus and a perilous crossing of the Ganges. Here they were carried across on boats barely bigger than they were. The jungles of Burma (Myanmar) were traversed along remnants of the Stilwell Road built more than 10 years earlier during the Second World War. Both arrived in Singapore in early 1956 after a journey of nearly 18,000 miles.

1956 The 10-seater 107in (271.8cm) wheelbase Station Wagon was introduced. The body had landmark Land Rover features, such as roof-mounted so-called Alpine Lights, and a tropical roof as well as heavy galvanised steel cappings. To make room for a new diesel engine under development, Land Rover wheelbases were also extended by 2in (2.5cm) to 88in (223cm) and 109in (277cm) by remounting the front spring hanger brackets further forward. The first part of the North Works at Lode Lane, at the western edge of the site, was a 100,000sq ft dispatch centre completed in January 1956. Formerly a rectification and trimming block, it later became part of the large section used for production of the Rover 2000 car, from 1963 to 1977. The demands of the management on Road Rover's development continued, since it had been expected to be in production for 1957, but doubts about it were increasing in view of constant need for improving its appearance. Minerva production in Belgium ended when the firm went on to make its own 4x4, the C20. Similarly Tempo in West Germany ceased production although continued selling British-made Land Rovers. The British army adopted the Land Rover as its light 4x4 in succession to the Austin Champ and in a landmark case the Law Lords judged that Land Rovers were "car-type" vehicles. Hitherto when they had used red-dyed commercial fuel, they had been subject to a 30mph speed restriction, an anomaly henceforward rescinded.

Shortly after concluding his relationship with HRH Princess Margaret, Battle of Britain pilot Group Captain Peter Townsend set off round the world alone, in a short wheelbase Station Wagon. His 57,000-mile journey took him from Paris to Singapore, Perth to Sydney, and Vancouver to Buenos Aires. He took a boat around the impassable jungles of the Darien Gap, completing the circumnavigation in 1957 with a drive from Cape Town to Paris, recording his adventures in a book *Earth, My Friend*. Another solo around the world trip got under way a matter of days after Townsend. Barbara Toy in her nine-year old Land Rover "Pollyanna" undertook it but was beset with mechanical problems. These included brake failure, which bizarrely prevented her from stopping in an attempted hold-up. She was unable to use the Stilwell Road to cross Burma due to a local revolt, so shipped her ageing vehicle to Thailand, subsequently crossing Australia and the United States before bringing it back to Britain.

Land Rover Santana began manufacture in Spain, making a variety of vehicles including normal and forward control, some with locally designed and made bodywork. Metalurgica de Santa Ana SA, or MSA, was the only firm that made Land Rovers from its own raw materials rather than from completely knocked down (CKD) components from Solihull. The Franco government was eager to create a motor industry, especially with a manufacturer capable of supplying vehicles for the military and agriculture, and subsidised the new factory at Jaén. Santana was registered on 24 February 1955 and in 1956 signed a licence contract with Rover. Production did not begin until 1958, with only 5400 being built in ten years.

1957 The first factory diesel engine for a Land Rover was introduced with a capacity of 2052cc, producing 52bhp (39kW) and 87lbft (118Nm) of torque. It had a cast iron cylinder head and block, and overhead valves with roller tappets. Spencer Wilks was appointed chairman of Rover.

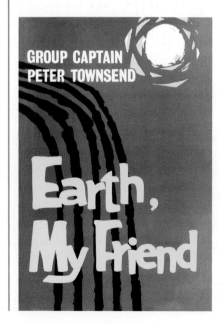

Townsend's book told of his epic 57,000-mile journey in a short wheelbase Station Wagon. Epic journeys like this provided valuable press coverage.

History of a Legend

1958 The Land Rover Series II was unveiled 10 years after the launch of the first Land Rover, appropriately also at the same Amsterdam Motor Show. Rover's styling department under David Bache provided a wider body, with barrelled sides, and sills that hid the chassis. Other changes included an external fuel filler, and glass replaced Perspex in the sliding side windows. A wider track gave a bigger turning circle, and the option of free-wheeling hubs saved wear on the front drive shafts, while improving fuel consumption. A new petrol engine for the Series II, closely related to the diesel, had a capacity of 2286cc and raised power output to 77bhp (57kW). An important contributor to the appearance of Land Rovers for many years Bache had been a student apprentice of engineering at Austin in 1948, spending six years at Longbridge, together with courses at Birmingham University and Birmingham College of Art. He went to work at Solihull aged 26, with an ambition to graduate to what was sometimes called styling but which he firmly regarded as "design". His first job, getting the Rover P5 to Maurice Wilks's liking, proved difficult. Work on the Road Rover was suspended and within a year it was consigned to oblivion. Land Rover annual production exceeded 30,000 for the first time.

1959 After 11 years in production, the 250,000th Land Rover rolled off the line. The Australian army had adopted the Land Rover as a standard vehicle in 1958 and the 109in

The Land Rover Series II was launched in 1958, and the same year annual production exceeded 30,000 vehicles for the first time.

Station Wagon was introduced. Austin, which had made the Rolls-Royce-engined and technically sophisticated military Champs between 1952 and 1955, embarked on its own competitor in 1958. The Austin Gipsy was never a great rival. Two versions were made, a 2199cc petrol and a 2178cc diesel, with utility bodywork but only 21,208 were produced before production ended in 1968.

1960 Rover factories proliferated in the 1950s and 1960s, with one at Perry Bar purchased in 1952, Percy Road in 1954, while transmission and chassis manufacture was dispersed from Solihull, and more buildings were acquired at Tyburn Road in 1964, Garrison Street in 1965, and Tyseley No2 in 1969.

1961 The Swiss army adopted the Land Rover. A revised range known as the Land Rover Series IIA was launched. The capacity of the diesel was increased to 2286cc, in line with the petrol unit, raising power to 62bhp (46kW).

1962 The Series IIA 109in Forward Control version was introduced. The Forward Control, like its American counterpart introduced by the American Jeep company, was designed to appeal to customers demanding a bigger payload. Despite the Forward Control's radically different appearance, Rover claimed it had a lot in common with standard Land Rovers. As well as the 4-cylinder petrol and diesel engines, a car-derived, 6-cylinder, 2.6-litre overhead inlet side exhaust valve engine was offered to help power the large vehicle. Spencer Wilks retired and was succeeded by William Martin-Hurst. Santana Land Rover began to export; its production reached a point where the Spanish market was being well catered for, and it began shipping to Colombia and other parts of South America.

1963 On a fact-finding tour to discuss production of a marine version of the Land Rover engine for fishing boats in the Far East, Martin-Hurst visited Mercury Marine's experimental department at Fond du Lac, Wisconsin. The new managing director had joined Rover in 1960 as executive director for production, and progressed swiftly. His call was to Carl Kiekhaefer, head of Mercury and on the shop floor he spotted a compact aluminium V8 being made ready for one of Mercury's boats. This was a Buick, taken out of production after only three years in the Buick Special, Pontiac Tempest, and Oldsmobile F-85 Cutlass. General Motors had abandoned it after contriving thin-walled iron castings for V8 blocks, which were almost as light, and a good deal cheaper than the elegant die-cast aluminium unit at Mercury Marine.

Martin-Hurst knew of difficulties with the development of the Rover 3 Litre saloon, and was concerned about programmes taking shape for the later 1960s. The sales department had misgivings about a large 4-cylinder engine in the proposed P6 saloon and a 6-cylinder was too long to fit the space available. The board was informed that: "Engineering was investigating the merits of a 5-cylinder 2½ litre, with a view to possible use in P6". But it presented as many difficulties as it solved, so when Martin-Hurst caught sight of the little redundant aluminium Buick, he was interested. It was only half an inch longer than the 4-cylinder for the projected P6, and would leave space to spare in the wide engine bay of both it and the current P5.

The customer is always right. A host of Land Rover variants lined up in the early Sixties show just how versatile the vehicle was.

GM made three quarters of a million 3.5 litre V8s before forsaking it, together with a 5.0 litre, large-bore cast iron unit of similar design. Martin-Hurst learned that the 3.5litre weighed only 12lb (5.4kg) more than the P6 four cylinder, and it would be lighter and 8in (20.3cm) shorter than Rover's proposed 6-cylinder. Kiekhaefer agreed to air-freight an engine to England, while Martin-Hurst hastened to the New York Motor Show to get in touch with General Motors. He sought to negotiate terms of a licence to make it. The question of whether it could be manufactured to Rover standards of silence and refinement could wait. A V8 was still something of a novelty in Europe, except for the old side-valve Ford by then out of production. BMW had all but abandoned a 2.6 and 3.2 litre aluminium V8 introduced in 1954. Nearly all V8s such as Jensen, Facel-Vega, and Bristol, had engines made in America, but two important exceptions, in the eyes of the Rover chief executive, were critical. One was Rolls-Royce. The 6.2 litre 90 degree V8 introduced for the Silver Cloud II in 1959 had an aluminium cylinder block and hydraulic tappets. Rolls-Royce had wanted to use thin walled cast iron for the cylinder block, but discovered the foundry techniques unavailable outside America, so made it in aluminium. To GM with money to spare, this cast-iron route remained open, so the aluminium engine could be forsaken. The only other V8 that concerned Martin-Hurst was the 2548cc Daimler, designed by Edward Turner, which Jaguar was squeezing into a Mark 2 Jaguar saloon body.

On 8 September 1963 Maurice Wilks died suddenly at his

In 1965 Rover acquired the rights to produce the compact Buick V8. This shows the 1968 version with automatic gearbox used in the Rover 3500.

holiday home in Anglesey. Born on Hayling Island in 1904 and educated at Malvern College, at age 13 he worked with Don Francis on a motorcycle with a pressed steel frame, which formed the basis of the Francis-Barnett. He gained experience of the motor industry in Detroit with GM from 1926 to 1928, joined Hillman as planning engineer in 1928, then rejoined his brother at Rover as chief engineer in 1930.

1964 Among the individuals who played key roles in developing Rover's and Land Rover's technology under Maurice Wilks, were cousins Spencer King and Peter Wilks. Nephews of Spencer and Maurice Wilks, neither relied on family connections to make their way. Peter Wilks died prematurely after a brilliant engineering career, and Spen King went on to become engineering director of BL Cars, but

Another milestone year in 1966.
William Martin-Hurst is behind
the wheel, with Tom Barton in the
centre seat next to A.B.Smith.
Peter Wilks is on the far left.

History of a Legend

his best work took place when he had the freedom of action his brilliance deserved at Land Rover. An apprentice at wartime Rolls-Royce, he became involved in the gas turbine programme following Rover's withdrawal from aircraft engines. He described Rolls-Royce as a generous university. "Rolls-Royce was in the process of learning a lot about the gas turbine engine itself. It was fundamentally new, no one had a text book, and a lot of bright people were wrapped up in the new subject."

1965 Negotiations with General Motors for the rights to the aluminium V8 were concluded. Rover gained the manufacturing licence together with all the production planning sheets, drawings, and machinery to make it. The engines' service records, and 39 that remained in stock were handed over, so that Rover could start development. The main changes were a new exhaust manifold, and semi-downdraught SU carburettors in place of the multi-choke Rochester. Included in the agreement with GM was an American engineer Joe Turley who, within a year or two of retirement, no longer worked on new projects. He had forty years' experience of GM, and knew enough about the history of the 215 cu in V8 to brief Rover on its history, and the reasons behind many of its features. Turley's advice proved invaluable in shortening the time it took to get the engine into production, incorporating many of the modifications and improvements GM had built into it. The main difference was changing the cylinder blocks from gravity die-castings to sand castings and a foundry was specially built by the Birmingham Aluminium Casting company to make them, and press-in the centrifugally cast cylinder liners. This proved unsatisfactory, and after an initial batch of some 600 the process was changed, and the liners inserted by heating the

block and leaving them fixed in place on cooling. In the meantime Rover took over Alvis of Coventry, which provided a well-equipped machine shop to make the V8's components, and assembly took place at Acocks Green until it was closed and later demolished. Other changes included raising the compression ratio to a formidable 10.5:1, and the engine became one of the building blocks on which a new model known as the 100in Station Wagon, which reached production as the Range Rover, was being developed.

1966 Land Rover production reached the half million mark in April. Rover celebrated the 500,001st vehicle, with managing director William Martin-Hurst driving an 88in off the production track with Tom Barton, one of its creators, squeezed alongside him in the centre seat. Rover now reckoned that the Land Rover had earned more than £230,000,000 in foreign currency. The Forward Control was revised with wider track, heavy-duty axles, revised rear springs and a front anti-roll bar. These changes were designed to improve stability and manoeuvrability, and they also altered the wheelbase so the vehicle became the Series IIB 110 Forward Control.

1967 The 6-cylinder 2.6-litre engine was also made available as an option on 109in wheelbase models. Minor improvements were made to the interior and a negative earth electrical system adopted. A derivative of the 109in, using heavy-duty axles from the forward control model was under development, and went on sale in 1969 with a one-ton payload. Rover could no longer afford to finance a forward model programme on its own, so merged with truck manufacturer Leyland, which had already acquired the Coventry-based car maker Triumph.

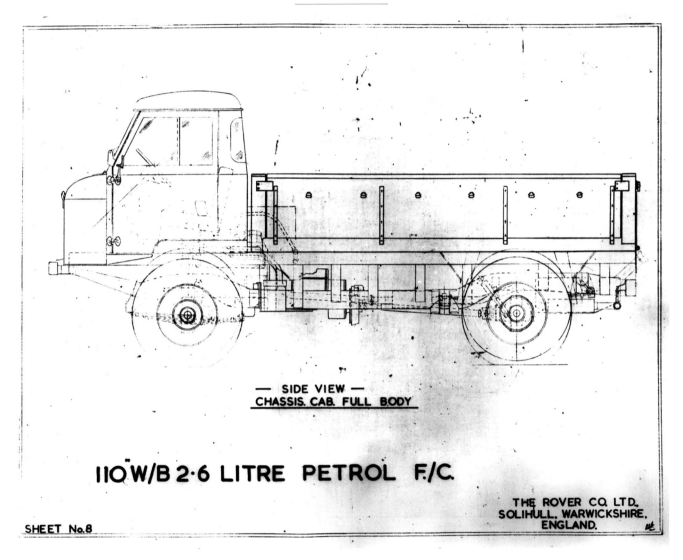

— SIDE VIEW —
CHASSIS. CAB. FULL BODY

110 W/B 2·6 LITRE PETROL F./C.

THE ROVER CO. LTD.
SOLIHULL. WARWICKSHIRE,
ENGLAND.

SHEET No. 8

Towards the end of 1966 the Forward
Control was revised to improve the
handling. The wheelbase was also
changed and the vehicle was known
as the Series 11B 110 Forward Control.

History of a Legend

1968 Following a three-year development the Truck Utility ½ Ton, better known as the Lightweight, entered service with the British Army. Designed jointly with the Ministry of Defence's Fighting Vehicles Research and Development Establishment (FVRDE), it provided British forces with the mobility of a vehicle, which could be transported by aircraft or even airlifted by helicopter. The basic 88in Land Rover was modified with a new body using flat detachable panels and a revised chassis. The ½ ton became one of the most successful Land Rovers, with production continuing until the mid

Lord Stokes was head of Leyland in 1968 when he was made chairman of the British Leyland Motor Corporation, later to become BL.

A Series 11A 109 experimentaly equipped as a shunter. The brakes were not quite up to the task of stopping a train.

1980s. Its detachable body panels provided a good platform for the US-designed 106mm Recoilless Rifle (RCL) in a conversion made in small numbers by Marshalls of Cambridge. In this form it went into action with the Iraqi armed forces, which were recipients of the final production vehicles. A full 35 years after the ½ ton entered service, it saw action defending Baghdad against the US Army and coalition forces.

The government encouraged the merger of the two major British vehicle manufacturing groups; Leyland (including Rover and Triumph), joined forces with British Motor Holdings (BMH), which incorporated BMC's Austin, Morris, MG and Jaguar, uniting much British vehicle manufacture under one management. British Leyland was created, chaired by Lord Stokes. At Solihull research was put in hand on the so-called Velar prototypes that led to the Range Rover. Land Rover annual production exceeded 50,000 for the first time.

1969 Following a revision to the headlamp position on export models to comply with new lighting regulations, headlamps

The Lightweight in stripped down form. It made an ideal platform for the 106mm Recoiless Rifle (RCL)

History of a Legend

In 1969 Land Rover celebrated 21
years. The first pre-production car is
on the left, with a Series 11A
showing the new headlamp position.

on all types of Land Rover were moved from their traditional well-protected position inside the radiator grille to the front wings. On the engineering side Rover remained convinced of a demand for a Land Rover that was better on the road, and approved plans for what was known internally as the 100-inch Station Wagon. Spen King, who had become director of engineering at Standard-Triumph in 1968, together with Gordon Bashford had already completed the layout of a new type of four wheel drive crossover, something closer to a car than an agricultural vehicle. On November 10 1967 the board was told: "…that the management had formulated its proposed product policy for the years 1968 to 1970 inclusive. The plan included the introduction of the 100-inch Station Wagon." Rover foresaw customers among what it called gentleman farmers. The basis of the new vehicle was a strong chassis different from a Land Rover's, a separate aluminium body, long-travel coil spring suspension to provide a better ride, without relinquishing a Land Rover's cross-country grip. It was to have closed bodywork and the appointments of a saloon car. The aluminium V8 engine provided the power for a useful turn of speed. Resources for development were slim at first, because the firm was preoccupied with new saloon cars, and King took responsibility for styling as well as engineering. The result was inspired, the proportions right, the performance spectacular, and when King passed the project to David Bache for finishing off in 1967 only detail changes were necessary. Bache fine-tuned it, indented the panel along the body sides, added the strikingly practical interior, and except for minor embellishments the Range Rover was complete.

Expeditions with Land Rovers flourished and there were so many requests for information on taking Land Rovers to remote parts of the world that the firm published *A Guide to Land Rover Expeditions*. The fifth edition in January 1969 ran to 15 pages of closely typed foolscap: "It is most important to organise your expedition by Land-Rover (the hyphen was still in use in 1969) well ahead as detailed planning will save time, trouble and money later on. These notes are only for guidance and every expedition will have its individual requirements. However one thing is certain. Providing you maintain and service your Land-Rover with care, and treat it with respect, you will reach your destination."

It contained advice on body style: "A Station Wagon or hard top on a long or short wheelbase chassis will not only be more dustproof but with locks and security catches fitted, pilfering is made more difficult. However if the hard top is fitted with windows, purchase tax must be paid unless the vehicle is to remain out of the country for at least twelve months." Under petrol versus diesel: "A petrol engine is a lot quieter. It is generally more easily understood than a diesel, but a diesel has no ignition system, which is an advantage in wading, and where there is a fire risk. Diesel fuel is generally less expensive, and fuel consumption is considerably better than that of a petrol engine."

History of a Legend

1970 In June the Range Rover was launched following extensive press appraisal in Cornwall that included using classic trials sections such as the famous Bluehills Mine hillclimb near Perranporth. Press reports were encouraging:

"If tar and Macadam were only now getting together to lay the dust and bind the stones, the Range Rover would have had to be invented. It is made for two elements: off the road and on it, and its duality is almost complete. The facilities for one environment are not encumbrances in the other. It carries its high clearance and elegant interior to each. You must assess its behaviour separately, but it deals well with both. Off the road it shows astonishing pace and agility. On the road it is comfortable, roomy, and above all fast. Refinement has attracted purchase tax, making the Range Rover expensive at £2 short of £2,000. It is aimed at a prosperous leisure market, which will use it for towing boats and horse-boxes, countryside pursuits, going on safari in comfort, or simply looking squirearchical. The Range Rover is one of the most cleverly styled, and cleverly named, estate cars ever."

An early Range Rover publicity shot. Its refinement meant that at launch its price came in at £2 short of £2,000 - twice the price of a Land Rover. It was a spectacular success.

"Driving the Range Rover is a revelation. You can take it straight into a field, and provided it is not actually ploughed, you need hardly slacken speed. The bumps disappear up the supple springs, and the permanent four wheel drive keeps the wheels gripping on almost anything. Almost anything probably includes mud of any practicable depth, deep snow, wet rocks, and potholes two feet deep from crest to crest; wet sand, loose boulders, clay combinations thereof up to gradients just under 1-in-1. Like any wheeled vehicle except tractors the only conditions likely to defeat it are wet grass and dry sand. But it will certainly deal better even with these than any ordinary car."

"The four wheel drive remains in operation all the time. For crawling out of craters you engage a low ratio with maximum speeds in each gear of 8, 14, 23, and 36mph instead of the normal 24, 41, 68, and 96mph. If one set of wheels loses its grip you operate a vacuum-assisted control, which locks up the centre differential. This prevents all the drive leaking away to one wheel, which may be hanging in mid-air over a hole, and keeps all four wheels rotating at the same speed."

"In less dramatic circumstances the Range Rover remains a stirring road performer. The 3½ litre V8 engine provides swift acceleration and most of the tranquillity you expect in a Rover. There is some whine from the transfer gears, seemingly endemic in four wheel drive arrangements, but Rover engineers are confident they can eliminate this once production gets properly under way. Tyre howl is less likely to be suppressed. Tyres that will maintain 95mph on motorways, cope with flints and sharp rocks off the road, and still grip on mud and snow, have to be tough above everything else. Our test car had Michelin XM+S tubed radials."

"The Range Rover is quite big, longer than most regular Land Rovers, but not quite so tall. You can see over a lot of other traffic. The interior has been well laid out with luxurious-looking but hard-wearing materials. Practicality takes precedence, but Rover has studied luxury for so long it comes almost naturally. The seats are superb with high backs and plenty of support for holding the driver in place on rough ground. They have their own built-in safety belts. It would finish the job more neatly though, if they were of the inertia-reel pattern."

"The steering is rather heavy, especially at parking speeds. The Range Rover is introduced after 21 years of Land Rovers. The customers asked for de luxe features, not the trappings of a saloon (there are no carpets in a Range Rover) and they got a car to drive in gum-boots or city slip-ons but which somehow feels best in brogues." Eric Dymock, *Motoring Guardian*, June 1970.

Range Rover was a bold design true to its marketing strap line "A Car for All Reasons". A gold medal was awarded for its coachwork at the London Motor Show while its safety features were recognised by the presentation of the Don Safety Trophy. Encouraged by its reception, development commenced on the SD5 leaf-sprung Land Rover hybrid.

History of a Legend

1971 The Royal Automobile Club awarded the Dewar Trophy to the Range Rover. Donated in 1906, by Sir Thomas Dewar MP of the whisky dynasty, it recognized significant achievements in motor engineering and manufacture. The year following Range Rover's launch also saw production of the 750,000th Land Rover. Series III was launched in 88in and 109in wheelbase versions with revised engines. In December the British Trans-Americas Expedition left Alaska for Tierra del Fuego. One of the last great car journeys of the world, its most strenuous challenge lay in the tropical forests of the Darien Gap in Central America. The team used two Range Rovers and was led by Major John Blashford-Snell. The expedition ran into trouble through collisions with a moose, and then a truck, before leaving Canada. Real problems began in Panama. The Darien Gap lived up to its reputation and difficulties abounded with frequent failures of the differentials, when the Range Rovers struggled with conditions scarcely envisaged by their designers, and also through the use of incorrect lubricants. An old locally purchased Land Rover was brought in to act as pathfinder, and with the aid of regular flights bringing in spare parts and engineers, the 250miles (402km) of the Darien were eventually conquered in 99 days.

Spencer Wilks died at his home on the Isle of Islay. Born at Rickmansworth in 1891, and educated at Charterhouse SB Wilks served as a captain in the First World War, entered the motor industry with Hillman in 1919, and married one of William Hillman's six daughters. In 1921 he was appointed managing director of Hillman jointly with his brother-in-law John (later Sir John) Black. Together they ran the firm until Rootes purchased it. In 1929 he replaced Peter Poppe as works director at Rover, becoming managing director in January 1933. It was Spencer Wilks's skill and enterprise that brought Rover successfully through the depression of the 1930s, and his volunteering to join the shadow factory scheme in the 1930s meant a great deal to the success of Land Rover.

When Range Rover road tests appeared in the technical press, the enthusiasm of the compilers was undimmed. *The Motor* called it The All-Together Car: "Remarkably versatile go-anywhere estate; excellent performance, heavy fuel consumption, good roadholding and ride, outstanding traction; heavy steering and gearchange; comfortable and well equipped. With the utilitarian Land Rover's indelible image firmly in mind, many people asked who we thought would pay £2000 (£1998) for what they saw as a superior cross-country tank. Their ignorance indicates that Rover still has a propaganda problem, to promote the Range Rover for what it really is, not what people imagine it to be."

After 23 years in production the 750,000th Land Rover, a Series 11A, was built in 1971. Tom Barton is third from right.

The functional lines of the 1972
Land Rover 1 tonne Forward
Control. Engine and gearbox were
from the Range Rover.

History of a Legend

1972 The Land Rover 1 Tonne Forward Control was announced at the Commercial Motor Show. Designed to a British Army specification for a vehicle to tow the new 105 mm Light Gun, it had a de-tuned, militarised version of the 3.5-litre V8 petrol engine used in the Range Rover, also inheriting its combined gear and transfer box. The driveline could be extended to the rear chassis cross member, forming a power takeoff that could be coupled to the live axle of a specially designed powered-axle trailer. Any resemblance to the Range Rover ended with the engine and transmission, for the new vehicle had traditional Land Rover semi-elliptic (but parabolic and different from the regular multi-leaf) spring suspension and a slab sided utility body, which could be partially dismantled to reduce weight for helicopter lifting.

1973 A press release from the Land Rover Public Relations Department on 11 April 1973, carried a message from AB Smith, managing director, Rover: "After 25 years of operation the Land Rover's do-anything, go-anywhere character has gained international respect that would be difficult to equal. Its name has become synonymous with British engineering and is now a household word virtually everywhere. Nearly every vehicle is built to its future owner's particular specification. The variety is such that in five years' complete production no two Land Rovers need be exactly alike. Celebrating the countless achievements made by the Land Rover is an honour with which we have happily become familiar throughout the vehicle's long history, and we are no less proud this month in announcing its quarter-centenary anniversary."

1974 New editions of *A Guide to Land Rover Expeditions* were published as stapled booklets from Rover Triumph British Leyland UK Ltd, Solihull, Warwickshire. Their real purpose, besides offering sound advice for travel to implausible destinations was to head off appeals, which arrived almost weekly, for free vehicles. A constant flow had been reaching Solihull from universities, adventure clubs, and safari organisers. The modest booklet was usually as much as they received however, with information on desirable extras, tools, spares, and equipment, based on the accumulated experience of hundreds of fellow-trekkers.

The publication carried plenty of fine detail, including the importance of passport photographs to placate bureaucrats, and the ambient temperatures at which Land Rovers could normally be started and operated. It included advice on what to take, what to leave behind, and where to put things. "Front-mounted jerricans should not be used to carry fuel due to the fire hazard in the event of an accident," it said. There were injunctions about looking inside sleeping bags for scorpions, and advice on washing clothes while travelling; tacitly admitting that a Land Rover's ride could be somewhat agitated. "Put them in a waterproof, sealed container in the back of the vehicle with a suitable amount of water and washing powder. After 100 miles they should be clean." The 1969 edition ended with an invitation to obtain further information. "The Public Relations Department in Solihull will be pleased to offer further advice." By the middle 1970s this had been deleted. Instead it said: "The Land Rover has been associated with expeditions for many years and the publicity we can gain from these ventures is now very minimal. Consequently, as a rule, any request for monetary or material assistance will not be considered."

History of a Legend

1975 To mark the entry into service of the 1 Tonne, Squadron Leader Tom Sheppard led an expedition to cross the Sahara from west to east. It used the first production 1 Tonne Land Rover and three other vehicles, equipped to tow their powered axle trailers. Leaving Dakar in Senegal at the end of January, the expedition covered nearly 12,177km (7550 miles) in 100 days carrying out scientific research on the way.

The government acquired the majority of British Leyland shares through the National Enterprise Board (later transferred to the Secretary of State for Industry), effectively nationalising it.

1976 In June an 88in Station Wagon at Solihull was the millionth Land Rover, its completion attended by the media, civic dignitaries from Cardiff and Birmingham where many of its parts were built, as well as from Solihull. Three out of every four Land Rovers had been exported. Making the first half million had taken 17 years, making the second 11.

In 1976 a Station Wagon was the millionth Land Rover, pictured here alongside the first pre-production car.

History of a Legend

1977 Don (later Sir Don) Ryder, head of the National Enterprise Board, which had been responsible for British Leyland, resigned, and Leslie Murphy his deputy replaced him. Murphy visited Alex Park, the managing director of British Leyland, to ask him what models to make, but when he found Park unable to frame a satisfactory reply Murphy knew it was time for change. He approached another member of the National Enterprise Board, South African Michael (later Sir Michael) Edwardes, to run British Leyland, which Edwardes accepted on a three-year secondment from his employer, Chloride Batteries. His mandate appeared to be to make British Leyland profitable or close it down. On 1 November 1977 Edwardes was put in charge, his arrival marked by resignations from amongst the old management team.

1978 Within weeks Edwardes negotiated loans from banks to keep the company, renamed BL Ltd, going. His rescue plan included factory closures but despite that, in February he gained support from BL shop stewards. Nevertheless the major plants, including Solihull, were affected by strikes. Edwardes planned first to scale down production at Speke in Liverpool, moving TR7 sports car assembly to Triumph at Canley, but here the necessary co-operation of the workforce was not forthcoming. Accordingly following sit-ins, and evidence of some sabotage, he closed the plant entirely. The TR7 survived, eventually being built at Solihull, although its V8 sibling the Lynx was cancelled. Although Speke did not wholly impress him, Edwardes was encouraged by what he found at Solihull, creating Land Rover Limited as a separate operating company within British Leyland. For the first time in its history, Land Rover was under independent management, and government funding of £200 million was promised to enable production to be doubled by the 1980s.

1979 In the first Paris-Dakar Rallye-Raid, a French-entered Range Rover crewed by Genestier, Tenbiat and Lemordant was fourth behind three motorbikes. It was the highest placed four-wheeler, closely followed by a Renault 4. A new version of the Land Rover 109in powered by the V8 petrol engine was launched. Within the company it was known as Stage 1, as it was the first part of a two-phase process to expand production, following the new funding. It used the V8 engine and gearbox from the Range Rover although the engine was detuned to suit the different handling and braking characteristics of the Land Rover. In September Michael Edwardes presented his recovery plan for British Leyland, calling for the closure of 13 factories including MG at Abingdon-on-Thames. In November 8 employees out of 10 voted on the plan, 87 per cent of whom approved it. In the first stage of a reorganisation of the Solihull site, the North Works was converted for storage, a massive undertaking that involved digging a gigantic hole for one of the first automated factory stocking and packing systems.

The 1980 Stage 1 using the Range
Rover V8 engine and gearbox to good
effect, especially off-road.

History of a Legend

1980 Demand for a 4-door Range Rover was so strong that specialists manufactured conversions, so a production option was put under development by the factory. Elsewhere in British Leyland a call for the Austin Longbridge workforce to strike in sympathy over the dismissal of shop stewards' leader Derek Robinson was defeated, and the power of the unions to dictate policy in BL effectively ended. Plant closures continued, and with them many symbolic British motor industry places were lost. For a time closure of Solihull was even contemplated. The expansion of the 1970s had included a new factory, the East Works planned for production of the Rover SD1 in 1982 and subsequently the Triumph TR7, which now lay empty after SD1 was transferred to Cowley. Solihull was therefore now a wholly Land Rover plant. In Spain production of Santana Land Rovers reached 18,000 a year and its export network covered 25 countries. It sent abroad 51,457 through 250 service and dealer outlets covering many territories not accessible to Solihull. New markets included Central America and the Middle East, and CKD kits were sent to Costa Rica for local assembly. Santana was even able to supply 200 4-cylinder powertrain units a week back to Solihull.

In Spain Santana were now building 18,000 vehicles a year. They were even producing powertrain units for Solihull.

1981 The Range Rover once again proved its quality in the Paris-Dakar rally. A VSD sponsored vehicle crewed by Metge and Giroux was first, with another Paris-Match supported vehicle driven by Simon and Boulanger fourth. In all, six Range Rovers finished in the top 20. After using Jeeps for the first event, Reynolds Tobacco chose Range Rovers for the second Camel Trophy, which covered 992 miles (1600km) and used a mere five vehicles. Subsequent events employed Land Rover products exclusively until 1998 with up to 20 of them involved, together with a fleet of supporting vehicles. Encouraged by its recent independence and a government cash injection, Land Rover had ambitious plans for Range Rover. First was the introduction of the 4-door, after many years when it had been made by specialist converters, such as FLM Panelcraft. The production model was based on the stylish conversion by Swiss coachbuilder Monteverdi, built on a new line in Solihull's North Works on facilities originally intended for the Rover P6. The next stage of reorganising Solihull included machining and assembly facilities for engines in North Works, 4-cylinder ones at first, but later V8s following the closure of Acocks Green. Range Rovers were assembled in an eastwards extension.

1982 Range Rover production reached 100,000. Following the introduction of the 4-door came an automatic gearbox option. Land Rover introduced the Series III County Station Wagon, named to appeal to what was popularly known as the County Set following concern over the threat from Japanese competitors. Also significant was the introduction of the High Capacity Pick Up body to the Land Rover 109in. Looking somewhat like its Toyota rival, the new body was sophisticated, made entirely of aluminium, with cast corners and double-skinned sides formed from extrusions.

1983 In January quietly-spoken Irishman Tony Gilroy, appointed managing director of Land Rover (still a BL subsidiary), made reassuring statements on its future. However, dismayed by complacency, he set about reorganising the company, and closed down seven satellite plants. Over the next two years a 16 per cent reduction in the workforce of 9,700 took place, as he concentrated instead on the core Solihull plant. Four years earlier when Land Rover was a separate company within BL it employed 14,200. Only the gearbox facility at Pengam, Cardiff where 600 were engaged, remained open for the time being. The local MP James Callaghan was nevertheless shocked, reported *The Financial Times*. "I suspect that these closures have been engineered to enable the government to privatise major sections of BL. Our community is already suffering high unemployment. I will be in touch with the trade unions urgently."

A key element of Gilroy's rationalisation was that Austin Rover, BL's car-making division, had no longer any use for the

Land Rover Managing Director Tony Gilroy took drastic action to rationalise the company. He closed seven satellite plants and cut 16 per cent of the workforce.

A production line for the One Ten.
In 1985 it was offered with a five-
speed Spanish-built Santana gearbox.

History of a Legend

car plant on the Solihull site. The £30 million factory had been opened in 1976, but was mothballed in 1982 after Rover SD1 production moved to Cowley. Nevertheless fixed costs were reduced by £14 million a year, and provided the momentum for an intense product development programme, the development of Range Rover into the luxury car sector and new markets abroad, and plans for the Discovery. A second stage of the expansion programme reached fruition in March with the introduction of the Stage 2 One Ten with coil spring suspension. There was also a 127, in effect a stretched One Ten, sold with a crew cab, or as a chassis cab. Land Rover's export markets suffered when a number of developing countries ran out of foreign currency, reducing their orders within a short space of time. From being one of BL's most consistently profitable parts, and having been listed as a likely candidate for privatisation, Land Rover suffered its first financial loss for 36 years. Output of vehicles and export kits dropped from 60,906 in 1980 to 51,181 in 1982, to only 40,768 in 1983. Production of CKD kits halved and total output was only 50 per cent of the factory's capacity of 100,000.

1984 In January a longer stroke version of the diesel engine took its capacity to 2.5 litres and power output to 67bhp (50kW). After experimenting with a number of short wheelbase options to partner the One Ten, a length of 92.9in (235.9cm) was settled on, and in June it was launched as the Land Rover Ninety. New doors with wind-up windows derived from those on Spanish Santana Land Rovers were introduced, with a galvanised steel trim strip to match the rear body capping. The first major contract for the One Ten came in the face of competition from Mercedes-Benz G-Wagen, from the Singapore Ministry of Defence for an initial

900. Land Rover was also up against Mercedes-Benz and Jeep, in a competitive trial for a large contract from the Australian Army, using Isuzu diesel engines. Further military orders came from the Ministry of Defence for 4-cylinder diesels, and the Swiss army for 4,100 vehicles over six years starting in 1990. Following a successful limited edition, the Range Rover Vogue was introduced, and as a result of the government's desire to rid itself of a costly nationalised motor industry, British Leyland sold Jaguar effectively privatised under the leadership of John (later Sir John) Egan.

1985 The Land Rover Ninety range was extended with the V8 engine, and as with the One Ten V8, this was now coupled to the LT85 5-speed gearbox sourced from Santana in Spain. *Autocar and Motor* described the Ninety V8 as "…one of the best off-road vehicles in the world," despite a fuel consumption that gave it a range of just 144 miles. Range Rover's automatic option was improved by the introduction of a refined ZF 4-speed transmission to replace the 3-speed Chrysler. The result was a noticeable increase in sales. Land Rovers were now sold in 120 countries with plans for even more expansion to come.

In March Spen King retired. Charles Spencer King, born 1925, came from the dynasty that founded the fortunes of Rover, although his engineering expertise transcended the family connections. Along with Peter Wilks, his work on the Rover 2000 approached that of genius and his Range Rover was no less inspired. In 1979 he became vice chairman of BL Technology, developing the ECV prototypes. In 1990 a limited edition Range Rover, the CSK, was named in his honour.

History of a Legend

1986 The introduction of a diesel was expected to increase penetration of Range Rover in Europe. Following cancellation of a joint venture with Perkins for a diesel version of the V8, Land Rover looked to the Italian state-owned company VM based at Cento near Bologna. Over £5 million and two years had been spent on developing the new engine from VM's standard offerings, but it proved noisy, rough and not very strong. Following a drubbing in the press, Land Rover responded with Project Bullet, a 24 hours run that broke 27 speed and endurance records, including maintaining over 100 mph (160kph) for an entire day and night. The government appointed a Canadian, Graham Day, as chairman of British Leyland. He renamed the company The Rover Group and endeavoured to force it up-market.

1987 Years of planning to re-enter North America came to fruition in March. The only model sold there was the Range Rover, equipped with a new, fuel-injected 150bhp (111kW) version of the V8. A new company, Range Rover of North America was set up, based in Maryland under its president Charlie Hughes. An initial network comprised 60 dealers and introduced new sales concepts. Despite continuing concerns over build quality, the Range Rover benefited from a 36,000-mile, three-year warranty in the USA, and with promises of a 24-hour response, Caterpillar managed its parts distribution service. The Swiss army annulled its £85 million order for 4,100 Land Rovers because, it was claimed, the company was unable to meet the required exhaust emission standards. The difficulty was not that it had been unable to meet the values, but that the timetable required by the Swiss was too short and Land Rover reacted angrily to a *Daily Mail* suggestion that it had been beaten by Steyr-Daimler-Puch to the contract.

A 1987 Land Rover 90. This year saw a major embarrassment when the Swiss Army cancelled its order for 4,100 Land Rovers because of concerns over exhaust emissions.

History of a Legend

1988 Land Rover's 40th anniversary was marked by total sales of over 1.6 million since 1948, but the celebrations were muted by a six-week strike. General Motors put in a bid to buy the company, leading to widespread indignation and political criticism, so managing director Tony Gilroy led a consortium of directors and financiers to buy it instead. General Motors pulled out and was replaced by others including JCB and Lonhro. The government acknowledged that without Land Rover, bidders for the loss-making car divisions of British Leyland might be limited, so the company was re-structured. In the end, Rover Group was sold to British Aerospace (BAe) on controversial terms, attracting attention from the European Union and the National Audit Office. The government wrote off debts of £2.6 billion and granted BAe £800 million of working capital. Stocks of unsold cars and parts were valued at £250 million. The British taxpayer received £150 million from BAe, which was able to recoup some of its investment by selling the Rover Group IT subsidiary ISTEL for £39 million, and getting a further £87 million from the flotation of Leyland-DAF. More came from a programme of disposals and building redevelopment, which

1988 saw the company celebrate 40 years of production. HUE 166, the first pilot – (or pre-) production Land Rover, (left), was wheeled out again to pose with a Ninety Station Wagon.

included the Triumph factory in Canley, Coventry and most of the old Morris plant at Cowley, Oxford. BAe posted modest profits for the Rover Group, but critics claimed it failed to invest strongly in future models. Instead it employed the established relationship with Honda to plan new cars based on Honda platforms.

In December Tony Gilroy, managing director for nearly six years, announced he would be leaving early in 1989 to join Perkins. His departure was made known less than three weeks after George (later Lord) Simpson was appointed managing director of Rover Group, still Land Rover's parent. Simpson had moved from being CEO of Leyland Daf and formerly, as managing director of Freight Rover he had spent a number of

years reporting to Gilroy, although colleagues attributed the departure to management reorganisation at Rover, rather than any animosity between them. Under this restructuring Graham Day remained chairman of Rover group but ceased to be chief executive, passing day to day running to George Simpson. Gilroy, then aged 48, felt that the additional tier of management would limit his prospects, and John Towers, Land Rover's director of manufacturing, filled his post. Gilroy left Land Rover with well integrated manufacturing facilities, record production, and a robust product plan.

The *Guide to Land Rover Expeditions* was still being published although downgraded slightly in appearance. It continued to offer good domestic advice such as "Creaseless

Land Rover continued to produce the useful expedition guides for serious travellers.

and non-iron clothes are a great boon, and present-day materials afford a combination of convenience and sartorial elegance." Land Rover expeditions were expected to be well dressed. Under Health it said: "Sensible measures in relation to the consumption of food and water will always be a help whilst travelling abroad, by reducing the incidence of tummy upsets. Before using any water for drinking purposes, mouth washes or cleaning teeth, be sure that it is safe. In large cities the water may be chlorinated but if doubt exists it is better to drink proprietary drinks and mineral water." It recommended "…an article in the *British Medical Journal* dated 17 January 1981 entitled Medical equipment for expeditions is worth reading."

1989 The first new Land Rover since the Range Rover in 1970 was launched at the Frankfurt Motor Show in September. Banished to Hall 9 together with the Japanese and East European makes, it tried to compensate for the slight by dressing up the stand with four enormous "By Appointment Royal Warrant" coats of arms, one more than Jaguar could claim. The new Discovery was similar in size but lighter than the Range Rover, to compete with the cheap and cheerful Japanese 4x4s, more recreational perhaps than hardworking. The Discovery had the same V8 as the Range Rover, with a 4-cylinder diesel alternative, but its success seemed to depend on which side of the £15,000 divide it would fall. Gilroy had planned for Discovery to move away from Land Rover's declining traditional markets, and into the burgeoning leisure sector. Energetic project manager Mike Donovan planned its production, with a team locked away in a special area at Solihull, using an innovative approach to deliver the new model on time. In order to keep below the £25 million authorised, Project Jay as the Discovery was code-named drew

heavily on the Range Rover, sharing its chassis, suspension, body frame, inner door panels and even the size of its windscreen. Yet the Discovery was still a significant addition to the range, its launch supported by a large marketing campaign designed to emphasise Land Rover as a brand. In order to distinguish the Discovery from the Range Rover, it gained extra power with its V8 enlarged to 3.9 litres. The Discovery production line was laid out in a U-shape, using bodies brought in from storage in the eastern part of the old shadow factory. They were trimmed, and at the base of the U lowered on to completed chassis, in the way of car factories since the time of the Model T Ford.

Dave Evans, one of the styling team that worked on the development of the Discovery, Land Rover's first launch for nearly 20 years.

History of a Legend

History of a Legend

1990 The traditional Land Rover range was renamed Defender, reflecting in some senses its long-standing military role, and went on sale with a version of the Discovery's 200 Tdi engine. A new 5-door Discovery gained a Design Council award and the 20th anniversary of Range Rover was celebrated with a four-wheel, four-channel ABS braking system, claimed the first ever designed to work off, as well as on-road. North America became the largest export market for the Range Rover, and it was well represented in the JD Power customer satisfaction survey. As a means of demonstrating the credentials of a leading manufacturer of off-road vehicles, the Land Rover Experience was opened at Solihull. Some of the spoil used in the construction of East Works had been put to use in laying down the test tracks and now the Land Track together with the older Jungle Track provided a 4.1 mile

(6.6km) circuit to show off the capabilities of the entire range. This enabled customers to be trained convincingly, with tuition on climbing, wading, driving over obstacles, through swamps where they faced 2 feet or more of water, earth banks with alarming 47 per cent side tilts, and even a flight of steps. Members of the presentations and demonstrations team, including Roger Crathorne and Don Green, showed how to tackle obstructions apparently insurmountable for anything with wheels. Courses costing £90 were run for drivers from the emergency services, on the track where the Land Rover, Range Rover and Discovery were all developed. Don Green, manager of demonstrations and a member of the driving team for 26 years, was awarded a BEM in 1991.

Honda acquired a 20 per cent share in the Rover Group, which included taking over virtually all its mainstream car development. Nobuhiko Kawamoto, who took over the presidency of Honda in 1990, said the company had no desire to dominate Rover's engineering. "Co-operation is the principle. Rover has many good engineers, but they are not trained in modern processes and the most advanced concepts. We want to help them by providing anything they need," he told Ray Hutton in an interview for *The Sunday Times*.

Charles Spencer King in 1990 with the CSK Range Rover, a special edition named after him.

An early rendering of Project
Challenger, which set out to provide
a replacement for the ageing Defender.

History of a Legend

1991 Project Challenger examined replacement of Defender with a design based on a Discovery platform, since the market appeared to be tending towards lighter vehicles. Challenger was projected to use the Discovery platform, and compete with the Toyota HiLux, using the sub-structure, chassis, suspension and power train, front wings and doors of the Discovery. A full range was planned across two wheelbase sizes, and although the design was widely regarded as attractive, Defender 2 as Challenger was to have been called, did not go down well in styling clinics. Attempts to extend the design also failed and BAe abandoned the project. However some elements of Challenger survived, as the design team was re-assigned to work on the Freelander.

1992 Following the Range Rover's American success, further expansion was planned. Range Rover North America changed its name to Land Rover North America, and marked the occasion by importing 500 Defender 110s, specially modified for the market. All were station wagons incorporating an external roll cage with integral roof basket, a front brush guard, lamp guards and a new rear step. A significant upgrade to the Range Rover, the LSE, was part of a programme to gain experience with features being developed for a planned new model. The wheelbase was extended to 108in (274cm) allowing larger rear doors and more legroom in the back. Air suspension was evaluated since the flexibility of a multi-height system would allow low-level access, a standard cruising height, and extra ground clearance for off-road. Electronic traction control used the ABS system to control slip at the rear wheels. The unpopular VM diesel engine was abandoned, and instead Range Rover was provided with a home-grown 200 Tdi diesel, available later with an automatic gearbox, an option also applied to Discovery.

1993 Signifying the close links between its proprietors, Discovery was launched in Japan as the Honda Crossroad, the first time the Japanese manufacturer had put its badge on a foreign product. Faced with increasing competition from the Japanese on the home market, positive moves were made to re-assert the position of Defender. The 90 County Station Wagon was re-introduced and the County range extended to include a 90 Hard Top. The 1.5 millionth Defender, a 90SV, was driven off the production line by pop star Bryan Adams.

Reviewing the British 4x4 market on 21 November, *The Sunday Times* said: "During the L-plate bulge in August, sales of recreational four wheel drive vehicles continued to soar. Almost 15,000 new off-roaders were registered, a rise of 66 per cent over last year, amounting to over 3.5 per cent of the entire car market. The Land Rover Discovery remained the best seller. A total of 3,161 were sold in August, followed by the Vauxhall Frontera, which overtook the Suzuki Vitara with 2,273. Isuzu Trooper, Jeep Cherokee, Land Rover Defender, Range Rover, and Mitsubishi Shogun also recorded sales of over 1,000. The new Ford Maverick outsold its near-identical twin the Nissan Terrano II, with 699 registrations, ahead of Nissan's 462, thanks largely to a bigger dealer network. Even Mercedes-Benz recorded an improvement. August's sales of its supremely efficient but rather severe and expensive Gelandewagen were up from 24 last year, to 29. The new car market has declined by nearly a third since 1988, but the four wheel drive sector has nearly doubled. *Glass's Guide*, the industry barometer of used car prices, reveals that demand for second-hand off-roaders remains high, prices are hardening, with the result that depreciation will remain low so long as the demand continues. Newcomers are challenging Land Rover. The number of twenty and thirty year-old Land Rovers still working not only show how strong they are, but also how

Canadian singer Bryan Adams joins
the celebrations at Lode Lane in a
limited edition SV90

easy they are to fix when something goes wrong. Yet the important feature of the new sort of 4x4 is its behaviour on the road rather than off it."

1994 The 2.5 litre Tdi diesel engine was modified to meet noise and emission standards and make it compatible with military requirements. This engine, now called the 300Tdi was common to Defender, Discovery and Range Rover. A new second generation Range Rover launched in October was codenamed 38A, after the building at Solihull housing the development team. The launch included a world wide TV broadcast on an in-house satellite network, yet Land Rover was apprehensive about it and kept the old model in production as the Range Rover Classic. UK dealers were invited to the new headquarters at Gaydon to pick up their initial stock, but some broke down on the way home, anticipating the quality issues that afflicted the new model. British Aerospace was accused of skimping on the project's development by trying to adapt corporate solutions to the complex design, but the principal culprit was the electrical system, based on that of the Rover 800.

British Aerospace sold the Rover Group over the heads of its Honda partner to BMW, and to the surprise of many people (including it was said his own), John Towers was promoted to CEO. BMW also had doubts about the new Range Rover, intending to replace it as soon as possible, so little was spent on its further development.

As BMW's takeover of Rover unfolded, the chairman of BMW's board of management Bernd Pischetsrieder told British motoring correspondents at Geneva he was determined to carry through his declared policy of keeping Rover and BMW separate, with different model ranges and independent dealer networks. Pischetsrieder was born in Munich, graduated in mechanical engineering at Munich technical University, and joined BMW in 1973 as a production planning engineer. Following Eberhard v. Kuenheim's elevation to the supervisory board he became chairman in May 1993. BMW's bid for Rover created potentially one of the world's most profitable car manufacturers, making a million or more cars a year, each in a premium-priced niche of the market. Nearly all its models were benchmarks in their class and the prospect of economies in engines and components persuaded Rover shareholders agreement to the sale, at a special meeting on March 15.

Right: The new shape 38A pictured at its launch at Cliveden in 1994.

History of a Legend

Top of the hill is the new 38A,
pictured with the previous four door
and two door versions.

1995 Production of Land Rover vehicles at Solihull exceeded 100,000 per annum for the first time. V8 petrol Defenders ceased production for the home market.

1996 After considering military versions of the Mercedes G-Wagen, the MoD settled on Land Rover for its future military fleet, but only after the German firm declined to bid. The contract was for 8,000 Defender 90s and 110s with an additional 800 Battlefield Ambulances based on the Defender 130. Powered by the 300 Tdi diesel engine and equipped with a 24 volt electrical system, the vehicles - codenamed Wolf for the Defender 90 and 110 and Pulse for the Defender 130 ambulance - were different from their civilian counterparts. The chassis was new and stronger, the body tougher, and it was designed to accept a variety of military equipment. Work done in the 1980s to modify Land Rovers for various weapons systems, resulted in a Weapons Mount Improvement Kit (WMIK). Designed by Ricardo, the WMIK carried various machine guns, grenade launchers and the MILAN anti-tank missile. Wolf and Pulse saw active service in both Iraq wars, Afghanistan and Sierra Leone. Walter Hasselkus replaced John Towers.

1997 The Freelander made its debut at the Frankfurt Motor Show in September, and despite a power failure at the moment of its press showing in the Frankfurt Messe it proved a best seller in both the UK and Europe. Freelander's origins lay in the Oden and Pathfinder projects of the 1990s, when Rover managers had been invited to the Gaydon test centre in the middle of the night to drive a Honda Shuttle converted to four wheel drive. Such nocturnal goings-on suggested that a car-based off-roader could be successful, and led to development of the Freelander. Once again codenamed after a

History of a Legend

Rather obviously posed publicity shot for the new Freelander, launched at Frankfurt in September 1997.

building in the old Triumph works at Canley housing the design team, plans were made to build CB40 at Longbridge. Land Rover prevailed however and the design was finalised at the time of the BMW acquisition. Incoming development executive Wolfgang Reitzle had his own ideas however, and ordered a re-design to introduce the barrelled sides he regarded as important. This delayed the project allowing Honda, which had been privy to the plans thanks to its investment in the group, to get into the 4x4 leisure sector first with its CR-V. Rover had tried negotiating with Valmet, the Finnish manufacturers of Porsche and Saab convertibles, to share the project, but BMW could afford the investment on its own, and withdrew from the discussions.

1998 April 30th was the 50th anniversary of Land Rover and special commemorative limited editions of all four models were produced. These included a Defender 90 Station Wagon, with V8 engine and automatic gearbox, derived from the now defunct NAS vehicle. Sales of Freelander began in Europe where it soon became the best selling 4x4. It took part in the 1998 Camel Trophy in Tierra del Fuego in South America. Three Rallye-Raid prepared Discoverys acted as support vehicles for the BMW Motorrad motorcycle team in the Paris-Dakar Rally. All the motorcycles dropped out, but two of the Discoverys entered in the event completed the course. A third was only ruled out of time through turning back to search for a lost BMW motorcyclist. The new Discovery went on an ambitious round-the-world journey called Tempest Trek after

Discovery II's code-name, and the first two Discovery Series IIs produced travelled through Europe, Asia, Australia, South America, North America and returned to Paris for the launch. Bernd Pischetsreider criticised high costs and inefficiency at the Rover Group, compromising the presentation of the Cowley-produced Rover 75.

1999 In January Ford bought Volvo for $6.45 billion and in March created Premier Automotive Group with Jaguar, Volvo, Aston Martin and Lincoln-Mercury. Discovery Series II was named Sport Utility of the Year at the Detroit Motor Show at the beginning of the year, and at Frankfurt the centrepiece of the Land Rover stand was the Defender SVX. Designed by Dave Saddington at the new Gaydon styling studio, it featured racy Recaro seats, upgraded suspension and large areas of aluminium chequer plate. A number of board members, including Wolfgang Reitzle, were forced out of BMW, along with Pischetsreider following his gloomy forecasts. Reitzle was recruited by Ford Motor Company to head the Premier Automotive Group. Meanwhile, BMW tightened its grip on Rover, running it directly from Munich and appointing Werner Sämann in an effort to make it profitable.

1998 Series 11 Discovery alongside its nautical namesake. Both were equally at home spanning the globe - the new Discovery went round the world on the Tempest Trek

The first £100,000 Range Rover had
a regal heritage. Introduced as an
exclusive variant in 1999 it was
designed by the late Princess
Margaret's son Lord Linley. Only six
were made.

History of a Legend

2000 Rumours abounded at the Detroit and Geneva Motor Shows concerning Rover's future. The Freelander was introduced with a Rover car V6 petrol engine, intended to lead the launch of the model into the USA and the Middle East, but the Group was unable to produce a viable business plan, and in March BMW disposed of it. MG and Rover were combined, and sold to a consortium led by John Towers, formerly of Land Rover, for £10. The deal included a substantial dowry, in loans and debt relief from BMW, for which it sold Land Rover to Ford Motor Company for 3 billion Euros. Ford made Land Rover part of the Premier Automotive Group with CEO Bob Dover, who had been its manufacturing director in the 1980s under Tony Gilroy. Dover had had a distinguished career with Ford, running Jaguar and Aston Martin, and for the first time Land Rover had its own board of directors. They were appointed from top positions in Ford, and following due diligence, Ford Motor Company officially took over on 1 July.

The acquisition included the Land Rover brand name, the manufacturing plant at Solihull, the design and development centre at Gaydon – where the company had established its headquarters – and the Heritage Motor Centre. At the press conference launching it, Dover announced that although Land Rover was making a loss, he expected a return to profit within two years under an ambitious new product programme. Land Rover had been completely integrated within the Rover Group but separating it, with the associated complex movements of staff and establishing new systems, was nevertheless achieved. Anomalies of the old order persisted. The new stamping plant at Solihull continued to supply body parts for the new BMW Mini plant at Oxford, and Land Rovers continued to use engines from MG Rover's Powertrain company, as well as BMW. The V6 derivative of the

Freelander was launched in the US, and whereas it had aimed at improving the lot of Land Rover dealers in America, its poor feature levels and uncompetitive price meant it never fulfilled its potential. In October Land Rover joined its fellow Ford Trustmark companies in an exclusive exhibition hall at the British International Motor Show in Birmingham.

History of a Legend

Left: From July 1st 2000 Land Rover came into the Ford fold as part of the Premier Automotive Group. The CEO was Bob Dover.

The Freelander was at one stage the best selling 4x4 in Europe. Within a year of introducing the Td4 engine, in 2000, BMW was struggling to keep up with demand. This cutaway shows the five door Station Wagon.

2001 The three millionth Land Rover came off the Solihull production line. The Freelander Td4 proved so popular that BMW struggled to keep up with engine supply; a situation partly overcome by diverting units earmarked for the Rover 75. Ford's World Rally Car team used Freelanders as scouts for gravel rallies. The ex-launch vehicles shared M-Sport's workshops with the Ford Focus rally cars, where they were prepared with modified engines, uprated suspension and full rally interiors. On 22 November the third generation Range Rover was revealed to the press at the London Design Museum. It cost £1 billion to develop, making it the most expensive project carried out by the British motor industry ever. Under Wolfgang Reitzle during his BMW days, developed in Munich by Land Rover engineers, the project was begun shortly after BMW took over in 1994 and took 6 years to reach production. It was the first major model after Ford's acquisition, and Reitzle launched it under circumstances that he could not have imagined at its commencement. Land Rover announced that a new one to be built at Solihull would replace the Discovery in due course. In Detroit Ford was affected by a slump in domestic demand and problems with Firestone tyres on the Ford Explorer were reputed to have cost $3 million. Jac Nasser, who founded Premier Automotive Group and was behind the Land Rover purchase, left the company, and his position as CEO was taken over by William Clay Ford.

2002 Ford revealed the new Range Rover, on what was now effectively home ground, at the Detroit Motor Show. It went on sale in the UK on 15 March. The Discovery also received a facelift with a new front that echoed the theme established with Range Rover. It also recovered, at least as an option, the central differential lock it lost with the Series II, restoring its

The third generation L322 Range Rover, developed with BMW input, but sold under Ford.

History of a Legend

off-road capability. In April Wolfgang Reitzle, head of the Premier Automotive Group and architect of the new Range Rover, left the company and was replaced by Mark Fields, former CEO of Ford subsidiary, Mazda. Fields cut costs by amalgamating Land Rover with Jaguar and in May Range Rover reached its 500,000th.

Above: The Series 11 Land Rover Discovery as it looked in 2003, the year Land Rover was voted "Greatest Car of All Time".

2003 Bob Dover retired and Matthew Taylor, who had been sales and marketing director, took his place. Land Rover's short existence as an effectively stand-alone company was now over, with many functions including manufacturing and engineering placed under joint management with Jaguar. Since the Camel Trophy had been discontinued, Land Rover took over the running of an extreme competition of its own, known as the G4 Challenge. Using specially-adapted Range Rovers, Discoverys and Freelanders with Defenders in support, competitors undertook a variety of tests, which started on the streets of New York. The G4 Challenge took them to the mountains and deserts of America and Australia, and the winner, Rudi Thoelen a Belgian fighter pilot, took home two Defenders as his prize. It was revealed that once the Freelander was replaced in 2006, it would be built at Halewood in Liverpool, alongside the Jaguar X-Type. Halewood's efficiency and capacity for bigger production numbers were the rationale for moving production out of Solihull, while viewers of the BBC's *Top Gear* television programme voted the Land Rover The Greatest Car of All Time.

2004 Land Rover had not made a publicly exhibited concept vehicle since the Defender SVX and the Range Stormer, with classic design hints such as a clamshell bonnet and so-called floating roof, was wrapped in the sportiest package ever seen on a Solihull product. Based on a 38A Range Rover, it showed new technology such as Terrain Response, which at the turn of a knob activated systems to gain wheel traction over a variety of surfaces. Design director Geoff Upex incorporated powered, upward hingeing doors, slim roof pillars and a glass roof with an interior dominated by a high centre console. The minor controls had clever aluminium detailing. Saddle leather seats completed a design initiative, which the company happily made known as the prelude to a new integrated platform. The first example of the new thinking would be the Discovery 3, at the British International Motor Show. The platform known at T5 marked a return to a separate chassis and body using elements from the Ford Explorer, providing flexibility over a range of models, while special care was given to maintaining the performance of a monocoque design. The Discovery 3 followed the design themes of the original Discovery and brought to production some of the features of the Range Stormer. These included equipment such as Terrain Response, and stylish proposals such as an all-glass roof, it also

This L322 Range Rover competed in the first G4 Challenge, initiated by Land Rover to replace the Camel Trophy.

marked the wide range of options provided by the array of Ford's engineering inventory with the introduction of a 2.7 litre V6 diesel shared with Jaguar. A 4.0 litre V6 petrol engine for the US and other markets was pooled with the Explorer and other Ford products. The suspension was independent all round and a flat floor gave plenty of rear compartment space, made feasible by having the rear drive shafts pass through the chassis side members. The Discovery 3 was launched in North America as the LR3.

2005 An entirely new model line, the Range Rover Sport introduced at the Detroit Motor Show early in the year, was based on the T5 platform with a shorter chassis than the Discovery 3 and better road holding. As a further

enhancement the Range Rover Sport could be specified with the Dynamic Response system, an improved version of Active Cornering Enhancement first used on the Discovery Series II. After just eight years' production the half millionth Freelander left the production line, a black Hardback, it was specially marked with paw prints and the logo of the Born Free Foundation. It was offered as a prize in an appeal for the animal welfare charity.

MG Rover collapsed after increasingly desperate attempts to find a partner failed, and its suppliers stopped supplying parts, which immediately affected engine supply for the Freelander. As soon as stockpiles of V6 engines, which came from the MG Rover subsidiary Powertrain were exhausted, production for North America ceased. Much the same fate

The dramatic concept vehicle the Range Stormer was first seen in Detroit in January 2004.

befell the 1.8-litre, whose engines came from the same source, and production had to be severely curtailed, after which most Freelanders were built with TD4 BMW diesels. International Motors of Brazil, which had been producing the 300 Tdi engine, announced that its production would cease, with the result that the 5-cylinder TD5 became the last in a long line of Land Rover designed engines. Nonetheless the company set an all time sales record, up 14 per cent on the previous year, and according to JD Power-LMC the brand built 175,78 units in 2005 against 149,764 in 2004.

2006 Land Rover liked to demonstrate its commitment to environmental concerns, and at the Geneva Motor Show went public with an innovatory piece of equipment, in a display emphasising the direction its research was taking. Land_e was the generic title for e-Terrain Technology, which aimed at reductions in both fuel consumption and CO_2 emissions, without apparently sacrificing a 4x4's capabilities. Outgoing managing director Matthew Taylor was able to make the point that nobody had marketed a diesel-electric hybrid SUV, and Land_e was effectively the only hybrid technology specially developed for them. It was expected to be available within a few years and was capable of reducing fuel consumption by 30 per cent, the equivalent of a Freelander doing 50mpg (5.65l/100km). Land_e combined mechanical and electrical developments in areas as diverse as cooling efficiency, battery power management, and power steering.

Notwithstanding improvements already wrought in fuel consumption and exhaust emissions, the exhibit at Geneva included an ingenious electric rear axle drive disconnecting the propeller-shaft power from the engine to the rear wheels. This provided electric propulsion alone at low speeds. A combined starter-generator stopped the engine in traffic, and a system designed to reduce mechanical losses also disconnected drive to the rear when it was not needed, leaving the front wheels alone to do the work. The e-Mode, shown for the first time, focussed mainly on road use but reconfigured all the e-terrain systems for economy. This retained instant access to four wheel drive, but moderated the driver's throttle movements, and selected lower gearshift speeds. Other initiatives, besides those directly affecting the drive-train, included the Intelligent Thermal Programme (ITP) controlling exhaust heat management and functions of the cooling system. This refined the old concept of a radiator blind, with vanes electronically closing off sections of the radiator to help warm-up, then re-opening them to sustain running temperature and prevent overheating . The Exhaust Heat Recovery System (EHRS) used waste heat from the exhaust for faster engine and gearbox warm-up. The Land_e research included an examination of renewable and sustainable fuels, with the aim of running engines on a 25 per cent bio-diesel mix.

Leaving Land Rover after six years, Matthew Taylor said: "Our biggest success has been turning a business from a significant loss to a significant profit, and taking a great brand into the 21st century by giving it the products it needs." Land Rover was the only Ford brand to show sales increases in Europe during the first quarter of 2006, up 13.3 per cent.

With Ford's premium SUV brand headed for record sales and profitability, Taylor's replacement was Phil Popham. He had been director of European operations, taking over on April 19, reporting to Goeff Polities CEO of Jaguar-Land Rover. Among his first tasks was the launch of the new Freelander, which although sales fell in 2005 following the collapse of MG Rover, at 41,440 was the brand's second best

History of a Legend

Above: Range Rover Sport doing what it does best. "The Range Rover Sport has the refinement and luxury once found in Rolls-Royces, together with the cross country agility of a gazelle."

Right: Early rendering of the Range Rover Sport. It marked the start of an entirely new model line.

seller after Discovery. Popham's challenges included involved moving Freelander production from Solihull to Halewood and completing modernisation and quality improvements at the old plant, which continued building Defender, Discovery, Range Rover, and Range Rover Sport.

The new Freelander was put on display at the London Motor Show in July and went on sale at the end of the year.

Series 1 to Defender

Available in bright AA Yellow, the
1993 NAS Defender 90 epitomised
the fun and leisure appeal which the
utility Land Rovers acquired over
the years.

1947 Jeep-based prototype, the J-model

Rover technical director Maurice Wilks used a friend's 1943 Willys Jeep from about March 1947, and by June he had acquired and registered it in his name. Photographs show the Wilks family using FWD 534 at home and at their farm, Tros-yr-Afon on Anglesey, North Wales. The Land Rover idea seems to have taken root there, and also on Llanddona Beach in Red Wharf Bay, where Wilks was said to have drawn the basic configuration of it with a stick in the sand. Back at Rover Cars in Solihull, Maurice Wilks set up a design team under his deputy Robert Boyle, who selected five designers Gordon Bashford, Tom Barton, Frank Shaw, Joe Drinkwater and Sam Ostler and gave them the task of tracking down two further war-surplus Jeeps. They produced the J-Model, essentially a Rover powered Jeep, to try the concept out. This was the foundation for the only real prototype. Surviving members of the project recalled an extensive test programme and wide-ranging modifications to the Jeep detail design to accept the Rover engine and gearbox. They also recollected Maurice Wilks's cavalier attitude to accounts and keeping records. Many different configurations were tried, using such components as were readily available, during the evolution of the J-model. Rover had to acquire 4x4 experience of its own, and the Jeep was invaluable in revealing many of the secrets of off-road driving.

INTRODUCTION (Jeep) 1941
BODY open utility vehicle, 3125lbs (1417.49kg) gross weight
ENGINES Jeep 'Go-Devil'; 4-cylinder in line, front. 3 1/8in x 4 3/8in; 3.125in (79.37mm) x 4.375in (111.112mm); 134.2 cu.in (2199 cc). 60bhp (44.74kW)@ 4000rpm, 105lb ft (140.8Nm) @ 2000rpm. Rover P3 'Sloping Head' 4-cylinder in line, front 65.5mm x 105mm, 1415 cc. 46bhp, 46bhp (34.3W), 74lb ft (99Nm)
ENGINE STRUCTURE Jeep; cast iron block and cylinder head. L-head with side valves. Carter W-O carburettor, Auto-Lite IGC-4705 distributor. Rover; cast iron block and cylinder head. sloping head with overhead inlet and side exhaust valves.
TRANSMISSION selectable four wheel drive, hydraulic single dry plate clutch 8in dia. Warner 3-speed gearbox with synchromesh on 2nd and 3rd gears (Rover gearbox 4-speed), 2-speed Spicer transfer box, Spicer front and rear axles, 4.88:1.

CHASSIS welded steel ladder frame. Front and rear beam axles with semi-elliptic springs and telescopic shock absorbers. Cam and lever steering. 4-wheel hydraulic 9in drum brakes, 6in drum transmission hand brake. 15 US gallon (12.5 Imperial gallon) fuel tank. 16in pressed steel combat wheels with 6.00 x 16 tyres.
DIMENSIONS wheelbase 80in (203.2cm), front and rear track 49in (124.46cm) with combat wheels, length; 132.75in (337.18cm) width; 62in, (157.48cm) height; 69.75in (177.16cm) with top up.

The wartime Jeep was the inspiration for the original Land Rover. This is a preserved example, with the legendary Willys Go-Devil engine.

1947 The centre-steer prototype

Once Wilks had made up his mind to proceed with the Land Rover, work began on a number of prototypes, some accounts say there were five, others seven. To save time, one was based on the chassis of one of the procured Jeeps, using its transfer box and axles. The engine was from an experimental Rover car built before the war, a sloping head design, later used in the P3 car. A member of the team confirmed that the Jeep's side valve engine, with a modified Rover flywheel to match up with the Rover gearbox , was retained for testing. Produced first as a wooden mock up, the body was simple, using readily available Birmabright aluminium panels and avoiding complex curves. To try and improve its chances of classification as an agricultural implement, it had a centre steering position like a tractor. This might also have provided economies in avoiding different versions for export markets. The steering was taken from the left hand side of the original Jeep to the centre, by means of a chain, and the pedals straddled the transmission tunnel. The prototype was tried out with a variety of farm machinery power take off (PTO) equipment, but the centre steer position was soon seen as impractical and abandoned. There were no doors but the sills were low so it was easy to get in and out. The windscreen was a one-piece affair, which could be folded flat on to buffers on the bonnet, and held there with spring-loaded catches. Weather protection was a primitive pram-type hood. The sole prototype was used to evaluate a number of features before Rover went straight into the pre-production phase of Land Rovers, and once its job was complete, the father of all Land Rovers was ignominiously scrapped.

INTRODUCTION 1947
BODY open utility 3 seats, 2588lbs (1174kg) – estimated gross weight
ENGINES Jeep 'Go-Devil'; 4-cylinder in line, front. 3.125in (79.37mm) x 4.375in (111.112mm); 134.2 cu.in (2199 cc). 60bhp (44.74kW) @ 4000rpm, 105lb ft (140.8Nm) @ 2000rpm. Rover P3 sloping head 4-cylinder in line, front 65.5mm x 105mm, 1415 cc. 46bhp, 46bhp (34.3W), 74lb ft (99Nm)
ENGINE STRUCTURE Jeep; cast iron block and cylinder head. L-head with side valves. Carter W-O carburettor, Auto-Lite IGC-4705 distributor. Rover; cast iron block and cylinder head. sloping head with overhead inlet and side exhaust valves.

TRANSMISSION selectable four wheel drive, hydraulic single dry plate clutch 8in dia. Rover gearbox 4-speed, 2-speed Spicer transfer box, Spicer front and rear axles, 4.88:1.
CHASSIS welded steel ladder frame. Front and rear beam axles with semi-elliptic springs and telescopic shock absorbers. Cam and lever steering. 4-wheel hydraulically operated 9in drum brakes, 6in drum transmission hand brake.12.5 gallon (57 litre) fuel tank.16in pressed steel combat wheels with 6.00 x 16 tyres.
DIMENSIONS wheelbase 80in (203.2cm), front and rear track 49in (124.46cm) with combat wheels, length; 132.75in (337.18cm) width; 62.5in, (159cm) height; 69in (175.0cm).

There was almost certainly just one centre-steer prototype, although other theories have been advanced over the years. Here it is outside the main office block at Solihull.

1948 Pre-production Land Rovers

Land Rover moved quickly from the J-model and centre-steer prototype, to building 48 pre-production vehicles in the Experimental Workshop at Solihull, while work was proceeding on a production line in South Works. Each was slightly different in detail, but they all had a fabricated box section galvanised steel chassis frame, and a body from Birmabright 2 alloy panels. This was the same material but of a thicker gauge than production vehicles. The sides were topped with galvanised steel cappings, front wings were now more upright and the rear body was of a box style. Lift-off doors were fitted and there was proper provision for a hood. Power came from the sloping head engine and gearbox from the Rover P3 60 car. The first pre-production Land Rovers had a transfer box with Jeep rotating parts inside a case machined from a solid aluminium billet. Later ones had a cast aluminium case, with new Rover designed gears that had a 15 per cent drive reduction, to make up for the lower power of the Rover engine. There was a freewheel in the drive to the front axle to control wind-up, which released drive to the front axle when in reverse, and could be locked only in low range. The axles were derived from the P2 car's, the front using the same differential as the rear, merely changing ends so that the axis of drive was in the same line, with the casing modified to suit the Tracta swivelling steering joints. After abandoning the centre steering position of the prototype both right and left-hand drive versions were built. Some were lent for evaluation to the Ministry of Supply and Overseas Food Corporation, which was running the ill-starred ground-nuts scheme in Africa. One was also used as a prototype for the Tickford Station Wagon while others were robbed of components to support the build-up of production.

INTRODUCTION 1947
BODY pickup, 4032lbs (1829kg).
ENGINE: 4-cylinder in line, front 69.5mm x 105mm, 1595cc. 55bhp (40kW) @4000rpm, 83lb ft (112Nm) @ 2000 rpm, compression 7.1:1.
ENGINE STRUCTURE cast iron block and cylinder head. Overhead inlet, side exhaust valves, chain-driven camshaft, pushrods and rockers, 3-bearing crankshaft.
TRANSMISSION permanent four wheel drive with lockable freewheel for front axle, hydraulic single dry plate clutch 9in (22.9cm) dia. Rover 4-speed gearbox and 2-speed transfer box, Rover front and rear axles, 4.88:1.

CHASSIS welded box section steel ladder frame – galvanised. Front and rear beam axles with semi-elliptic springs and telescopic shock absorbers. Worm and nut steering. 4-wheel hydraulically operated 10in (25.4cm) drum brakes, 6in (15.2cm) drum transmission hand brake. 10 gallon (45 litre) fuel tank. 16in detachable disc pressed steel wheels with 6.00 x 16 heavy traction tyres.
DIMENSIONS wheelbase 80in (203cm), front and rear track 50in (127cm), length; 132in (335cm), width; 61in (155cm), height; 72in (182cm).

The very first pre-production model, with chassis number R.01, was bought back by Land Rover and rebuilt.

1948 Land Rover initial production

Less than a year after Maurice Wilks drew the outlines of the Land Rover in the sand of a Welsh beach, the vehicle was revealed to the press and public in the halls of the RAI exhibition centre on April 30 1948 at Amsterdam Motor Show. It was an immediate success. With production getting into its stride, Rover chairman E Ransom Harrison reported to the 53rd Annual General Meeting on 26 November 1948, that the decision to go ahead with Land Rover had proved "very satisfactory". He claimed that Land Rovers were "just as exciting" as the cars with which they shared so many components. More importantly, it appeared that the response to the new product was such that it would be more than just a stop-gap. Prophetically he concluded that the Land Rover "may yet equal – and even exceed – our car output". In 1949 Commercial Motor gave a Land Rover a thorough testing. This included a 240-mile (386km) trip to Bodmin Moor in Cornwall, the battle course at the Army's proving ground at Long Valley towing a 250-gallon (1137 litre) water bowser, and agricultural work such as harrowing and ploughing. Testers, L J Cotton and T Hammond Cradock concluded that it "climbed like a cat and pulled like an ox". The farmer on whose acres it was used considered that it took the place of six good horses. They noted that the Land Rover weighed 3 cwt (336lbs or 152kg) more than the Jeep, but considered that the additional weight was all in the right places, and there was nothing skimpy in its construction. Their praiseworthy conclusion was that it would "take all punishment without flinching".

INTRODUCTION 1948
BODY pickup, 4032lbs (1829kg).
ENGINES 4-cylinder in line, front 69.5mm x 105mm, 1595cc. 50bhp (37kW) @ 4000 rpm, 80lb ft (108Nm) @2000 rpm, compression 7.1:1.
ENGINE STRUCTURE cast iron block and cylinder head. Overhead inlet, side exhaust valves, chain-driven camshaft, pushrods and rockers, 3-bearing crankshaft.
TRANSMISSION permanent four wheel drive with lockable freewheel for front axle, hydraulic single dry plate clutch 9in (22.8cm) dia. Rover 4-speed gearbox and 2-speed transfer box, Rover front and rear axles, 4.88:1, later 4.7:1.

CHASSIS welded box section steel ladder frame – galvanised. Front and rear beam axles with semi-elliptic springs and telescopic shock absorbers. Worm and nut steering. 4-wheel hydraulically operated 10in (25.4cm) drum brakes, 6in (15.2cm) drum transmission hand brake. 10 gallon (45 litre) fuel tank. 16in divided pressed steel wheels with 6.00 x 16 heavy traction tyres. One piece pressed steel wheels and 7.00 x 16 tyres also offered.
DIMENSIONS wheelbase 80in (203cm), front and rear track 50in (127cm), length; 132in (335cm), width; 61in (155cm), height; 73.5in (192cm).
PRICE £450 0s 0d

One of the first production Land Rovers was pictured inside the factory grounds at Solihull. This RHD example has the optional semaphore indicators and an early spare wheel mounting arrangement.

1948 Land Rover Tickford Station Wagon

Although Rover was launching an essentially utility vehicle, it did not overlook its heritage of luxury cars, which had been successful in the 1930s. It seemed natural to explore the possibility of extending Land Rover similarly up-market. Perhaps surprisingly this was done at an early stage, following a trend at the time for car manufacturers to produce wooden estate car bodies, when their sheet steel allocation would not stretch to cars. One pre-production Land Rover was dispatched to Newport Pagnell, to receive a prototype body, by coachbuilders Tickford who made a metal body on a wooden frame. What emerged owed something to a Jeep Station Wagon selling in America so it was well up to the minute. The body was wood framed, probably in mahogany, to resist wood boring insects in export markets. Aluminium panels with distinctive swage lines resembled the popular wooden styles. The familiar Land Rover front was retained, the bonnet mounted spare wheel concealed by a spun aluminium cover. There was a one-piece windscreen, and seven seats trimmed in green leather, the left front one cut away, and tilting forward to allow access to the rear. The fuel filler was under the right hand seat cushion, and the rear seats could be folded up or removed, to create more space. A two-piece tailgate again echoed the Jeep version but also foreshadowed the Range Rover, which was still 20 years away. The tailgate had an upper section secured by a friction nut, while the lower was held by chains, and had rubbing strips to make loading luggage easier. In the UK, the vehicle attracted purchase tax; its £1000 would be £20,000 in 21st century money, and sales were small. The bulk of production went overseas to various aid projects.

INTRODUCTION 1948
BODY 7-seat station wagon, aluminium panels on a wooden frame, 4424lbs (2006kg).
ENGINE 4-cylinder in line, front 69.5mm x 105mm, 1595cc. 50bhp (37kW), 80lb ft (108Nm), compression 7.1:1.
ENGINE STRUCTURE cast iron block and cylinder head. Overhead inlet, side exhaust valves, chain-driven camshaft, pushrods and rockers, 3-bearing crankshaft.
TRANSMISSION permanent four wheel drive with lockable freewheel for front axle, hydraulic single dry plate clutch 9in (22.8cm) dia. Rover 4-speed gearbox and 2-speed transfer box, Rover front and rear axles, 4.88:1, later 4.7:1.

CHASSIS welded box section steel ladder frame – galvanised. Front and rear beam axles with semi-elliptic springs and telescopic shock absorbers. Worm and nut steering. 4-wheel hydraulically operated 10in (254cm) drum brakes, 6in (15.2cm) drum transmission hand brake.10 gallon (45 litre) fuel tank.16in divided pressed steel wheels with 6.00 x 16 heavy traction tyres. One piece pressed steel wheels and 7.00 x 16 tyres also offered.
DIMENSIONS wheelbase 80in (203cm), front and rear track 50in (127cm), length; 132in (335.28cm), width; 61in (154.94cm), height; 76.75in (194.94cm).
PRICE £959 1s 8d

The vehicle illustrated in the Station Wagon sales brochure was in fact the prototype, which differed in a number of respects from the production models. Note, for example, the two-pane windscreen and the colour scheme with the body pressings picked out in darker paint.

THE FOUR WHEEL DRIVE

LAND
ROVER
STATION WAGON

"Meets every occasion"

1950 Land Rover Series I, 2 litre petrol

Production rose steeply to over 16,000 a year and by 1950 was fulfilling the chairman's prediction that it would be Solihull's major product. The most significant change was upgrading the engine in August 1951. The new unit had a wider bore, designed to increase low-speed torque, reduce gear changes and make towing easier. With experience, modifications were made, such as altering the grille so that the headlights no longer shone through it. This left them exposed, no longer protected by its mesh, which had been a useful feature when penetrating woods or driving over scrubland. Other changes came about through using so many car components. Early on, Rover had changed the final drive ratio to suit the Rover P3 axle, and the Land Rover also received the gearbox from the P4 Rover 75. However while Rover was traditionally keen on the transmission freewheel, fitting one in the 75 saloon, to save fuel by disconnecting the engine on the overrun, it decided to replace it on the Land Rover with selectable four wheel drive. Under the new system, the front axle was not driven in normal high range, as with the Jeep, but four wheel drive could be engaged in high range. It was however automatically engaged when shifting to the lower ratios.

INTRODUCTION 1951
BODY pickup, 4032lbs (1829kg).
ENGINES 4-cylinder in line, front 77.8mm x 105mm, 1997cc. 52bhp (38.8kW) @ 4000 rpm, 101lb ft (137Nm) @1500 rpm, compression 7.1:1.
ENGINE STRUCTURE cast iron block and cylinder head. Overhead inlet, side exhaust valves, chain-driven camshaft, pushrods and rockers, 3-bearing crankshaft.
TRANSMISSION selectable four wheel drive, hydraulic single dry plate clutch 9in (22.8cm) dia. Rover 4-speed gearbox and 2-speed transfer box, Rover front and rear axles, 4.7:1.

CHASSIS welded box section steel ladder frame, front and rear beam axles with semi-elliptic springs and telescopic shock absorbers, worm and nut steering. 4-wheel hydraulically operated 10in (25.4cm) drum brakes, 6in (15.2cm) drum transmission hand brake.10 gallon (45 litre) fuel tank.16in divided pressed steel wheels with 6.00 x 16 heavy traction tyres. One piece pressed steel wheels and 7.00 x 16 tyres also offered.
DIMENSIONS wheelbase 80in (203cm), front and rear track 50in (127cm), length; 132in (335cm), width; 61in (155cm), height; 73.5in (192cm).

The sales brochure certainly made the most of Land Rover's new engine.

...MORE POWER FOR THE LAND-ROVER

The LAND-ROVER

NEW 2-LITRE POWER UNIT

The powerful high efficiency four-cylinder engine of the Land-Rover is the result of many years' experience in automobile engineering.

Early examples of the new stretched Land Rover had the same 2 litre engine of the 80inch, but a new one was not long coming. It had the same bore and stroke as its predecessor and produced the same power and torque, but it was in reality quite different. It was a different version of the engine developed for the Rover P4 60, the cheaper and more economical version of the 6-cylinder Rover 75. It seemed only natural for the Land Rover to share the unit, although a cast iron cylinder head was substituted for the car's aluminium one and it was considerably de-rated. The construction was of the spread bore type, with a full water jacket between the cylinders, a technique developed originally to stop piston scuffing in the 6-cylinder car engines. The engineering team, now led by Tom Barton, had worked hard to improve the Land Rover, and the fruits of their labours appeared in September 1953 in time for the following season. The original wheelbase had been copied from the Jeep, but now Rover felt confident enough to extend it to 86 inches, and took the opportunity to add three inches to the body. This increased load space by 25 per cent although the payload remained the same. It was, contemporary sales literature said reassuringly; "ample for a vehicle of this kind". It came with a detachable, aluminium hard top, and a truck cab painted cream to keep the interior cool, as well as the normal full-length canvas hood. Drivers were made more comfortable by re-positioning the pedals, there was a new instrument cluster, dash ventilators, a full width shelf and better weatherproofing.

INTRODUCTION 1953
BODY pickup, 4142lbs (1879kg).
ENGINE: 4-cylinder in line, front 77.8mm x 105mm, 1997cc. 52bhp (38.8kW) @ 4000 rpm, 101lb ft (137Nm) @1500 rpm, compression 7.1:1.
ENGINE STRUCTURE cast iron block and cylinder head. Overhead inlet, side exhaust valves, chain-driven camshaft, pushrods and rockers, 3-bearing crankshaft.
TRANSMISSION selectable four wheel drive, hydraulic single dry plate clutch 9in (22.8cm) dia. Rover 4-speed gearbox and 2-speed transfer box, Rover front and rear axles, 4.7:1.

CHASSIS welded box section steel ladder frame. Front and rear beam axles with semi-elliptic springs and telescopic shock absorbers. Worm and nut steering. 4-wheel hydraulically operated 10in (25.4cm) drum brakes, 6in (15.2cm) drum transmission hand brake. 10gallon (45 litre) fuel tank. 16in divided pressed steel wheels with 6.00 x 16 heavy traction tyres. One piece pressed steel wheels and 7.00 x 16 tyres also available.
DIMENSIONS wheelbase 86in (218cm), front and rear track 50in (127cm), length; 140.5in (357cm), width; 61in (155cm), height; 76in (194cm).

The longer wheelbase of the 86-inch model allowed for a bigger load bed, and also made a Station Wagon variant more practical.

THE 86in. WHEELBASE LAND-ROVER GIVES 25% MORE CAPACITY

The above illustration shows graphically just what the 6-inch extension in the Land-Rover wheelbase means. The rear load-carrying section is extended by 9 inches, giving a 25% increase in carrying capacity and more space for bulky loads. In addition, riding and road-holding qualities—always outstanding—are now even better.

1953 Land Rover Station Wagon

The original Tickford-bodied Land Rover Station Wagon of 1948 was not regarded as a success with a mere 641 built. However Rover realised the potential of the style and set out to produce an in-house version. The 80inch wheelbase version had lasted until 1951, and now was reintroduced with the 86inch wheelbase, which offered more room. The new Station Wagon shared the same 7-seat capacity of the old 80inch, but there the resemblance ended. The new one was built at Solihull with an aluminium hard top, side windows for the rear passengers, and introduced the so-called tropical roof. This had an extra panel on top, so an insulating layer of air helped prevent the roof of the passenger compartment from overheating, and also allowed ventilation, claimed draught-proof, via a roof-mounted vent. The Station Wagon also marked the first appearance of a feature popular in years to come, the Alpine Light, which allowed more daylight into the rear. Later made of glass, these first ones were curved Perspex. Station Wagons lost convenient access to the rear through inheriting the full width seat base and interior bulkhead of the utility versions. Instead, they had a side opening rear door with a simple folding step. Since they also shared the chassis and lower body of the standard Land Rover, the rear cross member still had the "woodpecker" mounts for the downward hinging tailgate, while the body side kept now redundant cleats for tying down a non-existent hood. The only colour option was light grey with blue upholstery.

INTRODUCTION 1954
BODY all-steel station wagon, 4032lbs (1829kg) with aluminium fittings.
ENGINE: 4-cylinder in line, front 77.8mm x 105mm, 1997cc. 52bhp (38.8kW) @ 4000 rpm, 101lb ft (137Nm) @1500 rpm, compression 7.1:1.
ENGINE STRUCTURE cast iron block and cylinder head. Overhead inlet, side exhaust valves, chain-driven camshaft, pushrods and rockers, 3-bearing crankshaft.
TRANSMISSION selectable four wheel drive, hydraulic single dry plate clutch 9in (22.8cm) dia. Rover 4-speed gearbox and 2-speed transfer box, Rover front and rear axles, 4.7:1.

CHASSIS welded box section steel ladder frame, front and rear beam axles with semi-elliptic springs and telescopic shock absorbers, worm and nut steering. 4-wheel hydraulically operated 10in (25.4cm) drum brakes, 6in (15.2cm) drum transmission hand brake.10 gallon (45 litre) fuel tank.16in divided pressed steel wheels with 6.00 x 16 heavy traction tyres. One piece pressed steel wheels and 7.00 x 16 tyres also offered.
DIMENSIONS wheelbase 86in (218cm), front and rear track 50in (127cm), length; 132in (335cm), width; 62.5in (159cm), height; 76in (193cm).

The Station Wagon was based on the new 86inch wheelbase chassis and used many of the panels of the basic model in order to keep costs down. These two are on the later 88inch chassis.

1953 Land Rover Series 1 107inch Long Wheelbase

The most radically new production Land Rover since 1948 was a long wheelbase version stretched by 21inches (112cm). Initially available with a truck cab, the long wheelbase provided improvements in load space and payload up to 1500lb (680.4kg), compared with its "tough little partner". Except for the longer propeller shaft and bigger tyres, the mechanical specification was largely unchanged, but the rear body had higher sides and there were stowage lockers in the wheelboxes. Comfort was taken a little more seriously. There was a De Luxe version with a blue leather cloth trimmed cab, a plastic-covered felt headlining, door trim with pockets, plastic-covered felt floor mats, an interior light and thick padded seats covered with gingham-patterned plastic. Optional extras included a heater/demister, radio, tropical roof and a passenger windscreen wiper as well as practical items such as power take offs and seating for the rear. From 1956 there was also a long wheelbase Station Wagon, notable for its extraordinarily homespun appearance, with a plethora of galvanised cappings and reinforcements. The rear body was bespoke so was, at last, clear of redundant rope cleats. Accommodation was provided for 10 with two forward-facing bench seats, the front row with separate cushions allowing access to the fuel tank, while the back row could be folded. The rear compartment's inward facing bench seats could be folded to increase load-carrying capacity. Long Wheelbase vehicles were available in blue or grey, as well as the customary Land Rover green, with the wheels and chassis in a contrasting colour.

INTRODUCTION 1953
BODY long wheelbase pickup, 4556lbs (2080kg), 10-seat station wagon, 4938lbs (2240kg).
ENGINE 4-cylinder in line, front 77.8mm x 105mm, 1997cc. 52bhp (38.8kW) @ 4000 rpm, 101lb ft (137Nm) @1500 rpm.
ENGINE STRUCTURE cast iron block and cylinder head. Overhead inlet, side exhaust valves, chain-driven camshaft, pushrods and rockers, 3-bearing crankshaft.
TRANSMISSION selectable four wheel drive, hydraulic single dry plate clutch 9in (22.8cm) dia. Rover 4-speed gearbox and 2-speed transfer box, Rover front and rear axles, 4.7:1.

CHASSIS welded box section steel ladder frame, front and rear beam axles with semi-elliptic springs and telescopic shock absorbers, worm and nut steering, 4-wheel hydraulically operated 11in (27.9cm) drum brakes, 6in (15.2cm) drum transmission hand brake. 10 gallon (45 litre) fuel tank. One piece pressed steel wheels and 7.00 x 16 tyres.
DIMENSIONS wheelbase 107in (272cm), front and rear track 50in (127cm), length; 173.5in (441cm), width; 62.5in (159cm), height; 78in (198cm).
PRICE £615 0s 0d – £1186 7s 0d

The 107-inch long-wheelbase chassis arrived at the same time as the 86-inch model. Most were built as pick-ups.

1957 Land Rover. Petrol and new diesel

By the middle of the 1950s diesel was starting to take over from petrol in the truck and, more importantly, the agricultural sector. In the words of a contemporary brochure the Land Rover was, "primarily designed to help the farmer in his multifarious activities". Diesel fuel was not burdened by heavy taxation for agricultural activities, farms often acquired their own supply tank, so the demand for a diesel-powered Land Rover became so widespread that several companies began offering conversions. Rover began work on its own unit, the first engine designed solely for use in the Land Rover. The old overhead inlet side exhaust petrol engine was retained but the new diesel switched to a conventional overhead valve layout operated by pushrods from a block-mounted camshaft and adjusted by roller tappets. The engine produced the same power output as the petrol engine, which allowed the transmission to be used without change. However it was longer than the petrol engine so the wheelbase of Land Rovers was altered by 2inches (5cm), effected by moving the front spring hangers forwards. This change delayed the arrival of the diesel engine by several months, when it came it added £100 to the price, and the models were now known as Regular or Long.

INTRODUCTION 1957
BODY short wheelbase full hood, truck cab, 4190lbs (1900kg). Long Wheelbase truck cab or Station Wagon, 5185lbs (2352kg).
ENGINES petrol; 4-cylinder in line, 77.8mm x 105mm, 1997cc. 52bhp (38.8kW) @ 4000 rpm, 101lb ft (137Nm) @1500 rpm. Diesel; 4-cylinder in line, 85.7mm x 88.9mm 2052cc. 52bhp (38.8kW) @ 3500rpm, 87lb ft (118Nm) @2,000 rpm, compression ratio 22.5:1.
ENGINE STRUCTURE petrol; cast iron block and cylinder head, overhead inlet, side exhaust valves. Diesel; cast iron block and cylinder head, Ricardo Comet V combustion chambers with recesses in the piston crowns, pushrod overhead valves, camshaft chain driven with hydraulic tensioner. CAV fuel injection with Pintaux-type nozzles.
TRANSMISSION selectable four wheel drive, hydraulic single dry plate clutch 9in (22.8cm) dia. Rover 4-speed gearbox and 2-speed transfer box, Rover front and rear axles, 4.7:1.

CHASSIS welded box section steel ladder frame, front and rear beam axles with semi-elliptic springs and telescopic shock absorbers, worm and nut steering with recirculating ball. 4-wheel hydraulically operated drum brakes, Regular; 10in (25.4cm), Long; 11in (27.9cm), 6in (15.2cm) drum transmission hand brake. 10 gallon (45 litre) fuel tank. Pressed steel wheels with 6.00 x 16 tyres – 7.00 x 16 tyres on Long models.
DIMENSIONS regular; wheelbase 88in (224cm), front and rear track 50in (127cm), length; 140.75in (358cm), width; 62.56in (159cm), height; 76in (193cm). Long; wheelbase 109in (277cm), front and rear track 50in (127cm), length; 173.50in (441cm), width; 62.56in (159cm), height; 76in (193cm).
PRICES 88in and 109in £730-850

The big news in summer 1957, as this sales brochure makes clear, was that a diesel engine was now available as an alternative to the petrol type.

THE
WORLD'S
MOST
VERSATILE
VEHICLE

NOW AVAILABLE WITH ROVER DIESEL ENGINE

1958 Land Rover Series II

Thus far Land Rover had remained free from the attentions of Rover's styling designers, so some models such as the Long Station Wagon had been criticised for looking more like the product of a Meccano set than a styling studio. This changed with Land Rover's 10th anniversary although perhaps symptomatically, the package of changes was staggered, and was not complete until later in the year. The new Land Rover was dubbed Series II although Series I had never been called as much by the company. Chief designer David Bache altered the appearance of Land Rovers substantially creating some landmark designs. Straight slab sides were replaced by barrelling that continued the curvature of the front wing tops rearwards. This was not only a styling expedient it was also a practical means of catering for the new, wide-track axles. A new external fuel filler slightly spoilt the line, but it was better than having it under the driver's seat. Cast iron door hinges were needed to clear the new body sides, and sill panels helped to balance the proportions as well as hiding the exhaust and the more agricultural bits of the chassis. On the Long Land Rover there was a new curved truck cab and a well for the spare wheel. Glass replaced Perspex in the side windows. Wider track axles were supported by springs mounted on chassis outriggers to give greater stability. Lower rate springs in conjunction with new shock absorbers provided what was called "a well balanced ride for driver, passengers and load", and the turning circle was smaller.

INTRODUCTION 1958
BODY short wheelbase full hood, truck cab, hard top or Station Wagon. Kerb weight petrol; 2953lb (1339kg), diesel; 3097lb (1405kg). Long wheelbase truck cab or Station Wagon, kerb weight petrol; 3301lb (1497kg), diesel 3471lb (1574kg).
ENGINES petrol; 4-cylinder in line, 77.8mm x 105mm, 1997cc. 52bhp (38.8kW) @ 4000 rpm, 101lb ft (137Nm) @1500 rpm. Diesel; 4-cylinder in line, 85.7mm x 88.9mm 2052cc. 52bhp (38.8kW) @ 3500 rpm, 87lb ft (118Nm) @2,000 rpm.
ENGINE STRUCTURE petrol; cast iron block and cylinder head. Overhead inlet, side exhaust valves. Diesel; cast iron block and cylinder head. Overhead valves, Ricardo Comet V combustion chambers with recesses in the piston crowns, pushrod overhead valves, camshaft chain driven with hydraulic tensioner.
TRANSMISSION selectable four wheel drive, hydraulic single dry plate clutch 9in (22.9cm) dia. Rover 4-speed gearbox and 2-speed transfer box, Rover front and rear axles, 4.7:1.

CHASSIS welded box section steel ladder frame, front and rear beam axles with semi-elliptic springs and telescopic shock absorbers, worm and nut steering with recirculating ball. 4-wheel hydraulically operated drum brakes, Regular; 10in (25.4cm), Long; 11in (27.9cm), 9in (22.9cm) drum transmission hand brake. 10 gallon (45 litre) fuel tank – 16 gallon (73 litre) on Long Station Wagon. 16in pressed steel wheels with 6.00 x 16 tyres – 7.50 x 16 on Long models.
DIMENSIONS Regular; wheelbase 88in (224cm), front and rear track 51.5in (131cm); length; 142.4in (362cm), width; 66in (168cm), height; 77.5in (197cm). Long; wheelbase 109in (277cm), front and rear track 51.5in (131cm); length; 175in (444cm), width; 66in (168cm), height; 81in (206cm).
PRICE Regular; £640 0s 0d, Long; £730 0s 0d

David Bache's masterful re-style of the Land Rover, with the basic work done by Tony Poole, softened its edges and gave it a more integrated look, but without sacrificing any of its vital ruggedness. The same basic shape endured right through to the first decade of the 21st century in the Defender.

Land Rover 2.25 Petrol Engine

Despite its anxiety to get the Series II into the market to mark the 10th anniversary, Rover was unable to bring in all the changes at once. The major mechanical improvement was a new, 2.25litre petrol engine, introduced first on the Long models, leaving the Regulars to use up stocks of the old engine. The new one was essentially a petrol version of the diesel introduced the year before, sharing its pushrod overhead valves but with a larger capacity achieved by a wider cylinder bore. It also dispensed with the diesel's wet cast iron cylinder liners. Rover was exploring a new car range, and were able to install the Land Rover engine, virtually unchanged, into the Rover 80 P4 car of which 5900 were produced between 1960 and 1962. A surprisingly smooth economical unit in the P4 it boosted the power available to the Land Rover by nearly half as much again as the old unit. The increase in pulling power was also significant even though it peaked higher up the rev range.

INTRODUCTION 1958
BODY short wheelbase full hood, truck cab, kerb weight petrol; 2953lb (1339kg), diesel; 3097lb (1405kg). Long wheelbase truck cab or station wagon, kerb weight petrol; 3301lb (1497kg), diesel 3471lb (1574kg).
ENGINES petrol; 4-cylinder in line, 90.47mm x 88.9mm, 2286cc. 77bhp (57kW) @ 4250 rpm, 124lb ft (168Nm) @2500 rpm. Diesel; 4-cylinder in line, 85.7mm x 88.9mm 2052cc. 52bhp (38.8kW) @ 3500 rpm, 87lb ft (118Nm) @2,000 rpm.
ENGINE STRUCTURE cast iron block and cylinder head, pushrod overhead valves, camshaft duplex chain driven with hydraulic tensioner.
TRANSMISSION selectable four wheel drive, hydraulic single dry plate clutch 9in (22.8cm) dia. Rover 4-speed gearbox and 2-speed transfer box, Rover front and rear axles, 4.7:1.

CHASSIS welded box section steel ladder frame, front and rear beam axles with semi-elliptic springs and telescopic shock absorbers, worm and nut steering with recirculating ball. 4-wheel hydraulically operated drum brakes, Regular; 10in (25.4cm), Long; 11in (27.9cm), 6in (15.2cm) drum transmission hand brake.10 gallon (45 litre) fuel tank – 16 gallon (73 litre) on Long Station Wagon. 16in pressed steel wheels with 6.00 x 16 tyres – 7.50 x 16 on Long models.
DIMENSIONS regular; wheelbase 88in (224cm), front and rear track 51.5in (131cm), length; 142.4in (362cm), width; 66in (168cm), height; 77.5in (197cm). Long; wheelbase 109in (277cm), front and rear track 51.5in (131cm), length; 175in (444cm), width; 66in (168cm), height; 81in (206cm).

The much-loved "two and a quarter" petrol engine was an OHV design closely related to the existing Land Rover diesel engine.

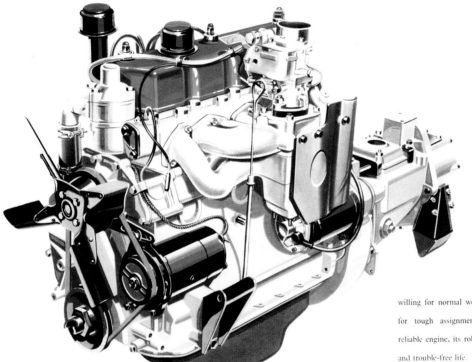

The 2¼-litre overhead valve petrol engine develops 77 b.h.p. at 4,250 r.p.m. and has a torque of 124 lb. ft. at 2,500 r.p.m. Thus, there is abundant power available for vehicle operation, hauling trailers or driving machinery. Power that is smooth and willing for normal work; slogging, determined power for tough assignments. This is an outstandingly reliable engine, its robust construction giving it a long and trouble-free life.

PETROL POWER TO GO ANYWHERE

1961 Land Rover Series IIA

A change to Rover's production planning system brought a new designation for a changed Series II. Adding an A meant it had undergone a major change, in this case a new, more powerful diesel engine. The new version incorporated some of the changes brought in with the petrol engine that had leapfrogged the diesel during development. Chief among these was an increase in bore, made easy by deleting the cylinder liners, and using bores machined directly into the cylinder block. The combustion chambers were revised to alleviate some of the stresses imposed inside the engine. The new chambers followed the Ricardo design of the original, but incorporated a Rover-patented hot plug, with pimples that had the effect of increasing its surface area. This innovation improved combustion and reduced diesel knock. Injection was by a CAV DPA pump while the Pintaux-type nozzles were of a two-jet design with an auxiliary jet spraying fuel into the hottest part of the combustion chamber. This improved cold starting, for which glow plugs, operated by a dash-mounted switch were also included. While power and torque increments were less dramatic than when the petrol derivative had replaced the old side exhaust valve unit, they were still useful, particularly as maximum torque was now developed below 2,000 rpm. This rugged engine served Land Rover for many years to come.

INTRODUCTION 1961
BODY short wheelbase full hood, truck cab, kerb weight petrol; 2953lb (1339kg), diesel; 3097lb (1405kg). Long wheelbase truck cab or Station Wagon, kerb weight petrol; 3301lb (1497kg), diesel 3471lb (1574kg).
ENGINES petrol; 4-cylinder in line, 90.47mm x 88.9mm, 2286cc. 77bhp (57kW) @ 4250 rpm, 124lb ft (168Nm) @2500 rpm. Diesel; 4-cylinder in line, 90.47mm x 88.9mm 2286cc. 62bhp (46kW) @ 4000rpm, 103lb ft (139Nm) @ 1800 rpm.
ENGINE STRUCTURE cast iron block and cylinder head, on diesels Ricardo Comet V combustion chambers with recesses in the piston crowns, Rover hot plugs, pushrod overhead valves, camshaft chain driven with hydraulic tensioner, CAV fuel injection.
TRANSMISSION selectable four wheel drive, hydraulic single dry plate clutch 9in (22.8cm) dia. Rover 4-speed gearbox and 2-speed transfer box, Rover front and rear axles, 4.7:1.

CHASSIS welded box section steel ladder frame, front and rear beam axles with semi-elliptic springs and telescopic shock absorbers, worm and nut steering with recirculating ball. 4-wheel hydraulically operated drum brakes, Regular; 10in (25.4cm), Long; 11in (27.9cm), 6in (15.2cm) drum transmission hand brake. 10 gallon (45 litre) fuel tank – 16 gallon (73 litre) on Long Station Wagon. 16in pressed steel wheels with 6.00 x 16 tyres – 7.50 x 16 on Long models.
DIMENSIONS regular; wheelbase 88in (224cm), front and rear track 51.5in (131cm), length; 142.4in (362cm), width; 66in (168cm), height; 77.5in (197cm). Long; wheelbase 109in (277cm), front and rear track 51.5in (131cm), length; 175in (444cm), width; 66in (168cm), height; 81in (206cm).

Although the revised Series II became a Series IIA in recognition of the new major unit numbering system, the letter suffix did not change to keep pace with new chassis number suffixes: a IIA remained a IIA, right the way through to H-suffix chassis in 1971.

1962 Forward Control Land Rover

Military and fleet customers were always pressing for more carrying capacity. Experimental vehicles such as a 129-inch (327cm) wheelbase version were stillborn, but a forward control development of the Long Land Rover went into production, initially for export markets only. A purposeful-looking vehicle, it could carry up to a 30 cwt (3360lb or 1524kg) payload in a high-sided cargo body, with the option of sides that could be folded down and a flat load bed. The cab had standard Land Rover doors, truck cab and windscreen with a unique front. A supplementary sub-frame provided a flat floor clear of any need for wheel boxes. Despite these changes, the contemporary sales brochure claimed that the Forward Control used a very high percentage of standard Land Rover parts a fact, it said, of great significance to fleet owners. The extra weight demanded more power and the Forward Control was fitted with a 6-cylinder engine derived from the one used in the Rover 100 P4 car. This brought a reversion to the overhead inlet and side exhaust arrangement of early Land Rovers, as it belonged to the same family as the first 4-cylinder. Power was reduced compared to the car engine, as the compression ratio was lower and timing altered, to take account of the poorer quality of fuel that the Forward Control was likely to encounter, particularly in export markets. The gearbox remained standard, except for its selector mechanism, and the transfer box ratio changed to give lower overall gearing.

INTRODUCTION 1962
BODY forward control truck cab with detachable loadspace body sides, kerb weight; 4,200lb (1904kg), gross weight (on road); 8000lb (3625kg).
ENGINE: 6 cylinders in-line, 77.8mm x 92.075mm, 2625cc, 90bhp (67kW) @ 4500 rpm, 132lb ft (179kW) @ 1500rpm.
ENGINE STRUCTURE cast iron block, alloy cylinder head. Overhead inlet and side exhaust valves chain-driven camshaft, pushrods and rockers, 5-bearing crankshaft.
TRANSMISSION selectable four wheel drive, hydraulic single dry plate clutch 9.5 in (24.1cm) dia. Rover 4-speed gearbox and 2-speed transfer box, Rover front and rear axles, 4.7:1.

CHASSIS welded box section steel ladder frame with additional body mounting frame, front and rear beam axles with semi-elliptic springs and telescopic shock absorbers, worm and nut steering with recirculating ball 4-wheel hydraulically operated drum brakes, 11in (27.9cm), 9in (22.9cm) drum transmission hand brake. 16 gallon (73 litre) fuel tank. 16in pressed steel wheels with 9.00 x 16 tyres.
DIMENSIONS wheelbase 109in (277cm), front and rear track 53.3in (136cm), length; 193in (490cm), width; 68.5in (174cm), height; 102in (260cm)
PRICES: £1426 – £1520

Initially available only for export, the 109 Forward Control had more parts in common with the contemporary Series IIA 109 than a first glance might suggest.

The Forward Control Land-Rover is available for overseas markets only. It has been designed to combine the accepted Land-Rover four-wheel drive mobility and toughness with a carrying capacity up to twice that of the Long model. It will deal easily with a 30-cwt. payload on roads and tracks and with 25-cwt. across rough country. Its high ground clearance and excellent weight distribution make it ideal for cross-country travel. It has the same speed range as the Long Land-Rover, can climb a 1 in 2 slope fully laden and has a side tipping angle of over 40 degrees. Although unlike other Land-Rover models in appearance, the Forward Control vehicle uses a very high percentage of standard Land-Rover parts, a fact of great significance to fleet owners. Various body styles are available.

Forward Control with drop-side body.

1966 Land Rover 110 Forward Control

Even though the first Forward Control Land Rover had not been a large-volume seller it was developed further. A major concern was stability. Although a 40 degree side angle before the vehicle tipped was claimed, there had been incidents, including one where a Rover employee witnessed a Forward Control fire engine conversion actually falling over when stationary, due to the movement of water in the tank. The solution was to fit wider-track, heavy-duty axles, which were being made by ENV. This improved the turning circle and a front anti-roll bar was also fitted. At the rear, the springs were now mounted on outriggers to widen the spring base, and the rear axle was slung under the springs to improve ground clearance. The changes altered the wheelbase slightly and the improved vehicle was known as the 110inch Wheelbase Forward Control. A changed instrument panel now included a combined ignition key and starter switch, and gear lever and hand brake were re-positioned. The cab was fully trimmed and dual rack driven windscreen wipers were standard for the first in a Land Rover. De-luxe seats, a heater and an additional fuel tank were among the options. To comply with new regulations the front lighting was changed along with other detail changes to the body. There was a wide range of engine options although the 4-cylinder petrol engine was only available for export markets.

INTRODUCTION 1966
BODY forward control truck cab with detachable loadspace body sides, kerb weight; 4,200lb (1904kg), gross weight (on road); 8000lb (3625kg).
ENGINE: petrol (export only); 4-cylinder in line, 90.47mm x 88.9mm, 2286cc, 77bhp (57kW) @ 4250 rpm, 124lb ft (168Nm) @2500 rpm. 6-cylinder in-line, 77.8mm x 92.075mm, 2625cc, 90bhp (67kW) @ 4500 rpm, 132lb ft (179kW) @ 1500rpm. Diesel; 4-cylinder in line, 90.47mm x 88.9mm 2286cc, 62bhp (46kW) @ 4000rpm, 103lb ft (139Nm) @ 1800 rpm.
ENGINE STRUCTURE 4-cylinder petrol and diesel; cast iron block and cylinder head, overhead valves, 3-bearing crankshaft. 6-cylinder petrol; cast iron block, alloy cylinder head, overhead inlet and side exhaust valves. chain-driven camshaft, pushrods and rockers, 5-bearing crankshaft.

TRANSMISSION selectable four wheel drive, hydraulic single dry plate clutch 9.5 in (24.1cm) dia. Rover 4-speed gearbox and 2-speed transfer box, ENV front and rear wide track axles, 4.7:1.
CHASSIS welded box section steel ladder frame with additional body mounting frame, front and rear beam axles with semi-elliptic springs and telescopic shock absorbers, worm and nut steering with recirculating ball. 4-wheel hydraulically operated drum brakes, 11in (27.9cm), 9in (22.9cm) drum transmission hand brake. 16 gallon (73 litre) fuel tank. 16in pressed steel wheels with 9.00 x 16 tyres.
DIMENSIONS wheelbase 109.75in (279cm), front and rear track 57.5in (146cm), length; 193in (490cm), width; 68.5in (174cm), height; 102in (260cm)
PRICE (in 1969): £1,426 0s 0d – £1,456 0s 0d (6-cylinder petrol), £1,490 0s 0d – £1,520 0s 0d (diesel).

Lower-mounted headlamps were the easiest way of distinguishing the 110 Forward Control - somewhat perversely known as a Series IIB – although there were other important differences, not least in the cab.

103

1967 Land Rover Series IIA 6-cylinder

The success of the 6-cylinder petrol engine in the Forward Control encouraged Rover to offer it in normal control versions of the Long Land Rover. By this time however the Rover 100 P4 car, for which it had been developed, was out of production so the 2.6-litre engine was being built solely for 4x4s. The engine produced less horsepower than the one in the Forward Control but had the same pulling power, and since this came in at a meagre 1500 rpm, it provided good driving characteristics for the job in hand. It went on sale with a choice of compression ratios – the same 7:1 as the Forward Control had for export markets and 7.8:1 for places where higher quality fuels could be expected. The 6-cylinder normal control Land Rovers also received the Forward Control's larger clutch to cope with the extra power and torque. To celebrate the evolution of Britain's new road network, publicity material suggested that the Land Rover was capable of "cruising down the motorway". It was certainly capable of 70 mph (112kph) although it took more than a minute to get there. Travelling at these higher speeds in a Land Rover was novel, so to make it safer and less fatiguing, servo-assisted brakes were made standard, together with laminated windscreen, twin horns and a new speedometer, which extended to a rather optimistic 90 mph (144 kph). The facia was re-styled and the new instrument cluster included a temperature gauge. Door sealing was improved to "make the Land Rover cosier" while the Station Wagon at last gained de-luxe trim and, after a time, a new profiled seat for driver and front passenger. To comply with impending rules they also gained the security of static seat belts.

INTRODUCTION 1967
BODY long wheelbase truck cab or Station Wagon, kerb weight petrol; 3459lb (1569kg).
ENGINE: 6 cylinders in-line, 77.8mm x 92.075mm, 2625cc, low (7:1) compression; 81bhp (60kW) @ 4500 rpm, high (7.8:1) compression; 85bhp (63kW), 132lb ft (179Nm) @ 1500rpm.
ENGINE STRUCTURE cast iron block, aluminium cylinder head. Overhead inlet and side exhaust valves, chain-driven camshaft, pushrods and rockers, 5-bearing crankshaft.
TRANSMISSION selectable four wheel drive, hydraulic single dry plate clutch 9.5in (24.1cm) dia. Rover 4-speed gearbox and 2-speed transfer box, Rover front and rear axles, 4.7:1.

CHASSIS welded box section steel ladder frame, front and rear beam axles with semi-elliptic springs and telescopic shock absorbers, worm and nut steering with recirculating ball, 4-wheel hydraulically operated drum brakes, 11in (27.9cm), 6in (15.2cm) drum transmission hand brake. 16 gallon (73 litre) fuel tank. 16in pressed steel wheels with 7.50 x 16 tyres.
DIMENSIONS wheelbase 109in (277cm), front and rear track 51.5in (131cm), length; 175in (444cm), width; 66in (168cm), height; 81in (206cm)
PRICE £1220 (12-seater) £1580 14s 2d (10 seater).

The six-cylinder engine was smoother than the four-cylinder, and was more appropriate for Station Wagons.

6 CYLINDER

109" WHEELBASE LONG LAND-ROVER

NOW LAND-ROVER TAKES THE SMOOTH WITH THE ROUGH

New 6-cylinder option for the 109" range makes the Land-Rover comfortably at home cruising down the motorway. A 6-cylinder, 2.6 Litre petrol engine that gives Land-Rover power to cruise faster, accelerate quicker, run quieter. All this and improved fuel economy.

And this new power is matched by a host of other improvements to the 109" range. There's a heavy duty 9½" diaphragm spring clutch to cope with the extra power. It bristles with new safety features. Servo-assisted brakes. Safety-belts. Laminated windscreen and twin horns.

The door sealing has also been improved to make the Land-Rover cosier. A new speedo and temperature gauge have been incorporated in the re-styled facia and de-luxe trim adds the finishing touch.

The Land-Rover has 38 body styles with options of 4- or 6-cylinder petrol engine or 4-cylinder diesel engine. So see your Land-Rover dealer now. He's the man in the know.

1949 –1974 Land Rovers for the United States

In order to gain vital dollar sales Land Rovers were exported to North America from the earliest days. Compared with the indigenous Jeep, sales were insignificant, although British expats and American anglophiles sought them out enthusiastically. As production progressed, a fuller more convincing range was built up, reaching its peak in the early 1970s with the most popular Series III 88in Station Wagon, known in the US as the DeLuxe Hard Top. As the influence of lobbyists such as Ralph Nader took hold, and the US government grew increasingly concerned with automobile safety, it was difficult for the Land Rover to comply with increasingly onerous and sometimes contradictory regulations. It was eventually forced out of the market although it would return many years later. The Series III DeLuxe Hard Top differed from other marker specifications in a lighting arrangement to comply with US regulations, which included larger direction indicators, side marker and repeater lamps and reversing (back up) lamps. Land Rover's 16in wheels were replaced with 15in as these were more common in North America. Easily available Goodyear Ultra Grip tyres were fitted as standard, and the old Series II blade bonnet was retained, with an optional spare wheel carrier. The interior was fully trimmed, with De Luxe seats as standard, made to federal flame retardant specifications, and all seven seats were provided with safety harnesses. The fascia boasted an ashtray; a supplementary panel provided a hazard warning switch, and uniquely a heater/demister was standard. Less obvious qualities included equipping the engine with emission control equipment, and the fuel system with evaporative loss control. Brakes were dual line with servo assistance. Factory fitted options included side and rear steps, sun visors and towing equipment. US dealers were able to fit free-wheeling front hubs, an electric winch, and even a snow plough.

INTRODUCTION 1972
BODY short wheelbase station wagon (sold as 'DeLuxe' Hard Top), kerb weight; 2900lb (1315kg).
ENGINES petrol; 4-cylinder in line, 90.47mm x 88.9mm, 2286cc. 67bhp (50kW) SAE @ 4000 rpm, 115lb ft (156Nm) SAE @1500 rpm.
ENGINE STRUCTURE 4-cylinder, pushrod overheadvalves, cast iron block and cylinder head.
TRANSMISSION selectable four wheel drive, hydraulic single dry plate clutch 9.5 in (24.1cm) dia. Rover 4-speed gearbox and 2-speed transfer box, Rover front and rear banjo axles.

CHASSIS welded box section steel ladder frame, front and rear beam axles with semi-elliptic springs and telescopic shock absorbers, worm and nut steering with recirculating ball, 4-wheel hydraulically operated dual circuit drum brakes, 10in (25.4cm), 6in (15.2cm) drum transmission hand brake.10 UK gallon (12 US gallon – 45 litre) fuel tank.15in pressed steel wheels with 7.10 x 15 tyres.
DIMENSIONS Regular; wheelbase 88in (224cm), front and rear track 51.5in (131cm), length; 142.4in (362cm), width; 66in (168cm), height; 77.5in (197cm).

The large indicator lamps and side markers on the wings instantly identify this North American Series III 88-inch DeLuxe Hardtop from the early 1970s.

Land-Rover

1969 Land Rover Series IIA revised

Most noticeable among a package of improvements on the Series IIA was the repositioning of the headlamps from the grille to the front wings. New lighting regulations required the change although it was not done without some opposition. Early Land Rovers had protected them behind the grille at the expense of some lighting brightness, then they were moved alongside the grille, now they looked more vulnerable than ever to damage in the rough and tumble world Land Rovers lived in. However they were slightly recessed and enclosed, with a finishing bezel housing the side and direction indicator lamps. The new-style instrument cluster was standardised, and the electrical system changed to negative earth, although it was still dynamo powered with an alternator available as an option. Modest improvements to engine power and torque outputs were also made. There were now 38 models in the Land Rover range from the basic 88in Regular to 110in Forward Control, and few places in the world where the vehicle was not sold. The company was granted a Queen's Award to Industry in 1966 and its new advertising strap-line was "The World's Most Versatile Vehicle".

INTRODUCTION 1969
BODY short wheelbase full hood, truck cab, kerb weight petrol; 2953lb (1339kg), diesel; 3097lb (1405kg). Long wheelbase truck cab or Station Wagon, kerb weight petrol; 3301lb (1497kg), diesel 3471lb (1574kg).
ENGINES petrol; 4-cylinder in line, 90.47mm x 88.9mm, 2286cc. 81bhp (60kW) @ 4250 rpm, 124lb ft (168Nm) @2500 rpm. 6-cylinders in-line (Long only); 77.8mm x 92.075mm, 2625cc, low (7:1 compression) – optional on Long, standard on Forward Control ; 91bhp (68kW) @ 4500 rpm, 130lb ft (176Nm) @ 1750 rpm, high (7.8:1) compression – only available on Long; 95bhp (71kW) @ 4500 rpm, 134lb ft (182Nm) @ 1500rpm. Diesel; 4-cylinder in line, 90.47mm x 88.9mm 2286cc. 67bhp (50kW) @ 4000rpm, 105lb ft (142Nm) @ 1800 rpm.
ENGINE STRUCTURE 4-cylinder; cast iron block and cylinder head, 3-bearing crankshaft, overhead valves. 6-cylinder; cast iron block, alloy cylinder head. Overhead inlet and side exhaust valves chain-driven camshaft, pushrods and rockers, 5-bearing crankshaft.

TRANSMISSION selectable four wheel drive, hydraulic single dry plate clutch 9in (22.8cm) dia. 4-speed gearbox and 2-speed transfer box, Rover front and rear axles, 4.7:1.
CHASSIS welded box section steel ladder frame, front and rear beam axles with semi-elliptic springs and telescopic shock absorbers, worm and nut steering with recirculating ball, 4-wheel hydraulically operated drum brakes, Regular; 10in (25.4cm), Long; 11in (27.9cm), 6in (15.2cm) drum transmission hand brake.10 gallon (45 litre) fuel tank – 16 gallon (73 litre) on Long Station Wagon. 16in pressed steel wheels with 6.00 x 16 tyres – 7.50 x 16 on Long models, 9.00 x 16 on Forward Control.
DIMENSIONS Regular; wheelbase 88in (224cm), front and rear track 51.5in (131cm), length; 142.4in (362cm), width; 66in (168cm), height; 77.5in (197cm). Long; wheelbase 109in (277cm), front and rear track 51.5in (131cm), length; 175in (444cm), width; 66in (168cm), height; 81in (206cm)
PRICE (1969): £806 – £1,520

A brand-new Series IIA with the front-end configuration introduced in April 1969 poses with the first pre-production Land Rover from 1948.

1971 Land Rover Series III

Changes introduced in 1971 were of such magnitude that a new model designation was introduced. The Land Rover Series III was destined to be one of the longest-lived models and one that would sustain the range throughout the troubled 1970s. Externally similar to the Series IIA with the new wing-mounted headlamps, the metal grille was replaced by one in styled moulded plastic, to the chagrin of Australian customers at least, who used the strong metal mesh of the old grille as an extemporised barbeque. Once again a big change was carried out on the facia, with a full-width upper crash roll, inspired by what was specified to comply with German market regulations. One curiosity throughout Land Rover history was that despite changes in the appearance of the interior, homespun touches remained. In this case a unique finishing strip of black cloth tape and the foam rubber jammed between the instrument console and the steering column. The instruments were now housed in a plastic moulded console in front of the driver, carrying toggle switches for the lights, instrument lighting and the heater fan. A push knob catered for the washer and wipers and a cowl was placed round the steering column with a stalk for the indicators, horn and main beam. Sliding cable-operated controls adjusted the heater, standard in the UK. A trimmed parcel shelf had plenty of places for things to get lost in and pre-punched holes covered with trim provided a means of adding extra instruments. Mechanically, the Series III moved to an all-synchromesh gearbox, which gave a shorter throw between gear changes, although the gearshift still felt far from pleasant. Clutch durability and disengagement pressure was improved by standardising the bigger clutch of the 6-cylinder and heavy-duty variants.

INTRODUCTION 1971
BODY short wheelbase full hood, hard top, truck cab, Station Wagon, kerb weight; 2953 – 3425lb (1342 – 1556kg), long wheelbase full hood, hard top, truck cab or Station Wagon, kerb weight; 3301 – 3922lb (1500 – 1783kg).
ENGINES petrol; 4-cylinder in line, 90.47mm x 88.9mm, 2286cc. 81bhp (60kW) @ 4250 rpm, 124lb ft (168Nm) @2500 rpm. 6-cylinders in-line (Long only); 77.8mm x 92.075mm, 2625cc, low (7:1 compression) – optional on Long, standard on Forward Control ; 91bhp (68kW) @ 4500 rpm, 130lb ft (176Nm) @ 1750 rpm, high (7.8:1) compression – only available on Long; 95bhp (71kW) @ 4500 rpm, 134lb ft (182Nm) @ 1500rpm. Diesel; 4-cylinder in line, 90.47mm x 88.9mm 2286cc. 67bhp (50kW) @ 4000rpm, 105lb ft (142Nm) @ 1800 rpm.
ENGINE STRUCTURE 4-cylinder; cast iron block and cylinder head, 3-bearing crankshaft, overhead valves. 6-cylinder; cast iron block, alloy cylinder head, overhead inlet and side exhaust valves, chain-driven camshaft, pushrods and rockers, 5-bearing crankshaft.

TRANSMISSION selectable four wheel drive, hydraulic single dry plate clutch 9.5 in (24.1cm) dia. 4-speed gearbox and 2-speed transfer box, Regular; Rover front and rear axles, Long; Salisbury rear axle with cast differential, 4.7:1.
CHASSIS welded box section steel ladder frame, front and rear beam axles with semi-elliptic springs and telescopic shock absorbers, worm and nut steering with recirculating ball, 4-wheel hydraulically operated drum brakes, Regular; 10in (25.4cm), Long; 11in (27.9cm), 6in (15.2cm) drum transmission hand brake.10 gallon (45 litre) fuel tank – 16 gallon (73 litre) on Long Station Wagon. 16in pressed steel wheels with 6.00 x 16 tyres – 7.50 x 16 on Long models, 9.00 x 16 on 109in One Ton.
DIMENSIONS Regular; wheelbase 88in (224cm), front and rear track 51.5in (131cm), length; 142.4in (362cm), width; 66in (168cm), height; 77.5in (197cm). Long; wheelbase 109in (277cm), front and rear track 51.5in (131cm), length; 175in (444cm), width; 66in (168cm), height; 81in (206cm)
PRICE (1979): £5459.05 – £9163.10

The most obvious distinguishing feature of the Series III was its new ABS plastic grille. Flat door hinges, not visible here, were another clue.

1975 Land Rover SD5

Land Rover could scarcely have been accused of having a radical culture in the 1970s, although its engineers were still capable of innovation. Their inventiveness was exemplified by the SD5 project, which looked at a potential replacement for the Series III Land Rover. By now part of the Specialist Division of British Leyland, Rover-Triumph's engineering director Spen King was turning his mind to projects such as the 16-valve version of the Triumph Slant 4 engine for the Dolomite Sprint, so he instructed a Solihull styling team to look at a new Land Rover. Rover head of design David Bache was busy refining the SD1 Rover 3500, so the task fell to another designer, Tony Poole. The work was not confined to styling. During the gestation of the Range Rover studies were going on of foreign competition to see what lessons could be applied to Land Rover. It was concluded that it was worth trying out combinations of leaf and coil spring suspensions, some of which provided highly unsatisfactory handling according to Roger Crathorne, an engineer who worked on them. The research eventually lead to a formal Stage 2 of the venture, but meantime the current semi-elliptical springs seemed the best choice.

Poole was given the job of creating a dramatic body style to signify change. His concept was of a modular construction, using a range of base units, around which a variety of vehicles could be constructed. It was rather like the way Land Rover had evolved in the first place, but the shapes were advanced for the time, with elements echoing those of the Range Rover. Bucks made out of wood and clay showed a distinct family resemblance. Poole's team also proposed new materials such as moulded plastic for hard tops. The innovations were not confined to the exterior. Some of the artistic renderings showed a modular seating concept, with moulded plastic seats, and an experimental interior buck was built of a short wheelbase hard top/station wagon. The designers sketched a variety of vehicles, including a long wheelbase station wagon, and a sporty soft top with a mesh grille and large wheels.

Plans for SD5 were bold and exciting, but it soon became obvious that they would be expensive. The style was judged too close to the Range Rover and there were worries that a production SD5 might attract sales away from what was becoming a vital source of revenue for the whole of British Leyland. The creation of an overall Product Planning function for Leyland Cars spelt the end for SD5, as it was felt that Land Rover's condition was broadly satisfactory, and that attention was urgently required elsewhere.

The full-size SD5 short-wheelbase mock-up was not driveable, but looked realistic enough in these pictures. It was posed with contemporary Land Rover products for comparison purposes.

1976 Land Rover Stage 2 hybrid prototypes

The release of funds to support expansion provided an opportunity to use the results of a world wide market study as a foundation of a product plan. This had concluded that the integration of the Range Rover chassis with its long-travel coil spring suspension, and a Land Rover body, would open up new market sectors by providing a robust and capable vehicle with higher levels of comfort. A small project team was formed to build some test vehicles. It procured some Range Rover chassis and Land Rover body sets and built four hybrid vehicles. One chassis was shortened by 10inches (25.4cm) to construct a short wheelbase derivative, two were left alone and the fourth acquired a 10inch (25.4cm) extension to provide a long wheelbase version close to the existing Land Rover 109. The driveline was essentially Range Rover. The Land Rover body panels were fitted to produce a short wheelbase soft top, a 4-door command car, a hard top on the mid-length chassis and a long wheelbase hard top. They all used the long bonnet and flat front from the Stage 1 V8, and one was fitted with a deeper, one-piece windscreen being developed to meet new legislation on visibility. Wheel arch extensions made up for the wider track of the Range Rover axles. Thanks to the hybrid project, the building blocks of the Stage 2 were already in place, when the vehicles were dispatched to the Eastnor Castle off-road proving ground for further development and evaluation by senior management. While the hybrids used V8 petrol engines from the Range Rover, one so-called skunk project used the 2.5 litre petrol engine and evaluated a remote gearbox concept.

INTRODUCTION 1976/77
BODY Short wheelbase: Soft top, Mid length: (1) Hard Top, (2) 4-door Command Car Station Wagon, Long wheelbase: Hard Top (with export side windows).
ENGINE petrol; V8, 88.9mm x 71.1mm, 3528cc.134bhp (100kW) @ 5000 rpm, 187 lb ft (253Nm) @ 2500 rpm, compression ratio 8.5:1.
ENGINE STRUCTURE pushrod overhead valves with single central camshaft; aluminium block and cylinder heads; two SU HIF 44 or Solex 175CDSE; Lucas 35DLM8 electronic ignition system; five main bearings.
TRANSMISSION permanent four wheel drive. single dry plate hydraulically operated diaphragm spring clutch; 4-speed integrated manual gearbox and transfer box with vacuum operated centre differential lock. Land Rover front and rear banjo type axles, 3.54:1 final drive ratio.

CHASSIS welded steel ladder frame, front and rear beam axles with coil springs and telescopic shock absorbers, recirculating ball steering with PAS, Servo assisted, single circuit, hydraulic brakes, discs all round, drum transmission parking brake, short and mid length wheelbase; 10 gallon (45 litre) fuel tank, long wheelbase; 18 gallon (80 litre) fuel tank. 16in wheels with 7.50 x16 tyres.
DIMENSIONS short wheelbase 90in (228.6cm), mid length wheelbase 100in (254.0cm), long wheelbase 110in (279.4cm), front and rear track 58.7in (149.0cm)58.5in (148.6cm). Short wheelbase; length 155.2in (394.2cm), mid length 165.2in (419.6cm), long wheelbase 175.2in (445cm) width 70.5in (179.0cm), height 77.36/78.5 in (196.5/200cm) depending on specification, ground clearance (min) 7.5in (19.0cm).
CAPABILITIES (estimated) Max gradient 45deg, approach angle (max) 51.5deg departure angle (max) 53deg.

Hastily built to test the concept of mating Land Rover body to Range Rover chassis, this is one of the 100-inch hybrids. It survives today in the Dunsfold Collection of Land Rovers.

1979 Land Rover Stage 1 V8

An ambitious plan to introduce new models, and recover some of the market lost to Japanese manufacturers, brought Land Rover Ltd an injection of government money. The plan was for a two-stage increase in production, the first naturally enough codenamed Stage 1, which was expected to offer a high-power derivative for Middle East customers and expand Land Rover's market. The result was essentially a 109inch wheelbase Land Rover, with the aluminium V8 engine from the Range Rover, de-tuned by restricting the carburettor throats, to give approximately the same as the by now out-dated 6-cylinder. Introducing the V8 also overcame a production bottleneck with the 4-cylinder engines. The V8 was 60 per cent lighter than the six, but fitting it into the Land Rover's engine compartment required a number of changes. Most obvious was a flush front end and full-length bonnet, later adopted for the Stage 2 Land Rover One Ten then under development. The V8 retained the LT95 one-piece gear and transfer box of the Range Rover so it had permanent four wheel drive. The transfer box range change lever was mounted on the heelboard making it difficult to see and operate. A vacuum operated switch adjacent to the range control lever locked the centre differential. Emphasising its role in trying to reconquer lost markets, the Land Rover V8 was available in a range of bright colours from the Triumph sports car range. In addition to the normal monotonous Land Rover paintwork, Inca Yellow, Java Green and Pageant Blue may never have been popular with conservative Land Rover customers, yet they certainly enhanced the large vehicle's no-nonsense lines.

INTRODUCTION 1979
BODY long wheelbase full hood, hard top, truck cab and station wagon, gross weight; 5974lbs (2710kg) 6658lbs option (3020kg).
ENGINES petrol; V8, 88.9mm x 71.1mm, 3528cc. 91bhp (68kW) @ 3500rpm, 166lb ft (225.6Nm) @ 2000 rpm, compression ratio 8.5:1.
ENGINE STRUCTURE pushrod ohv with single central camshaft; aluminium alloy LM25 block and cylinder heads; twin Stromberg/Solex 175CDSE; Lucas 35DM8 distributor; electrical fuel pump; 5-bearing crankshaft.
TRANSMISSION permanent four wheel drive. 10.5 in (26.7cm) hydraulically operated diaphragm spring clutch; LT95 4-speed integrated manual gearbox and transfer box with vacuum operated centre differential lock. Rover banjo front axle, Salisbury rear axle with cast differential, 4.7:1.

CHASSIS welded box section steel ladder frame. Front and rear beam axles with semi-elliptic springs and telescopic shock absorbers. Worm and nut steering with recirculating ball. 4-wheel hydraulically operated drum brakes, 11in (27.9cm), 7.25in (18.4cm) drum transmission hand brake. 15 gallon (68 litre) fuel tank. 16in pressed steel wheels with 7.50 x 16 tyres.
DIMENSIONS wheelbase 109in (277cm), front and rear track 51.5in (131cm), length (truck cab); 175in (444.5cm), width; 66.54in (169cm), height; 80in (203cm).
PRICE (1983): £8706.65 – £10240.75

The addition of V8 power to the long-wheelbase Land Rover brought less performance than some had hoped: the engine had to be detuned to stay within the vehicle's braking capabilities.

1981 Land Rover Stage 1 V8 88 inch

When the local sales manager from the West Indies saw an opportunity to sell a short wheelbase version of the Stage 1 V8 Solihull was quick to oblige. Fitting the engine proved straightforward. The front portion of an 88inch wheelbase was much the same as the 109inch, and although such extemporised engineering would probably have been impossible in the later stages of a heavily regulated industry, in the 1980s it was still possible to put a special project together thanks to Land Rover's S (for Special) specification system. The still relatively unsophisticated nature of the chassis build area, housed in an old rope factory in Garrison Street, Birmingham smoothed the progress of obtaining components, with instructions passing to and fro informally. Special chassis had to be clearly identified to avoid mistakes. For the Stage I 88inch it proved difficult to find a propeller shaft to drive the rear axle. The gap between the driving flange of the LT95 gearbox and the rear axle pinion was short. Hardy Spicer met the challenge with a double Hookes jointed arrangement. Product planning manager Mike Gould took a prototype for a weekend trial, and recalled that it was spectacularly quick for a Land Rover, although finding that the standard brakes were barely up to the task. The short rear prop shaft proved not good for refinement, and recalled the unpleasant shunting sensation from which Land Rover transmissions sometimes suffered. Only 29 88inch V8s were built, the majority going to Trinidad.

INTRODUCTION 1981
BODY short wheelbase Station Wagons, gross weight 4462.11lb (2024kg)
ENGINE V8, 88.9mm x 71.1mm, 3528cc. 91bhp (68kW) @ 3500rpm, 166lb ft (225.6Nm) @ 2000 rpm, compression ratio 8.5:1.
ENGINE STRUCTURE pushrod ohv with single central camshaft; aluminium alloy LM25 block and cylinder heads; twin Stromberg/Solex 175CDSE; Lucas 35DM8 distributor; electrical fuel pump; 5-bearing crankshaft.
TRANSMISSION permanent four wheel drive. 10.5 in (26.7cm) hydraulically operated diaphragm spring clutch; LT95 4-speed integrated manual gearbox and transfer box with vacuum operated centre differential lock. Rover banjo front axle, Salisbury rear axle with cast differential, 4.7:1.

CHASSIS welded box section steel ladder frame, front and rear beam axles with semi-elliptic springs and telescopic shock absorbers, worm and nut steering with recirculating ball, 4-wheel hydraulically operated drum brakes, 11in (27.9cm), 7.25in (18.4cm) drum transmission hand brake, 15 gallon (68 litre) fuel tank, 16in pressed steel wheels with 7.50 x 16 tyres.
DIMENSIONS wheelbase 88in (224cm), front and rear track 51.5in (131cm), length 142in (362cm), width; 66.54in (169cm), height; 76in (194cm).

This V8 engine is in its production installation for the Stage 1 V8 109 models; the underbonnet view of the rare short-wheelbase derivative would have been exactly the same.

1982 Land Rover High Capacity Pick up

By the middle of the 1970s competition was intense, in particular from the Toyota Land Cruiser which could claim a heritage almost as long as Land Rover's. The Land Rover may have already passed its sales peak, but the company was not about to give up, despite the industrial relations crises in its parent British Leyland. A new crop of young engineers was challenging the established approach, among whom was Mike Donovan, whose first project at Land Rover was the High Capacity Pick Up. Although introduced as a variant of the Long Wheelbase, 109inch Land Rover, its back body had the capacious wheel arches designed for the Stage 2 Land Rover One Ten and some distinctive traditional Land Rover features. The rear body tray was aluminium, with the major body sections made of extrusions, which already incorporated the strengthening swages. In order to avoid damage from the loads it would carry, the body sides had a separate inner liner, and were attached to thin-wall aluminium castings forming the corners. The floor was swaged aluminium sheet and wheel arches were pressed and localised rather than ran full length. There was a spare wheel carrier forward of the wheel arch and a removable ladder rack. A hood was available and, later a resin Truckman Top. Besides the standard suspension a heavy-duty option was offered so that owners could take advantage of the 2-metre load space. Mike Donovan went on to manage Project Jay, which became the Land Rover Discovery.

INTRODUCTION 1982
BODY long wheelbase truck cab with high capacity rear body, gross weight;5974lbs (2710kg) 6658lbs option (3020kg).
ENGINES petrol, 4-cylinder in line, 90.47mm x 88.9mm, 2286cc. low (7:1) compression 65bhp (48kW) DIN @ 4250 rpm, 114lb ft (154Nm) DIN @ 2000 rpm, high (8:1) compression 70bhp (52kW) DIN @ 4250 rpm, 117lb ft (159Nm) DIN @2000 rpm. diesel; 4-cylinder in line, 90.47mm x 88.9mm 2286cc. 60bhp (45kW) DIN @ 4000rpm, 103lb ft (140Nm) DIN @ 1800 rpm.
ENGINE STRUCTURE 4-cylinder, cast iron block and cylinder head, pushrod overhead valves.
TRANSMISSION selectable four wheel drive, hydraulic single dry plate clutch 9.5 in (24.1cm) dia. Rover 4-speed gearbox and 2-speed transfer box, Regular; Rover front and rear axles, Long; Salisbury rear axle with cast differential, 4.7:1.

CHASSIS welded box section steel ladder frame, front and rear beam axles with semi-elliptic springs and telescopic shock absorbers, worm and nut steering with recirculating ball, 4-wheel hydraulically operated drum brakes, 11in (27.9cm), 6in (15.2cm) drum transmission hand brake, 15 gallon (68 litre) fuel tank,16in pressed steel wheels with 7.50 x 16 tyres.
DIMENSIONS wheelbase 109in (277cm), front and rear track 51.5in (131cm), length; 183in (464cm), width; 67.7in (172cm), height; 80in (203cm)
PRICE (1982): £7873–£8608

- Increased payload area
- 2 metre bed length
- Easy access tailgate
- Aluminium body

LAND ROVER 109" HIGH CAPACITY PICK-UP

- Optional suspension/Payload
- Localised wheel arches
- Low floor height

**LAND ROVER 109" HIGH CAPACITY PICK-UP
+ ¾ HOOD (EXPORT)**

The main target of the Hi-Cap, as it soon came to be known, was the Toyota FJ45 four wheel drive pick-up.

1982 Land Rover County Station Wagon

The marketing department of Land Rover Ltd was always concerned that its utility products were a little too basic to appeal to the leisure, rather than the purely commercial, user. The appearance of increasing numbers of highly specified Japanese competitors however offered even commercial customers more comfort. Land Rover's answer was the County Station Wagon. Available in either the 88inch or 109inch versions, the County was distinguished externally by two unique colours – the rather drab Russet Brown and the brighter Masai Red, and by a decal treatment consisting of a broad, four-band stripe down the flanks of the 88 and a more restrained double stripe along the waist of the 109. The front was distinguished by silver or black headlamp bezels to match the grille. Lucas driving lamps were fitted to the front bumper. Tinted glass was provided to cool the interior and enhance the appearance. The County seat had been developed in-house and was notably comfortable. It had rake adjustment even though this was restricted to a few degrees by the bulkhead of the short wheelbase version. The squab was adjustable for height and was also removable. There were head restraints and, on the County Station Wagons, all the seats were trimmed in a grey, hound's tooth tweed. A centre cubby box was available where market regulations allowed it. Other standard features included inertia reel front seat belts, reversing lights and a spare wheel cover. Recognising that these vehicles would see more on-road usage than the basic Land Rover, options available included free-wheeling hubs and overdrive, for all except the permanent four wheel drive V8, and 7.50 x 16 tyres for the 88in.

INTRODUCTION 1982
BODY short wheelbase station wagon, kerb weight; 3199 – 3288lb (1451 – 1491kg), long wheelbase station wagon, kerb weight; 3777 – 4070lb (1713 – 1850kg).
ENGINES petrol; 4-cyl in line, 90.47mm x 88.9mm, 2286cc. 69bhp (51.5kW) @ 4000 rpm, 117lb ft (159Nm) @2000 rpm. V8, 88.9mm x 71.1mm, 3528cc. 91bhp (68kW) DIN @ 3500rpm, 166lb ft (225.6Nm) @ 2000 rpm. Diesel; 4-cyl, 90.47mm x 88.9mm 2286cc 60bhp (45kW) @ 4000rpm 103lb ft (140Nm) @ 1800 rpm.
ENGINE STRUCTURE 4-cylinder petrol and diesel; cast iron block and cylinder head. Overhead valves, three main bearings. V8; pushrod ohv with single central camshaft; aluminium alloy block and cylinder heads; twin Stromberg/Solex 175CDSE; Lucas 35DM8 distributor; electrical fuel pump; 5-bearing crankshaft.
TRANSMISSION 4-cylinder petrol and diesel; selectable four wheel drive, hydraulic single dry plate clutch 9.5 in (24.1cm) dia. Rover 4-speed gearbox and 2-speed transfer box, V8; permanent four wheel drive. 267mm (10.5 in) hydraulically operated diaphragm spring clutch; LT95 4-speed integrated manual gearbox and transfer box with vacuum operated centre differential lock. 88"; Rover front and rear axles, 109"; Salisbury rear axle with cast differential, 4.7:1.
CHASSIS: welded box section steel

ladder frame, front and rear beam axles with semi-elliptic springs and telescopic shock absorbers, worm and nut steering with recirculating ball. 4-wheel hydraulically operated drum brakes, 88in wb; 10in (25.4cm), 109in wb; 11in (27.9cm), 6in (15.2cm) drum transmission hand brake. 88in wb; 10 gallon (45 litre) fuel tank, 109"; 15 gallon (68 litre). 16in pressed steel wheels. 88"; 205 x 16 tyres – 7.50 x 16 available as an option. 109"; 7.50 x 16.
DIMENSIONS 88in wb; wheelbase 88in (224cm), front and rear track 51.5in (131cm), length; 142in (362cm), width; 66in (169cm), height; 76in (194cm). 109in wb; wheelbase 109in (277cm), front and rear track 51.5in (131cm), length; 175in (444cm), width; 66.5in (169cm), height; 79in (201cm)
PRICE (1983): 88in; £8978.72 – £10022.73, 109in; £9536.95 – £10240.75

Land Rover used the County Station Wagons to add side-stripes like those becoming fashionable on Japanese 4x4s. Suddenly, it seemed, customers were interested in cosmetics on their Land Rovers.

1983 Land Rover One Ten Stage 2

Work done on the so-called hybrids proved that combining the coil springs of the Range Rover, with a Land Rover body, provided an effective platform for development. The company did not have the engineering resources to design a full range, all at the same time, so the long wheelbase version was chosen to be first. The result had the 110inch (279.4cm) wheelbase of the hybrids, but the chassis side frames were deeper section than Range Rover, to cope with the more arduous duty cycle expected of a Land Rover. Essentially the suspension of the Range Rover was retained, although the coil springs were larger diameter. Initial vehicles had these staggered dampers of the Range Rover and the rear dampers both faced forward. County Station Wagons for Europe had a larger version of the Boge levelling unit. Other models kept its A-frame as an indispensable part of the suspension set-up. Both permanent and selectable 4-wheel drive was developed, and although permanent prevailed, some were built with selectable transmissions. The body was essentially the old Series III, modernised with a new grille below the long Stage 1 bonnet. It also had wheelarch eyebrows and a taller, one-piece windscreen. The doors had detachable tops fabricated from aluminium extrusions, and the station wagon lost its tropical-pattern roof once the necessary insulation was provided by new internal trim. Incoming Managing Director Tony Gilroy expressed some disbelief when told that the Land Rover One Ten was a poor man's Range Rover, and his doubts were justified by indifferent build quality.

Publicity called it "Land Rover's New Land Rover". Much of the One Ten really was new despite the deliberate visual resemblance to earlier Land Rovers.

INTRODUCTION 1983
BODY long wheel base soft top, truck cab, high capacity pick up, hard top or station wagon, gross weight 6722lbs (3050 kg), 6504lbs ((2950 kg) with ride levelling unit.
ENGINES 3.5-litre all-alloy V8 petrol; 113bhp (84kW) @ 4,000 rpm – later 134bhp (100kW) @ 5000 rpm, 185lb ft (250Nm) – later 187lb ft (253Nm) @ 2500 rpm. 2.3-litre 4-cylinder petrol; 74bhp (55kW) @4,000 rpm, 120lb ft (163Nm) @ 2000 rpm. Later (1985) 2.5-litre 4-cylinder petrol; 80bhp (60kW) @ 4,000 RPM, 129lb ft (175Nm) @ 2000 rpm. 2.3-litre 4-cylinder diesel; 59bhp (43kW) @4,000 rpm, 100lb ft (136Nm) @ 1800 rpm. Later (1984) 2.5-litre 4-cylinder diesel; 65.5bhp (48kW) @ 4,000 RPM, 113lb ft (153Nm) @ 1800 rpm. 1986 – 2.5-litre 4-cylinder diesel turbocharged; 85bhp (63kW) @ 4,000 RPM, 150lb ft (203Nm) @ 1800 rpm.
ENGINE STRUCTURE V8: pushrod ohv with single central camshaft; aluminium alloy LM25 block and cylinder heads; twin SU HIF 44 or Solex 175CDSE; Lucas 35DM8 or 35DLM8 electronic ignition system; electrical fuel pump; five main bearings. 4-cylinder: pushrod ohv with timing chain; cast iron cylinder block and head. Petrol ENGINES Weber carburetter, Lucas 45D4 distributor. Diesel ENGINES CAV distributor pump, turbocharged engine used Garrett turbocharger.
TRANSMISSION permanent four wheel drive. V8 engine: 10.5 in (26.7cm) hydraulically operated diaphragm spring clutch; LR95 4-speed integrated manual gearbox and transfer box with vacuum operated centre differential lock. 4-cylinder petrol; 9.53in (24.21cm) (later – also 2.5-litre turbocharged); 9.25in (23.5cm) hydraulically operated diaphragm spring clutch; 4-cylinder diesel; 9.53in (24.21cm) hydraulically operated diaphragm spring clutch; LT77 5-speed manual gearbox, LT230 2-speed transfer box with lever operated centre differential lock. Land Rover front banjo axle, Salisbury rear with cast differential housing. 3.54:1 final drive ratio.
CHASSIS welded steel ladder frame. Front and rear beam axles with coil springs and telescopic shock absorbers, recirculating ball steering, PAS optional, servo assisted, dual circuit, hydraulic brakes. 11.81 in (30cm) front disc brakes, 11in (28cm) rear drum brakes. 10in (25.4cm) drum transmission parking brake. 17.5 gallon (79.5 litre) fuel tank. 16in pressed steel wheels with 7.50x16 tyres.
DIMENSIONS wheelbase; 110in (279.4cm), front and rear track; 58.5in (148.6cm), length Soft Top and Pick Up; 152.9in (443.8cm), Hard Top and Station Wagon; 181.1in (459.9cm), High Capacity Pick Up; 182in (463.1cm), width 70.5in (179.0cm), height; with levelling unit; 80.1in (203.5cm), normal suspension; 81.9in (207.9cm), ground clearance (min) 8.5in (21.5cm), turning circle; 42ft (12.8m).
CAPABILITIES Max gradient; 45 deg, approach angle; 50deg, departure angle (max); 34.5deg.
PRICE £7990.20 – £10680.05.

1983 Land Rover 127

Designed to some extent in the field, the 127 was the result of Military Product Planning Manager Mike Gould's attendance at a bidder's conference, for the Australian Army's Project Perentie. Double-cabs prevailed in Australia, so he improvised one with cutout profile drawings from a technical manual for the upcoming One Ten. His original proposal required that the new bodies were re-skinned but production vehicles had fillets to make the rear door profile match up. Everything else was already in existence or could be easily modified. A One Ten front, with station wagon body sides, was secured to the rear of a truck cab. The roof was modified from station wagon and truck cab components, and the rear tray came from a High Capacity Pick Up. Marketing Manager Steve Westwood supported the concept, and it was sent to the engineering division back at Solihull for assessment. A two-piece propeller shaft was recommended, so an engineer was dispatched to the trade counter of nearby Hardy Spicer, to buy the longest one they had. This determined the wheelbase of 127inches (322.6cm), which was shorter than the original idea, so the rear tray was cropped. The chassis was common to the One Ten, apart from a 17inch (43cm) splice in the frame, and in the beginning it was offered with only the V8 petrol engine. Early versions had a ride-levelling unit to increase load carrying capacity. A Birmingham coachbuilder built a prototype, which was shown at the launch of the Land Rover One Ten, and attracted the attention of trade representatives from the Southern Electricity Board. The SEB thus became the first customer of a product that enjoyed significant sales among utility, military and private clients.

INTRODUCTION 1983
BODY extended wheelbase crew cab with rear load tray, gross weight 6722lbs (3050kg)
ENGINE 3.5-litre all-alloy V8 petrol; 134bhp (100kW) @ 5000 rpm, 187lb ft (253Nm) @ 2500 rpm compression ratio 8.5:1.
ENGINE STRUCTURE pushrod ohv with single central camshaft; aluminium alloy LM25 block and cylinder heads; twin Stromberg/Solex 175CDSE or SU HIF 44; Lucas 35DM8 or 35DLM8 electronic ignition; electrical fuel pump; 5-bearing crankshaft.
TRANSMISSION permanent four wheel drive. V8: 26.7cm 10.5in (26.7cm) hydraulically operated diaphragm spring clutch; LR95 4-speed integrated manual gearbox and transfer box with vacuum operated centre differential lock. Land Rover front banjo axle, Salisbury rear with cast differential housing. 3.54:1 final drive ratio.

CHASSIS Welded steel ladder frame with sleeved extension puddle-welded in place. Front and rear beam axles with coil springs and telescopic shock absorbers. recirculating ball steering, PAS optional. Servo assisted, dual circuit, hydraulic brakes. 11.81 in (300mm) front discs, 11in (28cm) rear drums. 10in (25.4cm) drum transmission parking brake. 17.5 gallon (79.5 litre) fuel tank.16in pressed steel wheels with 7.50x16 tyres.
DIMENSIONS Wheelbase 127in (322.6cm), front and rear track 58.5in (148.6cm), length; 202in (513.2cm), height; 80.1in (203.5cm), ground clearance (min) 8.5in (21.5cm), turning circle 49.5ft (15.1m).
CAPABILITIES Max gradient 45 deg, approach angle 50deg, departure angle 34deg.
PRICE Initial vehicles sold on a contract basis at about £15,000.

This very early 127 had a straight trailing edge on its rear door. The design was quickly changed to use a Station Wagon rear door with angled trailing edge,

1984 Land Rover Stage 2 Ninety

Since over 70 per cent of Land Rover's production was long wheelbase, it was natural that the One Ten should be the first to reach production Stage 2. Some internal debate took place, over what exactly a short wheelbase should measure, which delayed its introduction. There was a strong argument in favour of 254cm (100in), but concern over costs and possible conflict with Range Rover, meant that the choice fell on the shortest of the hybrid proposals. In the end packaging constraints, and the need to keep the rear propeller shaft's so-called "angle of dangle" within practical limits to avoid excessive noise and wear, dictated the adoption of 236cm (92.9in). The Land Rover Ninety kept the deeper section chassis side members of the One Ten, together with its suspension, even though the levelling unit, and roll bar were not fitted. However a new, smaller side mounted fuel tank was required. The driveline was the same, except for the shorter rear propshaft, and a Land Rover rear axle rather than the stronger Salisbury type. The Ninety was equipped with new one-piece doors and winding windows. Derived from those on the Santana Land Rovers, these made a welcome change from the short-lived sliding windows of the One Ten, which were now consigned to military vehicles. The Ninety came in all the body versions of its predecessor, including the County Station Wagon. To match the rear body cappings, the doors were fitted with a feature perhaps unique in the annals of the British motor industry – a galvanised steel trim strip.

INTRODUCTION 1984
BODY short wheel base soft top, truck cab, hard top or station wagon, gross weight 5291lbs (2400 kg), 5622lbs (2550 kg) with heavy duty suspension
ENGINES 2.3-litre 4-cylinder petrol; 74bhp (55kW) @4,000 rpm, 120lb ft (163Nm) @ 2000 rpm. Later (1985) 2.5-litre 4-cylinder petrol; 80bhp (60kW) @ 4,000 RPM, 129lb ft (175Nm) @ 2000 rpm. 2.5-litre 4-cylinder diesel; 65.5bhp (48kW) @ 4,000 RPM, 113lb ft (153Nm) @ 1800 rpm. 1986 2.5-litre 4-cylinder diesel turbocharged; 85bhp (63kW) @ 4,000 RPM, 150lb ft (203Nm) @ 1800 rpm.
ENGINE STRUCTURE pushrod ohv with timing chain; cast iron cylinder block and head. Petrol engines: Weber carburetter, Lucas 45D4 distributor. Diesel engines: CAV distributor pump, turbocharged engine used Garrett turbocharger.
TRANSMISSION permanent four wheel drive. 4-cylinder petrol; 9.53in (24.21cm) (later also 2.5-litre turbocharged); 9.25in (23.5cm) hydraulically operated diaphragm spring clutch; 4-cylinder diesel; 9.53in (24.21cm) hydraulically operated diaphragm spring clutch; LT77 5-speed manual gearbox, LT230 2-speed transfer box with lever operated centre differential lock. Land Rover banjo axles. 3.54:1 final drive ratio.

CHASSIS welded steel ladder frame. Front and rear beam axles with coil springs and telescopic shock absorbers. Recirculating ball steering, PAS optional. Servo assisted, dual circuit, hydraulic brakes. 11.81in (30.0cm) front discs, 11in (28.0cm) rear drums. 10in (25.4cm) drum transmission parking brake. 12 gallon (54.5 litre) fuel tank. 16in pressed steel wheels with 205x16 tyres – 7.50x16 tyres optional.
DIMENSIONS wheelbase 92.9in (236cm), front and rear track 58.5in (148.6cm), length Soft Top and Pick Up; 146.5in (372.2cm), Hard Top and Station Wagon; width 70.5in (179cm), height (nominal); normal suspension; 77.4in (196.5cm), heavy duty suspension; 78.7in (200cm), ground clearance (min); 9in (22.9cm), turning circle (min); 42ft (11.7m).
CAPABILITIES max gradient 45 deg, approach angle 50deg, departure angle (max) 49deg.
PRICE (1985): £7747–£11,324

The Ninety offered important improvements over the Series III 88 that it replaced, and went on to become one of the best-loved of all Land Rovers.

1984 Land Rover Ninety V8

Almost as soon as the One Ten was launched, it was obvious that worries over its effect on Range Rover sales were unfounded, and the company felt confident enough to offer the short wheelbase utility model as a V8 too. At the same time, the Santana-sourced LT85 gearbox was introduced in all V8 Land Rovers, offering the advantages of five gears. It was used in conjunction with Land Rover's own LT230 transfer box, rather than having the integrated gear and transfer box arrangement of the LT95, which it replaced. The engine was still de-tuned compared with that used in the Range Rover, yet it gave the Ninety a sprightly performance for a Land Rover with a Motor road test recording a 0 – 60mph (0 – 96kph) time of 14.7sec and a top speed of 90mph (145kph). Using all this extra power did nothing for the fuel consumption however, with the same test only recording 11.9mpg (4.2km per litre) under hard driving, giving a range of only 143 miles (229km) from the 12 gallon (54.5 litre) fuel tank The Ninety V8 was considered by motoring journalists to be a credible response to emerging competition from both Japan and Europe. Within the company, it stimulated the desire to conquer the emerging off-road leisure sector – a process that would lead to the Discovery.

INTRODUCTION 1985
BODY short wheel base soft top, truck cab, hard top or station wagon, gross weight 5291lbs (2400 kg), 5622lbs (2550 kg) with heavy duty suspension
ENGINE 3.5-litre V8; 113bhp (84kW) @ 4,000 rpm – later 134bhp (100kW) @ 5000 rpm, 185lb ft (250Nm) – later 187lb ft (253Nm) @ 2500 rpm.
ENGINE STRUCTURE pushrod ohv with single central camshaft; aluminium block and cylinder heads; twin Stromberg/Solex 175CDSE or SU HIF 44; Lucas 35DM8 or 35DLM8 electronic ignition system; electrical fuel pump; five main bearings.
TRANSMISSION permanent four wheel drive. 10.5 in (26.7cm) hydraulically operated diaphragm spring clutch; LT85 5-speed gearbox, LT230 transfer box with lever operated centre differential lock. Land Rover front and rear banjo axles. 3.54:1 final drive.

CHASSIS welded steel ladder frame. Front and rear beam axles with coil springs and telescopic shock absorbers. Recirculating ball steering, PAS optional. Servo assisted, dual circuit, hydraulic braking system. 11.8in (30cm) front disc brakes, 11in (28.0cm) rear drum brakes. 10in (25.4cm) drum transmission parking brake. 12 gallon (54.5 litre) fuel tank. 16in pressed steel wheels with 205x16 tyres – 7.50x16 tyres optional.
DIMENSIONS Wheelbase 92.9in (236cm), front and rear track 58.5in (148.6cm), length Soft Top and Pick Up; 146.5in (372.2cm), Hard Top and Station Wagon; width 70.5in (1790mm), height (nominal); normal suspension; 77.4in (196.5cm), heavy duty suspension; 78.7in (200cm), ground clearance (min); 9in (22.9cm), turning circle (min); 42ft (11.7m).
CAPABILITIES Max gradient 45 deg, approach angle 50deg, departure angle (max) 49deg.
PRICE (1985): £8878–£11,702

This cutaway of a V8-powered 90 County Station Wagon shows the optional air conditioning

1986 Land Rover Stage 2 Diesel Turbo

Considerable advances had been made across the range but in the face of increasing competition a package of improvements was introduced, principally a turbocharged version of the diesel engine. This entailed a major redesign. A new cylinder block had an integral oil feed for the turbocharger, a revised crankshaft with cross drillings to improve lubrication, new pistons and nimonic exhaust valves. The turbocharger was a Garrett AirResearch T2 with an integral wastegate. A boost control capsule for the injector pump, and a new starter motor provided higher cranking speeds. Engine temperatures were countered with a standard oil cooler and a new breathing system developed. Some of the changes were fed back into the naturally aspirated diesel, and also to the 4-cylinder petrol engine, while the V8 engine gained a new electronic injection system for a useful increase in power. Other changes included new push button door locks, replacing the lift up style that had been used since the early days. The interior door trims were redesigned to provide more elbow room and the new flush door locking buttons enhanced security and prevented inadvertent locking. Other improvements to the Ninety County included a radio cassette player in yet another new facia console, and styled steel wheels. Autocar praised the Ninety County as a superb off-roader with good handling and an excellent ride, yet the refinements brought problems. The new engine breathing system had a tendency to ingest its own lubricating oil, which burnt pistons out, and the new door locks could jam when contaminated with mud or sand.

INTRODUCTION 1986
BODY short wheelbase soft top, truck cab, hard top or station wagon, long wheel base soft top, truck cab, high capacity pick up, hard top or station wagon, extended wheelbase crew cab. Gross weight: Land Rover 90; 5291lbs (2400 kg), 5622lbs ((2550 kg) with heavy duty suspension, Land Rover 110; 6722lbs (3050 kg) 6504lbs (2950 kg))with ride levelling unit, Land Rover 127; 6722lbs (3050kg).
ENGINES 3.5-litre all-alloy V8 petrol; 134bhp (100kW) @ 5000 rpm, 185lb ft (250Nm) – later 187lb ft (253Nm) @ 2500 rpm, 2.5-litre 4-cylinder petrol; 80bhp (60kW) @ 4,000 RPM, 129lb ft (175Nm) @ 2000 rpm, 2.5-litre 4-cylinder diesel; 65.5bhp (48kW) @ 4,000 RPM, 113lb ft (153Nm) @ 1800 rpm, 2.5-litre 4-cylinder diesel turbocharged; 85bhp (63kW) @ 4,000 RPM, 150lb ft (203Nm) @ 1800 rpm.
ENGINE STRUCTURE V8: pushrod ohv with single central camshaft; aluminium alloy LM25 block and cylinder heads; twin SU HIF 44 carburettors; Lucas 35DLM8 electronic ignition system; electrical fuel pump; five main bearings. 4-cylinder: pushrod ohv with timing chain; cast iron cylinder block and head. Petrol engines: Weber carburetter, Lucas 45D4 distributor. Diesel engines: CAV distributor pump (DPA on naturally aspirated, DPS on turbocharged) turbocharged engine used Garrett T2 turbocharger.

TRANSMISSION permanent four wheel drive. Hydraulically operated diaphragm spring clutch; V8; 10.5in (26.7cm) dia; 4-cylinder petrol; 9.53in (24.21cm) dia; all diesel engines; 9.25in (23.5cm) dia; V8; LT85 5-speed gearbox, all petrol and diesel 4-cylinder engines; LT77 5-speed manual gearbox, all vehicles; LT230 2-speed transfer box with lever operated centre differential lock. Land Rover front banjo axle, Land Rover 90; Land Rover rear banjo axle, Land Rover 110 and 127; Salisbury rear axle with cast centre differential. 3.54:1 final drive ratio.
CHASSIS welded steel ladder frame. Front and rear beam axles with coil springs and telescopic shock absorbers. Recirculating ball steering, PAS optional. Servo assisted, dual circuit, hydraulic braking system. 11.81in (30 cm) front disc brakes, 11in (28cm) rear drum brakes. 10 in (25.4cm) drum transmission parking brake. Land Rover 90; 12 gallon (54.5 litre) fuel tank, Land Rover 110 and 127; 17.5 gallon (79.5 litre) fuel tank. Land Rover 90; 16in pressed steel wheels (styled on County models) with 205x16 tyres. Land Rover 110 and 127; 16in pressed steel wheels with 7.50x16 tyres.

DIMENSIONS Land Rover 90;
Wheelbase 92.9in (236cm), front and
rear track 58.5in (148.6cm), length Soft
Top and Pick Up; 146.5in (372.2cm),
Hard Top and Station Wagon; width
70.5in (179cm), height (nominal);
normal suspension; 77.4in (196.5cm),
heavy duty suspension; 78.7in (200cm),
ground clearance (min); 9in (22.9cm),
turning circle (min); 42ft (11.7m). Land
Rover 110; Wheelbase; 110in
(279.4cm), front and rear track; 58.5in
(148.6cm), length Soft Top and Pick Up;
152.9in (443.8cm), Hard Top and
Station Wagon; 181.1in (459.9cm),
High Capacity Pick Up; 182in
(463.1cm), width 70.5in (179.0cm),
height; with levelling unit; 80.1in
(203.5cm), normal suspension; 81.9in
(207.9cm), ground clearance (min) 8.5in
(21.5cm), turning circle; 42ft (12.8m).
Land Rover 127; Wheelbase 127in
(322.6cm), front and rear track 58.5in
(148.6cm), length; 202in (513.2cm),
height; 80.1in (203.5cm), ground
clearance (min) 8.5in (21.5cm), turning
circle 49.5ft (15.1m).
CAPABILITIES Land Rover 90; Max
gradient 45 deg, approach angle 50deg,
departure angle (max) 49deg. Land
Rover 110; Max gradient; 45 deg,
approach angle; 50deg, departure angle
(max); 34.5deg. Land Rover 127; Max
gradient 45 deg, approach angle 50deg,
departure angle 34deg.
PRICE £9568–£13,317

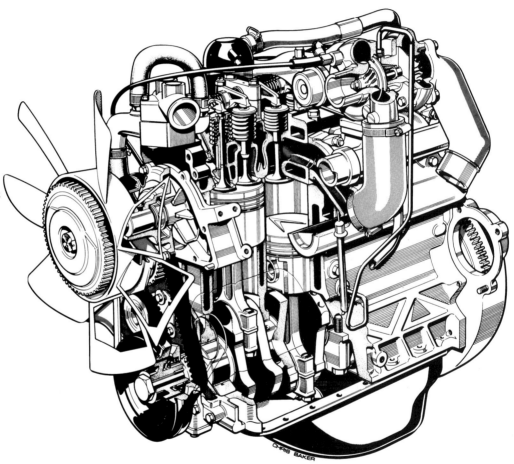

Turbocharging the old 2.5-litre
diesel engine brought welcome
performance increases, although in
fact Land Rover had started looking
at turbocharging their diesel engine
as long ago as 1957.

1990 Land Rover Defender

The debut of Discovery in 1989 brought major changes to the rest of Land Rover's product line. Market research revealed that the brand name had significant value, which the Discovery exploited, but it seemed to make little sense to have an alternative product with the same name as the company. The traditional-style Land Rover had to have a name, Defender had been an unused project code and, although somebody else formally owned it, they were willing to sell. Research indicated that Defender was understandable in major languages and customer clinics seemed to approve. To get the best out of it, such a major change needed to be co-ordinated to an event, in this case the 200Tdi diesel engine that had been in the Discovery since 1989. Equipping the utility models with the Tdi was not yet decided, and although it was equipped with an intercooler from the beginning of its development, that did not rescue its somewhat fragile nature. The 200Tdi remained the standard Defender diesel until 1994, but following its failure to pass durability tests, it was abandoned. Changes associated with the exhaust meant that the Defender engine had a slightly lower power output at 80kW (107bhp). This was still 26 percent better than the old engine as was the increase in torque to 264Nm (195lb ft). Achieved with a 25 percent improvement in fuel economy, the Defender package was completed with a bold decal treatment, bearing the new name. The 300 Tdi was a direct descendent and retained its high mounted turbocharger, different from the lower one on the Discovery.

INTRODUCTION 1990
BODY short wheelbase soft top, truck cab, hard top or station wagon, long wheel base soft top, truck cab, high capacity pick up, hard top or station wagon, extended wheelbase crew cab. Gross weight: Land Rover 90; 5291lbs (2400 kg) 5622lbs (2550 kg) with heavy duty suspension, Land Rover 110; 6722lbs (3050 kg) 6504lbs (2950 kg) with ride levelling unit, Land Rover 127; 6722lbs (3050k).
ENGINES 3.5-litre all-alloy V8 petrol; 134bhp (100kW) @ 5000 rpm, 185lb ft (250Nm) – later 187lb ft (253Nm) @ 2500 rpm, 2.5-litre 4-cylinder petrol; 80bhp (60kW) @ 4,000 RPM, 129lb ft (175Nm) @ 2000 rpm, 2.5-litre 4-cylinder diesel; 65.5bhp (48kW) @ 4,000 RPM, 113lb ft (153Nm) @ 1800 rpm, 2.5-litre 4-cylinder direct injection diesel turbocharged with intercooler; 107bhp (80kW) @ 4,000 RPM, 195lb ft (264Nm) @ 1800 rpm.
ENGINE STRUCTURE V8: pushrod ohv with single central camshaft; alloy block and cylinder heads; twin SU HIF 44 carburettors; Lucas 35DLM8 electronic ignition system; electrical fuel pump; five main bearings. 4-cylinder petrol and naturally aspirated diesel: pushrod ohv with timing chain; cast iron cylinder block and head. Turbocharged diesel engine: cast iron block, aluminium cylinder head. Petrol engines: Weber carburettor, Lucas 45D4 distributor. Diesel engines: naturally aspirated; CAV DPA distributor pump, turbocharged; Bosch rotary injection pump, Garrett T25 turbocharger.

TRANSMISSION permanent four wheel drive. Hydraulically operated diaphragm spring clutch; V8; 10.5 in (26.7cm) dia; 4-cylinder petrol; 9.53in (24.21cm) dia; all diesel engines; 9.25in (23.5cm) dia; V8; LT85 5-speed gearbox, all petrol and diesel 4-cylinder engines; LT77 5-speed manual gearbox, all vehicles; LT230 2-speed transfer box with lever operated centre differential lock. Land Rover front banjo axle, Land Rover 90; Land Rover rear banjo axle, Land Rover 110 and 127; Salisbury rear axle with cast centre differential. 3.54:1 final drive ratio.
CHASSIS Welded steel ladder frame. Front and rear beam axles with coil springs and telescopic shock absorbers. Recirculating ball steering, PAS optional. Servo assisted, dual circuit, hydraulic braking system. 11.81in (30cm) front disc brakes, 11in (28cm) rear drum brakes. 10 in (25.4cm) drum transmission parking brake. Land Rover 90; 12 gallon (54.5 litre) fuel tank, Land Rover 110 and 130; 17.5 gallon (79.5 litre) fuel tank. Land Rover 90; 16in pressed steel wheels (styled on County models);
205x16 tyres. Land Rover 110 and 130; 16in pressed steel wheels; 7.50x16 tyres.

DIMENSIONS Land Rover 90;
Wheelbase 92.9in (236cm), front and
rear track 58.5in (148.6cm), length Soft
Top and Pick Up; 146.5in (372.2cm),
Hard Top and Station Wagon; width
70.5in (179cm), height (nominal);
normal suspension; 77.4in (196.5cm),
heavy duty suspension; 78.7in (200cm),
ground clearance (min); 9in (22.9cm),
turning circle (min); 42ft (11.7m). Land
Rover 110; Wheelbase; 110in
(279.4cm), front and rear track; 58.5in
(148.6cm), length Soft Top and Pick
Up; 152.9in (443.8cm), Hard Top and
Station Wagon; 181.1in (459.9cm),
High Capacity Pick Up; 182in
(463.1cm), width 70.5in (179.0cm),
height; with levelling unit; 80.1in

(203.5cm), normal suspension; 81.9in
(207.9cm), ground clearance (min) 8.5in
(21.5cm), turning circle; 42ft (12.8m).
Land Rover 127; Wheelbase 127in
(322.6cm), front and rear track 58.5in
(148.6cm), length; 202in (513.2cm),
height; 80.1in (203.5cm), ground
clearance (min) 8.5in (21.5cm), turning
circle 49.5ft (15.1m).
CAPABILITIES Land Rover 90; Max
gradient 45 deg, approach angle 50deg,
departure angle (max) 49deg. Land
Rover 110; Max gradient; 45 deg,
approach angle; 50deg, departure angle
(max); 34.5deg. Land Rover 127; Max
gradient 45 deg, approach angle 50deg,
departure angle 34deg.
PRICE (1990): £10,309–£17,007

An early Defender 110 County
Station Wagon demonstrates its
off-road ability at a Land Rover
company event in Scotland.

The launch of Defender reinvigorated Land Rover's utility market but it was an ageing design. A newly created brand management organisation contemplated the market and it looked as though a lot of the rivals were lighter, less complex, and more modern. Codenamed Challenger, a programme was started to produce something that was to be known as Defender II. This aimed to improve Land Rover's penetration into the utility market, using the sub-structure, chassis, suspension and power train of the Discovery together with its front wings and doors. Defender's traditional purpose was kept in mind, and the bumpers were hefty, made of composite materials, and based on truck designs. A full range was planned, including double and what was termed king-size cabs. Hard tops and Station Wagons used composite roof assemblies, while a new universal tailgate was designed, capable of being hinged downwards or on either side, to cater for left or right hand drive. The interior included a new facia which, with different materials, would be used on the approaching new Discovery and Range Rover, while the roomy cab was capable of seating three in comfort. Challenger was a striking design but it was not well received by focus groups. A further problem lay in the Ministry of Defence's doubts over Land Rover quality and reliability, which worried the government and military sales team. It looked as though any new model would have to meet more stringent contract requirements. Although prototypes were built, costs were rising, and Challenger struggled to meet the demands that were being made of it. British Aerospace, for its part, refused further funding and the project was effectively abandoned.

This 1990 design rendering shows the tough look that Land Rover wanted for its short-wheelbase Defender II. The resemblance to the Discovery is also clear.

1992 Land Rover Defender SV90

While work was going on to revitalise Defender in the UK, emphasising the introduction of the County models, Land Rover realised it needed to show that this was more than just a utility model. Soft-top versions of short wheelbase Land Rovers had always been popular, encouraging concept vehicles such as the ill-starred Cariba. A soft-top leisure vehicle for the UK now seemed opportune and the SV90 took its name from the Special Vehicles department at Solihull, and from its limited edition of just 90 examples. It used many of the features under development for the NAS90, and shared new ones such as the roll cage, hood, front seats and the rear door spare wheel carrier. A full-height door with winding windows was deemed more suitable for the UK. The SV90 was finished in Caprice Blue metallic paint and special decals. It also used Discovery wheels, but in a different style, and with smaller tyres than the North American version. The main change came under the bonnet and instead of the powerful 3.9-litre petrol V8, SV90 had a 2.5-litre 200 Tdi diesel. The use of the SV90 as a development platform for the NAS90 delayed its appearance in dealers' showrooms until after the summer. Work done installing the 2.0-litre Mpi engine into Defenders for the Italian Carabinieri , gave rise to a proposal for a similar follow-up to the SV90, but following the indifference shown to the engine in Discovery it was never pursued.

INTRODUCTION 1993
BODY short wheelbase convertible, gross weight 5291lbs (2400kg)
ENGINE: 200 Tdi, 4-cylinder, 90.47mm x 97mm, 2495cc, compression ratio 19.5:1, 107bhp (80kW) @ 4000 rpm, 195 lbft (264Nm) @ 1800 rpm.
ENGINE STUCTURE: pushrod ohv with belt driven camshaft; cast iron cylinder block, aluminium cylinder head; Bosch rotary VE 4/11F 1900R 347-1 direct fuel injection pump; Garrett T25 turbocharger with intercooler, max boost 0.82bar (12psi).
TRANSMISSION permanent four wheel drive. 10.5 in (26.7cm) hydraulically operated diaphragm spring clutch; LT77 5-speed gearbox, LT230 transfer box with lever operated centre differential lock. Land Rover banjo front and rear axles. 3.54:1 final drive ratio.

CHASSIS welded steel ladder frame, front and rear beam axles with coil springs and telescopic shock absorbers, recirculating ball steering,with PAS, servo assisted, dual circuit, hydraulic brakes. 11.81in (30cm) front disc brakes, 11.4in (29.0cm) rear disc brakes. 10 in (25.4cm) drum transmission parking brake. 12 gallon (54.5 litre) fuel tank. 16in styled alloy wheels with 205 X 16 tyres.
DIMENSIONS Wheelbase 92.9 in (236.0cm), front and rear track 58.5in (148.6cm), length 146.5in (372.2cm), height (max) 77.3in (196.5cm), ground clearance (min); 9.0in (22.9cm), turning circle (min); 37.7ft (11.5m).
CAPABILITIES Max gradient 45 deg, approach angle 50deg, departure angle 49deg.
PRICE £18,995

Framed door windows certainly detracted from the sporty look of the SV90, and reliance on the Tdi engine gave it no special performance appeal. It was nonetheless strikingly different from the standard soft-top Defender 90 of the day.

1993 Land Rover Defender County

When Defender sales in the UK seemed to decline Land Rover evaluated two concepts based on the Ninety Hard Top. The first represented a return to the model's essentially utility heredity, and was stripped back to essentials with military doors instead of winding windows, no roof or floor trim, slab seats and with even the dash ventilators deleted. These reductions enabled the Defender to be offered cheaper. A second initiative proceeded in the opposite direction. It had the full County trim package, a fully-trimmed roof complete with alpine lights and sun roof, floor trim, County cloth seats and radio. There were body coloured wheel arch trims, distinctive decals and Rostyle wheels, which meant it had all the features of competitors such as the Daihatsu Fortrak, at a higher price justified by the Land Rover build and reputation. The wide range of options won the approval of customers and it was introduced as part of a revised range, which included County versions of the Defender Ninety Station Wagons and Hard Tops, and the Defender One Ten Station Wagon. For the first time Defenders were available with clear over base black and metallic paint finishes. There was some opposition from Solihull manufacturing staff, worried at the prospect of big bills for paintwork rectification, but the new colours proved popular and paved the way for a revival of interest in the make and the model.

INTRODUCTION 1993 produced to 1998
BODY Short wheel base hard top, gross weight 5291lbs (2400kg) 5622lbs (2550kg) heavy duty option.
ENGINES V8, 88.9mm x 71.1mm, 3528cc, compression ratio 8.13:1, 134bhp (100kW) @ 5000 rpm, 187 lb ft (253Nm) @ 2500 rpm. 200 Tdi, 4-cylinder 90.47mm x97mm 2495cc, compression ratio 19.5:1, 107bhp (80kW) @ 4000 rpm, 195 lb ft (264Nm) @ 1800 rpm. Later L R 300 Tdi 111bhp (83kW) @ 4000 rpm, 195 lb ft (254Nm) @ 1800 rpm.
ENGINE STRUCTURE V8: pushrod ohv with single central camshaft; aluminium block and cylinder heads; twin SU HIF 44 or Solex 175CDSE; Lucas 35DLM8 electronic ignition system; Facet electrical direct injection fuel pump; 5-bearing crankshaft. 200 Tdi: pushrod ohv with belt driven camshaft; cast iron cylinder block, aluminium cylinder head; Bosch rotary VE 4/11F 1900R 347-1 injection pump; Garrett T25 turbocharger with intercooler, max boost 0.82bar (12psi); 300 Tdi: Bosch R509 rotary fuel pump; Allied Signal turbocharger.
TRANSMISSION permanent four wheel drive. V8: Borg and Beck 10.5in (26.7cm) single dry plate hydraulically operated diaphragm spring clutch; Land Rover LT85 5-speed manual gearbox,

Tdi: Valeo 9.25in (23.5cm) hydraulically operated diaphragm spring clutch; Land Rover LT77S 5-speed manual gearbox, LT230 2-speed transfer box with centre differential lock. Land Rover front and rear banjo type axles, 3.54:1 final drive ratio.
CHASSIS welded steel ladder frame. Front and rear beam axles with coil springs and telescopic shock absorbers, Gemmer recirculating ball steering with optional power assistance, servo assisted, dual circuit, hydraulic brakes, 11.81in (30.0cm) front discs, ventilated on V8 and heavy duty vehicles, 11in (28.0cm) rear drums – 11.42 in (29cm) disc brakes from 1994. 10in (25.4cm) drum transmission parking brake. 12.5 gallon (54.5 litre) fuel tank. 16in wheels with 205x16 tyres.
DIMENSIONS Wheelbase 92.9in (236.0cm), front and rear track 58.5in (148.6cm), length 152.9in (388.3cm), width 70.5in (179.0cm), height 77.36/78.5 in (196.5/200cm) depending on specification, ground clearance (min) 7.5in (19.0cm), turning circle 37.7ft (11.5m).
CAPABILITIES Max gradient 45deg, approach angle 48/51.5deg, departure angle 49/53deg depending on specification.
PRICE (1994): County Station Wagon Tdi £16,826

By the mid-1990s, it had become commonplace to see high-specification Defenders with alloy wheels – unthinkable not many years earlier.

1992 Land Rover Defender

Defender was not allowed to stagnate. Aggressive marketing was matched by real progress, and throughout the following years, significant improvements were introduced as well as formalising the One Ten and One Thirty name tags introduced in 1989, the last year before it was called Defender. Innovations included disc brakes all round, One Ten, One Thirty and heavy-duty derivatives of the Ninety had ventilated ones on the front. Power assisted steering was also standardised and a new, smaller steering wheel based on the Discovery's, provided more elbow room although moving the outer seats inward slightly reduced centre seat width. As a further enhancement, the clutch pedal was provided with spring assistance to reduce disengagement pressure. The Ninety Hard Top and Station Wagon and the One Ten Station Wagon became available in County form, with a sunroof, cloth seats, radio cassette player, tinted glass, rear wash wipe and heated rear window. They were distinguished by new decals and on Ninety variants styled steel wheels. A range of clear over base colours comprising County Red metallic, County Green metallic and County Black proved popular.

A major development in 1994 was the 300 Tdi engine, already used in Discovery, now installed in Defender with increased horsepower and torque. As a result of new emission regulations it was the only Land Rover diesel sold in the UK and Europe, and for the same reason Ninety Station Wagons had to have an EGR and exhaust catalyst. The turbocharger was moved lower and a full width acoustic engine cover was provided to reduce noise. Although the 200Tdi engine had been a step forward, it had been essentially a re-working of the old turbocharged diesel to accept direct fuel injection. In contrast the 300Tdi was virtually new. It was now common to the Discovery, the main change between the two installations was that the Defender had a lower-mounted turbocharger and

a full width acoustic cover to reduce noise. The front was completely revised with a new belt-driven vacuum pump to eliminate problems hitherto with a skew-gear driven unit. There was provision for military 24-volt alternators and a new front cover meant that the timing belt could be changed without breaking into the water jacket. The new cylinder head had revised porting to improve combustion. Compliance with new European regulations was achieved by an exhaust gas recirculation (EGR) system. The necessary new engine mounts were fitted further back to reduce the bending tendency of the powertrain and to make it feel more refined.

INTRODUCTION 1992
BODY short wheelbase soft top, truck cab, hard top or station wagon, long wheel base soft top, truck cab, high capacity pick up, hard top or station wagon, extended wheelbase crew cab. Gross weight: 90; 5291lbs (2400 kg) 5622lbs (2550 kg) with heavy duty suspension, 110; 6722lbs (3050 kg) 6504lbs (2950 kg) with ride levelling unit, 130; 7496lbs (3400kg).
ENGINE (UK and Europe): 2.5-litre 4-cylinder direct injection diesel turbocharged with intercooler; 111bhp (83kW) @ 4,000 RPM, 195lb ft (265Nm) @ 1800 rpm.
ENGINE STRUCTURE cast iron block, aluminium cylinder head. Bosch rotary injection pump, Garrett T25 turbocharger.
TRANSMISSION permanent four wheel drive. Hydraulically operated diaphragm spring clutch; 9.25in (23.5cm) dia; LT77 5-speed manual gearbox, all vehicles; LT230 2-speed transfer box with lever operated centre

differential lock. Land Rover front banjo axle, Land Rover 90; Land Rover rear banjo axle, Land Rover 110 and 127; Salisbury rear axle with cast centre differential. 3.54:1 final drive ratio.
CHASSIS welded steel ladder frame, front and rear beam axles with coil springs and telescopic shock absorbers, recirculating ball steering with PAS. Servo assisted, dual circuit, hydraulic braking system. 11.8in (30.0cm) front disc brakes, ventilated on 90 heavy duty, 110 and 130, 11.4in (29.0cm) rear disc brakes. 10in (25.4cm) drum transmission parking brake. 90; 12 gallon (54.5 litre) fuel tank, 110 and 130; 17.5 gallon (79.5 litre) fuel tank. 90; 16in pressed steel wheels (styled on County models) with 205x16 tyres. 110 and 130; 16in pressed steel wheels with 7.50x16 tyres.
DIMENSIONS Land Rover 90; Wheelbase 92.9in (236cm), front and rear track 58.5in (148.6cm), length Soft Top and Pick Up; 146.5in (372.2cm), Hard Top and Station Wagon; width

70.5in (1790mm), height (nominal); normal suspension; 77.4in (196.5cm), heavy duty suspension; 78.7in (200cm), ground clearance (min); 9in (22.9cm), turning circle (min); 42ft (11.7m). Land Rover 110; Wheelbase; 110in (279.4cm), front and rear track; 58.5in (148.6cm), length Soft Top and Pick Up; 152.9in (443.8cm), Hard Top and Station Wagon; 181.1in (459.9cm),

High Capacity Pick Up; 182in (463.1cm), width 70.5in (179.0cm), height; with levelling unit; 80.1in (203.5cm), normal suspension; 81.9in (207.9cm), ground clearance (min) 8.5in (21.5cm), turning circle; 42ft (11.7m). Land Rover 127; Wheelbase 127in (322.6cm), front and rear track 58.5in (148.6cm), length; 202in (513.2cm), height; 80.1in (203.5cm), ground

clearance (min) 8.5in (21.5cm), turning circle 49.5ft (15.1m).
CAPABILITIES Land Rover 90; Max gradient 45 deg, approach angle 50deg, departure angle (max) 49deg. Land Rover 110; Max gradient; 45 deg, approach angle; 50deg, departure angle (max); 34.5deg. Land Rover 127; Max gradient 45 deg, approach angle 50deg, departure angle 34deg.

A 1992 Defender scales some picturesque rocks. Land Rover was always aware of environmental concerns, and the company went to great lengths to take account of pressures on off-road tracks and damage to green lanes in the countryside.

1992 Land Rover Defender 110 North American Specification (NAS 110)

Given the size of the North American market, Land Rover needed something else besides the Range Rover. So once the brand was well established, it looked like time to change the name of the Maryland-based business. The creation of Land Rover of North America in 1992 was marked by the launch of a limited edition Defender based on the 110. While it would not have been impossible to adapt Defender with a driver's airbag to meet forthcoming legislation (it had after all been achieved on the Morgan with a wooden body structure), the company did not consider the work to be an effective investment, so the production run was restricted to 500. The NAS 110 looked dramatic, with Alpine White paintwork, the tough image emphasised by a full external safari-style cage, the effectiveness of which had been assessed by rolling a prototype down a hill at Solihull. Defender's stability was so good that it required a great deal of persuasion to roll at all. A rear ladder gave access to the roof cargo rack, a front brush bar was matched with side runners, and lamp guards emphasised the prairie chic. It was fully carpeted, there were nine cloth-trimmed seats, a radio cassette player with four speakers, air conditioning and extra instrumentation. The 3.9-litre V8 was fitted with a catalytic converter and Land Rover Owner writer Jim Allen assessed the five-speed manual gearbox as being "as slick as oiled spaghetti". The unique rear step incorporated a US-style receptacle for a towing hitch.

INTRODUCTION 1992 (Sold as 1993 Model Year)
BODY long wheel base station wagon, gross weight 6504lbs (2950kg)
ENGINE: V8, 94mm x 71.1mm 3947cc; 185bhp (138kW) @ 4,750 rpm, 227lb ft (308Nm).
ENGINE STRUCTURE pushrod ohv with single central camshaft; aluminium block and cylinder heads; Lucas L-Jetronic electronic fuel injection; electrical fuel pump; five main bearings.
TRANSMISSION permanent four wheel drive. 10.5 in (26.7cm) hydraulically operated diaphragm spring clutch; LT77 5-speed gearbox, LT230 transfer box with lever operated centre differential lock. Land Rover banjo front axle, Salisbury rear axle with cast differential. 3.54:1 final drive ratio.

CHASSIS welded steel ladder frame. Front and rear beam axles with coil springs and telescopic shock absorbers. Recirculating ball steering, with PAS. Servo assisted, dual circuit, hydraulic braking system. 11.8in (30.0cm) front disc brakes, 11.4in (27.9cm) rear drum brakes. 10in (25.4cm) drum transmission parking brake. 17.5 gallon (79.5 litre) fuel tank. 16in pressed steel wheels with 7.50 X 16 Michelin 4 x 4 tyres.
DIMENSIONS Wheelbase 110in (279.4cm), front and rear track 58.5in (148.6cm), length 181.1in (459.9cm), height (with rack) 90.0in (228.6cm), ground clearance (min); 8.5in (21.5cm), turning circle (min); 43.6ft (13.3m).
CAPABILITIES Max gradient 45 deg, approach angle 50deg, departure angle 34deg.
PRICE $40,575 inc delivery.

The NAS 110 was a striking-looking vehicle, its rollover cage giving an aura of toughness even though painting it in the body colour had the effect of partially concealing it.

Owing to some impending air bag legislation the North American version of the Defender One Ten was faced with a limited period on the market. However so far as the regulations were concerned the Defender Ninety was light enough to fall into a different category. Accordingly a suitable version was developed, which lasted until the legislation eventually caught up with it too in 1997. Initially the only body style was a soft top reinforced by a roll cage. The first ones had hoods manufactured by Tickford but, after problems making them fit properly, a US-sourced BesTop accessory replaced them. Later still a resin hard top and a Station Wagon went on sale. The NAS 90 had the brush bar, rear step, and the American market lighting of the 110, but was improved by aluminium wheels from Discovery. It also had a swing away carrier on the side hinged rear door, which had been developed for the Turkish Army, and detachable door tops taken from the military spare parts bin. A special frame on the rear door carried a high mounted stop lamp on soft tops, and the seats were trimmed in weatherproof material. The in-car entertainment system was protected for the outdoor life owners were expected to enjoy. A wide range of accessories, such as curiously named Surrey and Bimini tops, were aimed at Californian customers, who could also have air conditioning fitted by the dealer. Accessories included lifestyle items such as bike racks and rear seats for additional passengers.

INTRODUCTION 1993 (Sold as 1994 Model Year)
BODY short wheel base convertible, gross weight 6003lbs (2723kg).
ENGINE: V8, 94mm x 71.1mm 3947cc; 182bhp (135kW) @ 4,750 rpm, 232lb ft (315Nm).
ENGINE STRUCTURE pushrod ohv with single central camshaft; aluminium block and cylinder heads; Lucas L-Jetronic electronic fuel injection; in-tank electrical fuel pump; five main bearings.
TRANSMISSION permanent four wheel drive. 10.5 in (26.7cm) hydraulically operated diaphragm spring clutch; LT77 5-speed gearbox, LT230 transfer box with lever operated centre differential lock. Land Rover banjo front and rear axles. 3.54:1 final drive ratio.

CHASSIS Welded steel ladder frame. Front and rear beam axles with coil springs and telescopic shock absorbers. Recirculating ball steering,with PAS. Servo assisted, dual circuit, hydraulic braking system. 11.81in (30cm) front ventilated disc brakes, 11.4in (29.0cm) rear disc brakes. 10in (25.4cm) drum transmission parking brake. 12 gallon (54.5 litre) fuel tank. 16in styled alloy wheels with 265/75 X 16 BF Goodrich Mud Terrain (later All Terrain) tyres.
DIMENSIONS Wheelbase 92.9in (236.0cm), front and rear track 58.5in (148.6cm), length 160.5in (407.2cm), height (max) 80.2in (203.7cm) (with rack), ground clearance (min); 9.0in (22.9cm), turning circle (min); 40.0 ft (12.2m).
CAPABILITIES Max gradient 45 deg, approach angle 50deg, departure angle 49deg.
PRICE $28,495 inc delivery.

Bright colours added to the open-air appeal of the NAS 90. Note the old-style door handles which went with the half-doors with their detachable tops.

1994 Land Rover Defender 90 Carabinieri 2.0 Station Wagon

Italy was always a big market for Land Rover, and their influence was enhanced when Fiat ended production of the Campagnola in 1985. The Carabinieri operated all over Italy, had established its own fuel infrastructure based on petrol-engined vehicles, so when its old Fiats needed replacement wanted to buy Land Rovers. Unfortunately they were only offered in Europe with the Tdi diesel. The difficulty was overcome with the petrol engine from the recently introduced Discovery Mpi, a twin overhead camshaft 1994cc 4-cylinder derived from one used in Rover cars. With such a large order at stake (700 later increased to 840), engineering resources were found to make the engine fit, and vehicles were built on the normal Defender production line. Final preparation to Carabinieri specification was carried out in Italy. The chassis was modified from the Defender NAS 90, incorporated its rear mounted plastic fuel tank, and the engine came straight from the Discovery. It had a revised version of the ECU settings to reproduce the characteristic intake depression and exhaust back pressure of the Discovery. Concerned that the transfer gear ratio of the Discovery Mpi would compromise performance, a lower Defender gear set was recommended, and the vehicles eventually had Discovery Mpi gearbox ratios coupled with a Defender Tdi transfer box. These provided a relatively lively performance. The exhaust system was fitted with a catalyst, requiring a new chassis cross member, and the fuel pipes, evaporative loss control and sensors all came from the NAS 90. The vehicle proved popular with the Carabinieri although it overcame its petrol prejudice and later contracts went back to the Tdi diesel engine. A Defender Mpi was nearly two seconds quicker to 60 mph (96kph) than a Discovery, prompting a revival of the leisure vehicle concept, pioneered by the SV90 with the Mpi engine. This was only shelved following the poor sales achieved by the Discovery Mpi.

INTRODUCTION 1994
BODY short wheel base, 6-seat station wagon, gross weight 5291lbs (2400kg).
ENGINE: petrol, 4-cylinder in line 84.45mm x 89.00mm 1994cc. Compression ratio 10:1, 134 bhp (100kW) @ 6000 rpm, 140 lb ft (190Nm) @ 3600.
ENGINE STRUCTURE Austin-Rover twin overhead belt-driven camshaft, 16-valve, aluminium cylinder head, cast iron block with five main bearings, electronic fuel injection.
TRANSMISSION permanent four wheel drive. 10.5 in (26.7cm) hydraulically operated diaphragm spring clutch; LT77 5-speed gearbox, LT230 transfer box with lever operated centre differential lock. Land Rover banjo front and rear axles. 3.54:1 final drive ratio.

CHASSIS welded steel ladder frame, front and rear beam axles with coil springs and telescopic shock absorbers, recirculating ball steering, with PAS. servo assisted, dual circuit, hydraulic braking system, 11.81in (30.0cm) front ventilated disc brakes, 11.4in (29.0cm) rear disc brakes. 10in (25.4cm) drum transmission parking brake, 13 gallon (59 litre) fuel tank. 16in styled steel wheels with 205 x 16 tyres.
DIMENSIONS Wheelbase 92.9in (236.0cm), front and rear track 58.5in (148.6cm), length 152.9in (388.3cm), height (max) 77.3in (196.3cm), ground clearance (min); 9.0in (22.9cm), turning circle (min); 40.0 ft (12.2m).
CAPABILITIES Max gradient 45 deg, approach angle 48deg, departure angle 38deg (with towbar fitted).

As always, Solihull was prepared to bend over backwards when there was the prospect of a large fleet order. The Carabinieri got the petrol engine they wanted.

1998 Land Rover Defender Td5 90, 110, 130

Discovery Series II had been the publicity platform for the 5-cylinder Electronic Unit Injector Td5 diesel, and now the same engine was quietly introduced in the Defender. Here it provided a useful nine per cent gain in power and 13 per cent more torque. It was designed, like so many automotive creations, to be sold throughout the world but some territories remained unconvinced about the reliability of its electronics. Tdi production was licensed to Maxion (later International) in Brazil, and the Td5 turned out to be exceptionally reliable, the worries unjustified. Defender underwent other improvements. The issue of better traction had preoccupied Land Rover and its customers for some time. Air locking differentials were a popular and well established after-market accessory, and the company had experimented with Torsen differentials, fitting some to vehicles used by the South Western Electricity Board. Concern about traction was met by ABS coupled with Electronic Traction Control (ETC). Just as important, given the wide spread of Defender load conditions, was another ABS offshoot, Electronic Brakeforce Distribution (EBD). To cope with the extra torque and to quieten the intrusive whine from the transmission, the R380 transfer box was upgraded with new bushes, revised material specifications, new gear profiles and a cable-operated gear change. Complementing the new power and refinement, the cabin received extra sound deadening as well as a new air conditioning system and revised electronic instrumentation.

INTRODUCTION 1998
BODY short wheelbase soft top, truck cab, hard top or station wagon, long wheel base soft top, truck cab, high capacity pick up, hard top or station wagon, extended wheelbase crew cab. Gross weight: 90; 5291lbs (2400kg) 5622lbs (2550kg) with heavy duty suspension, 110; 6722lbs (3050 kg) 7716lbs (3500kg) with Heavy Duty suspension, 110 Station Wagon; 6504lbs (2950kg 6722lbs (3050kg) with 'Freestyle' alloy wheels, 130; 7716lbs (3500kg).
ENGINE (UK and Europe): 84.5mm x 89mm 2495cc, straight 5-cylinder electronic unit injector diesel turbocharged with intercooler;124bhp (90kW) @ 4,200 rpm, 221lb ft (300Nm) @ 1950 rpm.
ENGINE STRUCTURE cast iron block, aluminium cylinder head. Electronically controlled pump injectors, Garrett turbocharger.
TRANSMISSION permanent four wheel drive, hydraulically operated diaphragm spring clutch; 9.25in (23.5cm) dia; LT77 5-speed manual gearbox, all vehicles; LT230Q 2-speed transfer box with lever operated centre differential lock. Land Rover front and rear banjo axles, heavy duty 110 and 130; Salisbury rear axle with cast centre differential. 3.54:1 final drive ratio.
CHASSIS welded steel ladder frame, front and rear beam axles with coil springs and telescopic shock absorbers. Recirculating ball steering with PAS. Servo assisted, dual circuit, hydraulic brakes. 11.81in (30.0cm) front disc brakes, ventilated on 90 heavy duty, 110 and 130, 11.42in (29.0cm) rear disc brakes. 10in (25.4cm) drum

transmission parking brake. 90; 13.2 gallon (60 litre) fuel tank, 110 and 130; 16.5 gallon (75 litre) fuel tank. 90; 16in pressed steel wheels with 205x16 tyres – optional styled alloy wheels with 265/75 x 16 tyres. 110 and 130; 16in pressed steel wheels with 7.50 x 16 tyres or optional styled alloy wheels with 265/75 x 16 tyres.
DIMENSIONS 90; Wheelbase 92.9in (236cm), front and rear track 58.5in (148.6cm), length Soft Top and Pick Up; 146.5in (372.2cm), Hard Top and Station Wagon; width 70.5in (1790 mm), height (nominal); normal suspension; 78.5in (193.3cm), heavy duty suspension; 81.7in (207.6cm), ground clearance (min); 9in (22.9cm), turning circle (min); 42ft (11.7m). 110; Wheelbase; 110in (279.4cm), front and rear track; 58.5in (148.6cm), length Soft Top and Pick Up; 152.9in (443.8cm), Hard Top and Station Wagon; 181.1in (459.9cm), High Capacity Pick Up; 182in (463.1cm), width 70.5in (179.0cm), height; 81.7in (207.6cm), ground clearance (min) 21.5cm 8.5in (21.5cm), turning circle; 42ft (12.8m). 130; Wheelbase 127in (3226mm), front and rear track 58.5in (148.6cm), length; 202in (513.2cm), height; 81.7in (207.6cm), ground clearance (min) 8.5in (215mm), turning circle 49.5ft (15.1m).
CAPABILITIES 90; Max gradient 45 deg, approach angle 50deg, departure angle (max) 49deg. 110; Max gradient; 45 deg, approach angle; 50deg, departure angle (max); 34.5deg. 130; Max gradient 45 deg, approach angle 50deg, departure angle 34deg.
PRICE £17,170 – £26,550

The Td5 engine's electronics led to mistrust by many Land Rover traditionalists. Pictured at the top, the Braemar was a special limited-edition hardtop sold only in Scotland.

2002 MY Land Rover Defender

At the 2001 Frankfurt Motor Show a number of changes were introduced aimed at bringing Defender into the new century. Some tried to correct deficiencies that had been with it for a long time, others improved comfort, and a new variant was introduced. The conception of the 90 County Station Wagon was not unlike that of the Tickford Station Wagon of 1948, with the removal of the bulkhead enabling the front seat to recline more, and provide extra space behind. New side and rear doors of zinc-plated steel, scorning Land Rover's trademark aluminium, were also introduced. While they looked the same, they offered a better and consistent fit, curing a long-standing Defender bugbear. They also allowed the addition of electric window lifts and central locking. The new rear door had a continuous seal for the rear window, replacing the old-style framework. Another benefit was a revised facia with a new centre console housing a bank of switches, and an unheard-of luxury at extra cost, heated front seats. Chassis improvements included larger suspension bushes and revised rear brakes for the 110 and 130. The new model was the 110 Double Cab, begun as a Special Vehicles project for developing world markets and now introduced as a mainstream variant. The changes emphasised Land Rover's commitment to its oldest model in its 54th year. While still powered by the redoubtable Td5 engine, impending legislation led to the announcement that this would be replaced within a few years by a version of the US Ford Puma engine from the Ranger. At the same time the Defender's future at Solihull was affirmed.

INTRODUCTION 2001
BODY short wheelbase soft top, truck cab, hard top or station wagon, long wheel base soft top, truck cab, high capacity pick up, hard top, double cab or station wagon, extended wheelbase crew cab. Gross weight: 90; 5291lbs (2400kg) 5622lbs (2550kg) with heavy duty suspension, 110; 6722lbs (3050 kg) 7716lbs (3500kg) with Heavy Duty suspension), 110 Station Wagon; 6504lbs (2950kg) 6722lbs (3050kg) with 'Freestyle' alloy wheels, 130; 7716lbs (3500kg).
ENGINE (UK and Europe): 2.5-litre 5-cylinder electronic unit injector diesel turbocharged with intercooler; 124bhp (90kW) @ 4,200 rpm, 221lb ft (300Nm) @ 1950 rpm.
ENGINE STRUCTURE cast iron block, aluminium cylinder head. Electronically controlled pump injectors, Garrett turbocharger.
TRANSMISSION permanent four wheel drive. Hydraulically operated diaphragm spring clutch; 9.25in (23.5cm) dia; LT77 5-speed manual gearbox, all vehicles; LT230Q 2-speed transfer box with lever operated centre differential lock. Land Rover front and rear banjo axles, heavy duty 110 and 130; Salisbury rear axle with cast centre differential. 3.54:1 final drive ratio.
CHASSIS Welded steel ladder frame. Front and rear beam axles with coil springs and telescopic shock absorbers. Recirculating ball steering with PAS. Servo assisted, dual circuit, hydraulic braking system. 11.81in (30.0cm) front disc brakes, ventilated on 90 heavy duty, 110 and 130, 11.42in (29.0cm) rear disc brakes. 10in (25.4cm) drum

transmission parking brake. 90; 13.2 gallon (60 litre) fuel tank, 110 and 130; 16.5 gallon (75 litre) fuel tank. 90; 16in pressed steel wheels with 205x16 tyres – optional styled alloy wheels with 265/75 x 16 tyres. 110 and 130; 16in pressed steel wheels with 7.50 x 16 tyres or optional styled alloy wheels with 265/75 x 16 tyres.
DIMENSIONS 90; Wheelbase 92.9in (236cm), front and rear track 58.5in (148.6cm), length Soft Top and Pick Up; 146.5in (372.2cm), Hard Top and Station Wagon; width 70.5in (1790mm), height (nominal); normal suspension; 78.5in (193.3cm), heavy duty suspension; 81.7in (207.6cm), ground clearance (min); 9in (22.9cm), turning circle (min); 42ft (11.7m). 110; Wheelbase; 110in (279.4cm), front and rear track; 58.5in (148.6cm), length Soft Top and Pick Up; 152.9in (388.3cm), Hard Top and Station Wagon; 181.1in (459.9cm), High Capacity Pick Up; 182in (463.1cm), width 70.5in (179.0cm), height; 81.7in (207.6cm), ground clearance (min) 8.5in (21.5cm), turning circle; 42ft (12.8m). 130; Wheelbase 127in (322.6cm), front and rear track 58.5in (148.6cm), length; 202in (513.2cm), height; 81.7in (207.6cm), ground clearance (min) 8.5in (21.5cm), turning circle 849.5ft (15.1m).
CAPABILITIES 90; Max gradient 45 deg, approach angle 50deg, departure angle (max) 49deg. 110; Max gradient; 45 deg, approach angle; 50deg, departure angle (max); 34.5deg. 130; Max gradient 45 deg, approach angle 50deg, departure angle 34deg.
PRICE £17,480 – 24,995

Discovery

Discovery 3 in convoy in Oman
2006 during the Biosphere
Expedition

1988 Prototypes and Range Rover bucks

By the middle of the 1980s, Land Rover was casting an envious eye on cars like the Mitsubishi Pajero-Shogun and the Isuzu Trooper, which were selling strongly in the big price and marketing gap between the Defender and the Range Rover. An effort was made to fill this by employing funds available following the Gilroy Review. There was still not enough money for a completely new model, so a choice had to be made, between the chassis of a One-Ten Land Rover or something derived from the Range Rover. The choice fell on Range Rover, because it was better on-road, offered the prospect of superior refinement, even though it would mean a lot of work in developing a new style of body. At all times the designers looked on the Japanese as their major competition, yet it was still necessary to make the new machine different from the up-market Range Rover. The first clay models of Project Jay were built in 1986, using the 100in (254cm) wheelbase of the Range Rover, together with a few of its expensive-to-tool components such as floor-pan, and windscreen. Flat and stepped-roof estate cars with plain or sculpted sides were tried. Variants with three or five doors were all attempted, together with (to save money) Sherpa van headlamps and Austin-Rover Maestro van tail lamps. What was inescapable, given the Range Rover's chassis and running gear, was that the new vehicle's basic size and bulk would be much the same, even though the body shell was quite different. Making the distinction taxed the designers but after deep appraisal, a stepped roof style with extra glass above the drip rails was chosen, and the interior was aimed at what had come to be known as life-style (in the jargon of the Sunday supplements) rather than the working-off-road market.

Above: Early thoughts on the fascia.
Right: Many different styling proposals were made. This clay model, different on both sides, dates from 1986.

1989 Land Rover Discovery

Launched in September 1989, the Discovery was available only in 3-door estate style, with a choice of V8 petrol or 4-cylinder turbo-diesel engines. It seemed obvious that a 5-door was a logical derivative, but this did not happen for a further year. Although the underpinnings were unmistakably derived from the Range Rover, the Discovery was carefully planned to be slower, and therefore lower down the price scale. There was no disguising the entire chassis, suspension, steering and brakes, although there was no self-levelling strut at the rear, and a new-type of pressed steel road wheel was used. To emphasise the dissimilarity from the faster, more expensive Range Rover, the engine had SU carburettors, and was rated at 145bhp (108.13kW). The alternative was a much-improved, 26 per cent more powerful, version of the 2.5-litre turbo-diesel engine (the 200TDi), which had an aluminium head, and direct fuel injection. It was a good deal livelier than Land Rover's earlier turbo-diesel, became known as the 200Tdi (code-named Gemini by the engineering team), and represented a fresh approach to diesel power. Convinced that a lot more of this was required for the bulky Discovery – as delivered, it had 111bhp (82.77kW) instead of 85bhp (63.39kW) and, more importantly, 195lbft (264Nm) instead of 150lbft (203Nm) – Land Rover provided a belt-driven overhead camshaft to keep the timing precise, and an air-to-air intercooler to help keep down the temperature of the pressurised inlet gases. In the transmission the dual-range transfer box was the LT230T, which had recently been displaced by a more sophisticated system on the Range Rover.

INTRODUCTION 1989, produced to (carburetted-V8) 1990, or 1994
BODY estate, 3-doors, 7-seats; weight from 4359lb (1932kg).
ENGINE V8-cylinder petrol, in-line; front; 88.9mm x 71.1mm, 3528cc; compr 8:1; 145bhp (108.2kW) @ 5200rpm; 41.1bhp/l (30.7kW/l); 192lbft (260.3Nm) @ 2800rpm. 4-cyl turbo-diesel, in-line, front, 90.47mm x 97mm, 2495cc; compr 19.5:1, 111bhp (82.8kW) @ 4000rpm; 195lbft (264.3Nm) @ 1800rpm. Turbo-diesel with automatic transmission 120bhp (89.5kW); 221lbft (299.6Nm) @ 2000rpm.
ENGINE STRUCTURE V8 petrol, 2 overhead valves per cylinder; chain-driven camshaft in centre of block; aluminium cylinder heads and block; two SU carburettors, 5-bearing crankshaft; water-cooled. 4-cyl turbo-diesel, overhead valves, belt-driven camshaft; aluminium cylinder head, cast iron block. Bosch fuel injection and Garrett turbocharger, 5-bearing crankshaft, water-cooled.
TRANSMISSION Permanent four-wheel-wheel drive; diaphragm spring clutch; manual gearbox, 5-speed all-synchromesh; final drive 3.538:1, transfer box ratios (High Range) 1.222:1 or (Low Range) 3.321:1.

CHASSIS separate box-section chassis frame, steel and aluminium-panelled body; beam axle front suspension by coil springs, radius arms, Panhard rod; live axle rear suspension by coil springs, radius arms, A-bracket, telescopic dampers; hydraulic servo brakes, front 11.8in (30.0cm) dia discs, rear 11.4in (28.95cm) dia discs; transmission drum parking brake; power-assisted recirculating ball steering; 19.5gal (89l) fuel tank; 205R-16in.tyres or 235/70-16in tyres on steel rims.
DIMENSIONS wheelbase, 100in (254cm); track front and rear, 51.5in (148.6cm); length 178in (452.1cm); width 70.6in (179.3cm); height 75.6in (192cm); ground clearance 8.1in (20.4cm); turning circle 37.5ft (11.4m)
PERFORMANCE maximum speed V8, 95mph; 4-cyl turbo-diesel, 92mph 25.1mph (40.4kph) @ 1000rpm; 0-60mph (96kph) V8, 12.8sec; 4-cyl turbo-diesel, 17.1sec; fuel consumption V8, 14mpg; 4-cyl turbo-diesel, 23.9mpg
PRICE £15,750

The original Discovery was only available as a three-door station wagon, with a somewhat decorative colour scheme.

At this stage automatic transmission was not yet available. The exterior style was fresh, subtly different from the Range Rover, still with a steel shell and aluminium panels, but the interior design and choice of materials and colours (in association with Conran Design) was light, bright, and much more car-like than the more expensive model. In the rear inward-facing foldaway seats made it into a 7-seater, unusual in the category though at the expense of some luggage space when the seats were in use. The Discovery's appeal lay not just in performance and looks, but also in its price. Both models sold for £15,750, whereas Range Rover prices started at £23,784 – £8,034 or 51 per cent more. More than 20,000 would be sold within a year, and before the first major changes were made. It was small wonder that *Autocar & Motor's* road test stated that: "Faster, more economical, better riding and with the extra traction and balance of permanent 4WD, Discovery has the measure of its rivals. With the right build quality, this new champion of Britain's motor industry is good enough to send the Japanese back to the drawing board."

The 200Tdi turbo-diesel engine produced 111bhp, which helped deliver a top speed of 92mph.

1990 Land Rover Discovery 5-door

A steady and persistent programme of up-grades began only a year after Discovery was launched. In the autumn of 1990, following a great deal of rumour and speculation, the 5-door version of the new style appeared without any changes to the overall estate car profile. The original carburetted V8 engine was dropped in favour of one with fuel injection. For the time being the 200Tdi diesel remained unchanged. Fuel injection of petrol-engined cars was not new to Rover and Land Rover; it had been seen first on the Rover 3500 Vitesse SD1 of 1982. Bosch/Lucas fuel injection had already been fitted to Triumph TR8s for the USA in 1981, and was adopted on the Range Rover Vogue from late 1985. This was a joint enterprise between Bosch of Germany, which provided the technology, and Joseph Lucas, which built it in the Midlands. Not only did it improve the performance of the 3.5-litre engine – peak torque, for instance, was up from 192lbft (260Nm) with carburettors to 212lbft (288Nm) – but the precision of its engineering also limited exhaust emissions. This prepared the Discovery for eventual sale into tough emission-controlled markets like North America and Japan. With this in mind an exhaust system catalytic converter became optional, although demand for it was low at first on the home market. Discovery now had an impressive array of optional extra items, including alloy wheels and air-conditioning. Further improvements came with the choice of a 4-speed ZF automatic transmission (from autumn 1992 with the V8 engine, from autumn 1993 with the Tdi), while an enlarged 180bhp (134.23kW), 3,947cc version of the V8 took over in September 1993. In every case, these dates followed (not led) those made to the Range Rover, and never outgunned the top-of-the-line model in any way. Discovery production was often over 700 cars a week (more than 35,000 a year) before the entire 1990-1994 range was displaced by a face-lifted model in the spring of 1994.

INTRODUCTION 1990, produced to 1994
BODY estate, 5-doors, 7-seats; weight from 4363lb (1975kg).
ENGINE V8-cylinders, in-line; front; 88.9mm x 71.1mm, 3528cc; compr 9.35:1; 164bhp (122kW) @ 4750rpm; 46.5bhp/l (34.6kW/l); 212lbft (288Nm) @ 3000rpm; (1993-1994) 94mm x 71.1mm, 3947cc; compr 9.35:1; 180bhp (134kW) @ 4750rpm; 45.6bhp/l (33.9kW/l); 230lbft (312Nm) @ 3100rpm.
ENGINE STRUCTURE V8, 2 overhead valves per cylinder; chain-driven camshaft in centre of block; aluminium cylinder heads and block; Bosch-Lucas fuel injection; 5-bearing crankshaft; water-cooled.
TRANSMISSION permanent four-wheel drive; diaphragm spring clutch; manual all-synchromesh 5-speed gearbox; final drive 3.538:1, transfer box ratios (High Ratio) 1.222:1, or (Low Range) 3.321:1. From 1992 (V8i models) and 1993 (TDi models), optional four-speed ZF 4HP22 automatic transmission.

CHASSIS separate box-section chassis frame, steel and aluminium panelled body; beam axle front suspension by coil springs, radius arms; Panhard rod; live axle rear suspension by coil springs, radius arms, A-bracket, telescopic dampers; hydraulic servo-assisted brakes, front 11.8in (30cm) dia ventilated discs, rear 11.4in (28.95cm) dia discs; transmission drum parking brake; power-assisted recirculating ball steering; 19.5gal (89l) fuel tank; 205R-16in. or 235/70-16in. tyres on steel or alloy rims.
DIMENSIONS wheelbase 100in (254cm); track front and rear 51.5in (148.6cm); length 178in (452.1cm); width 70.6in (179.3cm); height 75.6in (192cm); ground clearance 8.1in (20.4cm); turning circle 37ft (11.4m).
PERFORMANCE maximum speed 105mph (168.56kph) 25.1mph (40.4kph) @ 1000rpm; 0-60mph (96kph) 11.7sec; fuel consumption 16.5mpg (17.12l/100km).
PRICE (3-door) £17,985 (5-door) £20,470

The five-door version of the Discovery was launched at the end of 1990, and soon became the best-selling type in the range.

1993 Land Rover Discovery Mpi 2.0-litre petrol

The 2-litre petrol engined Mpi Discovery launched in April 1993, came as something of a surprise. Not only was it the first non-Land Rover 4-cylinder engined type to be marketed for some years – it used a car-based Rover T16 power unit – but it was a sophisticated, high-revving engine of a type not previously linked with heavy four-wheel-drive models. It was introduced, fair-and-square, as a tax-break model in certain countries (Italy was a perfect example) where taxation laws penalised petrol engined cars of more than 2litres. Although the T16 was powerful and technically advanced (it had four-valves per cylinder and a narrow angle twin-overhead-camshaft cylinder head), it lacked the torque of both the V8 and the 200Tdi turbo-diesel, and needed to be revved much higher to produce the same performance. For that reason, it featured lower overall gearing, the step-down ratio being 1.41:1 instead of 1.222:1 – and it was not suitable for automatic transmission. According to 4x4 expert James Taylor the Mpi was: "…disappointing off-road, or as a tow car, but its top speed of 98mph (157.32kph) helped it to appeal to a certain type of buyer," This proved that there was no substitute for torque where heavy four-wheel-drive machines were concerned, and not even an attractive price could make the difference. Even so, it remained in the Discovery range until 1998, but was not continued with the Discovery 2.

INTRODUCTION 1993, produced to 1998
BODY estate, 5-doors, 5-seats or 7-seats; weight 4175lb (1890kg)
ENGINE 4-cylinders, in-line; front; 84.45mm x 88.9mm, 1994cc; compr 10.0:1; 134bhp (100kW) @ 6000rpm; 67.2bhp/l (50kW/l); 137lbft (185.7Nm) @ 2500rpm .
ENGINE STRUCTURE Rover T16; 4-valves per cylinder; twin overhead camshafts, cogged-belt camshaft drive; aluminium cylinder head, cast iron block; Bosch/Lucas fuel injection; 5-bearing crankshaft; water-cooled.
TRANSMISSION Permanent four-wheel-drive; diaphragm spring clutch; manual gearbox; 5-speed all-synchromesh; final drive 3.538:1, transfer box ratios (High Range) 1.41:1, (Low Range) 3.760:1. Automatic transmission not available.

CHASSIS separate box-section chassis frame, steel and aluminium-panelled body; beam axle front suspension by coil springs, radius arms, Panhard rod; live-axle rear suspension by coil springs, radius arms, A-bracket, telescopic dampers; telescopic dampers; hydraulic servo-assisted brakes, front 11.8in (30cm) dia ventilated disc, rear 11.4in (28.95cm) dia discs; transmission drum parking brake; power-assisted recirculating ball steering; 19.5gal (89l) fuel tank; 205R-16in. or 235/70-16in. tyres on steel or alloy rims.
DIMENSIONS wheelbase 100in (254cm); track front and rear 58.5in (148.6cm); length 178in (452.1cm); width 70.6in (179.3cm); height 75.6in (192cm); ground clearance 8.1in (20.4cm); turning circle 37.5ft (11.4m).
PERFORMANCE
maximum speed 98mph (157.32kph); 21.2mph (34.1kph) @ 1000rpm; 0-60mph (96kph) 15.3sec; fuel consumption, approx 20mpg (7.08km/l)
PRICE £16,695

Powered by the high-revving 16-valve Rover T16 2-litre engine, the Discovery Mpi could reach nearly 100mph.

1993 Honda Crossroad

Although British Leyland formed a strategic alliance with Honda in 1979, the Japanese showed little interest in Land Rover's 4x4s until the early 1990s. At that point Honda noted the success of the Discovery and, envious of the success of rivals like Mitsubishi and Isuzu, decided to market a re-badged Discovery - the Honda Crossroad - for sale in Japan where the off-road market reached 300,000 a year, more than the whole of Europe. It was the first foreign vehicle ever to be sold there bearing the name of a local manufacturer and Rover Group managing director John Towers took the opportunity to pay tribute to the workforce: "Japan is the world's most demanding market in the world for quality," he said. This was a very simple re-badging exercise, for there was only one type of Crossroad, which was a Discovery V8i in all but name. All the cars had the same emissions-compliant 3947cc V8 engine, and every one had ZF automatic transmission: the usual five-speed manual transmission was not available. There were no style changes at all, which meant that the same product was effectively on sale in Japan through Honda dealerships (as Hondas) and through Rover dealerships (as Land Rover Discoverys). Honda had hoped to sell up to 1,200 Crossroads every year – it was apparently costly in the domestic market, but the Japanese public realised what was going on, and rarely bought more than 600 a year. Crossroads arrived in Japan unbadged but a close observer could see the Land Rover logo moulded in the headlamp lenses. This was a short-lived experiment, which effectively expired when the Series 2 Discovery appeared in 1998.

INTRODUCTION 1993, produced to 1998
BODY Estate; 5-doors, 5 or 7-seats; weight from 4234lb (1920kg).
ENGINE V8-cylinders; in-line; front; 94mm x 71.1mm, 3947cc; compr: 9.35:1; 180bhp (134kW) @ 4750rpm; 45.6bhp/l (33.95kW/l); 230lbft (313Nm) @ 3100rpm.
ENGINE STRUCTURE V8, 2-overhead valves per cylinder; central chain-driven camshaft; aluminium cylinder heads and block; Bosch-Lucas fuel injection and engine management; 5-bearing crankshaft; water-cooled.
TRANSMISSION permanent four-wheel drive; four-speed ZF 4HP22 automatic transmission; final drive ratio 3.538:1. transfer box ratios (High Range) 1.222:1, Low range (3.321:1).

CHASSIS separate box-section chassis frame, steel and aluminium-panelled body shell; beam axle front suspension by coil springs, radius arms, Panhard rod; live axle rear suspension by coil springs, radius arms, A-bracket, telescopic dampers; hydraulic servo-assisted brakes, front 11.8in (30cm) dia ventilated disc, rear 11.4in (28.95cm) dia rear discs, transmission drum parking brake; power-assisted recirculating ball steering; 19.5gal (89l) fuel tank; 235/70-16in radial-ply tyres, on alloy rims.
DIMENSIONS wheelbase 100in (254cm); track front and rear 58.5in (148.6cm); length 178in (452.1cm); width 70.6in (179.3cm); height 75.6in (192.0cm); ground clearance; 8.1in (20.4cm); turning circle 37.5ft (11.4m).
PERFORMANCE
maximum speed 106mph (170.16kph) 26.5mph (42.6kph) @ 1000rpm; 0-60mph (96kph) 10.8sec; fuel consumption 16.5mpg (17.12l/100km).
PRICE. Not sold in UK

Except for the badges, the Honda Crossroad was utterly identical to the existing Land Rover Discovery V8i of the period. This model was sold only in Japan.

1993 Land Rover Discovery Commercial

Meeting a small but definite demand for a purely load-carrying version of the Discovery, the Commercial derivative was kept in the lists until 1998. Cheaper than the regular Discovery, visually and mechanically almost identical, it retained the 4x4 virtues for trade and industrial users who required urgent transport for components or spares over both road and track. Developed by the Special Vehicles team at Solihull the Commercial's performance was much the same as any other Discovery and was one of several variants which were produced. Technically the Commercial was like the normal Discovery, with a choice of petrol and diesel engines (most sales were diesels), and a manual transmission. Based on the three-door body shell, and with a bare and businesslike interior, the Commercial had panelled-over side windows, and normally there were no rear seats. Somewhat different versions of the Commercial were available in territories where CKD assembly took place. The Commercial's arrival coincided with a facelift for the passenger Discovery in 1993-1994. There were larger headlights, a slimmer grille did away with the awkward black frames, and a full width body-coloured band below the grille were made ready for the 1994 model year. A new deeper spoiler had room for extra driving lamps, and there were 5-spoke alloy wheels and bigger badges. Impending lighting legislation shifted the tail, brake, and indicator lamps on to a new rear bumper. This prevented the outside spare wheel obscuring the lights when viewed at an angle or when the tailgate was open. High-intensity rear foglamps and reversing lamps replaced the original clusters of lights. For 1994 model year passenger Discoverys the Conran interior was discarded for something more traditional, and the front seat frames were redesigned to improve access to the back. The old Maestro instruments were forsaken for clearer ones and a driver's airbag was fitted as standard.

INTRODUCTION 1993, produced to 1998
BODY Van; 3-doors, 2-seats; weight from 4418lb (2000kg) (approx), payload 1654lb (750kg)
ENGINE V8-cylinder petrol, in-line, front, 88.9 x 71.1mm, 3528cc, compr 9.35:1; 164bhp (122 kW) @ 4750rpm, 46.5bhp/l (34.8 kW/l); 212lbft (288 Nm) @ 3000rpm. Turbo-diesel, 4-cylinders, in-line; front; 90.47mm x 97mm, 2495cc; compr 19.5:1; 113bhp (83kW) @ 4000rpm; 45.3bhp/l ((33,3 kW/l); 195lb ft (265Nm) @ 1800rpm .
ENGINE STRUCTURE (V8 petrol) 2 overhead valves per cylinder, chain-driven camshaft in centre of block, aluminium cylinder heads and block, Bosch-Lucas fuel injection, 5-bearing crankshaft, water-cooled. Turbo-diesel 2 overhead valves per cylinder; belt-driven camshaft drive; aluminium cylinder head, cast iron block; Bosch fuel injection and Garrett turbocharger, 5-bearing crankshaft; water-cooled .
TRANSMISSION permanent four-wheel drive; diaphragm spring clutch; manual gearbox, 5-speed all-synchromesh; final drive 3.538:1, transfer box ratio (High Range) 1.222:1, (Low range) 3.321:1.

CHASSIS separate box-section chassis frame, steel and aluminium-panelled body; beam axle front suspension by coil springs, radius arms, Panhard rod, anti-roll bar; live-axle rear suspension, coil springs, radius arms, A-bracket, anti-roll bar; telescopic dampers; hydraulic servo-assisted brakes, front 11.8in (30cm) dia discs, rear 11.4in (28.95cm) dia discs; transmission drum parking brake; power-assisted recirculating ball steering; 19.5gal (89l) fuel tank; 205R-16in. tyres on steel wheels.
DIMENSIONS wheelbase 100in (254cm); track front and rear 58.5in (148.6cm); length 178.6in (453.8cm); width 70.6in (179.3cm); height 75.6in (192cm); ground clearance 8.1in (20.4cm); turning circle 37.5ft (11.4m).
PERFORMANCE maximum speed; V8, 105mph (168.56kph); turbo-diesel, 92mph (147.69kph); 25.1mph (40.4kph) @ 1000rpm; 0-60mph (96kph) V8, 11.7sec; turbo-diesel, 17.1sec; fuel consumption V8, 16.5mpg, turbo-diesel 24 mpg.

The Discovery Commercial was a relatively-simple van conversion of the 3-door Discovery, with blanked out sides, front seats only, and a bare but servicable interior.

1993 Land Rover Discovery 3.9 V8i S

By its fourth year the Discovery was a firm success. United Kingdom sales were up 15 per cent on 1992, the launch in Japan of the Honda Discovery/Crossroad gave its makers confidence, Solihull had to enrol a third shift to keep, up with demand, and making 900 Discoverys a week represented an increase in output of almost one-third. With diesels out-selling petrol engined examples by five to one, a new V8 of 3.9litres was expected to enhance the petrol car's appeal and even things up a bit. The first carburettor Discovery had 134bhp (99.92kW), the next fuel injected version 164bhp (122.3kW) and now the 3.9litre raised this to 180bhp (134.22kW) providing, it was hoped, power to spare for the 4-speed automatic ZF. This V8i S was available only as a 5-door. The result was a useful, although scarcely dramatic increase in performance, described by *Autocar & Motor* as , "a measly five per cent improvement... Discovery 3.9 auto drivers have about the same performance as a 1.6litre Vauxhall Cavalier." The testers heaped praise on the smooth-shifting automatic however, finding that knocking the lever into third gear hold exploited the useful pulling power around 3,000 rpm for swift overtaking. Further backing for Discovery's good road manners came with improvements to its ride and handling on a weight distribution of 48per cent front, 52 to the rear, "...strengthening Discovery's role as a credible alternative to a luxury saloon or estate. It's surprising just how subtle a live axle suspension system can be; all but the worst road imperfections are nicely mopped up." Tyre noise, wind noise, and transmission whine still emphasised the Discovery's off-road credentials but the all-purpose 4x4 was well acknowledged as fulfilling any number of roles besides the obvious. Worries about equipping the Discovery with Range Rover-style power were not fulfilled. Both species of Land Rover were doing well.

INTRODUCTION 1994, produced to 1998
BODY estate; 3-doors or 5-doors, 5-seats/7-seats; weight from 4234lb (1920kg).
ENGINE V8-cylinders, in-line; front; 94mm x 71.1mm, 3947cc; compr 9.35:1; 182bhp (135.5kW) @ 4750rpm; 46.1bhp/l (34.3kW/l); 231lbft (314Nm) @ 3100rpm.
ENGINE STRUCTURE V8, 2-overhead valves per cylinder, central chain-driven camshaft; aluminium cylinder heads and block; Bosch-Lucas fuel injection and engine management, 5-bearing crankshaft; water-cooled.
TRANSMISSION permanent four-wheel drive; diaphragm spring clutch; manual gearbox, 5-speed all-synchromesh; final drive 3.538:1, transfer box ratios (High Range) 1.222:1, (Low Range) 3.321:1; four-speed ZF 4HP22 automatic transmission.

CHASSIS separate box-section chassis frame, steel and aluminium-panelled body; beam axle front suspension by coil springs, radius arms, Panhard rod, anti-roll bar; live-axle rear suspension by coil springs, radius arms, A-bracket, anti-roll bar; telescopic dampers; hydraulic servo brakes, front 11.7in (29.8cm) dia ventilated front discs, rear 11.4in (28.95cm) dia rear discs; transmission drum parking brake, ABS anti-lock standard on ES, optional on other models; power-assisted recirculating ball steering; 19.5gal (89l) fuel tank; 205R-16in or 235/70-16in. tyres on cast alloy rims.
DIMENSIONS wheelbase 100in (254cm); track front and rear 51.5in (148.6cm); length 178.6in (453.8cm); width 70.6in (179.3cm); height 75.6in (192.0cm); ground clearance 8.1in (20.4cm); turning circle 37.5ft (11.4m).
PERFORMANCE maximum speed V8, 106mph (170.16kph); 26.5mph (42.6kph) @ 1000rpm; 0-60mph (96kph) 12.9sec; fuel consumption 16.5mpg (17.12l/100km).
PRICE: £21,494; automatic £1,150; metallic paint £283; CD player £499; air conditioning £1347 front £1949 front and rear, handling pack with wide tyres £400.

The introduction of the 182bhp 3.9-litre V8i S gave Discovery's performance image a further boost in 1994. It was built until 1998.

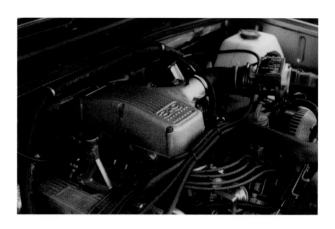

1994 Land Rover Discovery

Less than five years after the first Discovery, Land Rover introduced a face-lifted model, internally coded Romulus. Externally there was little to see - enlarged headlamps and different bonnet and front bumper pressings, modified tail lamps - the major innovations being technical, and inside the cabin. There was a new fascia, more curvaceous and car-like, with a Rover 800-style steering wheel incorporating an air bag, with a matching air bag ahead of the front passenger. Not only that, but there was a more integrated heater/fresh-air controls/sound-system layout, along with new (and perhaps more practical for heavy use) fabrics and colour schemes in the cabin together with an even longer list of optional features. The enhanced suspension/chassis package included ABS anti-lock braking (standard on the flagship ES version, optional on other models), and anti-roll bars at front and rear. The most important advance, however, was a completely re-designed diesel engine (the 300Tdi in place of the 200di), and a new R380 5-speed manual transmission. The 300Tdi, also used in 1995 model Range Rovers and Defenders, was still a 2.5-litre 4-cylinder turbo-diesel, with the same bore and stroke as before, but was much improved in all respects, especially those of exhaust emissions. Rover claimed that 208 engine components had been changed, including a new aluminium cylinder head, and fuel injection. Because much work had gone into stiffening up components and castings, and into noise control, it was much more refined than the outgoing 200Tdi. The new gearbox (R380 stood for Rover design, with a 380Nm (280lbft) torque capacity) was a replacement for the long-running LT77/LT77S transmission, and had been developed to be quieter, and with a slicker and easier gearchange. All in all this was an impressive package, which formed the basis of the first Discovery to be sold in North America (qv). The public and the media was impressed, for nearly 70,000 Discoverys would be built in 1995, while Auto Express made it the Best Off-Roader in its New Car Honours list. For the next four years this revised Discovery became the fastest-selling 4x4 built at Solihull. Running changes included the evolution of a more powerful 300Tdi engine for use with automatic transmission. This was a period in which several special editions, including Camel Trophy, Goodwood, and Horse and Hound were put on sale. The final special edition, which celebrated half-a-century of Rover 4x4s, was the Anniversary 50.

INTRODUCTION 1994, produced to 1998
BODY estate; 3-doors or 5-doors, 5-seats/7-seats; weight from 4234lb (1920kg).
ENGINE V8-cylinders, in-line; front; 94mm x 71.1mm, 3947cc; compr 9.35:1; 182bhp (135.5kW) @ 4750rpm; 46.1bhp/l (34.3kW/l); 231lbft (314Nm) @ 3100rpm. 4-cyl petrol, in-line, front, 84.45mm x 88.9mm, 1994cc, compr 10.0:1, 134bhp (100kW) @ 6000rpm, 67.2bhp/l (50.15kW/l); 140lbft (190Nm) @ 2500rpm. 4-cylinder turbo-diesel, in-line, front, 90.47mm x 97mm, 2495cc; compr 19.5:1; 113bhp (83kW) @ 4000rpm, 45.3 bhp/l (33.3 kW/l); 195lbft (265Nm) @ 1800rpm.
ENGINE STRUCTURE V8, 2-overhead valves per cylinder, central chain-driven camshaft; aluminium cylinder heads and block; Bosch-Lucas fuel injection and engine management, 5-bearing crankshaft; water-cooled. 4-cyl (MPi) petrol; 4-valves per cylinder; twin overhead camshafts, cogged belt camshaft drive; aluminium cylinder head, cast iron block; Bosch/Lucas fuel injection; 5-bearing crankshaft; water-cooled. 4-cyl (300TDi turbo-diesel): 2 overhead valves per cylinder, belt-driven camshaft, aluminium cylinder head, cast iron block; Bosch KBEL fuel injection, Garrett turbocharger, 5-bearing crankshaft, water-cooled.
TRANSMISSION permanent four-wheel drive; diaphragm spring clutch; manual gearbox, 5-speed all-synchromesh; final drive 3.538:1, transfer box ratios (High Range) 1.222:1, or 1.41:1 on four-cylinder petrol.(Mpi), (Low Range) 3.321:1 or 3.76:1 on 4-cylinder petrol). Optional four-speed ZF 4HP22 automatic transmission on V8 and 300TDi turbo-diesels.
CHASSIS separate box-section chassis frame, steel and aluminium-panelled body; beam axle front suspension by coil springs, radius arms, Panhard rod, anti-roll bar; live-axle rear suspension by coil springs, radius arms, A-bracket, anti-roll bar; telescopic dampers; hydraulic servo brakes, front 11.7in (29.8cm) dia ventilated front discs, rear 11.4in

(28.95cm) dia rear discs; transmission drum parking brake, ABS anti-lock standard on ES, optional on other models; power-assisted recirculating ball steering; 19.5gal (89l) fuel tank; 205R-16in or 235/70-16in. tyres on cast alloy rims.

DIMENSIONS wheelbase 100in (254cm); track front and rear 51.5in (148.6cm); length 178.6in (453.8cm); width 70.6in (179.3cm); height 75.6in (192.0cm); ground clearance 8.1in (20.4cm); turning circle 37.5ft (11.4m)

PERFORMANCE maximum speed V8, 106mph (170.16kph); Mpi, 106mph (170.16kph); Tdi, 91mph (146.08kph) V8, 26.5mph (42.6kph) @ 1000rpm; Mpi, 21.2mph (34.1kph); Tdi, 25.1mph (40.6kph) 0-60mph (96kph): V8, 10.8sec; Mpi, 15.3sec; Tdi, 17.2sec fuel consumption; V8,16.5mpg (17.12l/100km); Mpi, 20mpg (14.12l/100km); Tdi, 26mpg (10.87l/100km) approx PRICE; From 3-door 2.0Mpi £17,995; 5-door, £19,590; V8ES £27,375

In 1994 the Discovery received its first facelift with many detail style changes, a much-modified diesel engine, and with a new fascia/instrument panel.

1994 Land Rover Discovery NAS spec

Following the successful launch of the Range Rover into the USA market in 1987, Land Rover followed up with the NAS (North American Specification) Discovery in 1994. Based closely on the revised and face-lifted model, which went on sale in the UK and the elsewhere, for North America there was to be only one dedicated version - a 5-door model with the powerful 182bhp (135.72kW), 3.95-litre V8 engine. No other types were considered. Not only were the turbo-diesel and the MPi both regarded as under-powered for this demanding market, but the NAS Discovery had to support the larger, and distinctly more expensive second-generation Range Rover (which would reach the USA in 1995). This strategy worked well, for later in the 1990s more than 15,000 Discoverys would be sold in North America every year. Luxury and convenience features such as leather upholstery (not yet available elsewhere), air conditioning, cruise control, central locking and electric window lifts were all standard for this market, and as expected a majority of sales were with the ZF automatic transmission. To meet stringent crash test regulations, but hidden away, were crash cans at the front of the chassis frame, and side impact doors. There was a third, high-level, brake light at the top of the tail door glass. Over in the USA, Four Wheeler magazine made the new model its Four-Wheeler of the Year in 1995, which was a real fillip for the marque's fortunes. Even though the two big 4x4s from Solihull - Discovery and Range Rover - had to compete head on with America's own Jeep, they were soon well-established, and later models built on that base.

INTRODUCTION 1994 produced to 1998
BODY estate, 5-doors, 5-seats or 7-seats; weight 9874.4lb (4479kg).
ENGINE V8-cylinder, in-line; front; 94mm x 71.1mm, 3947cc; compr 9.35:1; 182bhp (135kW) @ 4750rpm; 46.1bhp/l (34.3kW/l); 231lbft (314Nm) @ 3100rpm.
ENGINE STRUCTURE 2-overhead valves per cylinder; centre chain-driven camshaft; aluminium cylinder head and block; Bosch-Lucas fuel injection and engine management, 5-bearing crankshaft; water-cooled.
TRANSMISSION permanent four-wheel drive; diaphragm spring clutch; manual 5-speed all-synchromesh gearbox; final drive 3.538:1, transfer box ratios (High Range) 1.222:1, (Low Range) 3.321:1. Optional four-speed ZF 4HP22 automatic transmission.

CHASSIS separate box-section chassis frame, steel and aluminium-panelled body; beam axle front suspension by coil springs, radius arms, Panhard rod, anti-roll bar; live axle rear suspension by coil springs, radius arms, A-bracket, anti roll bar; telescopic dampers; hydraulic servo brakes, front 11.7in (29.8cm) dia ventilated discs, rear 11.4in (28.95cm) dia discs; transmission drum parking brake, ABS anti-lock; power-assisted recirculating-ball steering; 19.5gal (89l) fuel tank; 235/70-16in. tyres on cast alloy rims.
DIMENSIONS wheelbase 100in (254cm); track front and rear 58.5in (148.6cm); length 178.6in (453.8cm); width 70.6in (179.3cm); height 75.6in (192.0cm); ground clearance 8.1in (20.4cm); turning circle 37.5ft (11.4m).
PERFORMANCE
maximum speed; 106mph (170.16kph) 26.5mph (42.6kph) @ 1000rpm 0-60mph (96kph); 10.8sec fuel consumption approx 16.5mpg (17.12l/100km).
PRICE Sold only in North America.

When the Discovery went on sale in
North America, the 182bhp engine,
leather upholstery, air conditioning
and cruise control were all standard
equipment.

1998 Land Rover Discovery Series II

No sooner had BMW taken control of the Rover Group in 1994, than it concentrated on updating and enlarging the Land Rover operation at Solihull. The next-generation Range Rover was almost ready, the Freelander was approved at once, and it was immediately followed by a comprehensive revision of the Discovery. There were few styling innovations; yet although the second-generation Discovery looked very similar to the outgoing original model, the body and chassis was reworked in many respects. Based on the existing 100in (254cm) wheelbase chassis, with an extra cross-member to add stiffness and 2in (5.08cm) wider wheel tracks, it had a Watts linkage instead of A-bracket location for the back axle. The revised body shell was only produced as a 5-door, had a 5in (12.7cm) increase in rear overhang (enlarging the practical load-carrying capacity), and had changes to almost every external as well as some internal body panels. According to Land Rover it had no fewer than 200 new pressings, along with 100 carried over or lightly modified ones. Taller by 2.4in (6.09cm), it was easily recognised from the front by the new grille/bumper, and from behind by the high-mounted tail lamps introduced earlier. Land Rover was proud that the panel gaps on the new machine were much tighter than before, a certain sign of improved quality. The interior was more completely equipped, with yet another fascia style and instrument layout, along with a generously padded steering wheel. Since the shell was now longer, there was more space for the sideways facing third row of seats in the rear. Mechanically the 3.9-litre fuel-injected V8 engine was little changed, with the detail improvements found on recent Range Rovers, and later-model Discovery types. An innovation was a new, in-line, 5-cylinder turbo-diesel engine, the Storm also used in the Defender, closely related to the 4-cylinder diesel of the original Freelander. This time the

high-revving petrol-powered MPi 4-cylinder was not offered. The smoother, more fuel-efficient and more powerful diesel, with 136bhp (101.41kW) instead of 111bhp (82.77kW) made a substantial difference to the Discovery's appeal and buoyed up the sale of diesel-engined versions. The BMW regime was strong on acronyms, and the three introduced with this model told the story of technological advance: Active Cornering Enhancement (ACE) was standard on high-specification models, optionally extra on others. Added chassis-mounted anti-roll bars and hydraulic actuators, electronically controlled and speed-sensed, stiffened the handling at enterprising speeds, cutting roll considerably, but were not operative at low speeds off-road. Self-levelling air suspension took the place of coil springs when ACE was specified. This may have sounded unfeasible, but it worked well. As *Autocar* reported: "The new Discovery makes its rivals look backward and seriously under-developed ..." Electronic Traction Control (ETC) used the wheel-mounted ABS sensors to detect slip under power. As already proven on the existing Range Rover, electronic controls could then instruct the disc brake on that particular wheel to hold things in check. This meant that a central differential could be eliminated completely. Hill Descent Control (HDC) was another electronic masterpiece, which controlled the speed of Discovery descending steep hills, by enabling the ABS sensors and brakes to limit speeds to 14km/h (8.8mph). It was an exemplary combination, and served the Discovery well, for there would be only one more face-lift before an entirely new type took over in 2004.

Compared with the original, Discovery II had a longer tail, a new five-cylinder turbo-diesel engine, and a new type of rear suspension.

177

INTRODUCTION 1998, produced to 2002

BODY estate; 5-doors, 7-seats; weight from 4453lb (2020kg)

ENGINE V8-cylinder, in-line; front; 94mm x 71mm, 3947cc; compr 9.35:1; 182bhp (136 kW) @ 4750rpm; 46.1bhp (34.3 kW/l); 250lbft (340Nm) @ 2600rpm . 5-cylinder turbo-diesel, in-line, front, 84.5mm x 89mm, 2495cc; compr 19.5:1, 136bhp (101.5kW) @ 4200rpm; 54.5bhp/l (40.7kW/l); 221lbft (300 Nm) at 1950rpm with manual transmission, or 232lbft (315 Nm) with automatic.

ENGINE STRUCTURE V8: 2 overhead valves per cylinder, central chain-driven camshaft, aluminium cylinder heads and block; Bosch Motronic fuel injection and engine management, 5-bearing crankshaft, water-cooled. 5-cylinder Td5 turbo-diesel: 2-valves per cylinder, single chain-driven overhead camshaft; aluminium cylinder head, cast iron block; Lucas fuel injection, Garrett turbocharger, 6-bearing crankshaft, water-cooled.

TRANSMISSION permanent four-wheel drive; diaphragm spring clutch; manual gearbox, 5-speed all-synchromesh; final drive 3.538:1, transfer box ratios (High range) 1.211:1, (Low range) 3.269:1). Optional four-speed ZF 4HP22 automatic transmission.

CHASSIS separate box-section chassis frame, steel and aluminium-panelled body; beam axle front suspension by coil springs, radius arms, Panhard rod, anti-roll bar; live-axle rear suspension by coil springs, radius arms, Watts linkage, anti roll bar; telescopic dampers. ACE control, some models, including rear air suspension; hydraulic servo-assisted brakes, front 11.8in (30cm) dia ventilated front discs, rear 11.8in (30cm) dia discs; transmission drum parking brake, ABS anti-lock; power-assisted re-circulating ball steering; 20.9gal (95l) fuel tank; 237/70-16in. Radial ply tyres on alloy wheel rims.

DIMENSIONS wheelbase 100in (254cm); track front 60.6in (154cm); track rear;61.4in (156cm); length 185.2in (470.5cm); width 70.6in (179.3cm); height 76.4in (194cm); ground clearance 8.1in (20.4cm); turning circle 39ft (11.9m).

PERFORMANCE maximum speed; V8, 106mph (170.16 kph); Td5, 96mph (154.11kph) 25.2mph (40.5kph) @ 1000rpm; 0-60mph (96kph) V8, 10.5sec; Td5, 14.1sec; fuel consumption V8, 16.3mpg (17.33l/100km), Td5, 26.6mpg (10.62l/100km)

PRICE; Td5 From £25,520; V8 From £28,320

With a re-styled nose, and with a revised interior, Discovery II was a major update of the original model.

2002 Land Rover Discovery Series II facelift

As a means of freshening up the Discovery II range, and to maintain sales until a new model appeared in 2004, a face-lifted version was introduced in the spring of 2002. Although there were no major structural or mechanical changes, the style got a new nose, and there was a more powerful engine for sale only in North America. Land Rover said that it had spent £24million on new tooling and equipment. Without altering the proportions of the body shell, the nose was given the same paired jewel headlamp treatment of the new-generation Range Rover, there was a new front bumper, and yet more changes to the rear lights. Although it scarcely seemed possible, the list of paint, trim, and options was even longer than before, while the interior, fascia style and equipment layout was not changed. In the UK, fuel-injected V8 and Td5 turbo-diesel engines were unaltered, but for the USA there was a new 220bhp (162kW) 4.6-litre version of the V8 engine. Chassis changes included new suspension springs, and a locking centre differential as an optional extra. In Europe most Discoverys were sold with the Td5 turbo-diesel engine. Testers suggested that the on-road handling was an improvement, but the exemplary off-road capabilities were un-affected. The last iteration of the original 100in. chassis frame Discovery was discontinued in the autumn of 2004.

INTRODUCTION 2002, produced to 2004
BODY estate; 5-doors; 7-seats; weight from 4453lb (2020kg).
ENGINE V8-cylinder, in-line; front; 94mm x 71mm, 3947cc; compr 9.35:1; 182bhp (136kW) @ 4750rpm; 46.1bhp/l (34.3kW/l); 250lbft (340 Nm) @ 2600rpm . (V8, USA only) 94mm x 82mm, 4554cc. compr 9.35:1, 220bhp (162kW) @ 4/50rpm; 48.3bhp/l (35.6kW/l); 300lbft (407Nm) @ 2600rpm. 5-cylinder turbo-diesel, in line, front, 84.5mm x 89mm, 2495cc; compr 19.5:1, 136bhp (101.5kW) @ 4200rpm; 54.5bhp/l (40.7 kW/l); 221lbft (300Nm) @ 1950rpm with manual transmission, or 232lbft (315Nm) with automatic.
ENGINE STRUCTURE V8: 2 overhead valves per cylinder, central chain-driven camshaft; aluminium cylinder heads and block; Bosch Motronic fuel injection and engine management, 5-bearing crankshaft; water-cooled. 5-cylinder Td5 turbo-diesel; 2-valves per cylinder, single overhead camshaft, chain camshaft drive, aluminium cylinder head, cast iron block, Lucas fuel injection, Garrett turbocharger, 6-bearing crankshaft, water-cooled.
TRANSMISSION permanent four-wheel drive; diaphragm spring clutch; manual gearbox, 5-speed all-synchromesh; final; drive 3.538:1, transfer box ratios (High range) 1.211:1 (Low range) 3.269:1. Optional four-speed ZF 4HP22 automatic transmission.

CHASSIS separate box-section chassis frame, steel and aluminium-panelled body; beam axle front suspension by coil springs, radius arms, Panhard rod, anti-roll bar; live axle rear suspension by coil springs, radius arms, Watts linkage, anti-roll bar; telescopic dampers: ACE suspension control including rear air springs, some models; hydraulic servo-assisted brakes, front 11.8in (30cm) dia ventilated front discs, rear 11.8in (30cm) dia discs, transmission drum parking brake, ABS anti-lock; power-assisted recirculating ball steering; 20.9gal (95l) fuel tank; 235/70-16in tyres on alloy wheel rims.
DIMENSIONS wheelbase 100in (254cm); track front 60.6in (154cm); rear; 61.4in (156cm); length 185.2in (470.5cm); width 70.6in (179.3cm); height 76.4in (194cm); ground clearance 8.1in (20.4cm); turning circle 39ft (11.9m).
PERFORMANCE
maximum speed; 3.9 V8, 106mph (170.16kph); 4.6 V8, approx 115mph (185kph); Td5, 96mph (154.11kph) 40.5kph (25.2 mph) @ 1000rpm; 0-60mph (96kph) 3.9 V8, 10.5sec; 4.6 V8, 9.5sec; Td5, 14.1sec
fuel consumption 3.9 V8, 17.33L/100km (16.3mpg); Td5 10.62L/100km (26.6mpg)
PRICE; Td5 from £21,995; 3.9 V8 from £27,295

From 2002 to 2004, the Discovery was treated to a modified front-end style, with re-arranged headlamps.

2004 Land Rover Discovery 3

Following the purchase of Land Rover from BMW in 2000 by Ford's Premier Automotive Group, the third-generation Discovery was totally different from any of the foregoing, or even any Range Rover for that matter. Although it remained faithful to the original Discovery concept of a roomy 5/7-seater estate car, with a choice of petrol and diesel engines, permanent four-wheel drive and exceptional on and off-road ability, it was much larger, heavier, more powerful and more costly. Its skin styling was smoother, with a massive rear window glass, and since it ran on a wheelbase of 113.5in (288.5cm) it was much more roomy. For the first time too it had independent suspension all round and among its engines was one power unit intended specifically for sale in North America.

Not a single existing component was carried over for the new model, which had a choice of three engines, two petrol and one diesel. The flagship model's power was provided by a much modified 32-valve Jaguar V8, similar to that used in XJ saloons and XK Coupes, while for sale only in North America there was what Ford devotees knew as the 4litre Cologne V6, a single-overhead-camshaft power unit made in Germany, but fitted to Ford-USA products like the Explorer 4x4. Pride of place though went to the new 2.7-litre V6 turbo-diesel, a joint Ford/Peugeot/Citroen (PSA) product intended for widespread use, already found in Jaguar S-Type and Jaguar XJ cars. Light and powerful, with heads and block in aluminium, it was also fuel efficient and environmentally clean. At 190bhp (140kW) it was a good deal more powerful than any previous Discovery diesel.

INTRODUCTION Spring 2004
BODY estate, 5-doors, 5-seats; weight 5590lb (2535kg).
ENGINES V8-cylinder, petrol, front; in-line; 88mm x 90.3mm, 4394cc; compr 10.5:1; 300bhp (220kW) @ 5500rpm; 68.2bhp/l (50kW/l); 313lbft (425Nm) @ 4000rpm; V6-cylinder petrol, front, in-line, 100mm x 84.3mm, 4015cc; compr 9.7:1; 219bhp (161kW) @ 4500rpm; 54.4bhp/l (40.1kW/l); 265.5lbft (360Nm) @ 3000rpm; V6-cylinder turbo-diesel, front, in-line, 81mm x 88mm, 2720cc, compr 17.3:1, 190bhp (140kW) @ 4000rpm; 51.5bhp/l (69.9kW/l); 324.5lbft (440Nm)
ENGINE STRUCTURE V8, Jaguar 32 valves; twin chain-driven overhead camshafts; aluminium cylinder heads, and block; electronic fuel injection and engine management; 5-bearing crankshaft; V6 petrol, Ford-USA, single overhead camshaft, chain camshaft drive, aluminium cylinder heads, cast iron block, electronic fuel injection and engine management, 4-bearing crankshaft; V6 turbo-diesel, Ford/PSA, twin overhead camshafts, chain camshaft drive, aluminium cylinder heads and block, Bosch electronic fuel injection and engine management, KKK turbocharger, intercooler, 4-bearing crankshaft..
TRANSMISSION four wheel drive; six-speed ZF automatic transmission; final drive V8 and V6 petrol 3.73:1; V6 turbo-diesel 3.54:1. Six-speed synchromesh manual gearbox V6 turbo-diesel, 3.07:1 final drive ratio.

CHASSIS steel frame welded to steel and aluminium-panelled body shell; independent front suspension by coil springs (air suspension, some variants), wishbones, telescopic dampers when coil springs fitted, independent rear suspension; by coil springs (air suspension, some variants), wishbones, telescopic dampers when coil springs fitted; hydraulic servo-assisted brakes, front 12.5in (31.7cm) dia ventilated disc, rear 12.8in (32.5cm) dia ventilated discs, drum parking brake, ABS anti-lock; power-assisted rack-and-pinion steering; 18.1gal (82l) fuel tank; 235/70-17in. radial ply tyres on cast alloy wheel rims; larger wheels/tyres optional.
DIMENSIONS wheelbase 113.5in (288.5cm); track front 63.2in (160.5cm); track rear 63.5in (161.3cm); length 176.4in (484.8cm); width 86.2in (219cm); height 74.3in (188.7cm); ground clearance 9.4in (24cm); turning circle 37.7ft (11.5m).
PERFORMANCE
maximum speed; V8, 121mph (194.24kph); TDV6, 109mph (174.98kph); V6 petrol, 112mph (179.79kph)
33.8mph (54.4kph) @ 1000rpm
0-60mph (96kph) V8, 8.0sec; TDV6, 12.2sec; V6 petrol, 11.0sec
fuel consumption V8, 15mpg (18.83l/100km); TDV6, 20.5mpg (13.78l/100km); V6 petrol, 18mpg (15.69l/100km)
PRICE; V8 from £37,995; TDV6 from £26,995

All the new models had independent front and rear suspension by double wishbones, but only the entry-level ones used metal coil springs: the majority of the more costly cars had air suspension and self-levelling, with adjustment of ride-height built in. Not only that, but a variety of features including Dynamic Stability Control, Electronic Brake Force Distribution, Emergency Brake Assist and Hill Descent Control, six airbags in the cabin, and optional adaptive headlamps (which steered into the corner as the front wheels were turned) made this an exceptionally safe machine to drive on all types of surface and conditions. Even by comparison with the latest-generation Range Rover, this was a strikingly versatile and advanced 4x4 so it was no wonder that *Autocar's* commented that: "Quite simply, the car has such an exceptional spread of abilities ....it is almost impossible not to be swayed by the Discovery's compelling blend of character and practicality."

Discovery 3 in conditions for which it was ideal – looking for wild leopards in Oman.

Military Vehicles

Land Rover military 80, 86 and 88

There is a certain irony that the Land Rover, having been conceived as a civilian version of the military Jeep, would score some of its greatest successes with the military. The company once estimated that military forces bought 40 per cent of all the utility models it ever built, and by the 1960s it was sparing no effort to meet military requirements. On the understanding that once British forces bought a new or special model, it was likely that further orders would be generated elsewhere, although at first Solihull made few concessions to the military. Those delivered to the War Department in 1949 were more or less civilian models painted dark green. The military preferred this to the standard light green but it was a foretaste of things to come. Rover came to attention, saluted the colours, and switched to dark green as the standard house paintwork. The British were the first to buy Land Rovers for military purposes and sure enough multiple overseas orders followed. The 1.6-litre 80in (Rover Mk1 the War Department called it) was followed by the 2-litre 80in (Rover Mk2), the 86in (Rover Mk3) and then the 88in (Rover Mk5). The Series II 88 was a Rover Mk6, the IIA version initially a Rover Mk8 and then a Rover Mk10 to reflect changes from 1967. Series III 88s followed in British Army procedure as Rover Series 3s. The army never believed in Roman numerals. Military users liked the carrying capacity of long-wheelbase Land Rovers, so orders for the 88s thinned out after a time. The armed forces bought large numbers in civilian CL specification, tending to use them for rear-echelon duties. Units that really needed short-wheelbase models then converted to the Lightweight (qv) when it became available. Most short-wheelbase military Land Rovers were soft-tops, although some users obtained hardtops and even Station Wagons for special duties. Diesel engines became available as early as 1956, but most military users preferred the petrol option because the diesels were simply too

slow. A reinforced rear cross-member was available on 88s from the early 1960s to improve the towing capability, and also a 24-volt electrical system allowing the vehicles to be radio-equipped. Military-specification 88s had extra quarter-bumpers at the front.

Technical specifications for Rover Mk10, 1967
BODY: short wheelbase full hood, truck cab, kerb weight 2953lb (1339kg).
ENGINE: 4-cylinder in line, 90.47mm x 88.9mm, 2286cc. 77bhp (57kW) @ 4250 rpm, 124lb ft (168Nm) @2500 rpm.
ENGINE STRUCTURE: cast iron block and cylinder head, pushrod overhead valves, camshaft chain driven with hydraulic tensioner, single Solex carburettor, 3-bearing crankshaft.
TRANSMISSION: selectable four wheel drive, hydraulic single dry plate clutch 9in (22.8cm) dia. Rover 4-speed gearbox and 2-speed transfer box, Rover front and rear axles, 4.7:1.

CHASSIS: welded box section steel ladder frame, front and rear beam axles with semi-elliptic springs and telescopic shock absorbers, worm and nut steering with recirculating ball. 4-wheel hydraulically operated 10in (25.4cm) drum brakes, 6in (15.2cm) drum transmission hand brake. 10 gal (45l) fuel tank. 16in pressed steel wheels with 6.00 x 16 tyres.
DIMENSIONS: Wheelbase 88in (224cm), track 51.5in (131cm), length; 142.4in (362cm), width; 66in (168cm), height; 77.5in (197cm).

Cutaway front wings and a distinctive brush guard identify this as a Series IIA 88-inch model destined for the Australian military.

Land Rover military Lightweight

The so-called Lightweight was a military-only Land Rover known to the British army as the Half-Ton or Rover 1. It was developed in the mid-1960s to meet an airportability requirement, when standard 88in models were found too wide to be carried two-abreast in transport aircraft, and too heavy to be suspended under the helicopters then in service. The Lightweight was designed on the existing 88in chassis, with a narrower body to meet the first requirement, and to comply with the second, its body was made with demountable sections. Doors, upper rear body and other elements unbolted or lifted off to leave a stripped-down but still driveable vehicle light enough to be heli-lifted. The design necessary to achieve this resulted in a distinctive-looking, square-rigged Land Rover. Later transport aircraft and stronger helicopters removed the original requirements before the Lightweight entered service, but the army was so impressed with the vehicle's simple, stripped-down design that it standardised it as its short-wheelbase Land Rover. Early Lightweights had headlamps mounted in the grille panel, but from 1969 the headlamps moved to the wings. Series III Lightweight production began in April 1972, later than that of civilian models, because Solihull had to complete outstanding orders for the Series IIA. Series IIIs had all-synchromesh gearboxes, a larger clutch plate, and an alternator in place of the dynamo on 12-volt models. They also retained the central Series IIA instrument panel. Most Series IIA and Series III models were delivered as GS (12-volt) or Fitted For Radio (FFR 24-volt) soft tops, but the military converted some into hardtops or Station Wagons. Every Series IIA was delivered to the British armed forces, and all British Lightweights had the 4-cylinder petrol engine. The Dutch and Danish military took diesel Series IIIs from 1976. Marshalls of Cambridge developed a gunship version.

INTRODUCTION
1968 (Series IIA); 1972 (Series III); produced to 1984
(Specifications for Series III)
BODY: full hood or hard top, weight from 3210lb (1456kg) with petrol engine in full trim; from 2660lb (1206kg) stripped-out for air transportation.
ENGINES: Petrol; 4-cylinder in line, 90.47mm x 88.9mm, 2286cc. 81bhp (60kW) @ 4250 rpm, 124lb ft (168Nm) @2500 rpm. Diesel; 4-cylinder in line, 90.47mm x 88.9mm 2286cc. 67bhp (50kW) @ 4000rpm, 105lb ft (142Nm) @ 1800 rpm.
ENGINE STRUCTURE: 4-cylinder; cast iron block and cylinder head, 3-bearing crankshaft, overhead valves.
TRANSMISSION: selectable four wheel drive, hydraulic single dry plate clutch 9.5 in (24.1cm) dia. 4-speed gearbox and 2-speed transfer box, Regular; Rover front and rear axles, Long; Salisbury rear axle with cast differential, 4.7:1.

CHASSIS: welded box section steel ladder frame, front and rear beam axles with semi-elliptic springs and telescopic shock absorbers, worm and nut steering with recirculating ball, 4-wheel hydraulically operated drum brakes, 10in (25.4cm) dia, 6in (15.2cm) drum transmission hand brake.10gal(45l) fuel tank, 16in pressed steel wheels with 6.00-16 tyres (6.50-16, 7.00-16, 7.50-16 and 8.20-15 sand tyres all optional).
DIMENSIONS: Wheelbase 88in (224cm), track 51.5in (131cm), length; 144in (365cm); width, 60in (152cm); height, 77in (195cm) with soft top erect; ground clearance, 8.5in (21cm); turning circle, 42ft (12.8m)
PRICE
Not sold on the civilian market.
PRODUCTION
2989 (Series IIA); 15,000 approx (Series III)

The Lightweight came in many guises. The top picture shows an early Series IIA type with lights alongside the grille. Lower left is a diesel Series III for the Dutch military, and far right is the Marshalls gunship version which mounted a 106mm recoilless rifle.

Land Rover Military 109

Compared with their short-wheelbase counterparts relatively few of the Series I 107in models saw military service. Some Station Wagons were used on special duties by the army, and the RAF took some with special bodywork, for use as Mountain Rescue ambulances. However it was not until the 109in model that the long-wheelbase Land Rover really made its mark on military fleets worldwide. The Series III version was bought by the armed forces of 140 nations. The Series I 109 was fairly short-lived, and in British service (when it was called a Rover 4 or FV 18007) it was uncommon. The value of the long-wheelbase Land Rover's extra load-carrying capacity had become apparent by the time of the Series II in 1958, and from then on this was the Land Rover, which was most numerous in military service. The British army gave the name Rover 7 to its Series II 109s; the Series IIAs, which followed were Rover 9s, and the Series IIIs Rover Series 3s. Although they looked broadly similar to civilian Land Rovers, there were many special details which distinguished the military 109 from its civilian counterpart, such as a reinforced rear cross-member (for towing) with bumperettes, additional quarter-bumpers at the front, twin fuel tanks, lashing eyes front and rear, waterproofed lights with quick-change lenses, and an engine oil cooler. Some had jerrycan lockers in the body sides behind the cab doors. Some were converted for special duties by unit workshops, or specialists such as Marshalls of Cambridge, which developed a particularly successful ambulance conversion. The typical military 109 was a soft-top, delivered in either GS (General Service) form with a 12-volt electrical system or in FFR (Fitted For Radio) outline with a 24-volt system, in forces nomenclature. The 4-cylinder engines were always most common, and British military 109s almost always petrol-powered because the British would not embrace diesel power for this class of vehicle until years later. Some

nations preferred 6-cylinders and even the V8-engined Stage 1 models when these became available. Overseas forces bought 109s, some of which had been locally assembled. A notable overseas user was Australia, for whose 109s a special drop-shackle suspension was developed in the early 1960s to give more ground clearance. A version of this suspension became standard on the 109 One Ton models. In Spain, Santana built a special 109 Militar for the local military from 1977 (qv).

INTRODUCTION 1958
BODY Long wheelbase truck cab or station wagon, kerb weight petrol; 3301lb (1497kg), diesel 3471lb (1574kg).
ENGINES petrol; 4-cylinder in line, 90.47mm x 88.9mm, 2286cc. 77bhp (57kW) @ 4250 rpm, 124lb ft (168Nm) @2500 rpm. Diesel; 4-cylinder in line, 85.7mm x 88.9mm 2052cc. 52bhp (38.8kW) @ 3500 rpm, 87lb ft (118Nm) @2,000 rpm.
ENGINE STRUCTURE cast iron block and cylinder head, pushrod overhead valves, camshaft duplex chain driven with hydraulic tensioner.
TRANSMISSION selectable four wheel drive, hydraulic single dry plate clutch 9in (22.8cm) dia. Rover 4-speed gearbox and 2-speed transfer box, Rover front and rear axles, 4.7:1.

CHASSIS welded box section steel ladder frame, front and rear beam axles with semi-elliptic springs and telescopic shock absorbers, worm and nut steering with recirculating ball. 4-wheel hydraulically operated 11in (27.9cm) drum brakes; 6in (15.2cm) drum transmission hand brake. Twin 10 gallon (45 litre) fuel tanks; single 16 gallon (73 litre) tank on Station Wagon. 16in pressed steel wheels with 7.50 x 16 tyres.
DIMENSIONS wheelbase 109in (277cm), front and rear track 51.5in (131cm), length; 175in (444cm), width; 66in (168cm), height; 81in (206cm).

Three British military Series III 109s line up for the camera. Far left is a GS soft top, in the middle a GS hardtop, and nearest the camera is a 24-volt FFR hardtop

Land Rover Shorland armoured car

Short Brothers and Harland (later Shorts) in Belfast, Northern Ireland built one of the most distinctive military specials on the Land Rover chassis. The Royal Ulster Constabulary needed a manoeuvrable armoured vehicle for internal security and border patrol duties, and created the first prototypes in its own workshops during the early 1960s. The design was taken over by Short Bros, which developed it in collaboration with Land Rover. The first production Shorlands were built in 1965, and had 4-cylinder petrol engines on a Series IIA 109 chassis, with reinforced suspension and axles. From the beginning, they had military-pattern headlights mounted on the wing fronts, to allow for a fully armoured radiator grille. The armoured body followed Land Rover lines with a small hand-operated turret mounting a 7.62mm machine gun. It could also be equipped with smoke or riot-gas dischargers and there was an armoured trunk in the rear for a spare wheel and the fuel tank. Mk1 gave way to the Mk2, which had a higher compression engine giving more power, but the armoured Shorland was heavy, with armour 0.3in (0.8cm) to 0.43in (1.1cm) thick, and much improved with the arrival of the 2.6-litre 6-cylinder engine for the Mk3 in 1969. From 1980, the 6-cylinder engine was replaced by the 3.5-litre V8, making the Mk4 Shorland better still. The ultimate development came with the switch to the coil-sprung One Ten, forming the Shorland Series 5 in the early 1980s. The RUC was the best-known customer in Britain, although a pair of Shorlands were also used by the army and an experimental version mounted a Vigilant anti-tank missile. Many RUC vehicles passed to the Ulster Defence Regiment in 1970, and some were modified by the removal of their hexagonal turrets to make them look less like tanks. The Shorland was a considerable success overseas, and Shorts went on to develop the basic concept, to create Armoured Personnel Carriers and anti-hijack vehicles.

INTRODUCTION 1965 specification details for 1965 Mk.1
BODY Fully armoured body with revolving turret; crew of three; weight from 6200 lb (2812 kg).
ENGINE Petrol 4-cylinders, in-line; front; 90.47mm x 88.9mm, 2286cc; compr 7.0:1; 67bhp (50kW) @ 4100rpm; 29.3bhp/l (21.9kW/l); 116lbft (157Nm) @1500rpm.
ENGINE STRUCTURE 2 valves per cylinder; overhead valves; single camshaft; chain camshaft drive; aluminium cylinder head, cast iron cylinder block; Solex 40PA carburettor; three-bearing crankshaft; water-cooled.
TRANSMISSION Selectable four-wheel drive; four-speed "76mm" manual gearbox, two-speed transfer box; final drive ratio 4.7:1. High ratio1.53:1, Low ratio 2.92:1.

CHASSIS Separate box-section chassis frame, armoured steel body shell; front and rear beam axles, suspension by semi-elliptic leaf springs; telescopic dampers; hydraulic servo-assisted brakes; front and rear 11in (28cm) drums; transmission drum parking brake; recirculating-ball steering; 14gal (64l) fuel tank; 9.00-16in cross-ply tyres on steel rims.
DIMENSIONS Wheelbase: 109in (277cm); track 53.5in (136cm); length: 181in (460cm); width: 70in (178cm); height: 90in (228cm); ground clearance: 8.75in (22.3cm); turning circle, 58ft 3in (17.75m).
PERFORMANCE maximum speed: 50mph; 0-60mph (96kph) N/A; fuel consumption: 10mpg (3.54km/l) approx
PRICE: Not sold on the civilian market.
PRODUCTION 100 (Mk.1 only); production of subsequent Marks was approximately 1000.

The Shorland armoured car was updated to keep pace with the development of the Land Rover through Series IIA to Series III and then to coil-sprung One Ten. Top is a 1960s sales brochure for the Series IIA; below is a Series 5 powered by the V8 engine.

SHORLAND Armoured Patrol Car

Short Brothers & Harland Limited, London and Belfast

Land Rover 101 one-tonne Forward Control

The One-Tonne or 101-inch Forward Control Land Rover was a military-only model designed for the British army to tow its 105 mm howitzer. Prototype work began in 1966, but delays in the delivery of the new gun led to protracted development, and deliveries of 101s into front-line service did not begin until 1975. This purpose-built machine bore little resemblance to any other production Land Rover. Notable features were the taper-leaf springs, six-stud wheels (other Land Rovers had five studs), permanent four-wheel drive (it shared its gearbox and transfer box with the Range Rover) and V8 petrol engine, which made the 101 Solihull's first V8-powered utility model. With high ground clearance and short overhangs, it had exceptional off-road ability. The 101s were built with both left and right hand drive, and with both 12-volt, and 24-volt electrical systems to suit them for radio operations. Most were delivered to the British armed forces, the majority as GS soft-tops. Some of these became tractors for the Rapier missile system. Special conversions included ambulances bodied by Marshalls of Cambridge, and the rare Vampire, a van-bodied variant designed for electronic warfare. Others were delivered to various overseas military or paramilitary users, including Brunei, Dubai, Egypt, Kenya, Luxembourg, Oman and Uganda. Some saw service as Rapier tractors in Australia. Production of the 101 stopped in 1978 when all the military orders had been met. There was no civilian production, as the 101 could not be made to meet Construction and Use regulations. However, the basic chassis was taken over by MSA in Spain, which fitted its own 6-cylinder engines, and sold it as a Santana 2000.

INTRODUCTION 1972; into service 1975; produced to 1978.
BODY Soft-top GS; box-body ambulance; box-body for various special uses; weight from 4040lb (1832kg).
ENGINE V8-cylinders, in-line; front; 88.9mm x 71.1mm, 3528cc; compr 8.5:1; 128bhp (94kW) @ 5000rpm; 36.3bhp/l (26.6kW/l); 185lbft (251Nm) @ 2500rpm.
ENGINE STRUCTURE V8, 2-valves per cylinder; overhead valves, central chain-driven camshaft; aluminium cylinder heads and block; two Zenith-Stromberg carburettors; five-bearing crankshaft; water-cooled .
TRANSMISSION permanent four-wheel drive; 4-speed manual gearbox; final drive ratio 5.57:1. High ratio 1.174:1, Low ratio 3.321:1.

CHASSIS separate box-section chassis frame, steel and aluminium-panelled body shell; front and rear beam axles, with taper leaf springs and telescopic dampers; hydraulic servo-assisted brakes, front and rear drums, 11in (28cm) dia; transmission drum parking brake; recirculating ball steering; 24gal (109l) fuel tank; 9.00-16in cross-ply tyres, on steel rims.
DIMENSIONS wheelbase: 101in (256.5cm); track, front 60in (152.4cm), rear: 61in (154.9cm); length: 162.5in (412.7cm); width: 72.5in (184.2cm); height: 88in (223.5cm); ground clearance: 10in (254cm); turning circle: 37ft (11.3m) approx.
PERFORMANCE maximum speed: 75mph (120kph); 0-60mph (96kph): approx 17 sec; fuel consumption: 14mpg (4.96km/l).
PRICE Not sold on the civilian market.
PRODUCTION 2669

Land Rover military One Ten and Defender 110

The first military One Ten demonstrators were prepared during 1983, but production did not begin until 1985, the first order for 900 vehicles having been placed a year earlier by a Middle Eastern country. The One Ten marked the transition to diesel for the British armed forces, and almost every example delivered had a 4-cylinder diesel, the 2.25-litre in the beginning, but its 2.5-litre derivative thereafter. In due course, more than 70 overseas military forces would order the One Ten and its successor the Defender 110. The military-specification One Ten was not fundamentally different from the civilian, although the exact specification depended on the requirements of whichever country ordered it. In British service, it had waterproofed quick-change light units, bumperettes at the rear, a towing pintle in the front bumper, and jerrycan lockers let into the body sides just ahead of each rear wheel. Most British military One Tens and Defender 110s were GS soft-tops, and some were delivered as Fitted For Radio (FFR) with 24-volt electrical systems. Hardtops were often used for dedicated communications duties. A small quantity of V8-powered One Tens were specially equipped as long-range desert patrol vehicles and delivered to 22 SAS Regiment in the mid-1980s as replacements for the long-serving Pink Panthers (qv). The overwhelming majority of military Defender 110s for all customers were diesels, primarily the 200 Tdi (to 1994) and the 300 Tdi (from 1994). After the First Gulf War in 1991, the British Commander Sir Peter de la Billière singled out the performance of the military Land Rovers for particular praise. The US Rangers in the same conflict were so impressed with them that they ordered a quantity of specially-prepared ones for their own use in preference to American Jeeps or Hummers. These were special Defender 110s, the Special Operations Vehicles (SOVs) (qv).

INTRODUCTION 1985; production to 1990 (Military One Ten)
BODY long wheel base soft top, truck cab, high capacity pick up, hard top or station wagon, gross weight 6724lb (3050kg) or 6504lb (2950kg) with ride levelling unit.
ENGINES V8 petrol; 113bhp (84kW) @ 4,000 rpm - later 134bhp (100 kW) @ 5000 rpm, 185lbft (250Nm) - later 187lbft (253Nm) @ 2500 rpm. 2.3-litre 4-cylinder petrol; 74bhp (55kW) @ 4,000 rpm, 120lbft (163Nm) @ 2000 rpm. Later (1985) 2.5-litre 4-cylinder petrol; 80bhp (60kW) @ 4,000 rpm 129lbft (175Nm) @ 2000 rpm. 2.3-litre 4-cylinder diesel; 59bhp (43kW) @ 4,000 rpm, 100lbft (136Nm) @ 1800 rpm. Later (1984) 2.5-litre 4-cylinder diesel; 65.5bhp (48kW) @ 4,000 rpm 113lbft (153Nm) @ 1800 rpm. 1986 - 2.5-litre 4-cylinder diesel turbocharged; 85bhp (63kW) @ 4,000 rpm, 150lbft (203Nm) @ 1800 rpm.
ENGINE STRUCTURE V8: pushrod ohv with single central camshaft; aluminium alloy LM25 block and cylinder heads; twin Solex 175CDSE, later SU HIF44; Lucas 35DM8 or 35DLM8 electronic ignition; electrical fuel pump; 5-main bearings. 4-cylinder: pushrod ohv with timing chain; cast iron cylinder block and head. Petrol engines: Weber carburetter, Lucas 45D4 distributor. Diesels: CAV distributor pump, turbocharged engine with Garrett turbocharger.

TRANSMISSION permanent 4-wheel drive. V8 engine: 10.5in (267mm) hydraulic diaphragm spring clutch; LT95 4-speed integrated manual gearbox and transfer box with vacuum operated centre differential lock. 4-cylinder petrol; 9.53in (242.1mm) (later - also 2.5-litre turbocharged); 9.25in (235mm) hydraulic diaphragm spring clutch; 4-cylinder diesel; 9.53in (242.1mm) hydraulic diaphragm spring clutch; LT77 (later R380) 5-speed manual gearbox, LT230 2-speed transfer box with lever operated centre differential lock. Land Rover front banjo axle, Salisbury rear with cast differential housing. 3.54:1 final drive ratio.
CHASSIS welded steel ladder frame. Front and rear beam axles with coil springs and telescopic shock absorbers, recirculating ball steering, PAS optional, servo assisted, dual circuit, hydraulic brakes. 11.81in (30cm) front discs, 11in (28cm) rear drums. 10in (254mm) drum transmission parking brake. 17.5gal (79.5l) fuel tank. 16in pressed steel wheels with 7.50x16 tyres.
DIMENSIONS wheelbase; 110in (279.4cm), track; 58.5in (148.6cm), length Soft Top and Pick Up; 152.9in (443.8cm), Hard Top and Station Wagon; 181.1in (459.9cm), High Capacity Pick Up; 182in (463.1cm), width 70.5in (179cm), height; with levelling unit; 80.1in (203.5cm), normal suspension; 81.9in (207.9cm), ground clearance 8.5in (21.5cm), turning circle; 42ft (12.8m).
CAPABILITIES Max gradient; 45 deg, approach angle; 50deg, departure angle (max); 34.5deg.
PRICE Not sold on the civilian market.

A very early One Ten destined for the
British military. With jerrycan locker
ahead of the rear wheel and radio
antenna above it.

Military Defender 110

INTRODUCTION 1990
BODY soft top, truck cab, high
capacity pick up, hard top or station
wagon; gross weight: 6724lb (3050kg)
or 6504lb (2950kg) with ride levelling
unit.
ENGINES V8 petrol; 134bhp (100
kW) @ 5000 rpm, 185lbft (250Nm) -
later 187lbft (253Nm) @ 2500 rpm,
2.5-litre 4-cylinder petrol; 80bhp
(60kW) @ 4,000 rpm, 129lbft
(175Nm) @ 2000 rpm, 2.5-litre 4-
cylinder diesel; 65.5bhp (48kW) @
4,000 rpm, 113lbft (153Nm) @ 1800
rpm, 2.5-litre 4-cylinder direct injection
diesel turbocharged with intercooler;
107bhp (80kW) @ 4,000 rpm, 195ftlb
(264Nm) @ 1800 rpm, 2.5-litre 5-
cylinder electronic unit injector diesel
turbocharged with intercooler; 124bhp
(90kW) @ 4,200 rpm, 221lbft
(300Nm) @ 1950 rpm.
ENGINE STRUCTURE V8: pushrod
ohv with single central camshaft;
aluminium block and heads; twin SU
HIF 44 carburettors; Lucas 35DLM8
electronic ignition; electrical fuel pump;
5-main bearings. 4-cylinder petrol and
non-turbo diesel: pushrod ohv with
chain; cast iron block and head.
Turbocharged diesel: cast iron block,
aluminium head. 5-cyl diesel: cast iron
block, aluminium head. Petrol engines:
Weber carburettor, Lucas 45D4
distributor. 4-cyl diesel; CAV DPA
distributor pump, turbocharged; Bosch
rotary injection pump, Garrett T25
turbocharger; 5-cyl diesel engine:
Electronically controlled pump
injectors, Garrett turbocharger.

TRANSMISSION permanent four
wheel drive. Hydraulic diaphragm
spring clutch; V8; 10.5in (26.7cm) dia;
4-cylinder petrol; 9.53in (24.21cm) dia;
all diesel engines; 9.25in (23.5cm) dia;
V8; LT77, later R380, 5-speed manual
gearbox, all vehicles; LT230 2-speed
transfer box with lever operated centre
differential lock. Land Rover front banjo
axle, Defender 90; Land Rover rear
banjo axle, Defender 90 and 130;
Salisbury rear axle with cast centre
differential. 3.54:1 final drive ratio.
CHASSIS welded steel ladder frame;
front and rear beam axles with coil
springs and telescopic shock absorbers;
recirculating ball steering, PAS
optional; servo assisted, dual circuit,
hydraulic brakes; 11.81in (30cm) front
disc brakes, 11in (28cm) rear drum
brakes; 10in (25.4cm) drum
transmission parking brake; 17.5 gal
(79.5l) fuel tank; 16in pressed steel
wheels with 7.50x16 tyres.
DIMENSIONS wheelbase; 110in
(279.4cm), track; 58.5in (148.6cm),
length Soft Top and Pick Up; 152.9in
(443.8cm), Hard Top and Station
Wagon; 181.1in (459.9cm), High
Capacity Pick Up; 182in (463.1cm),
width 70.5in (179cm), height; with
levelling unit; 80.1in (203.5cm),
normal suspension; 81.9in (207.9cm),
ground clearance 8.5in (21.5cm),
turning circle; 42ft (12.8m).
CAPABILITIES Max gradient; 45 deg,
approach angle; 50deg, departure angle
(max); 34.5deg.
PRICE Not sold on the civilian market.

Pictured is a window hardtop model
delivered to the Dutch during the
1980s.

Land Rover military Ninety and Defender 90

Military production of the Ninety lagged some way behind its 1984 introduction to the civilian market, and the first ones were built in 1986. It was less popular than the military One Ten, if only because being smaller it was less versatile. Its light weight was not much of an advantage at a time when most heavy-lift helicopters could easily carry a fully-loaded One Ten. In the British armed forces the Ninety was usually a diesel, sometimes with 24-volt Fitted For Radio (FFR) specification, quite often a hardtop although there were also many GS soft-tops. Both the Ninety and its Defender 90 successor (built with the original 2.5-litre diesel engine despite the availability of the new 200 Tdi, which could not manage a 24-volt military alternator) were mostly used on communications or liaison duties. Some specialist units, for whom shipping space was at a premium, also used them. In British service, the Ninety replaced the few remaining civilian-pattern Series III 88s and many of the long-serving 88in Lightweights. For overseas forces, the Ninety was also made available as a gunship, to replace adapted Lightweights mounting the 106mm recoilless rifle. Demonstrators were also built to show how the model made an ideal base for the Milan anti-tank guided weapon. In Defender 90 form, Land Rover developed a versatile weapons fit for it and marketed the vehicle as the Multi-Role Combat Vehicle (MRCV) (qv). Most military Defender 90s were supplied with the 200 Tdi, or later 300 Tdi, diesel engine. The 300 Tdi was re-worked to accept a 24-volt military generator. After 1998, the Td5 diesel became available as an alternative but could only be ordered with 12-volt electrics.

INTRODUCTION 1984 (Ninety); production to 1990
BODY soft top, truck cab, hard top or station wagon, gross weight 5291lb (2400kg) 5622lb (2550kg) with heavy duty suspension.
ENGINES 2.3-litre 4-cylinder petrol; 74bhp (55kW) @4,000 rpm, 120lbft (163Nm) @ 2000 rpm. Later (1985) 2.5-litre 4-cylinder petrol; 80bhp (60kW) @ 4,000rpm, 129lbft (175Nm) @ 2000 rpm. 2.5-litre 4-cylinder diesel; 65.5bhp (48kW) @ 4,000 rpm, 113;bft (153Nm) @ 1800 rpm. 1986 2.5-litre 4-cylinder diesel turbocharged; 85bhp (63kW) @ 4,000 rpm, 150lbft (203Nm) @ 1800 rpm.
ENGINE STRUCTURE pushrod ohv with chain-driven camshaft; cast iron block and head. Petrol engines: Weber carburetter, Lucas 45D4 distributor. Diesels: CAV distributor pump; turbo-diesel Garrett turbocharger.
TRANSMISSION permanent four wheel drive. 4-cylinder petrol; 9.53in (24.2cm) (later also 2.5-litre turbocharged); 9.25in (23.5cm) hydraulic diaphragm spring clutch; 4-cylinder diesel; 9.53in (24.2cm) hydraulic diaphragm spring clutch; LT77 5-speed manual gearbox, LT230 2-speed transfer box with lever operated centre differential lock. Land Rover banjo axles. 3.54:1 final drive ratio.

CHASSIS welded steel ladder frame;front and rear beam axles with coil springs and telescopic shock absorbers; recirculating ball steering, PAS optional; servo assisted, dual circuit, hydraulic brakes. 11.81in (30cm) front discs, 11in (28cm) rear drums; 10in (25.4cm) drum transmission parking brake; 12gal (54.5l) fuel tank; 16in pressed steel wheels with 205x16 tyres – 7.50x16 tyres optional.
DIMENSIONS wheelbase 92.9in (236cm); track 58.5in (148.6cm); length Soft Top and Pick Up 146.5in (372.2cm); Hard Top and Station Wagon, width 70.5in (179cm); height normal suspension 77.4in (196.5cm), heavy duty suspension 78.7in (200cm); ground clearance 9in (22.9cm); turning circle 42ft (11.7m).
CAPABILITIES max gradient 45 deg, approach angle 50deg, departure angle (max) 49deg.
PRICE Not sold on the civilian market.

The Ninety was more versatile than its size suggested. This one was equipped with the 106mm recoilless rifle and was probably destined for anti-tank duties.

INTRODUCTION Defender 90, 1990
BODY soft top, truck cab, hard top or
station wagon; gross weight: 5291lb
(2400kg) 5622lb (2550kg) with heavy
duty suspension.
ENGINES V8 petrol; 113bhp (84kW)
@ 4,000 rpm - later 134bhp (100 kW)
@ 5000 rpm, 185lbft (250Nm) - later
187lbft (253Nm) @ 2500 rpm. 2.3-
litre 4-cylinder petrol; 74bhp (55kW)
@4,000 rpm, 120lbft (163Nm) @ 2000
rpm. Later (1985) 2.5-litre 4-cylinder
petrol; 80bhp (60kW) @ 4,000 rpm,
19lbft (175Nm) @ 2000 rpm. 2.3-litre
4-cylinder diesel; 59bhp (43kW)
@4,000 rpm, 100lbft (136Nm) @ 1800
rpm. Later (1984) 2.5-litre 4-cylinder
diesel; 65.5bhp (48kW) @ 4,000 rpm,

113lbft (153Nm) @ 1800 rpm. 1986 -
2.5-litre 4-cylinder diesel turbocharged;
85bhp (63kW) @ 4,000 rpm, 150lbft
(203Nm) @ 1800 rpm.
ENGINE STRUCTURE V8: pushrod
ohv with single central camshaft;
aluminium alloy LM25 block and
cylinder heads; twin Solex 175CDSE,
later SU HIF44; Lucas 35DM8 or
35DLM8 electronic ignition; electrical
fuel pump; 5-main bearings. 4-cylinder:
pushrod ohv with chain-driven
camshaft; cast iron block and head.
Petrol engines: Weber carburetter, Lucas
45D4 distributor. Diesels: CAV
distributor pump, turbo-diesel Garrett
turbocharger.

TRANSMISSION permanent four wheel
drive. Hydraulically operated diaphragm
spring clutch; V8; 10.5in (26.7cm) dia;
4-cylinder petrol; 9.53in (24.2cm) dia;
diesel engines 9.25in (23.5cm) dia; V8;
LT85 5-speed gearbox, petrol and diesel
4-cylinders; LT77 5-speed manual
gearbox; all LT230 2-speed transfer box
with lever operated centre differential
lock. Land Rover front and rear banjo
axles. 3.54:1 final drive ratio.
CHASSIS welded steel ladder frame;
front and rear beam axles with coil
springs and telescopic shock absorbers;
recirculating ball steering, PAS optional;
servo assisted, dual circuit, hydraulic
brakes; 11.81in (30cm) front discs, 11in
(28cm) rear drums; 10in (25.4cm) drum

transmission parking brake; 12gal
(54.5l) fuel tank; 16in pressed steel
wheels with 7.50x16 tyres.
DIMENSIONS wheelbase 92.9in
(236cm); track 58.5n (148.6cm); length
Soft Top and Pick Up 146.5in
(372.2cm); Hard Top and Station
Wagon, width 70.5in (179cm); height
normal suspension 77.4in (196.5cm),
heavy duty suspension 78.7in (200cm);
ground clearance 9in (22.9cm); turning
circle 42ft (11.7m).
CAPABILITIES Max gradient 45 deg,
approach angle 50deg, departure angle
(max) 49deg.
PRICE Not sold on the civilian market.

Land Rover Defender XD Wolf

The Defender XD 90 and XD 110 were heavy-duty military derivatives of the standard Defender 90 and 110. The letters XD stood for Extra Duty, and the models were often known by their development code-name of Wolf. In 1996, Land Rover was winner of three out of four categories for the British armed forces' next generation of light 4x4 vehicles (the fourth category, for a gun tractor, was won by the Steyr-Puch Pinzgauer). The Defender XD 90 was accepted in the Truck, Utility, Light (TUL) category to replace the existing Lightweights, and the XD 110 was accepted in the Truck, Utility, Medium (TUM) category to replace existing One Tens. In the battlefield ambulance category, the XD 130 was declared the winner (qv). Both the XD 90 and the XD 110 were based on the contemporary civilian Defender, modified to improve payload capability and occupant safety. The chassis cross-members were reinforced, the differentials were uprated, a Salisbury heavy-duty rear axle was fitted and re-rated springs gave them a nose-down appearance. Body reinforcements included strengthening under the load bed (providing 20 per cent more payload), stronger sills, front bulkhead and cab top rails plus a demountable roll cage over the rear body. All had 24-volt electrical systems (although not all were FFR variants) and carried the spare wheel mounted on the side of the roll cage behind the driver's door. There was provision for carrying a second spare on the passenger's side. Other distinguishing features were triangular air intake boxes on each front wing and the heavy-duty wheels with circular perforations near the rims. Although developed specifically for the Defender XD, these were subsequently adopted on some heavy-duty civilian Land Rovers as well, notably the Defender 130. Defender XDs also entered service with the Dutch Marines, and other overseas military forces.

INTRODUCTION 1996; into service 1997

BODY Soft-top GS; demountable plastic hardtop; gross vehicle weight from 2600lb (1179kg; 90); 3350lb (1519kg, 110).

ENGINE Diesel 300 Tdi 4-cylinders, in-line; front; 90.47mm x 97mm, 2495cc; compr 19.5:1; 111bhp (83kW) @ 4000rpm; 44.4bhp/l (33.2kW/l); 195lbft (265Nm) @1800rpm.

ENGINE STRUCTURE 2-overhead valves per cylinder; single belt-driven camshaft; aluminium cylinder head, cast iron block; direct injection, turbocharger with air-to-air intercooler; 5-bearing crankshaft; water-cooled.

TRANSMISSION Permanent four-wheel drive; five-speed R380 manual gearbox, two-speed LT230 transfer box; final drive ratio 3.54:1. High ratio1.41:1, Low ratio 3.32:1.

CHASSIS separate box-section chassis frame with reinforcements, steel and aluminium panelled body shell; front and rear beam axles, suspension by coil springs; telescopic dampers; hydraulic servo-assisted brakes; 11.81in (30cm) front ventilated discs, 11.4in (29cm) rear discs; transmission drum parking brake; power-assisted recirculating-ball steering; 17.5gal (79.5l) fuel tank; 7.50-16in radial-ply tyres on heavy-duty steel rims.

DIMENSIONS wheelbase 92.9in (236cm; 90); 110in (279.5cm; 110). track, front: 59.9in (152.1cm), rear 59.5in (151.1cm); length: 90: 151.18in (384cm); 110: 179.1in (455cm); width: 90: 81.9in (208cm); 110: 85.3in (216.8cm). height: 90: 80.27in (203.9cm); 110: 81.89in (208cm). ground clearance: 90: 9in (22.9cm), 110: 8.5in (21.5cm); turning circle: 90 and 110 42ft (11.7m).

CAPABILITIES Max gradient 45 deg, approach angle 90, 51deg, 110, 50deg, departure angle (max) 90, 53deg, 110 34deg.

PRICE Not sold on the civilian market.

The three varieties of Defender XD line up for the camera: nearest is an XD 90, in the middle an XD 110, and farthest away is the 130-based ambulance. The cutaway drawing illustrates some of the XD's special features

Land Rover Military 127, Defender 130 and Defender XD 130

The ultra-long wheelbase derivative of the coil-sprung Land Rover found a role with the armed forces towards the end of the 1980s as a support vehicle for the Rapier tracked missile system. The first to enter service were 127s, but by the time the last ones were delivered, Land Rover had switched over to the Defender 130 name. All had 3.5-litre V8 petrol engines, plus a special back body by Marshalls of Cambridge, with canvas tilt and cab roof. They were operated by the RAF Regiment, and also by some USAF units.

Typically the Rapier tractors operated in pairs, with a One Ten FFR hardtop to act as a communications vehicle, towing a trailer with the crew's kit and equipment. The 127s were used to tow the Rapier launcher and fire control units, to carry additional missiles, and transport the crew. They were also fitted with front-mounted winches to aid in the positioning of the Rapier trailer units. More than 200 127 Rapier tractors were at one time operating with British units. The 127 was also bodied as a military ambulance in the later 1980s, with examples by Marshalls of Cambridge entering service with the army while some by Locomotors of Andover were taken on by the RAF. Every one was powered by a V8 petrol engine. The next ultra-long wheelbase Land Rover variant to enter service was the Defender XD 130 battlefield ambulance. This was developed during the first half of the 1990s in conjunction with Marshalls to meet a Ministry of Defence deadline for replacing its existing 101 ambulances. Although it was designed at the same time as the Wolf vehicles (qv) and shared much of their specification, it was known by the separate code-name of Project Pulse. The XD 130 battlefield ambulance entered service towards the end of the 1990s, with distinctive, square-rigged bodywork, and was designed to carry four stretchers. Gas struts were used to assist loading of the upper pair of stretcher racks.

INTRODUCTION 1987 (127), 1997 (XD130)

BODY extended wheelbase with rear load tray (Rapier tractors) or ambulance body; gross weight 8267lb (3750kg) (XD130 ambulance)

ENGINE V8 petrol; 134bhp (100kW) @ 5000 rpm, 187lb ft (253Nm) @ 2500 rpm, compression ratio 8.5:1 (127s); 300 Tdi, 4-cylinder turbocharged diesel; 90.47mm x 97mm 2495cc, compression ratio 19.5:1, 111bhp (83kW) @ 4000 rpm, 195 lbft (264Nm) @ 1800 rpm.

ENGINE STRUCTURE V8 pushrod ohv with single central camshaft; aluminium alloy LM25 block and cylinder heads; twin Solex 175CDSE, later SU HIF 44; Lucas 35DM8 or 35DLM8 electronic ignition; electrical fuel pump; 5-bearing crankshaft; (300 Tdi) belt-driven camshaft, cast iron block, aluminium cylinder head. Bosch rotary injection pump, Garrett T25 turbocharger.

TRANSMISSION permanent four wheel drive. V8: 10.5in (26.7cm) hydraulic diaphragm spring clutch; LT85 5-speed manual gearbox; later R380 5-speed; LT230 2-speed transfer gearbox. Land Rover front banjo axle, Salisbury rear with cast differential housing. 3.54:1 final drive ratio. 300 Tdi: 9.25in (23.5cm) hydraulic diaphragm spring clutch; Land Rover R380 5-speed manual gearbox, LT230 2-speed transfer box with centre differential lock. Land Rover front and rear banjo type axles, 3.54:1 final drive ratio.

CHASSIS welded steel ladder frame with sleeved extension puddle-welded in place; front and rear beam axles with coil springs and telescopic shock absorbers; recirculating ball steering, PAS optional; servo assisted, dual circuit, hydraulic brakes; 11.81in (30cm) front discs, 11in (28cm) rear drums; 10in (25.4cm) drum transmission parking brake; 17.5 gallon (79.5l) fuel tank;16in pressed steel wheels with 7.50x16 tyres (heavy-duty types on XD130).

DIMENSIONS wheelbase 127in (322.6cm), track 58.5in (148.6cm); length 127: 202in (513.2cm), XD130 ambulance: 204.3in (518.9cm); height 127: 80.1in (203.5cm), XD130 ambulance 98.4in (250cm); ground clearance 8.5in (21.5cm), turning circle 49.5ft (15.1m).

CAPABILITIES Max gradient 45 deg, approach angle 50deg, departure angle 34deg XD130 ambulance 30deg).

PRICE Not sold on the civilian market.

The Defender XD 130 battlefield ambulance was developed in conjunction with Marshalls of Cambridge.

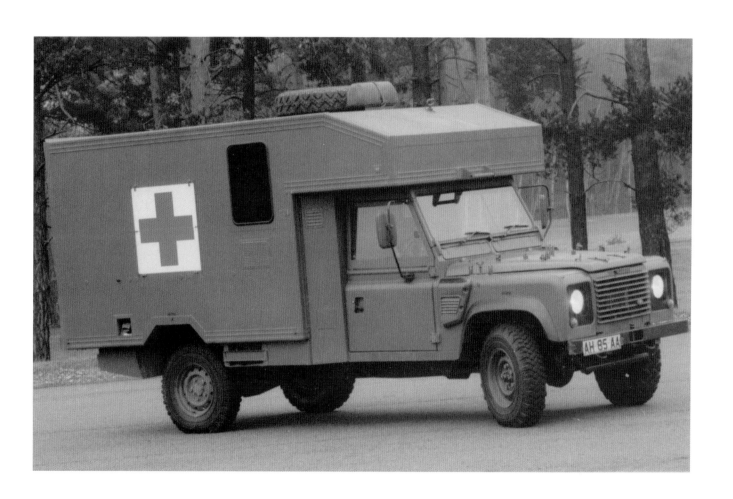

Land Rover Llama Forward Control

Towards the middle of the 1980s, the Ministry of Defence began to look for a vehicle to replace its ageing Land Rover 101s in the gun tractor role. Land Rover was among those who tendered for the supply, developing a special forward-control model, based on the coil-sprung One Ten. The vehicle was developed as a two-tonne truck under the code-name Project Llama. The first Llama prototypes had V8 petrol engines, but the military decided it wanted a diesel, and for the second-stage trials Land Rover submitted a Llama powered by its 2.5-litre 4-cylinder turbo-diesel. However, the Llama was not successful in these trials (the military eventually settled on a 4x4 truck built by Reynolds-Boughton) and the project went no further. There had been plans to offer the vehicle in civilian guise as the Land Rover 110 Forward Control, but these fell through when the military contract failed to materialise, because the sales potential was not great enough to justify the cost of tooling up for production. The Llama chassis was essentially a modified One Ten, with heavy-duty Salisbury axles as standard. Its side members were brought together in a point at the front to form a pivot for the tilting cab. This was made of glass reinforced plastic (GRP) panelling on a steel and aluminium frame, and was mounted right at the front so that the occupants sat above the engine. The forward-control layout allowed for a large load bed that was 299cm (nearly 118in) long at its maximum – more than a metre longer than the load-bed of a normal-control One Ten.

INTRODUCTION 1986
BODY Truck cab with dropside truck or fixed-side rear body and canvas tilt, or truck cab with box-body; weight from 4409lb (2000kg).
ENGINE V8, in-line; front; 88.9mm x 71.1mm, 3528cc; compr 8.13:1; 135bhp (100kW) @ 5000rpm; 38.6bhp/l (28.6kW/l); 182lbft (246Nm) @ 2500rpm.
ENGINE STRUCTURE 2-overhead valves per cylinder; central chain-driven camshaft; aluminium cylinder heads and block; two Zenith-Stromberg carburettors; 5-bearing crankshaft; water-cooled.
TRANSMISSION Permanent four-wheel drive; five-speed LT85 manual gearbox and two-speed LT230 transfer box; final drive ratio 4.7:1. High ratio 1.41:1, Low ratio 3.32:1.

CHASSIS Separate box-section chassis frame, steel cab frame with GRP panels; front and rear beam axles with coil springs and anti-roll bars; telescopic dampers; hydraulic servo-assisted brakes, front 11.8in (30cm) dia discs, rear 11in (28cm) dia drums; transmission drum parking brake; power-assisted recirculating ball steering; 28gal (127l) fuel tank; 9.00-16in cross-ply tyres, on steel rims.
DIMENSIONS Wheelbase: 110in (279.4cm); track 59in (151.1cm); length: 197in (500cm); width 73in (185cm); height 90in (229cm); ground clearance 9.4in (24cm); turning circle: 22.4ft (6.82m).
PERFORMANCE with V8, maximum speed: 95mph; 0-60mph (96kph): 9.45sec
PRICE Not put into production.

Land Rover SAS Pink Panther

Operations behind enemy lines were among the responsibilities of Britain's 22 Special Air Service Regiment. In the 1950s, the regiment adapted 86in Land Rovers for these purposes, and during the 1960s its own workshops modified some 109s, which offered more space and proved much more effective. By the middle of the 1960s, the regiment was operating in Oman, supporting the Sultan's forces against guerrillas in the country's southern district of Dhofar. Here a need was swiftly recognised for special vehicles, capable of carrying a three-man crew, weaponry for attack and defence, communications equipment and enough equipment and supplies of fuel, ammunition and water to remain self-sufficient for several days. A specification based on the Series IIA 109 Land Rover was drawn up in conjunction with Marshalls of Cambridge, which built the whole production batch. Most were delivered in bronze green, but those used in the desert during the Oman Dhofar Campaign were repainted matt pink, a colour that blended into the desert haze. They were nicknamed Pink Panthers after the popular film. They had heavy-duty suspension and a stripped-down body modified to take twin 40gal (181.8l) fuel tanks behind the front seats. The navigator's seat was raised to allow him to double as the front gunner, and a second machine-gun was mounted on a pedestal in the rear. The rest of the body was kitted out with radios, sand ladders, smoke dischargers, navigation equipment and a vast quantity of other equipment putting the operational weight up to more than three tons.

INTRODUCTION 1968; into service 1969.
BODY Stripped-out open pick-up type; 3-seats; full operational weight over 6720 lb (3048kg).
ENGINE 4-cylinders, in-line; front; 90.47mm x 88.9mm, 2286cc; compr 7.0:1; 77bhp (57.5kW) @ 4250rpm; 34.2bhp/l (25.5kW/l); 124lbft (168Nm) @ 2500rpm.
ENGINE STRUCTURE 2-overhead valves per cylinder; chain-driven camshaft; aluminium cylinder head, cast iron block; single Solex carburettor; three-bearing crankshaft; water-cooled
TRANSMISSION Selectable four-wheel drive in High range, permanent four-wheel drive in Low range; four-speed manual gearbox; final drive ratio 4.7:1. High ratio 1.148:1, Low ratio 2.89:1.

CHASSIS separate box-section frame; steel and aluminium-panelled body shell; beam axles front and rear, suspension by leaf springs; telescopic dampers; hydraulic brakes 11.5in (29.2cm) drums; transmission drum parking brake; recirculating ball steering; two 10gal (45.5l) fuel tanks plus two 40gal (182l) tanks; 9.00-16in tyres on steel rims (alternative 8.20-15in sand tyres on steel rims).
DIMENSIONS wheelbase 109in (276.8cm); track 51.5in (130.8cm); length 216in (548.6cm) approx; width 64in (162.5cm); height dependent on equipment; ground clearance 10in (25.4cm); turning circle: 45ft (13.7m) approx
PERFORMANCE Maximum speed: 45mph (72.4kph) approx
PRICE Not sold on the civilian market.
PRODUCTION 72.

Beautifully restored by the Dunsfold Collection, this Pink Panther is seen in as-delivered condition with Bronze Green paint.

Land Rover rapid-deployment weapons mounts

The worldwide emphasis on rapid deployment forces made Land Rover look at new ways of making the Defender suitable for the 1990s. There was a growing demand for vehicles to incorporate a fixed mount for machine-guns and other light weapons. The earliest publicly revealed was a Special Operations Vehicle, developed for the US Rangers, on the basis of a V8-engined Defender 110. Land Rover claimed it had been designed to meet the airportability and mobility needs of rapid reaction forces, as well as special forces for rapid-deployment roles in out-of-area or clandestine operations. Production began in 1992, and the vehicle was made available to other armed services. It had a stripped-down body, which allowed rapid deployment by its crew of up to six, while a tough tubular cage provided body strength, rollover protection and a ring-mount for a variety of weapons. These ranged from machine guns to anti-tank missiles. The low overall profile ensured an easy fit inside transport aircraft and had obvious benefits on the ground. For the Defender 90, Land Rover came up with a demountable system, which was both modular and extremely flexible. This was essentially a roll cage, with an integral weapons mount, and a hydraulic suspension lock-out system was available to provide a more stable firing platform. This system was known as the MRCV (Multi-Role Combat Vehicle). The essential principles of this were retained for the Weapons Mounted Installation Kit (WMIK), developed by Ricardo Specialist Vehicles for the Defender XD 110 and announced in 1999. The British military took more than 200 of these kits, which could be fitted to an XD 110 in four hours, and Land Rover sought additional sales through a WMIK-equipped XD 110, which it called the Rapid Deployment Vehicle (RDV). As with all specialist military vehicles, these were built to individual order, and Land Rover did not release full details of its military sales.

Defender 110 SOV:
INTRODUCTION 1992
BODY special low-profile body with tubular weapons mount and rollcage, no doors; 3-man crew; weight approximately 6720lb (3050kg).
ENGINE V8 petrol; 134bhp (100 kW) @ 5000 rpm, 187lb ft (253Nm) @ 2500 rpm.
ENGINE STRUCTURE: pushrod ohv with single central camshaft; alloy block and cylinder heads; twin SU HIF 44 carburettors; Lucas 35DLM8 electronic ignition system; electrical fuel pump; 5-main bearings.
TRANSMISSION permanent four wheel drive. Hydraulically operated diaphragm spring clutch; 10.5in (26.7cm) dia; LT77 5-speed manual gearbox; LT230 2-speed transfer box with lever operated centre differential lock. Land Rover front banjo axle; Salisbury rear axle with cast centre differential. 3.54:1 final drive.

CHASSIS welded steel ladder frame; front and rear beam axles with coil springs and telescopic shock absorbers; recirculating ball steering, PAS optional; servo assisted, dual circuit, hydraulic brakes, 11.81in (30cm) front discs, 11in (28cm) rear drums; 10in (25.4cm) drum transmission parking brake. Fuel tank capacity not revealed; 16in pressed steel wheels with 9.00-16 tyres.
DIMENSIONS wheelbase 110in (279.4cm); track 58.5in (148.6cm); length 152.9in (443.8cm) approximately; height not revealed ; ground clearance (min) 8.5in (21.5cm), turning circle 42ft (12.8m).
CAPABILITIES Max gradient; 45 deg, approach angle; 50deg, departure angle (max); 34.5deg.
PRICE Not sold on the civilian market.

The XD 110 RDV came with a Weapons Mounted Installation Kit developed with the help of Ricardo Specialist Vehicles.

Defender 90 MRCV:
INTRODUCTION 1998
BODY open type with integrated tubular rollcage and weapons mount. Gross weight not revealed.
ENGINES 300Tdi 2.5-litre 4-cylinder direct injection diesel turbocharged with intercooler; 111bhp (83kW) @ 4,000rpm, 195lb ft (265Nm) @ 1800 rpm; Td5 straight 5-cylinder with electronic unit injectors, turbocharger and intercooler; 124bhp (90kW) @ 4200rpm, 221 lb ft (300Nm) @ 1950rpm.
ENGINE STRUCTURE: 300Tdi cast iron block, aluminium head; Bosch rotary injection pump; Garrett T25 turbocharger. Td5 cast iron block, aluminium head. electronically controlled pump injectors; Garrett turbocharger.
TRANSMISSION permanent four wheel drive. hydraulic diaphragm spring clutch; 9.25in (23.5cm) dia; 4-cylinder petrol; R380 5-speed manual gearbox; LT230 2-speed transfer box with lever operated centre differential lock; Land Rover front and rear banjo axles. 3.54:1 final drive ratio.

CHASSIS welded steel ladder frame; front and rear beam axles with coil springs and telescopic shock absorbers; recirculating ball steering, PAS optional; servo assisted, dual circuit, hydraulic brakes, 11.81in (30cm) front discs, 11in (280 mm) rear drums; 10in (25.4cm) drum transmission parking brake; 12gal (54.5l) fuel tank; 16in pressed steel wheels with 7.50x16 tyres.
DIMENSIONS wheelbase 92.9in (236cm); track 58.5in (148.6cm); length 146.5in (372.2cm) approx; width 70.5in (179cm) approx; height not revealed; ground clearance 9in (22.9cm), turning circle 42ft (11.7m).
CAPABILITIES Max gradient 45 deg, approach angle 50deg, departure angle (max) 49deg.
PRICE Not sold on the civilian market.

Defender XD110 RDV:
INTRODUCTION 1999.
BODY special low-profile body with demountable tubular weapons mount and roll cage, no doors; 3-man crew; weight approximately 6720lb (3050kg).
ENGINE 300 Tdi diesel 4-cylinders, in-line; front; 90.47mm x 97mm, 2495cc; compr 19.5:1; 111bhp (83kW) @ 4000rpm; 44.4bhp/l (33.2kW/l); 195lbft (265Nm) @1800rpm; Td5 straight 5-cylinder with electronic unit injectors, turbocharger and intercooler; 124bhp (90kW) @ 4200rpm, 221 lb ft (300Nm) @ 1950rpm.
ENGINE STRUCTURE 300 Tdi, 2-overhead valves per cylinder; single belt-driven camshaft; aluminium cylinder head, cast iron block; direct injection, turbocharger with air-to-air intercooler; 5-bearing crankshaft; water-cooled. Td5 cast iron block, aluminium cylinder head. Electronically controlled pump injectors, Garrett turbocharger.
TRANSMISSION Permanent four-wheel drive; five-speed R380 manual gearbox, 2-speed LT230 transfer box; final drive ratio 3.54:1. High ratio1.41:1, Low ratio 3.32:1.

CHASSIS separate box-section chassis frame with reinforcements, steel and aluminium panelled body shell; front and rear beam axles, suspension by coil springs; telescopic dampers; hydraulic servo-assisted brakes; 11.81in (30cm) front ventilated discs, 11.4in (29cm) rear discs; transmission drum parking brake; power-assisted recirculating-ball steering; 17.5gal (79.5l) fuel tank.; 7.50-16in radial-ply tyres on heavy-duty steel rims.
DIMENSIONS wheelbase 110in (279.4cm); track 58.5in (148.6cm); length 152.9in (443.8cm) approximately; height 75.2in (191.0cm); ground clearance 8.5in (21.5cm), turning circle 42ft (12.8m).
CAPABILITIES Max gradient 45 deg, approach angle 50deg, departure angle 34deg
PRICE Not sold on the civilian market.

The surprising versatility of Land
Rover's short-wheelbase utility, the
an MRCV.

Specials

Land Rover Defender V8 50

During the 1990s, Solihull periodically came up with limited-edition Defenders to keep its oldest model-line fresh in the public eye. Many of these were put together in a straightforward way by clever use of the options list, but there were two derivatives of the Defender 90 that had some special features. The earlier of these was the Defender 90SV, built only for the UK market and released in the summer of 1993 . The later, and deliberately more glamorous model, was the Defender V8 50. Unlike the SV90, this very special edition was not confined to the UK. Built in 1998, it was made available in several overseas territories to help promote the 50th Anniversary of Land Rover, which was being celebrated that year. There were examples for Japan, Britain, Germany, France, Holland and Belgium. All of the V8 50 models were Station Wagons with the 4.0-litre petrol V8 and 4-speed automatic transmission pioneered on the 1997 NAS 90, and all had an integral roll cage, chequerplate panels on the body, and chromed side runners. The 4.0-litre V8 petrol engine and automatic box were not normally available for Defenders in any of the countries where the V8 50 was sold, which gave the model strong additional appeal. However, the V8 50 was never the performer that its specification promised, and some buyers reacted to this by upgrading the engine management chip to deliver more torque and power, or by swapping the engine for the larger 4.6-litre type used in the contemporary Range Rover. Some of the V8 50's specification differed from country to country. In Britain, the paintwork was Atlantis Blue and the wheels were Freestyle alloys with a gunmetal finish, while the upholstery was in leather. In Japan, which took the largest number, the paintwork was in the local favourite of white, the wheels were satin-finish Boost alloys, and the upholstery was cloth. All models carried a numbered limited-edition plaque on the right-hand rear body panel.

INTRODUCTION 1998
BODY: short wheel base Station Wagon, gross weight 3725lb (1690kg).
ENGINE: V8, 94mm x 71.1mm; 3947cc; 182bhp (135kW) @ 4,750 rpm, 232lb ft (315Nm) @ 3000rpm.
ENGINE STRUCTURE pushrod ohv with single central camshaft; aluminium block and cylinder heads; Lucas L-Jetronic electronic fuel injection; in-tank electrical fuel pump; 5-main bearings.
TRANSMISSION permanent four wheel drive four-speed ZF 4HP22 automatic, 2-speed LT230 transfer box with lever operated centre differential lock; transfer box ratios (High Range) 1.222:1, (Low Range) 3.321:1, Land Rover banjo front and rear axles, final drive 3.54:1,

CHASSIS welded steel ladder frame; beam axles with coil springs and telescopic shock absorbers; recirculating ball steering with PAS; servo assisted, dual circuit, hydraulic brakes. 11.81in (30cm) front ventilated discs, 11.4in (29cm) rear solid discs; 10in (25.4cm) drum transmission parking brake; 12 gal (54.5l) fuel tank; 16in styled alloy wheels with 265/75-16 BF Goodrich All Terrain tyres.
DIMENSIONS wheelbase 92.9in (236.0cm); track 58.5in (148.6cm); length 160.5in (407.2cm); height 77.3in (196.3cm); ground clearance 9.0in (22.9cm); turning circle 40ft (12.2m).
CAPABILITIES Max gradient 45 deg, approach angle 50deg, departure angle 49deg.
PRICE £25,995.
PRODUCTION 1071 of which 385 were for UK.

The Defender V8 50 was the only 4.0-litre V8-powered 90 with automatic transmission seen outside the USA.

Land Rover Discovery specials

Land Rover's Special Vehicles Division modified the first-generation Discovery in four ways. Best-known was the Discovery Commerical, but there were also Discovery Wheelchair Carriers, ambulances and a long-wheelbase Paramedic Discovery. Some countries had their own special versions of the Commercial adapted to meet local regulations. Ireland created its own "commercial" Discoverys even before Special Vehicles came up with the factory job, while Ter Berg in the Netherlands fitted high roofs and other special items, on behalf of the local importer, to meet Dutch commercial vehicle regulations. Constructed to special order, and introduced at about the same time, the Discovery Wheelchair Carrier was marketed by Land Rover as the Mobility Choice model. Normally made with the manual gearbox and diesel engine, this had a raised roof section, which provided headroom for a wheelchair passenger in the rear. There was a single second-row seat, the remaining space and the whole rear load area being dedicated to a wheelchair, carried on a special securing track with clamps. An electro-hydraulic wheelchair lift at the rear was part of the standard specification. The long-wheelbase Paramedic Discovery was built in limited numbers for the UK, and was equipped specially to meet a growing demand for fast-response medical aid vehicles for the emergency services. The wheelbase was extended to 116in (294.6cm), and it was available with either three or five doors. The majority were diesel-engined and two were equipped as mobile laboratories for a lubrication products company.

Technical Specification for Discovery 116in Paramedic vehicle
INTRODUCTION 1991
BODY 3-door or 5-door estate, 2-seats for crew, plus stretcher accommodation and optional attendant's seat in the rear.
ENGINES Petrol V8-cylinders, in-line; front; 88.9mm x 71.1mm, 3528cc; compr 9.35:1; 164bhp (122kW) @ 4750rpm; 46.5bhp/l (34.6kW/l); 212lbft (288Nm) @ 3000rpm; (1993–1994) 94mm x 71.1mm, 3947cc; compr 9.35:1; 180bhp (134kW) @ 4750rpm; 45.6bhp/l (33.9kW/l); 230lbft (312Nm) @ 3100rpm. Diesel 200Tdi (300Tdi from 1994) 4-cyl, in-line, front, 90.47mm x 97mm, 2495cc; compr 19.5:1, 111bhp (82.8kW) @ 4000rpm; 195lbft (264.3Nm) @ 1800rpm.
ENGINE STRUCTURE V8, 2 overhead valves per cylinder; chain-driven camshaft in centre of block; aluminium cylinder heads and block; Bosch-Lucas fuel injection; 5-bearing crankshaft; water-cooled. Diesel 200Tdi and 300Tdi in-line, overhead valves, belt-driven camshaft; aluminium cylinder head, cast iron block. Bosch fuel injection and Garrett turbocharger, intercooler; 5-bearing crankshaft, water-cooled.

TRANSMISSION permanent four-wheel drive; diaphragm spring clutch; manual all-synchromesh 5-speed gearbox; final drive 3.538:1, transfer box ratios (High Ratio) 1.222:1, or (Low Range) 3.321:1.
CHASSIS separate box-section chassis frame, steel and aluminium panelled body; beam axle front suspension by coil springs, radius arms; Panhard rod; live axle rear suspension by coil springs, radius arms, A-bracket, telescopic dampers; hydraulic servo-assisted brakes, front 11.8in (30cm) dia ventilated discs, rear 11.4in (28.95cm) dia discs; transmission drum parking brake; power-assisted recirculating ball steering; 19.5gal (89l) fuel tank; 205R-16in. tyres on steel or alloy rims.
DIMENSIONS: wheelbase 116in (294.5cm); track 51.5in (148.6cm); length 194in (492.7cm); width 70.6in (179.3cm); height 75.6in (192cm); ground clearance 8.1in (20.4cm); turning circle 37ft (11.4m).
PRICE: Varied according to specification and equipment.

The Mobility Choice wheelchair carrier and the extended-wheelbase Paramedic Discovery were two low-volume variants from Land Rover Special Vehicles.

Land Rover – Special Vehicles and the Autobiography scheme

Special Vehicle Operations (SVO) was the new title for the Special Projects Department from July 1985. It continued the old department's work of approving specialist aftermarket conversions, and also converted and assembled the Crew Cab 110 models on their 127in wheelbase until assembly became viable on the main production lines.

SVO also developed its own box-body conversion, variable in height, length, interior configuration and in number and position of access doors. From about 1990, this was marketed as the Quadtec body. Increasingly, it became policy for SVO to do as much of the conversion work as possible in-house, and many of the aftermarket specialists saw their traditional Land Rover work drying up. During 1992, SVO was re-organised as Land Rover Special Vehicles (LRSV) and added to its commercial conversion work responsibility for limited-edition and custom-building work for the passenger vehicle market. Thus it did the final assembly of vehicles like the 90SV as well as the Discovery Commercial. These and other LRSV conversions always carried "Land Rover Special Vehicles" badges. New for 1993 was the Autobiography custom-building service, a scheme that allowed customers to have their Range Rovers individually finished by LRSV in the style of a bespoke tailor or traditional coachbuilder. There was a limit to what LRSV would do however; special paint colours, upholstery material and wood trims were available, but special engines or transmissions were off the menu owing to difficulties with homologation. Nevertheless a batch of Autobiography Range Rovers was sold in the UK with the 4.2-litre engine otherwise reserved for the LSE, the 1992 long wheelbase air suspension model, and for the Middle Eastern market. Most Autobiography models carried special badging, although the only indication of LRSV involvement was on a build-plate under the bonnet. The Autobiography scheme

remained exclusive to Range Rovers, with the exception of 2001 Discovery and Freelander show models, which were publicised as Autobiography types. That project was cancelled however when the management decided that it would detract from the exclusiveness of the Range Rover Autobiography scheme. There were several limited-edition Autobiography Range Rovers, built in small batches to determine market acceptance of planned new features.

Overseas manufacturers

Derived from Santana's short-
wheelbase military model, the
Ligero was a leisure vehicle that
went down well in Spain.

Land Rover Tempo 80 and 86

Forbidden to build military-style vehicles of its own, under the terms of surrender imposed in 1945, West Germany in the early 1950s needed some light 4x4s for patrolling the East German border. Obliged to buy them from abroad, in early 1953 the Border Police force, Bundesgrenzschuutz (BGS), contracted for 189 Land Rovers to be supplied to Vidal und Sohn of Hamburg-Harburg, which had been making Tempo 3 and 4-wheeled delivery vans since 1933. Tempo's previous experience of military 4x4s had been the G1200, with a 600cc engine at each end, both driving their own axles, and with 4-wheel steering. Vidal converted the Land Rovers to BGS requirements, which involved switching to negative earth electrics with twin 6-volt batteries, the addition of twin fuel tanks at the rear, and the construction of a new, high-waisted rear body in steel with a cabriolet-style folding top. Four inward-facing seats were fitted in the back, and the spare wheel was mounted on the fixed rear panel. Map lockers were let into the front wings and there was a large flat map locker on the bonnet. These steel bodies were heavier, and also more prone to corrosion, than the Birmabright aluminium-bodied Land Rover of the time. When the switch was made from the 80in to 86in chassis in the middle of 1953, the German models made by Tempo of Hamburg for the BGS did the same. The 86-inch Tempos were very similar in specification to their 80-inch predecessors, but they had additional door hinges and the spare wheel was relocated to the bonnet in place of the large map locker. Exact production figures are uncertain; there may have been no more than 61 of these 86-inch Tempos. Vidal und Sohn also acted as the German importer for Land Rovers for many years, until Deutsche Rover took over in the early 1960s. West Germany was once again permitted to have a standing army, and it established its new force during 1956. One hundred Tempo Land Rovers were transferred to the new army.

INTRODUCTION: 80in 1953; 86in 1953

BODY: Open six-seater with cabriolet-type folding top, estimated weight from 4100lbs (1860kg).

ENGINES: 4-cylinder in line, front 77.8mm x 105mm, 1997cc. 52bhp (38.8kW) @ 4000 rpm, 101lb ft (137Nm) @1500 rpm, compression 7.1:1.

ENGINE STRUCTURE: cast iron block and cylinder head. Overhead inlet, side exhaust valves, chain-driven camshaft, pushrods and rockers, 3-bearing crankshaft.

TRANSMISSION: selectable four wheel drive, hydraulic single dry plate clutch 9in (22.8cm) dia. Rover 4-speed gearbox and 2-speed transfer box, Rover front and rear axles, 4.7:1.

CHASSIS: welded box section steel ladder frame, front and rear beam axles with semi-elliptic springs and telescopic shock absorbers, worm and nut steering. 4-wheel hydraulically operated 10in (25.4cm) drum brakes, 6in (15.2cm) drum transmission hand brake. Twin fuel tanks of undisclosed capacity. 16in divided pressed steel wheels with 6.00 x 16 heavy traction tyres.

DIMENSIONS: Wheelbase 80in (203cm) or 86in (218cm), track 50in (127cm), length; 132in (335cm) or 140.5in (357cm), width; 61in (155cm), height; 73.5in (192cm).

PRODUCTION: 189 (80in); exact production total of 86in models is uncertain, estimates vary between 61 and 287.

The high-sided bodywork and cabriolet-style folding top made the Tempo models for the BGS distinctively different.

Land Rover Minerva 80in and 86in

To meet the requirements of a Belgian military contract, Rover shipped 80in Land Rovers across the Channel in Completely Knocked Down (CKD) form. Assembly and completion was by Minerva, founded in 1899, of Mortsel near Antwerp. Minerva had made cars from 1902, some of very high quality and sold in Britain by no less than C S Rolls & Company. Minerva prospered throughout the inter-war years, right up to 1939, and Ettore Bugatti once proposed transferring his production there from Molsheim. After 1945 Minerva carried on by making commercials, and took up assembly of Land Rovers for the Belgian military, with a unique specification including a locally made steel body. They had unusual sloping front wings, a unique grille and a fixed rear panel instead of a drop-down tailgate, two 6-volt batteries and some time in 1953 changed from the standard positive earth to a negative earth. Solihull produced all the 1952-1953 CKD kits to 2-litre, 80in specification. However Minerva stockpiled them, only assembling them in later years, and the last examples to meet the Belgian military contract were not delivered until 1956 by which time Solihull had moved on to the 86in Land Rover. Out of the 8805 80in Minervas built, the best estimate is that 8440 went to the Belgian authorities and 365 were sold as civilian models with a standard drop-down tailgate, although still with the characteristic sloping front wings. From 1954, Minerva also assembled 86-inch Land Rovers from CKD components, but these were all for the civilian market. Just 1100 were built, and many of these - probably most - were exported. Minerva 86s had the same sloping front wings and steel bodywork as the 80in that the company assembled. The 1954 model year vehicles had the original siamese-bore 2-litre engine, later ones the spread-bore type. During 1954, there was a dispute between Minerva and Rover over the assembly contract, and it was terminated in June 1956.

INTRODUCTION: 80in 1952; 86in 1953
BODY: Pickup; weight (80in) from 4032lb (1829kg) or (86in) from 4142lb (1879kg).
ENGINES: 4-cylinder in line, front 77.8mm x 105mm, 1997cc. 52bhp (38.8kW) @ 4000 rpm, 101lb ft (137Nm) @1500 rpm, compression 7.1:1.
ENGINE STRUCTURE: cast iron block and cylinder head. Overhead inlet, side exhaust valves, chain-driven camshaft, pushrods and rockers, 3-bearing crankshaft.
TRANSMISSION: selectable four wheel drive, hydraulic single dry plate clutch 9in (22.8cm) dia. Rover 4-speed gearbox and 2-speed transfer box, Rover front and rear axles, 4.7:1.

CHASSIS: welded box section steel ladder frame, front and rear beam axles with semi-elliptic springs and telescopic shock absorbers, worm and nut steering; 4-wheel hydraulically operated 10in (25.4cm) drum brakes, 6in (15.2cm) drum transmission hand brake;10 gallon (45 l) fuel tank.16in divided pressed steel wheels with 6.00 x 16 heavy traction tyres.
DIMENSIONS: wheelbase 80in (203cm) or 86in (218cm), front and rear track 50in (127cm), length; 132in (335cm) or 140.5in (357cm), width; 61in (155cm), height; 73.5in (192cm).
PRODUCTION: 8805 (80in); 1100 (86in).

Sloping front wings made the Minervas unique among Series I Land Rovers.

229

Land Rover Santana

In the early 1950s Land Rover was intent on expanding its markets, but finding the Spanish government had erected trade barriers, it faced with approving manufacture from Completely Knocked Down (CKD) kits. The Spanish measures were taken to protect and encourage local industry, and the assembly plan, like many others of its type, was concluded on condition that the proportion of Spanish-sourced components increased over the years until the whole vehicle was actually made in Spain. Accordingly between 1959 and 1990, Land Rovers were produced by Metalurgica de Santa Ana in Spain, under the brand name Land Rover Santana. At first they were made wholly from CKD kits, and had no important differences from their Solihull equivalents, but as time went on Santana Land Rovers became more distinctive. Operations began with Series II models and limited local content. Over the next decade, Santana Land Rovers kept broadly in line with the Solihull varieties, but from 1967, under the terms of the agreement Santana began to build variants of its own. Notable among these were an adaptation of the Forward Control which lacked the sub-frame mounted above the chassis, and was sold as a Land Rover Santana 1300 – a name that reflected its kg payload. This remained in production during the 1970s, when the 88s and 109s switched to Series III. There was also a special 88 for the Spanish military, which drew on Solihull's own Lightweight, with distinctive differences. Following considerable input from Solihull, Santana developed 6-cylinder versions of the Land Rover ohv petrol and diesel engines for the 109 chassis. It introduced the diesel in 1976 for a military 109 and then launched both on the civilian market the following year. From 1978, the 1300 Forward Control was replaced by the 2000, a civilian development of Solihull's military 101 Forward Control that used the Spanish-built 6-cylinder engines. The Series III 88s and 109s continued to resemble

Technical Specifications were generally similar to those for Solihull-built vehicles, but there were three engines unique to Santana. These were the 3.4-litre 6-cylinder petrol and diesel, and the 2.25-litre turbocharged 4-cylinder diesel.

3.4-LITRE PETROL:
6-cylinder, in-line, front; 90.47mm x 88.9mm, 3429cc; compr 8.0:1 (7.0:1 optional); 103bhp (76.8kW) @ 4000rpm; 30bhp/l (22.39kW/l); 177lbft (240Nm) @1500rpm. 2 valves per cylinder; pushrod overhead valves; single chain-driven camshaft; aluminium cylinder head, cast iron block; single carburettor, 7-bearing crankshaft; water-cooled.

3.4-LITRE DIESEL:
6-cylinder, in-line, front; 90.47mm x 88.9mm, 3429cc; compr 23.0:1; 94bhp (70kW) @ 4000rpm; 27.4bhp/l (20.41kW/l); 152lbft (206Nm) @1800rpm. 2 valves per cylinder; pushrod overhead valves; single chain-driven camshaft; aluminium cylinder head, cast iron block; indirect injection, 7-bearing crankshaft; water-cooled.

2.25-LITRE TURBOCHARGED DIESEL:
4-cylinder, in-line, 90.477mm x 88.9mm, 2286cc; compr 20.5:1; 75bhp (55.9kW) @ 4000 rpm; 130lb ft (176.5Nm) @2000 rpm. Cast iron block and head, pushrod overhead valves, belt-driven camshaft; indirect injection with turbocharger; 5-bearing crankshaft; water-cooled.

A turbocharged version of the
2.25-litre diesel engine was unique
to Santana in the 1980s. This 109
betrays a host of detail differences
from the Solihull-built models of
the time.

Land Rover Santana continued

Solihull-built vehicles closely, although Santana went to metric dimensions long before Land Rover did in the UK, causing some problems for interchangeability of parts. Full local manufacture was achieved in the middle 1970s and Santana continued to diversify. From 1980 the Ligero was a civilian leisure-market derivative of the military 88, and the 4-cylinder engines gained five main bearings, like their Solihull equivalents, and gear-driven camshafts, a feature unique to Santana. The Spanish company decided not to follow Solihull's lead in going over to coil springs and permanent four-wheel drive in 1983. Instead the Series III models were upgraded to Series IIIAs with disc front brakes and an optional turbocharged version of the 2.25-litre engine with belt-driven camshaft. Luxury models gained a front end similar to that of the One Ten, but commercial variants retained the Series III front panels. The Series IIIA also had a unique (though not very effective) ventilation system, drawing air through slots cut into the bonnet, and had no ventilator flaps on the bulkhead. The Series IIIA range was expanded in the mid-1980s to include Santana's equivalent of the 127: the 119 Gran Capacidad on a 119-inch wheelbase. Santana developed its own gearboxes too, and the heavy-duty LT85 five-speed used in V8-engined Ninetys and One Tens from Solihull after 1985 was actually made by Santana and exported for fitment in the UK. From 1987, there were new names for the luxury (2500 and 3500) and workhorse (2.5 and 3.5) ranges, and the Land Rover name disappeared from all of them. Two years later, all models were restyled and re-named Series IV types, then from 1990 Land Rover severed its connection with Santana. Production of the Series IV models continued until 1994, and Santana subsequently re-started production with the PS-10 model, a vehicle of its own design which had no links – other than a strong visual resemblance – to Land Rover.

A brochure for the early Series II models shows how these closely resembled their Solihull equivalents, in complete contrast to the 2000 Forward Control, which was Santana's much-modified derivative of the 101 One Tonne military model.

Land Rover – Isuzu-engined Australians

CKD Land Rover assembly in Australia dated back to 1950, and for a long time those assembled by the Pressed Metal Corporation in Sydney closely resembled their UK equivalents. The first local variations came in the 1960s, initially for the Australian military, and by the end of the 1970s the Australian Land Rover importers were in a strong enough position to gain more autonomy. By then diesel engines were vital for 4x4 sales in Australia, but the standard factory-issue engines were not strong enough to compete with the big 6-cylinder offerings from rivals Toyota and Nissan. The Australian operation gained agreement from Solihull to offer a tough Japanese diesel in the One Ten from 1985. This was a 3.9-litre 4-cylinder, built by Isuzu, and it transformed Land Rover sales in Australia during the later 1980s, only making way for the 200 Tdi when the Defender arrived in 1990. This same engine was specified for special One Tens built in Australia to meet the one-tonne class requirements of a military contract called Project Perentie. Among a number of unusual features, these had splayed rear chassis members, allowing the spare wheel to be accommodated under the floor at the rear.

Even more exceptional were the 6x6 vehicles developed for the two-tonne class of Project Perentie. The 6x6 was very much an Australian confection, its rear chassis and leaf-sprung twin rear axles being developed locally in the early 1980s. The military 6x6 always had a widened cab, wide-track axles and a turbocharged version of the Isuzu diesel.

110 3.9D

INTRODUCTION: 1985

BODY: long wheel base station wagon, gross weight from 3050 kg (2950 kg) with ride levelling unit.

ENGINE: Diesel 4-cylinder, in-line, front; 102mm x 118mm, 3856cc; compr 17.0:1; 97bhp (72.3kW) @ 3200rpm; 25.1bhp/l (18.75kW/l); 188lbft (255Nm) @1900rpm.

ENGINE STRUCTURE: 2 valves per cylinder; pushrod overhead valves; single chain-driven camshaft; direct injection; 5-bearing crankshaft; water-cooled.

TRANSMISSION: permanent four wheel drive; 10.5in (26.7cm) hydraulically operated diaphragm spring clutch; LT95 4-speed integrated manual gearbox and transfer box with vacuum operated centre differential lock. Land Rover front banjo axle, Salisbury rear with cast differential housing. 3.54:1 final drive ratio.

CHASSIS: welded steel ladder frame; beam axles with coil springs and telescopic shock absorbers; recirculating ball steering, PAS standard; servo assisted, dual circuit, hydraulic brakes, 11.81in (30cm) front discs, 11in (28cm)

rear drums, 10in (25cm) drum transmission parking brake; 17.5 gal (79.5l) fuel tank; 16in pressed steel wheels with 7.50x16 tyres.

DIMENSIONS: wheelbase 110in (279.4cm); track 58.5in (148.6cm); length 181.1in (459.9cm); width 70.5in (179.0cm); height with levelling unit 80.1in (203.5cm), with normal suspension 81.9in (207.9cm; ground clearance 8.5in (21.5cm); turning circle 42ft (12.8m).

CAPABILITIES Max gradient; 45 deg, approach angle; 50deg, departure angle (max); 34.5deg.

The 6x6 Long Range Patrol Vehicle was developed specifically for the Australian SAS Regiment.

There were troop carriers, mobile workshops, and ambulance derivatives, but the most charismatic was the Long Range Patrol Vehicle developed specifically for the Australian SAS Regiment. There were just 27 of these, each with a special low-profile body, twin side-mounted spare wheels and a 250 cc motorcycle slung across the back for reconnaissance duties. Civilian versions of the 6x6 were made available as well, but these had the standard-width cab and standard-track axles. The 3.5-litre V8 engine was on offer as an alternative to the turbocharged Isuzu diesel. Land Rover attempted to market the Australian 6x6 worldwide as a military vehicle in the early 1990s, but without much success. The collapse of its Australian subsidiary in 1992 cannot have helped, and the last 6x6s were probably a batch for the Australian military built under Project Bushranger in the middle of the decade.

110 HEAVY-DUTY 6X6
INTRODUCTION: 1986
BODY: various, mostly built to special order.
ENGINES: Diesel 4-cylinder, in-line, front; 102mm x 118mm, 3856cc; compr 17.0:1; 97bhp (72.3kW) @ 3200rpm; 25.1bhp/l (18.75kW/l); 188lbft (255Nm) @1900rpm. Military versions 88.5bhp @3200rpm and 180lb ft @ 1900rpm. Turbocharged diesel 4-cylinder, in-line, front; 102mm x 118mm, 3856cc; compr 17.0:1; 121bhp (90.2kW) @ 3000rpm; 31.37bhp/l (23.39kW/l); 231lbft (313.7Nm) @2200rpm. V8 petrol, front; 88.9mm x 71.1mm, 3528cc; compr 8.13:1; 134bhp (100kW) @ 5000rpm; 37.9bhp/l (28.34kW/l); 187lbft (253Nm) @ 2500rpm.
ENGINE STRUCTURE: Diesel, 2 valves per cylinder; pushrod overhead valves; single chain-driven camshaft; direct injection; 5-bearing crankshaft; water-cooled. (V8) pushrod ohv with single central camshaft; aluminium block and heads; twin SU carburettors; Lucas electronic ignition; electric fuel pump; 5 main bearings.

TRANSMISSION: permanent four wheel drive with selectable drive to third axle; 10.5in (267mm) hydraulically operated diaphragm spring clutch; LT95A 4-speed integrated manual gearbox and transfer box with vacuum operated centre differential lock. Land Rover front banjo axle, Salisbury 8HA heavy-duty centre and rear axles. 4.7:1 final drive ratio.
CHASSIS: welded steel ladder frame at front, tubular at rear, all galvanised; front, middle and rear beam axles, with optional wider track; coil springs on front axle, rear twin-axle bogie with leaf springs and load-sharing rocker beam; telescopic shock absorbers all round; worm and peg steering, PAS standard; servo assisted, dual circuit, hydraulic brakes, 11.81in (30cm) front discs, 11in (28cm) drum brakes on centre and rear axles; 10in (25cm) drum transmission parking brake; 17.5gal (79.5l) fuel tank; 16in pressed steel wheels with 7.50x16 tyres.
DIMENSIONS: overall wheelbase 155in (394cm); intermediate wheelbase 119.67in (304cm), track 58.5in (148.6cm) (wide-track 66.85in (169.8cm) for military models) length 236.25in (600.1cm), width over rear cross-members 81.18in (206.2cm), cab height (with wide cab) 81.8in (208.0cm), ground clearance 8.5in (21.5cm), turning circle 67.7ft (17.2m).

The Isuzu engine was used in both
naturally-aspirated and turbocharged
forms. This is the turbocharged
version, seen in a 6x6 LRPV.

Land Rover South African specials

The assembly of Land Rovers from knocked-down kits in South Africa began in October 1963 and ended in December 2005. Like most other KD operations around the world, the South African one built Land Rovers, which were essentially the same as those built at Solihull, with a degree of locally manufactured content. However, it also built some unique models. The earliest of these were probably 109s built for the South African military from the later 1960s into the 1970s. These had an extended rear overhang to provide a bigger load-carrying area. Small numbers were equipped as long-range patrol and raiding vehicles known as Sabres. In the later 1970s, the South African operation developed its own derivatives of the Series III, known as the Series IIIS. These had Stage 1 V8 front-end panels but used a locally-made 2.6-litre 6-cylinder petrol engine called the R6, also used in locally-built Rover saloons, and a 3.8-litre diesel called the ADE4, which was actually a Perkins 4.236 built under licence in South Africa. Between 1996 and 2000, Defender 90s and 110s built in South Africa were made available with the BMW M52 2.8-litre 6-cylinder petrol engine, and were badged as the Defender 2.8i. The South African plant also provided Defender 90s with the 300 Tdi diesel engine for Australia from 2003, Safari tour vehicles were an important element of the South African market. Traditionally aftermarket specialists had manufactured these, but from 2001 Land Rover South Africa introduced a Station Wagon-like 12-seater tour bus on a Defender stretched to a wheelbase of 147in (373.38cm). This small-volume vehicle was homologated only for South Africa, but two examples were also made in the UK for use as tour buses within the grounds of Land Rover's Solihull factory, and a third was ordered for the Freelander plant at Halewood on Merseyside. From 2003, Land Rover South Africa also offered its own in-house model known as the Game Viewer.

R6 ENGINE:
Petrol 6-cylinder, in-line; front; 76.2mm x 95.76mm, 2623cc; compr 8.75:1, 110bhp (82kW)@4750rpm; 41.9bhp/l (31.2kW/l); 149lbft (202Nm) @2200rpm; 2 valves per cylinder; chain-driven single overhead camshaft; aluminium cylinder head, cast iron block; two SU HIF6 carburettors; 7-bearing crankshaft; water-cooled.

ADE4 ENGINE:
Diesel 4-cylinder, in-line; front; 98.4mm x 127mm, 3860cc; compr 16:1, 74bhp (55.2kW) @ 2800rpm, 19.17bhp/l (14.3kW/l); 179lbft (243Nm)@ 1400rpm; 2 valves per cylinder; chain-driven single overhead camshaft; cast iron cylinder head and block; indirect injection; 5-bearing crankshaft; water-cooled.

BMW M52 ENGINE:
Petrol 6-cylinder, in-line; front; 84mm x 84mm, 2793cc; compr 10.2:1, 193bhp (144kW)@5250rpm; 69.1bhp/l (51.5kW/l); 206lbft (279.7Nm) @3950rpm; 4 valves per cylinder; chain-driven twin overhead camshafts; aluminium cylinder head, cast iron block; electronic engine management; 7-bearing crankshaft; water-cooled.

Unique to South Africa: the 130-based Game Viewer, the BMW 2.8-litre petrol engine, and a special grille badge.

DEFENDER130 GAME VIEWER INTRODUCTION 2003.
BODY 10-passenger game viewer with fabric roof and drop-down sides; cab accommodation for 2 or 3 crew; maximum GVW 7716lb (3500kg)
ENGINE Diesel 300 Tdi 4-cylinders, in-line; front; 90.47mm x 97mm, 2495cc; compr 19.5:1; 111bhp (83kW) @ 4000rpm; 44.4bhp/l (33.2kW/l); 195lbft (265Nm) @1800rpm.
ENGINE STRUCTURE 2 overhead valves per cylinder; single belt-driven camshaft; aluminium cylinder head, cast iron block; direct injection, turbocharger with air-to-air intercooler; 5-bearing crankshaft; water-cooled.
TRANSMISSION permanent four-wheel drive; 5-speed R380 manual gearbox, 2-speed LT230 transfer box; final drive ratio 3.54:1. High ratio1.41:1, Low ratio 3.32:1.
CHASSIS separate box-section chassis frame with reinforcements, steel and aluminium panelled body; front and rear beam axles, suspension by coil springs; telescopic dampers; hydraulic servo-assisted brakes; 11.8in (30cm) ventilated front discs, 11.4in (29cm) rear discs; transmission drum parking brake; power-assisted recirculating-ball steering; 16.49gal (75l) fuel tank; 7.50-16in radial-ply tyres on heavy-duty steel rims.
DIMENSIONS wheelbase 127in (322.6cm), track 58.5in (148.6cm); length; 204.3in (518.9cm) approx; height 98.4in (250.0cm) approx; ground clearance 8.5in (21.5cm), turning circle 49.5ft (15.1m).

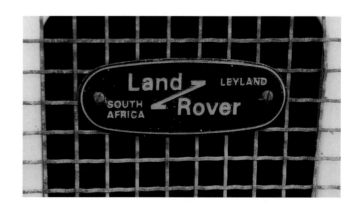

Show and Project Vehicles

Concept SVX built in 1999.

The Range Rover Olympic

Concept vehicles had never been Land Rover's style before the mid-1980s: there had been no need. However the impact made by Japanese manufacturers on the 4x4 market in the 1980s forced Solihull to think again. One result was the introduction of Discovery at the end of the decade, but in the meantime the company looked at the possibilities for a sporty Range Rover. Three prototypes were built. The first was displayed at the 1986 Motor Show at the NEC in Birmingham, partly at least because the 1987 model year changes were not going to be announced until a couple of months later. Birmingham was then in the running as the host city for the Olympic Games, and to capitalise on this Land Rover called it the Range Rover Olympic. Finished in gunmetal grey with red Olympic logos on the doors, the show model had a 2-door body with Recaro sports seats, the apron spoiler from the 1986-model Vogue, and body-colour three-spoke alloy wheels. Like the two later examples the NEC car had a high-compression prototype 3.9-litre V8 engine with a five-speed manual gearbox. The second vehicle was built to a similar specification, but painted red without the logos on the doors, and was known internally as the Kestrel prototype. The final example was built in 1987 and was again painted in gunmetal with red highlights on its side bump-strips. Essential features of the Olympic concept were seen again in the limited production Range Rover CSK introduced in 1990.

INTRODUCED 1986
BODY Two-door estate with five seats; weight estimated 3968lb (1800kg).
ENGINE V8-cylinders, in-line; front; 93.8mm x 71.1mm, 3947cc; compr 9.75:1; 188bhp (140kW) @ 4750rpm; 47.6bhp/l (35.4kW/l); 235lbft (319Nm) @ 2600rpm.
ENGINE STRUCTURE V8, 2 overhead valves per cylinder; central chain-driven camshaft; aluminium cylinder heads and block; Lucas-Bosch fuel injection and management system; 5-bearing crankshaft; water-cooled
TRANSMISSION permanent four-wheel drive; 5-speed manual gearbox; final drive ratio 3.54:1. High ratio 1.19:1, Low ratio 3.32:1.

CHASSIS separate box-section chassis frame, steel and aluminium-panelled body; beam axles front and rear with coil springs; telescopic dampers; hydraulic servo-assisted brakes, front 11.75in (29.8cm) dia discs, rear 11.42in (29.0cm) dia discs; transmission drum parking brake; power-assisted recirculating ball steering; 17.5gal (79.5l) fuel tank; 205-16in radial-ply tyres on alloy rims.
DIMENSIONS wheelbase 100in (254cm); track 58.5in (148cm); length 176in (447cm); width 70in (178cm); height 70in (178cm); ground clearance 7.5in (19cm); turning circle 37ft (11.3m).
PERFORMANCE maximum speed: 110mph; 0-60mph (96kph) 11sec; fuel consumption 18mpg.
PRICE Not put into production.

The third Olympic vehicle had most of the features but lacked the side decals (right) which distinguished the original model produced for Birmingham's Olympic bid.

Land Rover Cariba

The second of Land Rover's concept vehicles was announced in autumn 1987. Based on a V8-engined Ninety, it was prepared by Solihull's Public Relations department on the basis of a redundant press demonstrator, and was the first in a planned series of promotional vehicles. The Land Rover Cariba was conceived as a leisure-market 4x4, to exploit the opportunities opened up by much cheaper Japanese vehicles like the Suzuki SJ. It featured a roll over bar braced to the windscreen header rail, frameless door windows, wide tyres on aftermarket spoked wheels, specially-trimmed Range Rover leather seats at the front with rear seats retrimmed to match, and a unique metallic paint finish based on two contemporary Range Rover options. A military-specification swingaway spare-wheel carrier was mounted to the side-opening rear tailgate, a tough-looking bullbar to the front, and the Cariba was completed by a custom-made soft-top over the cab and a tonneau cover for the back body. The Cariba was given an enthusiastic reception from those members of the press who drove it, and Land Rover investigated the feasibility further with a modified second prototype, painted white and built by Special Vehicle Operations. However, the project was then shelved: the company had its hands full at the time, and was already gearing up for the 1989 introduction of the Discovery. The remaining promotional vehicles planned by the Press Department did not materialise, but the Cariba concept was nevertheless not a wasted opportunity. It paved the way for the NAS Defender 90 soft-tops of the early 1990s and for the 1993 UK-market Defender 90SV.

INTRODUCTION 1987.
BODY Open, 6-seats, with special front roll cage and side-hinged tailgate; special soft top for driving compartment and tonneau cover for rear; estimated weight 3600 lb (1633kg).
ENGINE V8-cylinders, in-line; front; 88.9mm x 71.1mm, 3528cc; compr 8.13:1; 134bhp (100kW) @ 5000rpm; 38.3bhp/l (28.6kW/l); 187lbft (254Nm) @ 2500rpm.
ENGINE STRUCTURE 2-valves per cylinder; overhead valves; central chain-driven camshaft; aluminium cylinder heads and block; two SU carburettors; 5-bearing crankshaft; water-cooled.
TRANSMISSION permanent four-wheel drive; five-speed LT77 manual gearbox, two-speed LT230 transfer box; final drive ratio 3.54:1. High ratio 1.41:1, Low ratio 3.32:1.

CHASSIS separate box-section chassis frame, steel and aluminium panelled body; front and rear beam axles, suspension by coil springs; telescopic dampers; hydraulic servo-assisted brakes; front 11.8in (30cm) dia discs, rear 11in (27.9cm) dia drums; transmission drum parking brake; power-assisted recirculating-ball steering; 12gal (54.5l) fuel tank; 205-16in radial-ply tyres on spoked steel rims.
DIMENSIONS Wheelbase: 92.9in (236cm); track: 58.5in (148.6cm); length: 152.9in (388.3cm); width: 70.5in (179cm); height: 78.7in (200cm) approx; ground clearance: 7.5in (19.1cm); turning circle: 37.8ft (11.5m)
PERFORMANCE Maximum speed: 85mph approx; 0-60mph (96kph) 14sec approx; fuel consumption: estimated 17mpg
PRODUCTION One prototype

The Cariba was breathtakingly adventurous for 1987, but by later standards this special soft-top 90 looks tame.

Land Rover Project SVX

Project SVX was built by Land Rover Special Vehicles and based on the Defender 90. It was prepared for the Frankfurt Motor Show in September 1999 but was not intended as the forerunner of a production vehicle. Its function was to lend some glamour to the Defender range, by now widely regarded as old-fashioned, and to help raise its profile with the BMW Group at the German company's home show. The host vehicle was a Defender 90 Td5, with its engine management system re-mapped to give a 25 percent increase in torque. All the latest features such as ABS, ETC and HDC were incorporated, and the vehicle featured a heavy-duty suspension with special 20in wheels and oversize tyres. The SVX was kitted out as a sharp-looking heavy-duty off-roader for the leisure market. Although it was readily recognisable as a Defender, an unusual alloy grille and aluminium dumb-iron cappings helped to transform the front, and a unique roll over cage incorporated a high-level air intake for the engine. The body was finished in Himalayan Green (a micatallic silver-green colour) with bright anodised cappings, door hinges and other fittings. Both doors and tailgate were removable, and there was no windscreen. The sill finishers were raised to give better ground clearance and the long-range fuel tanks were protected by rock sliders. There was a removable winch with front and rear attachment points, and the interior had individual seats, chequerplate flooring, and alloy knobs for the gear shift levers.

INTRODUCTION 1999
BODY short wheelbase open 4-seats; weight 6220lb (2400kg) approx.
ENGINE: 5-cylinder; 84.5mm x 89mm 2495cc; 124bhp (90kW) @ 4,200 rpm, 276lb ft (375Nm) @ 1950 rpm.
ENGINE STRUCTURE: cast iron block, aluminium cylinder head. Electronically controlled unit injectors, Garrett turbocharger with intercooler.
TRANSMISSION permanent four wheel drive, hydraulic diaphragm spring clutch; 23.5cm (9.25in) dia; R380 5-speed manual gearbox; LT230Q 2-speed transfer box with lever operated centre differential lock. Land Rover front and rear banjo axles; 3.54:1 final drive.

CHASSIS welded steel ladder frame, front and rear beam axles with coil springs and telescopic shock absorbers; recirculating ball steering with PAS; servo assisted, dual circuit, hydraulic brakes. 11.81in (30.0cm) ventilated front discs, 11.42in (29.0cm) rear discs. 25.4cm (10in) drum transmission parking brake; twin long-range fuel tanks; 20in alloy wheels with special tyres.
DIMENSIONS wheelbase 92.9in (236cm), track widened from standard; width 70.5in (179.0 cm); ground clearance 10.5in (266cm) estimated
PRICE: Not put into production.

Range Stormer

The Range Stormer exhibited at the Detroit Motor Show in January 2004 was Land Rover's most dramatic concept vehicle yet. Its main function was to arouse public interest, especially in the USA on behalf of owners Ford, in a more sporty Land Rover ahead of the Range Rover Sport's introduction a year later. However, there was little of the Range Rover Sport about the Range Stormer. The one-off concept car was built on a left hand drive Range Rover 38A chassis, which conveniently shared its 108.1in wheelbase with the forthcoming Sport. It also had the 38A's 4.6-litre V8 petrol engine and four-speed automatic gearbox, neither of which would appear in the production model. The Range Stormer was in fact designed after the Range Rover Sport had been signed off for production, and it was in many ways an exaggeration of what was to be expected. Its bright orange paintwork did reappear on the First Edition Supercharged models of the Sport, and the Range Stormer featured the swivelling Bi-Xenon Adaptive Front Lighting, which would appear on the Sport and the Discovery 3. It also offered the world a first glimpse of the forthcoming Terrain Response system – although in fact only the rotary control was present on the concept car. The Range Stormer's 22-inch alloy wheels were a couple of sizes larger than anything that would be seen on production models. Its full-length glass roof and 2-door configuration were imaginative but also not production items, and the ingenious door arrangement was designed as an effective show-stopper rather than a practical proposition. It split the door into two sections horizontally, the lower part folding down to make a step and the upper part hinging forwards, scissors-fashion, to allow entry and exit.

INTRODUCTION: 2004.
BODY: 2-door, 5-seats estate.
ENGINE: Petrol V8-cylinders; front; 93.98mm x 82mm, 4554cc; compr 9.35:1; 215bhp (160kW) @ 4750rpm; 47.2bhp/l (35.1kW/l); 294lbft (399Nm) @2600rpm.
ENGINE STRUCTURE: 2 overhead valves per cylinder; central chain-driven camshaft; aluminium cylinder heads and block; Lucas-Bosch fuel injection and engine management; 5-bearing crankshaft; water-cooled
TRANSMISSION permanent four-wheel drive; four-speed ZF automatic gearbox, 2-speed LT230 transfer box; final drive 3.54:1. High ratio1.22:1, Low ratio 3.27:1.

CHASSIS separate box-section frame; special body shell of steel, aluminium and glass panels; front and rear beam axles, suspension by coil springs; telescopic dampers; hydraulic servo-assisted brakes; 11.7in (29.7cm) dia front ventilated discs, 12in (30.5cm) dia solid rear discs; transmission drum parking brake; power-assisted recirculating-ball steering; 22gal (100l) fuel tank; 265/45-22 radial-ply tyres on special alloy rims.
DIMENSIONS wheelbase 108.1in (274.5cm); track, front 60.6in (154.0cm), rear 60.2in (153.0cm); length 185.5in (471.3cm) approx; width 87.7in (222.8cm) approx.
PRICE: Not put on sale.

Expeditions and Motorsport

One of the WRC Freelanders was later turned
into a Course Safety Car for the British Rally
Championship.

Land Rover 1955 Oxford and Cambridge Far Eastern Expedition

The Rover Company recognised the publicity value of sponsoring expeditions using Land Rover vehicles, at least during the 1950s although it entered a caveat in its Guide to Land Rover Expeditions, when entreaties for support became intolerable. However it did lend its support, and sometimes its vehicles, to the more ambitious ones of which the three Oxford and Cambridge Expeditions between 1955 and 1958 were the most significant. Best known is probably the one that set out in September 1955 and became the subject of a successful book, First Overland, written by one of the participants, Tim Slessor. Strictly the Oxford and Cambridge Far Eastern Expedition, it was composed of six graduates from the two universities, who aimed to drive overland from London to Singapore, in a pair of 86in Land Rovers they had persuaded Rover to lend them. This was a more ambitious undertaking in the mid-1950s than it might have been later. An overland journey all the way to Singapore had not been achieved before, owing to the difficulty of forcing a route through the jungles of Burma and Southern Thailand. The six adventurers carried out research into irrigation developments in Pakistan and India, and into the mineral resources of Upper Burma. The Royal Geographical Society, together with other foundations funded part of the cost of this, while a number of commercial sponsors also put up money to pledge success. For the Rover Company there was a double benefit. Not only did the exploits of adventurers like these spread the fame of the Land Rover but also reports on their return provided valuable feedback on how the vehicles behaved in tough conditions. Those were the days before manufacturers routinely took pre-production models to inhospitable corners of the earth for development testing.

INTRODUCTION The 86in Station Wagon was introduced in 1954
BODY All-steel station wagon with aluminium fittings; weight 4032lbs (1829kg) plus expedition equipment.
ENGINE 4-cylinder in line, front 77.8mm x 105mm, 1997cc. 52bhp (38.8kW) @ 4000 rpm, 101lb ft (137Nm) @1500 rpm, compression 7.1:1.
ENGINE STRUCTURE cast iron block and cylinder head, overhead inlet, side exhaust valves, chain-driven camshaft, pushrods and rockers, 3-bearing crankshaft.
TRANSMISSION selectable four wheel drive, hydraulic single dry plate clutch 9in (22.8cm) dia. Rover 4-speed gearbox and 2-speed transfer box, Rover front and rear axles, 4.7:1.

CHASSIS welded box section steel ladder frame, front and rear beam axles with semi-elliptic springs and telescopic shock absorbers, worm and nut steering. 4-wheel hydraulically operated 10in (25.4cm) drum brakes, 6in (15.2cm) drum transmission hand brake.10 gallon (45l) fuel tank.16in pressed steel wheels with 6.00 x 16 heavy traction tyres.
DIMENSIONS wheelbase 86in (218cm), track 50in (127cm), length; 132in (335cm), width; 62.5in (159cm), height; 76in (193cm).

Letting the Land Rover take the strain - London to Singapore in 1955.

Darien Gap Range Rovers

Between the sub-continents of North and South America, the Darien Isthmus was an area of swamp and jungle, which had defeated all attempts to build a road through it. This lack of communication had been a hindrance to trade, as well as the development of the adjacent countries. The Darien Action Committee was established, to promote attempts to create a pan-American highway linking the north and south parts of the continent, and in 1970 the British Trans-Americas Expedition Committee examined the feasibility of forcing a way with vehicles through this Darien Gap as it was called. The aim was to draw attention to the need for a road by gathering publicity for the expedition. It was an ideal opportunity, and one Rover seized as a means of promoting the then-new Range Rover to show that it was not only a luxury saloon, but also as tough and versatile as the traditional Land Rover. Two otherwise standard examples were therefore kitted out with a variety of expedition equipment and prepared for the task. The rear bench rear seats were removed to make room for utensils and paraphernalia, and a single reclining seat from a contemporary Rover P6 saloon was added, complete with headrest, to give one member of the crew a chance of sleeping on the move. Further glamour was lent to the project by turning it into a drive from Alaska to Cape Horn, along the full length of the American continent, crewed by teams drawn from the armed forces. The vehicles set out from Anchorage, Alaska at the head of the Cook inlet 290miles (465km) from the Canadian border in December 1971, and reached Ushuaia, the capital of Tierra del Fuego, in June 1972. Most of the 18,000mile (29,000km) journey was on metalled roads, but the crucial element of it – and the one for which the expedition is remembered – was the crossing of a 250mile (400km) region of almost impenetrable swamp and jungle. This included a scientific programme and occupied 99 days, and the two

Range Rovers emerged intact, although they suffered major problems on the way. Differential and half-shaft breakages had been caused by the use of over-sized swamp tyres. Plans to cross in the dry season were wrecked by late tropical rains, flooding the jungle tracks. An 88in Land Rover, bought second-hand in Panama, had to be flown in to act as a recce vehicle, one of a number of ploys including aluminium ladders and inflatable boats to cross rivers, which had to be adopted to secure the expedition's success. Both of the Darien Gap Range Rovers were preserved, although neither on its original chassis. When they returned to Solihull in 1972, their frames were removed and cut up to see how they had withstood the ordeal.

INTRODUCTION: Range Rover introduced June 1970
BODY: 3-door, 3-seat; weight 3800lb (1724kg) approximately, plus expedition equipment
ENGINE: V8 petrol; 88.9mm x 71.1mm; 3528cc; compression ratio 8.25:1; 135bhp (100.67kW) @ 4750 rpm; 38.26bhp/l (28.53kW/l); 185lb ft (248Nm) @ 2500 rpm
ENGINE STRUCTURE: pushrod ohv with single central chain-driven camshaft; aluminium alloy LM25 block and cylinder heads; two Zenith/Stromberg CD2 carburettors; Lucas 35DM8 distributor; mechanical fuel pump; 5-bearing crankshaft.
TRANSMISSION permanent four wheel drive; 10.5in (26.7cm) hydraulically operated diaphragm spring clutch; LT95 integrated 4-speed main gearbox and 2-speed transfer box with vacuum-operated centre differential lock; Rover front and rear banjo axles; 3.54:1 final drive ratio; low ratio 3.32:1, high 1.174:1.

CHASSIS welded steel ladder frame; front and rear live axles with coil springs and telescopic dampers, located by radius arms and Panhard rod; rear located by radius arms, support rods and central A-frame with Boge Hydromat strut; recirculating ball steering; dual circuit, servo-assisted hydraulic brakes, 11.75in (29.8cm) front discs, four-piston callipers, 11.42in (29.0cm) rear discs, 2-piston callipers, 10in (25.4cm) drum transmission parking brake; 19gal (86 litre) fuel tank; 16in pressed styled steel wheels with 205x16 tyres; wide swamp tyres also used on this expedition.
DIMENSIONS wheelbase 100in (254cm); front and rear track 58.5in (148cm); length; 176in (447cm); width 70in (178cm); height 70in (178cm); ground clearance 7.5in (19cm); turning circle 37ft (11.3m) with standard wheel and tyre set-up.
PERFORMANCE 0-60mph (96kph); 12.9 sec, top speed; 102mph. Approach angle; 45 deg, departure angle; 33 deg.
PRICE £2134.37 (inc purchase tax) for standard model, October 1971.

The Darien
Breakthrough

The Joint Services Expedition

The great Land Rover expedition tradition continued in 1975, when a team drawn from the armed forces took four early production 101 One-tonne models on the Joint Services Expedition across Africa. The lead vehicle was the first proper production 101, the new military Land Rover, which would not enter service until the following year. This was the first major trial of the 101 by its end-users, and proved a success even though it showed up a number of minor faults. The expedition, led by RAF Squadron Leader Tom Sheppard, took 100 days to cross the continent from the Atlantic coast on the West to the Red Sea on the East, covering 7494 miles (12,054 kilometres). The 101 had been developed with a facility for driving a powered-axle trailer, largely because the gun carriage of the new 105mm howitzer was originally planned with one. The British military had then taken an interest in the development of a powered-axle cargo trailer as well, an initiative Land Rover had taken as long ago as 1959 in conjunction with accessory firm Scottorn. Three of the four 101s were fitted with the necessary hardware to tow a powered-axle trailer, and two prototypes, specially refurbished by Rubery Owen which had taken over the project, were taken on the trip to carry the expedition's supplies. The powered-axle trailer offered additional traction in difficult going, in effect providing the vehicle-and-trailer combination a 6x6 capability. However, no production followed: Land Rover people owned up to one demonstration for the military, when a prototype trailer caused the towing vehicle to overturn, which must have discouraged the top brass from pursuing the project. The 105mm gun entered production with a conventional unpowered gun carriage.

INTRODUCTION 1972; into service 1975; produced to 1978.
BODY Soft-top GS (other 101 variants qv); weight from 4040lb (1832kg)
ENGINE V8-cylinders, in-line; front; 88.9mm x 71.1mm, 3528cc; compr 8.5:1; 128bhp (94kW) @ 5000rpm; 36.3bhp/l (26.6kW/l); 185lbft (251Nm) @ 2500rpm.
ENGINE STRUCTURE V8, 2-overhead valves per cylinder; central chain-driven camshaft; aluminium cylinder heads and block; two Zenith-Stromberg carburettors; 5-bearing crankshaft; water-cooled.
TRANSMISSION permanent four-wheel drive; 4-speed manual gearbox; final drive ratio 5.57:1. High ratio 1.174:1, Low ratio 3.321:1. Three expedition vehicles equipped with powered trailer drive.

CHASSIS separate box-section frame, steel and aluminium-panelled body; beam axles, with taper leaf springs and telescopic dampers; hydraulic servo-assisted drum brakes, 11in (28cm) dia; transmission drum parking brake; recirculating ball steering; 24gal (109l) fuel tank; 9.00-16in cross-ply tyres, on steel rims.
DIMENSIONS wheelbase: 101in (256.5cm); track, front 60in (152.4cm), rear 61in (154.9cm); length: 162.5in (412.7cm); width: 72.5in (184.2cm); height: 88in (223.5cm); ground clearance: 10in (254cm); turning circle: 37ft (11.3m) approx.
PERFORMANCE maximum speed: 75mph (120kph); 0-60mph (96kph) 17sec approx: fuel consumption: 14mpg (4.96km/l) approx.
PRICE Not sold on the civilian market.
PRODUCTION 2669 (all 101s)

The four Joint Services Expedition 101s lined up before embarking on their epic journey.

Range Rovers in the Paris-Dakar Rally

The gruelling Paris-Dakar Rally became something of a legend, a test of man and machine against the deserts of Africa over special stages in which only the fittest survived. Typically lasting between two and three weeks and covering up to 10,000 kilometres (6213 miles), it had a variety of classes for different vehicles. From the start it was a natural showcase for the Range Rover. A privately-entered Range Rover won its class on the very first in 1979, and throughout the 1980s Range Rovers were always among the competitors, taking podium places in the overall results in 1981 (first), 1983 (third), 1984 and 1987 (second) and 1988 (third). Some of the greatest names in African rallying sat behind the wheel of a Range Rover. However Land Rover remained ambivalent about its participation. There was never a proper factory team, until as the Range Rover came under pressure from new rivals in the early 1980s, the company decided it needed a rallying programme to strengthen its position in the market. The programme was conducted through Land Rover's French importers, allowing Solihull to maintain a discreet distance from the action. When it won Land Rover could reap the benefit; if it lost, it could be somebody else's fault. Between 1983 and 1986, there was semi-overt Land Rover support for the French Halt'Up! rally preparation specialists, and the Range Rovers that ran in the Dakar were readily recognisable. However, it became increasingly clear to Halt'Up! that to remain competitive their Range Rovers needed to be heavily modified, particularly against the lavishly-funded works teams from other 4x4 manufacturers. A longer wheelbase was needed so one was developed. An X-trac type replaced the standard gearbox, which had always given trouble on the Dakar, and the bodywork became a more aerodynamic composite of carbon fibre and Kevlar, resembling the Range Rover only in outline. Two more podium places with these heavily-modified vehicles

persuaded Land Rover UK to take a serious look at entering a proper works Range Rover team in the Dakar. A feasibility prototype (registered F201 NWK) was prepared during 1989 to meet the Group T regulations, with a 3.9-litre V8 engine prepared in the UK by John Eales, whose 4.2-litre V8s had featured in the 1988 Halt'Up! entries. However, no works team was ever sanctioned. Land Rover had too much on its plate during 1989 and 1990 with the worldwide rollout of the brand-new Discovery. The Range Rover was also scheduled to move further up into the luxury market, and the general feeling was that a competitions programme would not help its sales.

The Halt'Up! Range Rovers of the later 1980s were specially modified to suit long-distance desert rallies.

The Camel Trophy

Land Rover's close association with the annual Camel Trophy, over a period of 17 years, enhanced the company's image. The worldwide coverage it gained in the press and on television reminded potential buyers of the toughness inherent in Land Rovers, and it gave them a vital dash of glamour and adventure. During the 1990s the Trophy caught the mood of the times effectively by adding in tasks of environmental importance. It was only when the image of the Camel Trophy seemed to conflict with Land Rover's Tread Lightly philosophy, which actively discouraged damage to the environment, that the company withdrew its support. The first Camel Trophy was run in 1980 and had only three competing teams, all from West Germany, and all driving Jeeps. Its organisers obtained sponsorship from the makers of Camel cigarettes, then from 1981 Land Rover became a major co-sponsor, and provided the vehicles. Thereafter the Camel Trophy became intimately associated with Land Rover and everything the company and its products stood for, and Land Rover became its driving force as the makers of Camel cigarettes stepped back, and handed over to their associated company Worldwide Brands Inc. In essence the Camel Trophy was an international competition, with teams of two people driving off-road in extreme conditions. Vehicles had to be winched through near-impossible jungle terrain, transported across rivers on rafts made from whatever tree-trunks came to hand, and manhandled where necessary. Yet despite the element of competition between teams, the Camel Trophy was not an aggressive event. There were also awards for team spirit and for helping fellow-competitors in difficulties. There was no British team before 1986; the rationale was that since Camel cigarettes were not sold in Britain there was no publicity benrefit. Nor was there a team from the USA until the late 1980s, when Land Rover was mounting a big sales

Team vehicles and location of the events, year by year:

1981	Range Rover 2-door V8, Sumatra
1982	Range Rover 2-door V8, Papua, New Guinea
1983	Series III 88 Station Wagon, Zaire
1984	One Ten diesel Station Wagon, Brazil
1985	Ninety diesel Station Wagon, Borneo
1986	Ninety diesel Station Wagon, Australia
1987	Range Rover 4-door Turbo D, Madagascar
1988	One Ten Diesel Turbo, Sulawesi
1989	One Ten Station Wagon, Brazil (Amazon)
1990	Discovery 200 Tdi 3-door, Siberia
1991	Discovery 200 Tdi 5-door, Tanzania-Burundi
1992	Discovery 200 Tdi 5-door, Guyana
1993	Discovery 200 Tdi 5-door Sabah, Malaysia
1994	Discovery 200 Tdi 5-door, Argentina-Paraguay-Chile
1995	Discovery 300 Tdi 5-door, Mundo Maya
1996	Discovery 300 Tdi 5-door, Kalimantan
1997	Discovery 300 Tdi 5-door, Mongolia
1998	Freelander diesel 5-door, Chile and Argentina.

A pre-production Freelander heads Defenders in a recce group before the 1998 Camel Trophy.

push for the Range Rover in North America. It was only in its final years that the Camel Trophy embraced tasks that were not Land Rover-dependent, such as mountain biking and kayaking, and most onlookers thought the event the poorer for it. Land Rover ensured that the world's press was always on hand to report on the adventure, so the company gained maximum publicity advantage from what turned out to be a very expensive PR exercise. Each year Land Rover provided both the team vehicles (one for each of the 12-18 nations that took part) and the support vehicles to carry medics, supplies, PR staff, photographers, film crews, and media representatives. Most years the choice fell on the latest models, although the second-generation Range Rover was never considered appropriate. The entries were essentially to production specification but were always prepared by the Special Projects Division (later Special Vehicle Operations and then Land Rover Special Vehicles) with accessories such as heavy-duty roof racks, winches, additional lighting, underbody protection and internal roll cages. They were painted Camel Trophy Yellow, which was actually an old British Motor Corporation colour, originally known as Sandglow.

Probably the most fondly-remembered aspect of the Camel Trophy was its drama. Later environmental sensitivities made pictures like this one less powerful as a promotional tool.

The Land Rover G4 Challenge

Land Rover conceived the G4 Challenge as a marketing exercise to catch the attention of potential customers who had not so far shown interest in the marque. It was designed as the backdrop to the introduction of an entire range of new models in the first few years of the 21st century, namely the third-generation Range Rover (2002); the facelifted Freelander (2003); the Discovery 3 (2004); the Range Rover Sport (2005); and the second-generation Freelander (2006). It was also important in the run-up to an all-new Defender later in the decade. The G4 Challenge had some similarities to the Camel Trophy, and was clearly intended to emulate its impressive capacity to gather publicity. However it could not be the same as the Camel Trophy; worldwide environmental concerns and sensitivities had changed, and the G4 Challenge was altogether more moderate in its approach to the environment. Individuals representing competing nations were chosen after a gruelling round of selection trials, but the event was as much about such skills as orienteering, trail running, mountain biking, kayaking and abseiling as it was about driving Land Rovers and off-road navigation. Held in four different areas of the world (hence the 4; the G stood for Global), the event did feature driving events but these, like many of the more traditional sporting competitions, were carefully stage-managed for maximum publicity effect. The first G4 Challenge was held in 2003; the second in 2006. Standard production-line models were specially equipped with roof racks, additional lighting, winches and the latest Goodyear tyres - though without roll cages. All were painted a distinctive Tangiers Orange and emblazoned with distinctive livery. For 2003 a total of 154 vehicles was prepared, including four prototypes and six workshop-equipped Discoverys, and different models were used on various legs of the event. This was a ploy to give most exposure to the model best suited to the sales territory. The 2003 event featured Defenders, Freelanders, Series II Discoverys and Range Rovers. Special-edition G4 Challenge Defenders and Discoverys were announced that autumn for sale in various countries. The 2006 line-up included Freelanders despite its impending replacement by a new model by the year's end.

The 2003 G4 Challenge (right) was
followed by special-edition models
(left) available through the
showrooms.

Land Rover Freelander Rally Cars

Six Freelander V6s were prepared as reconnaissance vehicles to support the Ford World Rally Championship team's entry in the July 2001 Kenyan Safari Rally. Afterwards they were put to different uses: one became a Course Safety Car for the British Rally Championship, while most of the others were equipped with a 2004-style facelift and used to promote the 2004 Freelander press launch. Two were to give media representatives a taste of forest rallying. All were prepared by M-Sport, who built the Ford Focus WRC cars, with seam-welded bodyshells strengthened in key areas, and a custom-built M-Sport roll cage integrated into the main stress points. Additional strengthening also went into the framework, and strut braces were fitted front and rear.

The front carried a safari-specification brush bar, with mounts for additional spotlights, and this doubled as a support for a full-length aluminium sump guard. Kevlar sill protectors and a rear differential guard completed the underbody protection. To combat the high underbonnet temperatures expected in Africa, an engine space vent and additional transmission oil coolers were fitted. A new air-box and external snorkel were added, and the windows covered with reflective film to reduce cabin temperatures. Bespoke wheels from OZ Racing ran on Pirelli tyres. The suspension was fully adjustable race-car fashion, with strengthened links, cross-members and arms, while engine and gearbox mountings were also toughened up. A 120-litre bag-type fuel tank with a carbon cover in the back increased the range, and twin dry-cell batteries improved the weight distribution. The occupants had Sparco carbon kevlar seats with six-point harnesses, as used in the Focus rally cars, and the dashboard had an additional anti-glare coating. Navigation equipment was included, together with a fridge to keep the crew's drinks cold.

INTRODUCTION 2001
BODY 5-door estate with 2 seats only; weight not known
ENGINE petrol; 90deg V6; front; transverse; 80.0mm x 82.8mm, 2497cc; compr 10.5:1; 177bhp (132kW) @ 6250rpm; 70.9bhp/l (52.9kW/l); 177lbft (240Nm) @ 4000rpm.
ENGINE STRUCTURE: 4-valves per cylinder, twin-overhead camshafts driven by cogged belt; aluminium cylinder heads and block; Bosch fuel injection and engine management; 4-bearing crankshaft; water-cooled
TRANSMISSION permanent four-wheel-drive; diaphragm spring competition clutch; special 6-speed manual competition gearbox; final drive 3.66:1

CHASSIS steel monocoque structure with integrated roll cage, adjustable independent front suspension by coil springs, MacPherson struts, anti-roll bar; adjustable independent rear suspension by coil springs, MacPherson struts, wishbones and links, anti-roll bar; telescopic dampers; hydraulic servo-assisted brakes with ABS anti-lock, front 10.9in (27.7cm) dia ventilated discs, rear 10in (25.4cm) dia drums; power-assisted rack-and-pinion steering; 26.4 gal (120l) bag-type fuel tank; competition tyres on alloy rims.
DIMENSIONS wheelbase 100.5in (255.5cm); track front 60.4in (153.4cm), rear 60.8in (154.5cm); length175in (444.5cm); width 71in (180.5cm); height; 69.2in (175.7cm); ground clearance; 7.9in (20cm) approx; turning circle 38ft (11.6m).
PERFORMANCE: maximum speed113mph (181.39kph); 0-60mph (96kph) 10.1 sec; fuel consumption (for road car equivalent) 22.7mpg (12.44l/100km)
PRICE: Not available for sale.

The WRC recce Freelanders had the most powerful V6 engine option and were specially prepared for their role.

Bowler Wildcat

The Bowler Wildcat was a specialist off-road competition vehicle built up from components. Its distant ancestor, the first Bowler, was a private venture in 1981 on the basis of an 80in Land Rover, and over the following years Drew Bowler built up a thriving business around these modified vehicles. Experience led his company to develop its own skeleton chassis on a 100in wheelbase, and in 1996 this became the standard Bowler. The basic machine had Land Rover running gear and engine, and could be completed to meet a buyer's requirements. Four years later the Bowler Wildcat 200 had a 106in wheelbase and Discovery Series II axles. This was offered with a choice of Land Rover V8 or Td5 engine with five-speed manual or automatic gearbox. The Wildcat 200 maintained a clear visual relationship to the Defender, using aluminium and composite panels, on a combined space-frame and roll cage fabricated from T45 tubing. It quickly gained a reputation for durability and reliability in the toughest international rally-raid events. To the surprise of many, Land Rover Ltd gave Team Bowler, the Bowler factory's own three-car team its support for the 2002-2003 international rally season. The vehicles were painted in full Land Rover corporate livery and were entered into a number of events in Australia, France, Italy, Russia and the United Arab Emirates. One was fitted with a version of the Td5 engine developed to deliver 215 bhp; the other two had TVR 4-litre V8 petrol engines. These and other vehicles running with different sponsorship under the Team Bowler organisation recorded creditable finishes in the 2003 rally season, although there was to be no further sponsorship from Land Rover. Nevertheless the Bowlers had made an indelible mark on the international rally-raid scene. The Bowler Wildcat was a specialised competition vehicle, built to order, and no two were exactly the same.

INTRODUCTION: 2000.
BODY: Space-frame with aluminium and composite outer panels; weight not disclosed but dependent on specification.
ENGINE: to customer's choice; options included 4.0-litre and 4.6-litre Range Rover V8s and 2.5-litre Land Rover Td5 turbocharged diesel.
TRANSMISSION permanent four-wheel drive; 5-speed R380 manual gearbox or 4-speed ZF automatic gearbox, 2-speed LT230 transfer box, ratios for transfer box and final drive to customer's choice.

CHASSIS front and rear beam axles, suspension by coil springs; telescopic dampers; hydraulic servo-assisted brakes; disc brakes on all four wheels; transmission drum parking brake; power-assisted recirculating-ball steering; various fuel tank options to suit purpose; 16in competition tyres on steel or alloy rims.
DIMENSIONS: Wheelbase: 106in (296.2cm); track front; 60.6in (154cm) track rear; 61.4in (156cm); length, width and height not stated.
PRICE: In 2005, the three different models of Bowler Wildcat were the National (with 4.0-litre V8 petrol engine and 5-speed gearbox) at £34,500; the European Rally-Raid Specification at £39,800; and the African Rally-Raid Specification, at £49,000.

No two Wildcats were exactly the same; this one ran with Land Rover sponsorship in the 2002-2003 rallying season.

Range Rover

1968 Range Rover Velar prototypes

The Range Rover of the 1970s, like the Land Rover of the 1940s, was first of all an inspiration and later became a matter of expediency. In the 1960s William Martin-Hurst set up a market research department under economist Graham Bannock, who put forward a view that Land Rover markets could only expand at their leisure, and by implication higher-priced end. Sales to the military were about constant, farmers and light commercial users were buying steadily, but an emerging generation of private buyers were looking for a car that would tow a boat, caravan or horse-box, and they were not going for harshly sprung Land Rovers. In 1965, following a visit to the United States, Bannock convinced Rover management of the growing market for what would become Sports Utility Vehicles (SUVs). Here sophisticated off-road players were already in contention, such as the Jeep Wagoneer, International Harvester Scout and Ford Bronco. Spen King was in charge of Rover's new vehicle projects, and began work on new ideas in the middle of 1966. His team included chassis designer Gordon Bashford, who had worked on the original Land Rover, and almost every Rover car since 1945. He also recruited Geof Miller an expert in four wheel drive transmissions as project engineer.

Soon after Harold Wilson's government was re-elected in April 1966 the project took on a degree of urgency. The new administration imposed a standstill on wages and dividends, prices were frozen, and purchase tax rates increased, all affecting car sales. Cuts were imposed on overseas holiday allowances and curbs on hire purchase made things worse. The following year came the decision to withdraw militarily from East of Suez, and by November a financial crisis led to the devaluation of the pound. The immediate effect was cuts in defence spending. Contracts from the Ministry of Defence (MoD) for Land Rovers were reduced and the management grew anxious. Spen King's response was robust. He proposed a vehicle combining the comfort of a road car with a Land Rover's ability off-road, coinciding with the advice Bannock had already provided. A trial drive of a Rover 2000 across a bumpy field convinced King that the way to tackle the SUV market was with long-travel low rate coil spring suspension. A Land Rover with a V8 had pretty well been decided upon by the middle 1960s, so the ingredients of the Range Rover were falling into place.

King's principal challenge was to a long-held belief within the company, that the harsh ride, imposed by stiff semi-elliptic springs, was not only inescapable but also probably desirable. It slowed drivers down, keeping them from destroying fragile suspensions, wheels, and tyres. King persisted in his conviction that long-travel suspension was essential to provide a soft ride on the road, together with better articulation over uneven ground, keeping all the wheels in contact with it. Wheels that lost touch could have no traction.

Miller had Land Rover projects already in hand when he came into the project. A 2-door body was designed around a Rover saloon-sized interior and, following the example of the 2000, had a strong skeletal steel frame to which unstressed aluminium panels could be bolted. It would be self-supporting, safe in the event of a collision, and mounted on a rigid box-section frame stiffer than a 4-door, with all the structural integrity expected of a Land Rover. It was important that it could be easily adapted for construction overseas, which was much in King's mind, so for Completely Knocked Down (CKD) production King produced a box-like shape, using flattish panels that could be bolted on last. A variety of engines was examined, including a 6-cylinder 2.6litre, a 4-cylinder 2.25litre, and a Buick cast-iron V6 with

good low-speed pulling power, which had been used by Land Rover in testing during 1964. However the 3.5litre aluminium V8, another ex-Buick that Rover used in cars, found favour because it was light, compact and powerful. Land Rover gearbox and transfer drives were tried with selectable four wheel drive, however the power and torque of the V8 produced wheel spin, especially at the front along with axle tramp. Furthermore subjecting standard Land Rover axles to more power and torque than they had ever dealt with before would, during spells in two wheel drive, lead to failures. Spen King rejected heavy-duty axles; their greater unsprung weight would endanger his ambitions for handling and roadholding. Accordingly Miller resuscitated a prototype permanent four wheel drive transmission from a project dating back to the 1950s, and fitted it into an experimental 88in Land Rover, with a V8 engine. Tests showed this worked so transmission engineer Frank Shaw was given the job of designing a centre differential to allow front and rear axles to run at different speeds.

Among the other initiatives explored was a single box, 6-speed gearbox, but it was decided that one unit incorporating a 2-speed transfer box might have something in common with the Land Rover 1-Tonne Forward Control, then in progress for the MoD. Different sorts of suspension were studied, including multi-leaf springs similar to those on Land Rovers, tapered-leaf, and single-leaf springs under development for the Forward Control. However only long travel coil springs provided the right combination of on-road handling, and off-road articulation. One key ingredient was the Boge Hydromat self-levelling strut, spotted by King and Bashford on a Mercedes-Benz at a motor show, which promised consistent handling under all loads. Some of the original suspension layouts based on the Ford Bronco were developed into the characteristic C-Spanner radius arms and Panhard rod arrangement.

Since the styling department was preoccupied with cars, it was left to Phil Jackson the team's body engineer, to create prototypes using a number of proprietary components including Ford Transit bumpers. Early examples were demonstrated to executives from Leyland Motors, contemplating the 1967 merger with Rover, highlighting the abilities of Roger Crathorne who was involved in long distance hot-weather tests in the Sahara and cold-weather trials at minus 40deg in Alaska. Within the company the project was known sometimes as the Land Rover 100 Inch Station Wagon or sometimes Interim Station Wagon. When the styling department did get involved, it was so uncertain about what to call the thing that an experimental buck was labelled Road Rover, in homage to the Land Rover experiment of the 1950s.

In order to conceal their identity, prototypes bore the name Velar, a company created for secret trials of the Rover P6BS sports car. Mike Dunn at Alvis, where it was being developed, had the inspiration of using a Spanish-Italian word for hidden or secret, and VELAR was inscribed across the front. This was not a new ploy at Rover. During development testing in the 1960s, the P6 saloon was badged as a Talago, a name made up from the initials of T L Gawronski, the project engineer. In the same way as Velar, a Talago Motor Company was registered, so that the identity could be inscribed on the tax disc. Driving pre-production prototypes of the Talago before its launch as the Rover 2000, *The Motor* was surprised how little stir they created. "Most people probably summed it up as Italian, expensive, and unattainable," was as profound a compliment as could be conferred in 1963. *The Motor* would be just as adulatory of the approaching Range Rover.

The proportions of Spen King's prototype (see previous page) were pure Range Rover, square, practical, scarcely aerodynamic and perhaps a little severe especially in front. David Bache prettied it subtly without losing its essential rectitude. Pre-production prototypes above and right tentatively explore grassland not too far off-road.

1970 Range Rover

The first production Range Rover seemed a technological wonder. Permanent four wheel drive, dual line disc brakes, and lightweight V8 engines were unusual enough on road cars; thoroughly radical for anything that went off road. The body kept the proportions of the prototypes, King standing firm against David Bache's inclinations for an estate car appearance, in view of the practicalities of overseas assembly. Bache's design team did refine its lines, subtly recessing the sides to emphasise its length, adding castellations to the corners of the bonnet and refining the front. Bache also did a commendable job on the interior, which emerged as stylish yet practical, although due to pressure over getting it finished on time it scarcely matched the luxury that had been envisioned. The plastic-covered seats and floor coverings were extremely practical, and Land Rover made a virtue of necessity, suggesting they could be hosed-down when they got dirty. Most of the body panels were aluminium, except the bonnet, which was steel so that it could be pressed more easily to the deeply formed sections at the front. The lower tailgate too was a steel pressing. The V8 engine was modified for a cross-country role, with Zenith/Stromberg carburettors instead of SUs, a raised water pump lifting the fan clear of water for deep wading, and there was an aperture for a starting handle. The carburettor change was necessary because the Stromberg float chamber was concentric round the needle, so no matter what way the car tilted, the fuel supply was uninterrupted. The integrated gear and transfer box had a lockable centre differential after limited slip devices proved noisy. This was vacuum operated to eliminate problems with cables. Although the US market was not contemplated meantime, the Range Rover maintained the company's reputation for safety, with well-placed padding and a collapsible steering column. The marketing strap-line A Car for All Reasons highlighted versatility and its tough cross-country heritage was emphasised with an extra oval badge proclaiming it was By Land Rover. New owners, Leyland Motors, by 1968 British Leyland Motor Corporation, had pressed for the Range Rover to be launched in 1969 but among the difficulties that delayed it were development and testing of the front seats, with their complex integrated seat belt attachments.

INTRODUCTION: June 1970
BODY: 3-door, 5-seat 3800lb (1724kg)
ENGINE: 90deg V8 petrol; 88.9mm x 71.1mm; 3528cc; compression ratio 8.5:1; (1971 8.25:1) 130bhp (95kW) @ 5,000 rpm; 36.84bhp/l (27.47kW/l); 185lb ft (248Nm) @ 2500 rpm; (1971 135bhp (100.67kW) @ 4750rpm,)
ENGINE STRUCTURE: pushrod ohv with hydraulic tappets, single central chain-driven camshaft; aluminium alloy LM25 block and cylinder heads, dry liners; two Zenith/Stromberg CD2 carburettors; Lucas 35DM8 distributor; mechanical fuel pump; 5-bearing crankshaft.
TRANSMISSION permanent four wheel drive; 10.5in (26.7cm) hydraulically operated diaphragm spring clutch; LT95 integrated 4-speed main gearbox and 2-speed transfer box with vacuum-operated centre differential lock (1970 only with limited slip); Rover front and rear banjo axles; 3.54:1 final drive ratio; low ratio 3.32:1, high 1.174:1 (to 1976).

CHASSIS welded steel ladder frame; front and rear live axles with coil springs and telescopic dampers, located by radius arms and Panhard rod; rear located by radius arms, support rods and central A-frame with Boge Hydromat self-levelling strut; recirculating ball steering (left hand drive available from 1971); dual circuit, servo-assisted hydraulic brakes, 11.75in (29.8cm) front discs, four-piston callipers, 11.42in (29.0cm) rear discs, 2-piston callipers, 10in (25.4cm) drum transmission parking brake; 19gal (86 litre) fuel tank; 16in pressed styled steel wheels with 205x16 tyres.
DIMENSIONS wheelbase 100in (254cm); track 58.5in (148cm); length; 176in (447cm); width 70in (178cm); height 70in (178cm); ground clearance 7.5in (19cm); turning circle 37ft (11.3m).
PERFORMANCE (As tested by The Motor January 16 1971): 0-60mph (96kph); 12.9 sec, top speed; 102mph (165kph). Approach angle; 45 deg, departure angle; 33 deg.
EQUIPMENT 1971 optional towbar, Sundym tinted glass, laminated windscreen, heated rear window, 1972 new radio, rear seat belts.
PRICE £1998 0s 0d (inc purchase tax).

Articulation was the key. The third pre-production prototype displays the angles the coil-sprung axles could reach without losing their grip. YVB 153H, chassis 35500003A was whisked out for photography because it was the only one of the batch of 25 painted a photogenic blue. Tough-looking pleated PVC upholstery and floor coverings were not as robust as they looked.

1976 Range Rover

Rover miscalculated demand for the new product, and it quickly outstripped supply, with second hand vehicles selling at a premium. It also seemed that the market had been misunderstood, and farmers no matter how gentlemanly, were not carrying pigs to market in them, then hosing them out before going out to dinner. Instead the new model was starting a trend of its own in urban, suburban, and out-of-town 4x4s. The original smart but somewhat utilitarian interior was unsuitable, and some conversion companies seized the opportunity to produce luxurious special furnishings. Complaints from owners of country estates that their gun dogs slithered around in the untrimmed rear led to the installation of a non-slip mat. Other improvements inside included carpet trim for the gearbox tunnel, a moulded brushed nylon headlining, first as an option and then standard, nylon cloth for the seats. Further choices included a more powerful alternator, upgraded again in 1975, when split charging was introduced. The growing band of town drivers welcomed the option of power assistance, making the steering lighter at parking speeds. Vinyl trim on the rear quarter panels hinted at the upmarket stylish buyer, while disguising the patchy quality of the pressing. In 1978 came the option of an overdrive, already available on Land Rovers, and made by Fairey Winches. A two-shaft design, as opposed to the more usual epicyclic, it bolted straight on to the end of the transfer gearbox housing. Engaged by conventional dog clutches with baulk ring synchromesh, this provided a step-up ratio of 0.782:1 giving a 22.8 per cent drop in engine revs, operated on all gears, and provided a total of 16 forwards and four in reverse. The cost was £226. Claims of 25 per cent better overall fuel consumption were not realised however, *Autocar* recording gains at steady speeds but not much in everyday driving, only 0.1mpg better than the car tested in 1975.

INTRODUCTION: 1976
BODY: 3-door, 5-seat 3902lb (1770kg)
ENGINE: 90deg V8 petrol; 88.9mm x 71.1mm; 3528cc; compression ratio 8.25:1; 135bhp (67kW) @ 4750rpm; 38.25bhp/l (28.52kW/l); 185lbft (248Nm) @ 2500rpm (from 1977 CR lowered to 8.13:1, 132bhp (98.43kW) @ 5,000rpm; 186lbft (249.4Nm) @2500rpm)
ENGINE STRUCTURE: pushrod ohv with hydraulic tappets, single central chain-driven camshaft; aluminium alloy LM25 block and cylinder heads, dry liners; two Zenith/Stromberg CD2 carburettors; Lucas 35DM8 distributor; electric fuel pump; 5-bearing crankshaft (twin-pipe exhaust from 1976)
TRANSMISSION permanent four wheel drive; 10.5in (26.7cm) hydraulically operated diaphragm spring clutch; LT95 integrated 4-speed main gearbox and 2-speed transfer box with vacuum-operated centre differential lock; Rover front and rear banjo axles; 3.54:1 final drive ratio; low ratio 3.32:1, high 1.116:1 (from 1976); optional Fairey overdrive (from 1978).

CHASSIS welded steel ladder frame; front and rear live axles with coil springs and telescopic dampers, located by radius arms and Panhard rod; rear located by radius arms, support rods and central A-frame with Boge Hydromat self-levelling strut; recirculating ball steering, PAS optional, dual circuit, servo-assisted hydraulic brakes; 11.75in (29.8cm) front discs, four-piston callipers, 11.42in (29.0cm) rear discs, 2-piston callipers, 10in (25.4cm) drum transmission parking brake; 19gal (86 litre) fuel tank;16in pressed styled steel wheels with 205x16 tyres radial ply M+S.
DIMENSIONS wheelbase 100in (254cm); track 58.5in (148cm); length 176in (447cm); width 70in (178cm); height 70in (178cm); ground clearance 7.5in (19cm); turning circle 37ft (11.3m).
EQUIPMENT door-mounted mirrors 1977, black wiper arms.
PERFORMANCE (As tested by The Motor January 1976): 0-60mph (96kph); 15.0 sec, top speed; 100mph (162kph). Approach angle; 45 deg, departure angle; 33 deg. PRICE £3924.18 including car tax and VAT (As tested with overdrive by Autocar July 1978) 0-60mph (96kph) 14.3sec, top speed 96mph (151kph) overall 14.2mpg (19.9 l/100km). PRICE £8,528.13

Generous ground clearance and short front and rear overhangs with an approach angle of 45 deg, departure angle 33 deg, were essential for off-road agility.

Plain materials tried to give the fascia some out-of-town credentials but even by later models in 1980, when it had a four-spoke steering wheel, cloth upholstery, and head restraints, the build quality was still poor and the layout of the minor instruments somewhat haphazard.

1980 Range Rover 4-door Monteverdi

An omission of the original 1970 Range Rover was a failure to provide for four side doors. It was not thought important at the time. The motor industry calculated a model's life expectancy at about seven years if things went well. Any more would be a bonus, and there was no expectation of Range Rover continuing a good way into the 21st century, so too many choices were unnecessary. Such was the limited production capacity of the small facility in the South Works at Solihull two-doors-only seemed reasonable. However after ten years 11,000 were being sold annually, of which between 2,500 and 3,000 remained in the United Kingdom, and such was its success that even if production could not be stepped up, prices and profitability could be increased by adding choice. During most of the 1970s there was not much money available for development, but there seemed scant need since aftermarket converters were meeting the demand, such as it seemed to be, for bespoke Range Rovers. Still the sales department could see the potential for additional models with four doors, or automatic transmissions for leisure market customers, and professionals such as surveyors, architects and engineers. The field was being left open for Rapport, Carmichaels, and Wood & Pickett to produce aftermarket 4-door conversions. However the one made by Automobiles Monteverdi, of Basle, Switzerland met with Land Rover's approval and the firm was encouraged to test the market with a 4-door. A batch of 2-door Range Rovers was shipped to Monteverdi in white primer, where they were converted, luxuriously upholstered in leather, and sold in Switzerland for SwFr57,900 (£15,600) against the regular Range Rover's SwFr38,500. BL estimated at the Geneva Motor Show that the UK price would be 50 per cent more than a 2-door, approximately £18,600, and there were no plans to make one in-house. It went on sale through Land Rover dealers at £16,507.

INTRODUCTION: Geneva Motor Show 1980
BODY: 5-door, 5-seat 4078.5lb (1850kg).
ENGINE: 90deg V8 petrol; 88.9mm x 71.1mm; 3528cc; compression ratio 8.13:1; 132bhp (98.43kW) @ 5,000rpm; 37.41bhp/l (27.89kW/l); 186lbft (249.4Nm) @2500rpm.
ENGINE STRUCTURE: pushrod ohv with hydraulic tappets, single central chain-driven camshaft; aluminium alloy LM25 block and cylinder heads, dry liners; two Zenith/Stromberg CD2 carburettors; Lucas 35DM8 distributor; electric fuel pump; 5-bearing crankshaft
TRANSMISSION permanent four wheel drive; 10.5in (26.7cm) hydraulically operated diaphragm spring clutch; LT95 integrated 4-speed main gearbox and 2-speed transfer box with vacuum-operated centre differential lock; Rover front and rear banjo axles, 3.54:1 final drive ratio, low ratio 3.32:1, high 1.116:1; optional Fairey overdrive.

CHASSIS welded steel ladder frame; front and rear live axles with coil springs and telescopic dampers, located by radius arms and Panhard rod; rear located by radius arms, support rods and central A-frame with Boge Hydromat self-levelling strut; recirculating ball steering PAS; dual circuit, servo-assisted hydraulic brakes, 11.75in (29.8cm) front discs, four-piston callipers, 11.42in (29.0cm) rear discs, 2-piston callipers, 10in (25.4cm) drum transmission parking brake; 19gal (86 litre) fuel tank; 16in pressed styled steel wheels with 205x16 tyres radial ply M+S.
DIMENSIONS wheelbase 100in (254cm); track 58.5in (148cm); length 176in (447cm); width 70in (178cm); height; 70in (178cm); ground clearance 7.5in (19cm); turning circle 37ft (11.3m).
EQUIPMENT air conditioning (optional on regular Range Rovers), optional pleated leather upholstery
PERFORMANCE (As tested with overdrive by Autocar) 0-60mph (96kph) 14.3sec; top speed 96mph (151kph); overall 14.2mpg (19.9 l/100km); Approach angle; 45 deg, departure angle; 33 deg.
PRICE See text

The crisp outline remained the same when 4-doors enhanced the Range Rover's practicality. The sloping shut-line at the trailing edge of the rear door of the Monteverdi models gave a curiously lop-sided effect. Black grille and bumper (left) and repeater flashers on the front wings were new for 1980 UK models.

1981 Range Rover Fleet Line and police cars

A firm convention of the motor industry was that selling to police forces encouraged customers' confidence. It was a measure of the trust most people had, at least in the 1980s on the integrity of the constabulary, that manufacturers went to such lengths to make fleet sales to them. Wolseley discovered in the 1940s that it was a way into films, Jaguar made a stripped-down Mark V police model, and Ford had its Z-car television stars. Accordingly plans for police and emergency services' Range Rovers were laid even before its launch in 1970. The emergency services was already a flourishing market for Land Rover, and it was logical that it would be bigger for Range Rovers, which would be far faster in response times. A special projects department under George Mackie was set up, to advise outside specialists on what changes to incorporate, and award them the title of Land Rover Approved. Rover cars may never have been quite a policemens' lot, but the Range Rover with its high capacity boot and tall driver's eye, was ideal for motorway patrols. A police demonstrator was ready by September 1970 and the authorities in Cheshire had four by April 1971. It was the only vehicle capable of pursuing crooks along a motorway, then if necessary continue chasing them, when they abandoned cars and set off on foot across the countryside. It could tow (or even push) broken down or damaged vehicles off the road and was sold to the Belgian Gendarmerie, Dutch Rijkspolitie, Lichtenstein Police, Royal Malaysia Police, Oslo City Police, South Australia Police, Tasmania Police, Bahrain Police with FLN Panelcraft conversions, and City of Utrecht Police. By 1980 however the mounting cost of a Range Rover was putting buyers off, and the Fleet Line, effectively a basic equipment Range Rover for both police and commercial users was introduced. It was at an entry-level price for buyers seeking a long-range cruiser unconcerned about the trappings of luxury. Fleet Line cars had manual steering, rubber floor mats, and the upholstery was in a new material Ambla, which looked like leather, and was hard wearing enough for heavy coppers and the rough-and-tumble of emergency work. Fleet Line Range Rovers were also bought by converters who made them into specialist vehicles, sometimes like the Lomas coachbuilt private ambulance with a 10in (25.4cm) wheelbase extension. Fleet Lines carried on for four years or so, many with the Dale Stem-lite telescopic extending flashing blue light and floodlight, before the forces changed to 4-door versions. By then Land Rover image-makers were in any case growing nervous about Range Rovers with the trappings of trade eroding its exclusiveness.

Among the last batch of 2-door Range Rovers taken into service by the Metropolitan police was this 1980s example with extra lights, beacons, and signalling. A special wiring harness was designed to service the extra lights and radios, and police specification cars had larger alternators and an extra battery with clamps and cables for re-starting cars on the motorway hard shoulder. The high driving position gave police a commanding view over the roofs of most traffic and there was space inside for road cones, signs, and rescue gear. Range Rovers also saw service with coastguard, mountain rescue, ambulance and fire services.

INTRODUCTION: February 1981
BODY: 3-door, 5-seat 3902lb (1770kg)
ENGINE: 90deg V8 petrol; 88.9mm x
71.1mm; 3528cc; compression ratio
8.25:1; 135bhp (67kW) @ 4750rpm;
38.25bhp/l (28.52kW/l); 185lbft
(248Nm) @ 2500rpm
ENGINE STRUCTURE: pushrod ohv
with hydraulic tappets, single central
chain-driven camshaft; aluminium alloy
LM25 block and cylinder heads, dry
liners; two Zenith/Stromberg CD2
carburettors; Lucas 35DM8 distributor;
electric fuel pump; 5-bearing crankshaft

TRANSMISSION permanent four wheel
drive; 10.5in (26.7cm) hydraulically
operated diaphragm spring clutch; LT95
integrated 4-speed main gearbox and 2-
speed transfer box with
vacuum-operated centre differential
lock; Rover front and rear banjo axles;
3.54:1 final drive ratio; low ratio 3.32:1,
high 1.116:1 (from 1976)
CHASSIS welded steel ladder frame;
front and rear live axles with coil springs
and telescopic dampers, located by
radius arms and Panhard rod; rear
located by radius arms, support rods and
central A-frame with Boge Hydromat
self-levelling strut; recirculating ball

steering, dual circuit, servo-assisted
hydraulic brakes; 11.75in (29.8cm) front
discs, four-piston calipers, 11.42in
(29.0cm) rear discs, 2-piston calipers,
10in (25.4cm) drum transmission
parking brake; 19gal (86 litre) fuel
tank;16in pressed steel wheels with
205x16 tyres radial ply M+S.
DIMENSIONS wheelbase 100in
(254cm); track 58.5in (148cm); length
176in (447cm); width 70in (178cm);
height 70in (178cm); ground clearance
7.5in (19cm); turning circle 37ft
(11.3m).

EQUIPMENT for police model: 20ACR
60-amp alternator; communication radio
facility; electrical harness for roof
equipment; extra battery with clamps
and cables; extra switch panel; calibrated
speedometer in centre of fascia
PERFORMANCE : 0-60mph (96kph);
15.0 sec, top speed; 100mph (162kph).
Approach angle; 45 deg, departure
angle; 33 deg; overall fuel consumption
14.2mpg (19.9 l/100km)

1981 Range Rover In Vogue limited edition

Following the creation of Land Rover Ltd under new MD Mike Hodgkinson in July 1978, some £30million became available to expand production under the Phase 1 expansion programme, which eventually also brought a new generation of Land Rovers. It also enabled the creation of new production facilities to clear bottlenecks in V8 engine and LR95 transmission supply. This entailed a review of Range Rover strategy, taking it up-market, a move supported by the new Land Rover One Ten, which took on some of the Range Rover's refinement. Another result was the Range Rover In Vogue, the first of many limited edition Range Rovers. It came about following Vogue magazine's use of one HAC 414W, lent for the occasion and prepared by coachbuilders Wood & Pickett, as a prop for photography of the Lancôme and Jaeger collection in Biarritz. This provided an opportunity to produce 1000 2-door Range Rovers costing £800 more than standard offerings. They were essentially similar to the photo-shoot car, with the same pale blue metallic paintwork, twin grey coachlines, polished wood door cappings, full carpeting and luxurious upholstery. Air conditioning was standard as was a special picnic hamper in the back. The photo-shoot prototype's alloy wheels were not retained, but some of its innovations were continued for production, including the high compression engine, new high-ratio transfer box gearing, a central stowage box, seatback map pockets, and carpeted loadspace. The Vogue name was kept as a designation for later expensive derivatives. Another smaller 1980 special edition of 25 cars had explored the market for automatic transmission. The Schuler automatic Range Rover had a Chrysler A727 3-speed Torqueflite, a Schuler-Voith chain-driven transfer box, and Ferguson Formula anti-lock brakes made by Mullard. Schuler Presses of Sunningdale in Berkshire prepared the conversion, using a Morse chain drive to the transfer box driving the front wheels and a viscous coupling to the rears, which had the advantage, according to Autocar, of eliminating some of the transmission backlash that had bedevilled Range Rovers from the start. Land Rover dealers sold the package with a full warranty. A further transmission option was removal of the Land Rover 4-speed manual, replacing it with the newly developed corporate Jaguar-Rover-Triumph 5-speed gearbox. The cost of either manual or automatic was an additional £2,294 plus VAT on the Range Rover price. Anti-lock brakes with servo cost £1,380.

INTRODUCTION: 1981
BODY: 3-door, 5-seat 3802.9lb (1725kg) - 4034.4lb (1830kg)
ENGINE: 90deg V8 petrol; 88.9mm x 71.1mm, 3528cc; compression ratio 9.35:1; 125bhp (93.21kW) @ 4,000rpm; 35.43bhp/l (26.42kW/l); 185lbft (248Nm) @ 2500rpm.
ENGINE STRUCTURE: pushrod ohv with hydraulic tappets, single central chain-driven camshaft; aluminium alloy LM25 block and cylinder heads, dry liners; two Zenith/Stromberg CD2 carburettors; Lucas 35DM8 distributor; electric fuel pump; 5-bearing crankshaft.
TRANSMISSION permanent four wheel drive.10.5in (26.7cm) hydraulically operated diaphragm spring clutch; LT95 integrated 4-speed main gearbox and 2-speed transfer box with lockable centre differential, optional JRT 5-speed; Rover front and rear banjo axles; final drive ratio 3.54:1, low ratio 3.32:1, high 0.996 (options 1.116, 1.003, 0.996:1 with automatic: 5-speed manual LT77 from 1983, A727 automatic optional from 1982.

CHASSIS welded ladder frame; live axles, coil springs, tele dampers, radius arms and Panhard rod; rear radius arms, support rods and A-frame with Boge Hydromat strut; recirculating ball PAS; dual circuit, servo hydraulic disc brakes, 11.75in (29.8cm) front, four-piston callipers, 11.42in (29.0cm) rear, 2-piston callipers, 10in (25.4cm) drum parking brake; 19gal (86 litre) fuel; 16in steel wheels, 205x16 tyres.
DIMENSIONS w/b 100in (254cm); track 58.5in (148cm); length 176in (447cm); width 70in (178cm); height 70in (178cm); clearance 7.5in (19cm); turning circle 37ft (11.3m).
EQUIPMENT rear wash-wipe, inertia-reel belts, spare wheel cover, stainless steel-capped tailgate, Schuler Wilton carpets.
PERFORMANCE (The Motor 1976): 0-60mph (96kph); 15.0 sec, top speed; 100mph (162kph).
PRICE £13,788 including car tax and VAT; see also text.

Black centre caps on the wheels
and a two-tone grey coachline
distinguished the limited edition
In Vogue Range Rover that went
on sale in February 1981.

1981 Range Rover 4-door

After ten years' production, conversions of Range Rovers were widespread. They were made into stretched limousines complete with dummy hood irons (Scottorn), six-wheelers (Rapport Excelsior, Wood & Pickett) 4-doors (Safire), even pick-ups, convertibles and open hunting wagons costing anything up to £25,000. Experience with the Monteverdi convinced Land Rover that a production 4-door was viable and it was introduced along with changes to improve fuel economy. A 4-door prototype had been built back in 1972, and it was thought that a wheelbase stretch to 109in (276.9cm) might help, but cost ruled it out. In the event the extra pair of doors was done quite straightforwardly and looked better than Monteverdi's with a straight shut-line on the edge of the rear door. A black satin finish on the pillars was a clever cosmetic effect, but the splendid big door pulls of the 2-door, which could be opened with gloves on were abandoned in favour of cheap-looking recessed handles. Interior trim was improved, bare metal banished, and the back seat was moved 3in (7.6cm) rearwards to improve access and provide more legroom. Predicted sales for the 4-door, of four out of five new Range Rovers, were achieved in little more than a year and within three accounted for 9 out of 10. Autocar felt the changes effected in aid of fuel economy were so simple, "…that one could well question why it was never done before," although the change in compression ratio from 8.13 to 9.35:1 for MY1981 now required the use of 97-Octane 4-star fuel. Hitherto exports to territories with poor quality fuel had dictated the lower compression. The camshaft was redesigned for low lift, and with alterations to timing the engine developed peak power at a quieter and more refined 4,000, instead of 5,000rpm. A change of ratio in the transfer gearbox had the effect of making the gearing higher giving 23.7mph (38.04kph) per 1000rpm instead of 21.2mph (34.03kph) in top gear. Autocar failed to obtain the promised 20 per cent improvement in economy, and was lukewarm about a number of features such as the integral front seat belts, which precluded rake adjustment of the seat backs. Some rivals were also catching up in terms of noise especially howl from the transmission.

INTRODUCTION: 1981
BODY: 5-door, 5-seat, 3,942lb (1788kg)
ENGINE: 90deg V8 petrol; 88.9mm x 71.1mm, 3528cc; compression ratio 9.35:1; 125bhp (93.21kW) @ 4,000rpm; 35.43bhp/l (26.42kW/l); 185lbft (248Nm) @ 2500rpm.
ENGINE STRUCTURE: pushrod ohv with hydraulic tappets, single central chain-driven camshaft; aluminium alloy LM25 block and cylinder heads, dry liners; two Zenith/Stromberg 175CDE-SE carburettors; Lucas 35DM8 distributor; electric fuel pump; 5-bearing crankshaft.
TRANSMISSION permanent four wheel drive.10.5in (26.7cm) hydraulically operated diaphragm spring clutch; LT95 integrated 4-speed main gearbox and 2-speed transfer box with lockable centre differential, integral with primary gearbox on 4-speed models; Rover front and rear banjo axles; hypoid bevel final drive, ratio 3.54:1, low ratio 3.32:1, high ratio 1.003; 5-speed LT77 from 1983

CHASSIS welded steel ladder frame; front and rear live axles with coil springs and telescopic dampers, located by radius arms and Panhard rod; rear located by radius arms, support rods and central A-frame with Boge Hydromat self-levelling strut; recirculating ball steering PAS; dual circuit, servo-assisted hydraulic brakes, 11.75in (29.8cm) front discs, four-piston callipers, 11.42in (29.0cm) rear discs, 2-piston callipers, 10in (25.4cm) drum transmission parking brake; 19gal (86 litre) fuel tank; 16in pressed styled steel wheels with 205x16 tyres.
DIMENSIONS wheelbase 100in (254cm); track 58.5in (148cm); length 176in (447cm); width 70in (178cm); height 70in (178cm); ground clearance 7.5in (19cm); turning circle 37ft (11.3m).
EQUIPMENT option pack with 3-spoke alloy wheels, wood sill cappings, rear carpet, air conditioning £1682; lockable stowage box in front.
PERFORMANCE (As tested by Autocar October 1981): 0-60mph (96kph); 15.0 sec, top speed; 95mph (153kph); 16.2mpg (17.4l/100km).
PRICE £14,389 including car tax and VAT.

Land Rover's own 4-door had the vertical shut line down to the rear wheelarch. Door trims were much improved, and now concealed any bare metal. The rearwards movement of the back seat enhanced legroom in an interior which, year by year, was becoming more luxurious and refined earning it a Design Council Award in 1982 for "Excellence in design and in recognition of an outstanding product from British industry." (*Right*) Carpeting now extended throughout the rear load space and covered the spare wheel.

1982 Range Rover automatic

By February 1982 Schuler Presses of Sunninghill was claiming its 200th converted Range Rover with Chrysler A727 Torqueflite automatic transmission and Ferguson Formula (FF) anti-lock brakes. It must have known a factory equivalent was on the way, and pre-empted its arrival with a £400 discount, which brought its price down to £1995. However when the official automatic Range Rover came on stream in the autumn it only cost a £600 premium. In 1981 when the 25 tentative Schulers became 200, at the best part of £2,000 apiece, it did not take Land Rover long to know it was on to a good thing. The new key ingredient for the post-Schuler production Range Rover automatic was the 2-speed transfer box LT230R (LT for Leyland Transmissions, R for roller-bearings), which had the extra virtue of quietening the gear hum that had troubled the model for 12 years. It certainly transformed the driving experience; Range Rover was now firmly in the up-market luxury category, as the last vestiges of anything vaguely agricultural were abandoned. "You need a vehicle you can be proud of, which proclaims the fact that you have "arrived," ran an unblushing advertisement. "Luxury need not stop where adventure begins." Range Rover was now more grouse moor than ever, and High and Low ratios were best selected going slowly, with the stubby selector lever in neutral making off-road driving simpler than ever. Descents with engine braking were accomplished by a positive detent that held the automatic in first gear. A transmission oil cooler was fitted to deal with the higher fluid temperatures that could be expected with a hard-working automatic, especially off-road in Middle Eastern markets. The automatic was offered at first only on the luxurious Vogue Automatic Special Edition, but was soon extended throughout the range. Range Rover's comfort and luxury continued with its own colour coordinated cool-box.

INTRODUCTION: 1982
BODY: 5-door, 5-seat, 4078.5lb (1850kg)
ENGINE: 90deg V8 petrol; 88.9mm x 71.1mm, 3528cc; compression ratio 9.35:1; 125bhp (93.21kW) @ 4,000rpm; 35.43bhp/l (26.42kW/l); 185lbft (248Nm) @ 2500rpm.
ENGINE STRUCTURE: pushrod ohv with hydraulic tappets, single central chain-driven camshaft; aluminium alloy LM25 block and cylinder heads, dry liners; two Zenith/Stromberg 175CDE-SE carburettors; Lucas 35DM8 distributor; electric fuel pump; 5-bearing crankshaft.
TRANSMISSION permanent four wheel drive.10.5in (26.7cm) hydraulically operated diaphragm spring clutch; LT95 integrated 4-speed main gearbox and 2-speed transfer box with lockable centre differential, integral with primary gearbox on 4-speed models; LT230R on 5-speed and automatics; Rover front and rear banjo axles; hypoid bevel final drive, ratio 3.54:1, low ratio 3.32:1, high ratio 1.003:1; 5-speed LT77 from 1983.

CHASSIS welded ladder frame; live axles, coil springs, telescopic dampers, radius arms and Panhard rod; rear radius arms, support rods, A-frame with Boge Hydromat strut; recirculating ball PAS; dual circuit, servo hydraulic disc brakes, 11.75in (29.8cm) front, four-piston callipers, 11.42in (29.0cm) rear, 2-piston callipers, 10in (25.4cm) drum parking brake; 19gal (86 litre) tank; 16in steel wheels, 205 x16 tyres.
DIMENSIONS w/b 100in (254cm); track 58.5in (148cm); length 176in (447cm); width 70in (178cm); height 70in (178cm); gc 7.5in (19cm); turning circle 37ft (11.3m).
EQUIPMENT armrests and headrests, Philips AC807 stereo, American walnut door cappings, 3-spoke alloy wheels, rear carpet, a/c, front stowage box, Nevada Gold, Sierra Silver with coachlines.
PERFORMANCE 0–60mph (96kph); 16.7 sec, max; 95mph (153kph); 14mpg (20.17l/100km) – 16mpg (17.65l/100km).
PRICE £16,700 inc car tax, VAT.

New 3-spoke aluminium alloy wheels, first used for the In Vogue of 1980, became a Range Rover feature and were said to have been based on those of the American Ford Mustang. Required by marketing for a quick fix, styling rushed through the best design they knew. (*Below left*) The horizontally divided tailgate remained a popular Range Rover feature throughout, providing the basis of many a sporting fixture picnic, with the top half providing some shelter. (*Below right*) When air conditioning came in the minor instruments disappeared further under the fascia but the carpet on the transmission tunnel of this automatic is better-trimmed.

1983 Range Rover; powertrain upgrade, 5-speed manual and automatics

Economy was always problematical on Range Rovers; bringing in a 5-speed gearbox provided an opportunity for improvement, although in the event it did not amount to much except in the overdrive 0.77:1 top gear. Mid-range acceleration however was improved with the new overall gearing and Land Rover claimed a 25 per cent enhancement in 30-50mph (48 - 80kph), 40-60mph (64-96kph), and 50-70mph (80-112kph) range thanks to the ratios being better spaced. The new gearbox was an adaptation of the so-called 77mm Rover design, recently introduced on the Land Rover One Ten, and with its choice of effectively ten forward gears, was fitted as standard to all manual Range Rovers. It was part of a parcel of improvements, which included central locking, and a torsion bar counterbalanced lower tailgate. The shorter, more positive gearshift lever was a welcome break from the long-travel, rather spindly lever, and it was combined with the range-change lever and a centre diff lock in a new centre console. The LT230R transfer box had also been developed for the One Ten and was already in use on Range Rover automatics. An important bonus of the changes was a further reduction in the gear whine, something else that had disadvantaged Range Rover from the start, as well as transmission shunt in changing from drive to over-run. Diminished gear sounds demonstrated the relative quietness and refinement that were now being obtained. Wind noise, despite the bluff front and thanks to good door and window sealing was subdued, except for some commotion round the windscreen pillars. Claims by the factory that overall fuel consumption would be 10 per cent better were not borne out by an *Autocar* road test in the year of its introduction. Its 15.4mpg (18.34l/100km) of premium-grade 4-star was worse than the previous best of 16.4mpg (17.22l/100km), although the magazine did own up to having carried out a good deal of low-gear driving, and thought 17.6mpg (16.05l/100km) more likely in everyday driving. The higher top gear was a real advantage however, providing tranquil cruising with 70mph (112.4kph) on the motorway attained at a restful 2,700rpm or just a little over best torque.

INTRODUCTION: July 1983
BODY: 5-door, 5-seat, 4249lb (1927kg)
ENGINE: 90deg V8 petrol; 88.9mm x 71.1mm, 3528cc; compression ratio 9.35:1; 125bhp (93.21kW) @ 4,000rpm; 35.43bhp/l (26.42kW/l); 190ftlb (254.8Nm) @ 2500rpm.
ENGINE STRUCTURE: pushrod ohv with hydraulic tappets; single central chain-driven camshaft; aluminium alloy LM25 block and cylinder heads, dry liners; two Zenith/Stromberg 175CDE-SE carburettors; Lucas 35DM8 distributor; electric fuel pump; 5-bearing crankshaft.
TRANSMISSION permanent four wheel drive.10.5in (26.7cm) hydraulically operated diaphragm spring clutch; LT77 5-speed main gearbox and 2-speed LT230R transfer box with lockable centre differential; automatic optional; Rover front and rear banjo axles; hypoid bevel final drive, ratio 3.54:1, transfer box low ratio 3.32:1, high ratio 1.192:1
CHASSIS welded steel ladder frame; front and rear live axles with coil springs and telescopic dampers, located by radius arms and Panhard rod; rear located by radius arms, support rods and central A-frame with Boge Hydromat self-levelling strut; recirculating ball steering PAS; dual circuit, servo-assisted hydraulic brakes, 11.8in (30cm) front discs, four-piston callipers, 11.42in

(29.0cm) rear discs, 2-piston callipers, 10in (25.4cm) drum transmission parking brake; 19gal (86 litre) fuel tank; 16in pressed styled steel wheels with 205SRx16 Michelin XM+S tyres.
DIMENSIONS wheelbase 100in (254cm); track 58.5in (148cm); length 176in (447cm); width 70in (178cm); height 70in (178cm); ground clearance 7.5in (19cm); turning circle 37ft (11.3m).
EQUIPMENT Automatic £1031.55; alloy wheels £366.84; air conditioning £1159.07; metallic paint £1146.18; tow bar £94.57
PERFORMANCE (Autocar Dec 1983) 0-60mph (96kph); 14.4 sec, top speed; 96mph (154.1kph); 25.8mph (41.41kph) @ 1000rpm; 15.4mpg (18.34l/100km)(see text).
PRICE 4-door £15,373.58 including car tax and VAT; 2-door £14,483.

Range Rover's ascent up-market was accomplished by associations of grandeur such as this publicity picture by Simpson's famous emporium in Piccadilly. This is a 1983 limited-edition In Vogue, promoted with Daks autumn fashions.

1985 Range Rover Vogue with fuel injected engine

More than eight Range Rovers in ten were 4-door Vogues, and since only 20 2-door versions were sold in a year, it was discontinued. There seemed no limit to the sophistication and complexity, not to say expense, that the model could command. Orders for air conditioning doubled in 1984, and now engine power was increased by some 30 per cent in line with the Vitesse SD1 Rover saloon. The Zenith/Stromberg 175CDE-SE carburettor engine remained available, with a large bore pulsed air injection system, raising engine power to 127bhp (94.7kW) and torque to 194lbft (260.2Nm) but the pressure to comply with emission regulations world wide meant its days were numbered. Sensors on the injection engine included those for electronic management, housed in a cast aluminium manifold between the cylinder banks, and there was extra cooling with an 11-blade fan. Among the changes necessary for the Zahnradfabrik Friedrichshafen (ZF) automatic was a special sump and oil pick-up to cope with steep gradients but kick-down arrangements were unsatisfactory; it would drop a gear unexpectedly even at top speed. Suspension developments put in hand to reduce roll included replacing the single rate rear coil springs with dual rate units, which along with larger front radius arm bushes were aimed at increasing roll stiffness, although in the event not by much. Among the quality improvements introduced with the American market in mind, were jig-welded body frames enabling tighter shut-lines, unobtainable with the earlier bolted-up frames. Alterations made to the interior were all aimed at making Range Rover more like a car and less like a Land Rover. Electrically adjustable door mirrors with defrosting, and more accessible switchgear completed the transformation from something vaguely agricultural to something certainly in Vogue.

INTRODUCTION: October 1985
BODY: 5-door, 5-seat, 4259lb (1932kg)
ENGINE: 90deg V8 petrol; 88.9mm x 71.1mm, 3528cc; compression ratio 9.35:1; 165bhp (123kW) @ 4,750rpm; 46.77bhp/l (34.87kW/l); 206ftlb (276.25Nm) @ 3200rpm.
ENGINE STRUCTURE: pushrod ohv with hydraulic tappets; single central chain-driven camshaft; aluminium alloy LM25 block and cylinder heads, dry liners; Lucas L-Jetronic fuel injection; Lucas 35DM8 distributor; electric fuel pump; 5-bearing crankshaft.
TRANSMISSION permanent four wheel drive.10.5in (26.7cm) hydraulically operated single dry plate clutch; LT77 5-speed main gearbox and 2-speed LT230R transfer box with lockable centre differential; optional ZF HP22 4-speed automatic with overdrive top lock-up; Rover front and rear banjo axles; hypoid bevel final drive, ratio 3.54:1, transfer box low ratio 3.32:1, high ratio 1.222:1.
CHASSIS welded steel ladder frame; front and rear live axles with coil springs and telescopic dampers, located by radius arms and Panhard rod; rear located by radius arms, support rods and central A-frame with Boge Hydromat self-levelling strut; recirculating ball steering PAS; dual circuit, servo-assisted hydraulic brakes, 11.8in (30cm) front discs, four-piston callipers, 11.42in (29.0cm) rear discs, 2-piston callipers, 10in (25.4cm) drum transmission parking brake; 19gal (86 litre) fuel tank; 16in 3-spoke alloy wheels with 6in rims; 205x16 Michelin XM+S or Avon tyres.

DIMENSIONS wheelbase 100in (254cm) track 58.5in (148cm); length 176in (447cm); width 70in (178cm); height 70in (178cm); ground clearance 7.5in (19cm); turning circle 37ft (11.3m).
EQUIPMENT: Reversing lamp std; 2-speed wipers; electric screenwasher; air blending heater; optional air conditioning; cloth-faced seats; laminated windscreen; optional metallic paint; 4 speaker sound system.
PERFORMANCE 0-60mph (96kph), 11.9 sec, top speed; automatic 104mph (166.95kph), manual 107mph (171.76kph); manual 25.8mph (41.41kph) @ 1000rpm; automatic 27.23mph (43.71kph); fuel consumption Euromix (20.17mpg (14l/100km), automatic 14.73l/100km (19.17mpg).
PRICE £20,183 including car tax and VAT

Requirements of export markets sent testing crews to harsh climates and terrain to ensure Range Rovers stood up to deserts and searing heat. (Picture is from a photo shoot in Southern Spain.) Fuel injection became necessary to meet American emission regulations, which specified catalytic converters that had to last a car's lifetime.

1986 Range Rover Turbo D

A diesel engine was becoming obligatory in many European markets. Plans had been laid with Perkins Engines of Peterborough for Iceberg, a turbocharged version of the aluminium petrol V8 that had been under development for some five years. It promised 125bhp (93.21kW) like the petrol V8, together with a substantial 205lbft (275Nm) of pulling power, so not only would it have addressed the fuel consumption issue but it would also have offered a lively turn of speed through the gears. The engine was shown as a prototype at the Paris Motor Show in 1982 but the substantial tooling costs of converting the V8 to diesel put the management off. Diesel take-up was still uncertain in Britain, scarcely existed in America, and a good return on the investment was by no means guaranteed. Once again it fell to an outside source to take the initiative while Land Rover sat back and waited to see. In 1983 two diesel conversions were offered, one by Malcolm Cole of Poole using a Peugeot XD2S 2.5litre, which did not gain Land Rover approval, and one by Janspeed Engineering of Salisbury, which did. Janspeed retro-fitted Range Rovers with a turbocharged 2.4litre 4-cylinder diesel from Stabilimenti Meccanici VM SpA of Cento, Italy claiming a market at home and abroad including Japan, and 35mpg (8.07l/100km) at a steady 56mph (89.89kph) and an urban 26mpg (10.86l/100km). But with only 90bhp (67.11kW) it was a feeble performer and at £3089 for the conversion it would be a long time before it paid for itself in improved fuel consumption. The engine was the same as Rover had been using for its SD Turbo SD1 saloon since 1982 and after two years' work it found its way into the Solihull 4x4, the Turbo D. Supplied to Alfa Romeo as well as Rover for the lacklustre saloon car the HR492HI was alleged to be an improvement but it still felt and vibrated like a diesel. The main difference between the production version and the 1983 Janspeed was the addition of an intercooler, the cam profile was changed, nickel surface treatment for the four separate cylinder heads and exhaust valves of Nimonic alloy. Power was enhanced and torque was almost a match for the petrol V8. Conical engine mounts were tried to absorb the vibration and big production increases were cheerfully forecast. UK Range Rover sales were running at 3,300 a year, of which only one in ten was expected to be a diesel although there was more hope for sales on Continental Europe, where diesel Land Rovers had shown an increase of 30 per cent.

BODY: 5-door, 5-seat, 4408lb (2000kg) ENGINE: 4-cylinder, in-line, diesel; 92mm x 90mm, 2393cc; compression ratio 22:1; 112bhp (83.51kW) @ 4,200rpm; 46.8/l (34.9kW/l); 183ftlb (254.4Nm) @ 2400rpm.
ENGINE STRUCTURE: pushrod ohv; gear-driven camshaft; aluminium cylinder head; cast iron block, wet liners; water-cooled; indirect injection; KKK K16 turbocharger with air-to-air intercooler, boost pressure 12psi (0.83bar); 5-bearing crankshaft.
TRANSMISSION permanent four wheel drive.10.5in (26.7cm) hydraulically operated 10.5in (26.67cm) single dry plate clutch; LT77 5-speed main gearbox and 2-speed LT230T transfer box with lockable centre differential; automatic optional; Rover front and rear banjo axles; hypoid bevel final drive, ratio 3.54:1, transfer box low ratio 3.32:1, high ratio 1.192:1
CHASSIS welded steel ladder frame; front and rear live axles with coil springs and telescopic dampers, located by radius arms and Panhard rod; rear located by radius arms, support rods and central A-frame with Boge Hydromat self-levelling strut; recirculating ball steering PAS; dual circuit, servo-assisted hydraulic brakes, 11.8in (30cm) front discs, four-piston callipers, 11.42in (29.0cm) rear discs, 2-piston callipers, 10in (25.4cm) drum transmission parking brake; 19gal (86 litre) fuel tank; 16in alloy wheels, 6in rims with 205Rx16 Michelin XM+S tyres.
DIMENSIONS wheelbase 100in (254cm); track 58.5in (148cm); length 176in (447cm); width 70in (178cm); height 70in (178cm); ground clearance 7.5in (19cm); turning circle 37ft (11.3m).
PERFORMANCE 0-60mph (96kph); 18.1sec, top speed; 90mph (144.47kph); 25.8mph (41.41kph) @ 1000rpm; fuel consumption urban, 56mph (89.89kph), 75mph (120.39kph), 25.5mpg (11.07l/100km), 34.1mpg (8.28l/100km), 24.4mpg (11.57l/100km).
PRICE 4-door £18,109.43 including car tax and VAT.

A grille with horizontal slats came in for 1987, when a Vogue Turbo D was available with a whole range of appropriately luxury fittings. Land Rover was determined that a diesel was not regarded as a down-market option. Also in 1987 the bonnet hinges were concealed and the fuel filler, on the right rear quarter, had its own door as it had been designed to have back in 1970.

1988 Range Rovers for America and Vogue SE

What the news broke in late 1986 that Range Rovers were to be sold in America, 600 dealers applied for appointment. Land Rover tentatively aimed at East and West coasts, the South, Texas and the snow-belt ski resorts, and took on 60. The American market car was identifiable by a horizontal grille pattern, concealed bonnet hinges for the torsion bar assisted bonnet, and a locking flap for the petrol filler. Known internally as the Eagle when it was introduced to America in 1987 with 3,250 sold, it became Osprey with the engine enlarged from 3.5 to 3.9litres, and designed to run on unleaded fuel. All were automatics; there was no manual option, cloth upholstery was standard, leather optional. Power was up 19 per cent, torque by 13 per cent, and 0-60 acceleration came down from 13.2sec to 10.9sec. It was also faster, with Land Rover claiming that the engine change was intended purely to rectify the power loss due to the inclusion of a catalytic converter and there were no plans to sell the 3.9litre in Britain. For MY1988 came the new Borg Warner transfer box with Morse chain drive and viscous coupling centre differential, from which domestic-market cars were to benefit as well (qv). Cruise control was fitted as standard and there was a high-mounted stoplight on the tailgate to comply with American regulations. However even if the 3.9 was not sold in Britain meantime, the Vogue Special Equipment (SE) inherited a good deal of the US-market specification. The most luxurious and expensive Range Rover yet, air conditioning, electric seats, and and electric sunroof were all standard, it was trimmed in grey leather, and the plain wood door cappings were upgraded to polished burr walnut (called American walnut on US-market cars). Wheels were five-spoke alloys colour-matched to the blue or green paintwork.

INTRODUCTION: UK Vogue SE April, US spec November 1988
BODY: 5-door, 5-seat, 4259lb (1932kg)
ENGINE: US 90deg V8: 93.98mm x 71.1mm 3947cc; compression ratio 9.35:1; 178bhp (132.73kW) @ 4750rpm; 227ftlb(304.4Nm) @ 3500rpm; catalytic converter. Vogue SE: V8 petrol; 88.9mm x 71.1mm, 3528cc; 165bhp (123kW) @ 4,750rpm; 46.77bhp/l (34.87kW/l); 206ftlb (276.25Nm) @ 3200rpm.
ENGINE STRUCTURE: pushrod ohv with hydraulic tappets; single central chain-driven camshaft; aluminium alloy LM25 block and cylinder heads, dry liners; Lucas L-Jetronic fuel injection; Lucas 35DM8 distributor; electric fuel pump; 5-bearing crankshaft.
TRANSMISSION permanent four wheel drive.10.5in (26.7cm); VogueSE, 2-speed LT230T transfer box with lockable centre differential; US Borg-Warner transfer box with Morse chain drive, bevel central differential with viscous coupling lock; ZF HP22 4-speed automatic with overdrive top lock-up; Rover front and rear banjo axles; hypoid bevel final drive, ratio 3.54:1, transfer box low ratio 3.32:1, high ratio 1.222:1.

CHASSIS welded steel ladder frame; front and rear live axles with coil springs and telescopic dampers, located by radius arms and Panhard rod; rear located by radius arms, support rods and central A-frame with Boge Hydromat self-levelling strut; recirculating ball steering PAS; dual circuit, servo-assisted hydraulic brakes, 11.8in (30cm) front discs, four-piston callipers, 11.42in (29.0cm) rear discs, 2-piston callipers, 10in (25.4cm) drum transmission parking brake; 18gal (81.8l) fuel tank; 16in 5-spoke alloy wheels with 6in rims; 205x16 Michelin XM+S or Avon tyres.
DIMENSIONS wheelbase 102in (259cm); track 58.5in (148cm); length 176in (447cm); width 70in (178cm); height 70in (178cm); ground clearance 7.5in (19cm); turning circle 37ft (11.3m).
EQUIPMENT: cruise control; 6-speaker ICE; heated windscreen; tilt and slide sunroof
PERFORMANCE Vogue SE 0-60mph (96kph), 11.7 sec; top speed, 101mph (163kph); 26.6mph (42.7kph) @ 1000rpm; fuel consumption15.8mpg (17.87l/100km). US 0-60mph (96kph) 11sec; top speed 110mph (176.58kph) fuel consumption 15.8mpg (17.87l/100km)
PRICE $35,800 Vogue SE £27,349

At last a Rover that really was expected to be at home on the range. American market cars had a deep bib under the front fender, lots of lights, and lots of safety freatures as required by federal regulations. The Vogue SE inherited much of the US-market specification.

1988 Range Rover Borg Warner chain drive transfer

One of the most significant improvements of the Range Rover drive train's 18-year development was the replacement of the 2-speed LT230 helical transfer gearbox introduced in 1982. Developed by Borg Warner for US market 4x4s, where they were commonplace, and manufactured at its Kenfig plant in Wales, this took the drive from the output shaft of the manual or automatic gearbox to an epicyclic gear set, which provided the high and low ratios, then via an inverted tooth chain to the central differential. A silicone-filled viscous coupling across the outputs locked if wheelspin set in at front or back wheels. The effect was automatically to control the centre differential, so the driver no longer had to select diff-lock when wheelspin occurred. The immediate advantage was, at last, to banish the transfer gear whine that despite the engineers' best efforts, had been a feature of Range Rovers since the beginning. Noise was now really at saloon car levels and driveline shunt, the clunk between drive and over-run, was all but eliminated. Changing from high to low ratios for off-road driving could be accomplished smoothly, and although it was still necessary to stop for engagement, off-road driving was greatly simplified. *Autocar* remained disappointed with the degree of body roll the Vogue SE displayed, owing it was said to Land Rover's reluctance to fit anti-roll bars. The live axles meant no camber changes during fast cornering, so it felt more consistent than many saloon cars with independent suspension, and no abrupt changes from its natural slight understeer. The steering damper that was always necessary to prevent kick-back on rough ground made the recirculating ball steering feel rather lifeless and slow to respond. The ride remained supple and well controlled, effortlessly soaking up the bumps of badly patched roadworks it was claimed: "the rougher the road the better the suspension works." Furthermore off-road abilities were not compromised, although for what *Autocar* called serious work: "you should follow Land Rover's advice and remove the front spoiler ... a fiddly job that could be made much easier with some thoughtful design."

INTRODUCTION: UK Vogue SE April 1988
BODY: 5-door, 5-seat, 4192lb (1903kg)
ENGINE: 90deg V8 petrol, in-line, 88.9mm x 71.1mm, 3528cc; compression ratio 9.35:1; 165bhp (123kW) @ 4,750rpm; 46.77bhp/l (34.87kW/l); 206ftlb (276.25Nm) @ 3200rpm.
ENGINE STRUCTURE: pushrod ohv with hydraulic tappets; single central chain-driven camshaft; aluminium alloy LM25 block and cylinder heads, dry liners; Lucas L-Jetronic fuel injection; electronic ignition; electric fuel pump; 5-bearing crankshaft.
TRANSMISSION permanent four wheel drive.10.5in (26.7cm); VogueSE, 2-speed LT230T transfer box with lockable centre differential; Borg Warner transfer box with Morse chain drive, bevel central differential with viscous coupling lock; ZF HP22 4-speed automatic with overdrive top lock-up; Rover front and rear banjo axles; hypoid bevel final drive, ratio 3.54:1, transfer box low ratio 3.32:1, high ratio 1.222:1.

CHASSIS welded steel ladder frame; front and rear live axles with coil springs and telescopic dampers, located by radius arms and Panhard rod; rear located by radius arms, support rods and central A-frame with Boge Hydromat self-levelling strut; recirculating ball steering PAS 3.5 turns lock to lock; dual circuit, servo-assisted hydraulic brakes, 11.8in (30cm) front discs, four-piston callipers, 11.42in (29.0cm) rear discs, 2-piston callipers, 10in (25.4cm) drum transmission parking brake; 17.5gal (79.55l) fuel tank; 16in 5-spoke alloy wheels with 7in rims; 205x16 Michelin XM+S 244 or Avon tyres.
DIMENSIONS wheelbase 102in (259cm); track 58.5in (148cm); length 176in (447cm); width 70in (178cm); height 70in (178cm); ground clearance 7.5in (19cm); turning circle 37ft (11.3m).
EQUIPMENT: head restraints; reclining tilting height-adjustable leather seats; walnut trim; electric mirrors; heated rear window; sunroof; tinted glass; metallic paint; radio-cassette player all standard.
PERFORMANCE Autocar Nov 1988 0-60mph (96kph), 11.7 sec; top speed, 101mph (163kph); 26.6mph (42.7kph) @ 1000rpm; fuel consumption15.8mpg (17.87l/100km).
PRICE £28,885

Transmission noise was a perennial
problem with Range Rovers. Land
Rover's answer was the new Borg
Warner transfer box with a calming
chain drive instead of boisterous
gears.

1989 Range Rover 3.9litre V8, 2.5 Turbo D

It was only a matter of time before the 3.9litre engine became available in Britain, along with a further technical advance, anti-lock braking. Accompanied by price rises that went above £30,000 for the first time, this was a period which saw many manufacturers raising prices quarterly in order to keep pace with inflation. For the 1990 model year, besides the enlargement of the V8 by increasing the bore from 88.9mm to 94mm, the 4-cylinder diesel was also enhanced, although its lacklustre performance remained a drawback. The 200Tdi with which the Discovery was being equipped was disregarded for the time being, and the VM bore was increased from 90mm to 94mm, which not only increased power but augmented torque by some 14 per cent. ABS brakes however were a notable technical achievement, and their development occupied five years before Land Rover was satisfied that they were compatible with off-road driving. The worry was that slippery surfaces, together with the bumps and jolts of rocky ground would unnerve the system, and send the wrong messages to the callipers. Wabco, a German firm supplying ABS brakes to Porsche for its 959, was instrumental in solving the problem. The stiff viscous coupling in the centre differential and the low range in the transfer box had to be in a sense outmanoeuvred by a four-channel braking system sensor working at a very high 250 cycles per second sampling rate. High pressure brake fluid was supplied by an accumulator with an electrically powered hydraulic pump, and distributed to the four callipers by means of an electronically controlled valve block. When a wheel sensed lock-up its brake pressure was reduced by bleeding it back into the accumulator, cycling the fluid pressure 10 times a second. There was no means of switching the ABS off, as some had advocated for cross-country driving, although to help on snow or wet grass it did so automatically at under 2mph (3.21kph). It was even possible to re-write the off-roader's manual and apply the brakes on a downhill slippery slope. ABS was standard on Vogue SE and optional on the rest of the range. The 5-speed manual gearbox was strengthened through wider gears with forged dog teeth, the quality of the shift improved by a new guide plate, and top gear was made longer for more relaxed cruising. The ZF automatic acquired an inhibitor to stop worrying kick-downs at speed.

INTRODUCTIONS: October 1989
BODY: 5-door, 5-seat, 4365lb (1980kg); diesel 4442lb (2015kg)
ENGINE: 90deg V8 petrol, in-line; 94mm x 71.1mm, 3947cc; compression ratio 9.35:1; 185bhp (137.95kW) @ 4,750rpm; 46.9bhp/l (34.97kW/l); 235ftlb (315Nm) @ 2600rpm. Diesel 92mm x 94mm; 2499.5cc; compression 22.5:1; 119bhp (88.73kW) @ 4200rpm; 47.6bhp/l (35.49kW/l); 209lbft (280Nm) @ 1950rpm.
ENGINE STRUCTURE: V8 pushrod ohv with hydraulic tappets; single central chain-driven camshaft; aluminium alloy LM25 block and cylinder heads, dry liners; Lucas L-Jetronic fuel injection; electronic ignition; electric fuel pump; 5-bearing crankshaft. Diesel pushrod ohv; gear-driven camshaft; aluminium cylinder head; cast iron block, wet liners; water-cooled; indirect injection; KKK K16 turbocharger with air-to-air intercooler, boost pressure 12psi (0.83bar); 5-bearing crankshaft.

TRANSMISSION permanent four wheel drive.10.5in (26.7cm); Borg-Warner transfer box with Morse chain drive, bevel central differential with viscous coupling lock; Vogue SE, ZF 4HP22 4-speed automatic with overdrive top lock-up; Diesel 5-speed LT77 manual gearbox; Rover front and rear banjo axles; hypoid bevel final drive, ratio 3.54:1, transfer box low ratio 3.32:1, high ratio 1.222:1
CHASSIS welded steel ladder frame; front and rear live axles with coil springs and telescopic dampers, located by radius arms and Panhard rod; rear located by radius arms, support rods and central A-frame with Boge Hydromat self-levelling strut; recirculating ball steering PAS 3.5 turns lock to lock; dual circuit, servo-assisted hydraulic brakes with ABS, 11.8in (30cm) ventilated front discs, four-piston callipers, 11.42in (29.0cm) rear discs, 2-piston callipers, 10in (25.4cm) drum transmission parking brake; 17.5gal (79.55l) fuel tank; 16in 5-spoke alloy wheels with 7in rims; 205x16 Michelin XM+S 244 or Goodyear Wrangler tyres.

DIMENSIONS wheelbase 102in
(259cm); track 58.5in (148cm); length
176in (447cm); width 70in (178cm);
height 70in (178cm); ground clearance
7.5in (19cm); turning circle 37ft
(11.3m).
EQUIPMENT: Vogue SE, head
restraints; reclining tilting height-
adjustable leather seats; walnut trim;
electric mirrors; heated rear window;
sunroof; tinted glass; metallic paint;
radio-cassette player all standard

PERFORMANCE *Autocar* Nov 1988
Vogue SE 0-60mph (96kph), 11.7 sec;
top speed, 101mph (163kph); 26.6mph
(42.7kph) @ 1000rpm; fuel
consumption 15.8mpg (17.87l/100km).
Diesel 0-60mph (96kph) 15.8sec; top
speed 95mph (152.5kph) fuel
consumption Euromix 27.42mpg
(10.3l/100km)
PRICE Vogue SE £31,949, Diesel
£25,905

1990 Range Rover CSK 2-door limited edition

Special limited editions of cars were customary during their run-out phase, usually in an effort to clear stocks, and make way for a new model. Land Rover was not impervious from the pretext, although 20 years into the Range Rover's existence the motive was more to augment the profitability of a batch of cars, rather than merely sell them. It marked the second decade of a model, which unusually if not uniquely had undergone little real change, with a tribute to its progenitor Charles Spencer King by calling it the CSK. However the CSK was more than simply a special edition. It represented a new era in Range Rover philosophy. Anti-roll bars had long been resisted for the Range Rover on the grounds that they would impose limits the long-travel low rate coil spring suspension crucial to its performance especially off-road. There was concern that its articulation, the ability to keep opposing wheels touching uneven ground, would be compromised. Twisting bars connecting opposite wheels, effectively increasing spring stiffness when one wheel rose and the other fell (what happens when a car rolls), would in extreme conditions wind the bar up to its tightest, limiting roll. Stiff bars created roll oscillation at low speeds, an unpleasant waddle, or roll-rock but demand from the market was increasing. Racing driver Warwick Banks of the Koni shock absorber family among others, offered kits to improve Range Rover handling, and road testers had complained about the body roll on corners for years. Furthermore contemporaries were catching up, so developments were put in hand by suspension engineer Paul Markwick, who introduced front and rear anti-roll bars that reduced spring travel by no more than a negligible 0.5in (1.27cm). Front and real anti-roll bars and uprated dampers increased roll stiffness by 25 per cent. Work on air suspension for Range Rovers was well under way, and it had to be acknowledged that improving handling was an important objective for the long term, since good road performance had become so critical for many buyers. It soon transpired that if the change proved successful on the CSK it would soon be applied throughout the range. Thus the CSK was a significant step not only towards the next generation of Range Rovers, but the generation after that, reaching its apotheosis in 2005 with the Range Rover Sport. The CSK was the first new 2-door Range Rover for several years, and all 200 were finished in black with silver coachstripes, and had beige leather upholstery.

INTRODUCTION: September 1990
BODY: 2-door, 5-seat, 3872lb (1756kg); Vogue SE 4-door 4379lb (1988kg)
ENGINE: 90deg V8 petrol, in-line; 94mm x 71.1mm, 3947cc; compression ratio 9.35:1; 185bhp (137.95kW) @ 4,750rpm; 46.9bhp/l (34.97kW/l); 235ftlb (315Nm) @ 2600rpm.
ENGINE STRUCTURE: V8 pushrod ohv with hydraulic tappets; single central chain-driven camshaft; aluminium alloy LM25 block and cylinder heads, dry liners; Lucas L-Jetronic fuel injection; electronic ignition; electric fuel pump; 5-bearing crankshaft.
TRANSMISSION permanent four wheel drive.10.5in (26.7cm); Borg-Warner transfer box with Morse chain drive, bevel central differential with viscous coupling lock; 5-speed manual, or ZF 4HP22 4-speed automatic with overdrive top lock-up; Rover front and rear banjo axles; hypoid bevel final drive, ratio 3.54:1, transfer box low ratio 3.32:1, high ratio 1.222:1

CHASSIS welded steel ladder frame; front and rear live axles with coil springs, telescopic dampers and anti-roll bars, located by radius arms and Panhard rod; rear located by radius arms, support rods and central A-frame with Boge Hydromat self-levelling strut; recirculating ball steering PAS 3.5 turns lock to lock; dual circuit, servo-assisted hydraulic brakes with ABS, 11.8in (30cm) ventilated front discs, four-piston callipers, 11.42in (29.0cm) rear discs, 2-piston callipers, 10in (25.4cm) drum transmission parking brake; 17.5gal (79.55l) fuel tank; 16in 5-spoke alloy wheels with 7in rims; 205x16 Michelin XM+S 244 tyres.
DIMENSIONS wheelbase 102in (259cm); track 58.5in (148cm); length 176in (447cm); width 70in (178cm); height 70in (178cm); ground clearance 7.5in (19cm); turning circle 37ft (11.3m).

EQUIPMENT: Air conditioning;
electric sunroof, windows, and mirrors;
6-speaker stereo; chrome bumpers;
5-spoke alloy wheels, driving and fog
lamps, Vogue SE Triplex heated
windscreen, optional catalytic converter
£450
PERFORMANCE 0-60mph (96kph),
11.3 sec; top speed, 108mph
(173.37kph), manual 114mph
(183kph)(claim); 26.9mph (43.18kph)
@ 1000rpm; fuel consumption 14.6mpg
(19.3l/100km).
PRICE £28,995, automatic £30,319;
Vogue SE £31,949

By the 1990s the opposition was
catching up on Range Rover and the
angular cliff-like front was falling out
of fashion. Some more brash
competitors came out with trendy
nudge-bars, which were quickly
derided by safety campaigners as
unnecessary for those with no bulls
to nudge and no brushwood to fend
off. Land Rover took a more dignified
stance with the CSK's extra lights
and polished paintwork.

1992 Range Rover LSE 4.2litre long wheelbase, air suspension

An 8in (20.32cm) stretch, an extra 18bhp (13.42kW) with 18lbft (24Nm) more pulling power, and air suspension added up to a price that effectively broke £40,000 for the first time. "There are two certainties with a new Range Rover," said Autocar & Motor wryly. "That it won't cost any less than the previous model, and that everyone will still want one." However it doubted that something costing the equivalent of three Minis in 1972, four in 1982, and seven in 1992 was worth the money, notwithstanding its slow rate of depreciation compared with other luxury cars. Critics complained of wind noise, poor quality trim with exposed stapling, messy metal seams and panel gaps that were still large compared with the luxury BMWs, Mercedes-Benzes, and Jaguars with which Range Rover was now competing. The additional power came from a new crankshaft that increased the stroke from 71mm to 77mm, new camshafts, and high-compression pistons in an effort to keep fuel consumption under control. It was not very successful; the 4.2 litre was 2mpg (141.25l/100km) thirstier on the official cycle and the stretch and additional equipment increased the weight by 300lb (136kg) so its performance was much the same as before. Ride and handling were better, not in the car class with some insecurity in the steering on the straight, and the small lurch going into corners that had been acceptable at three Minis, was a good deal less so at seven Minis. The gains had come at a substantial price but there were no sacrifices in off-road performance. The air springing was a clever adaptation of a system already in use for trucks. Four variable-rate air springs replaced the steel coils while the live axles, dampers, radius arms and the new anti-roll bars continued much as before. An Electronic Control Unit (ECU) under the driver's seat gave notice to an air reservoir, which pumped up the springs through a series of valves, maintaining self-levelling whatever load was being carried in the large 2.16cu m (up by 6cu ft) load space. There were five different ride height settings controlled either automatically, or by fascia buttons, with a rise and fall of 5in (12.7cm). The ECU took account of everything, including door openings, lest a drop in ride height coincided with one open against a low wall or high kerbstone. Great play was made on the suspension's ability to lower itself by way of helping the less agile or downright infirm to get in and out, but its appeal was marginal. It also lowered the ride height for a supposed aerodynamic advantage above 50mph (80) but its effect was negligible. Range Rover sales were dropping in the UK from 6864 in 1989 to just over 4000 in 1991, and in the United States from a peak of 5000 to 3309 so a good deal depended on the new developments.

INTRODUCTION: September 1992
BODY 2-door, 5-seat, 4740lb (2150.06kg)
ENGINE 90deg V8 petrol, in-line; 94mm x 77mm, 4278cc; compression ratio 8.9:1; 200bhp (149.14kW) @ 4,850rpm; 47bhp/l (35.04kW/l); 250ftlb (335.25Nm) @ 3250rpm.
ENGINE STRUCTURE: V8 pushrod ohv with hydraulic tappets; single central chain-driven camshaft; aluminium alloy LM25 block and cylinder heads, dry liners; Lucas L-Jetronic fuel injection; electronic ignition; electric fuel pump; 5-bearing crankshaft.
TRANSMISSION permanent four wheel drive.10.5in (26.7cm); Borg-Warner transfer box with Morse chain drive, bevel central differential with viscous coupling lock; 5-speed manual, or ZF 4HP22 4-speed automatic with overdrive top lock-up; Rover front and rear banjo axles; hypoid bevel final drive, ratio 3.54:1, transfer box low ratio 3.244:1, high ratio 1.206:1
CHASSIS welded steel ladder frame; front and rear live axles with Electronically Controlled Air Suspension (ECAS), telescopic dampers and anti-roll bars, located by radius arms and Panhard rod; rear located by radius arms, support rods and central A-frame; worm and roller PAS; 3.75 turns lock to lock; dual circuit, servo-assisted hydraulic brakes with ABS, 11.8in (30cm) ventilated front discs, four-piston callipers, 11.42in (29.0cm) rear discs, 2-piston callipers, 10in (25.4cm) drum transmission parking brake; 17.5gal (79.55l) fuel tank; 16in 5-spoke alloy wheels with 7in rims; 205x16 Michelin XM+S 244 tyres.

DIMENSIONS wheelbase 108.07in
(274.5cm)); track 58.5in (148cm);
length 183in (464.8cm); width 70in
(178cm); height 72.2in (183.5cm);
ground clearance 7.5in (19cm); turning
circle 41.75ft (12.7m).
EQUIPMENT: Air conditioning;
electric sunroof, windows, and mirrors;
6-speaker stereo; chrome bumpers;
5-spoke alloy wheels, driving and fog
lamps.
PERFORMANCE 0-60mph (96kph),
9.9 sec; top speed, 112mph (179.8kph);
29.6mph (47.51kph) @ 1000rpm; fuel
consumption 13.1mpg (21.56l/100km),
24.2mpg (11.67l/100km), 18.7mpg
(15.1l/100km).
PRICE £39,995

Not quite stretched limo but the long
wheelbase certainly conferred greater
legroom and signified that an even
more luxurious Range Rover was in
the offing.

1992 Range Rover Vogue Tdi

It took three years for the Range Rover to be equipped with the Discovery's 200Tdi direct injection turbo-diesel engine. Rover claimed the power characteristics were not right, that it was not sufficiently refined, scarcely credible in view of the unevenness of the unloved VM. High demand and not enough engines were the real reasons for the delay. A moulded rocker cover, and inserting rubber and stainless steel sound damping pads in the sump tackled the 200Tdi's noise problem. It also got a two-part composite enclosure round the bellhousing for a claimed reduction in the clamour by five decibels at 3000rpm. The Tdi was less noisy than the VM starting from cold and fuel consumption was improved by some 30 per cent, giving it a 500mile range as well as the quieter cabin. By way of demonstrating its new-found economy a Range Rover Tdi on an economy run from Land's End to John O' Groats achieved 53mpg (5.3l/100km) at an average 44mph (70.6kph) for the 832miles (1339kms). Vogue specification turbodiesel Range Rovers were the only ones on offer, the makers asserting that there was no demand for a basic-spec one, although frugally minded drivers were likely to blink at a rise in the price of £1,500. For this they got a better stereo, extra foglights and high-intensity headlights, and the radio aerial was repositioned in a rear side window. The Tdi engine could trace its origins back to Land Rover's original diesel of 30 years before, and although it had a cast iron block and aluminium head like the VM, it was heavier. It raised the weight of the Vogue by 81.6lb (37kg) so the newcomer was slower off the mark despite the stronger torque. It needed less gearshifting but a further anomaly was that the new model was only available meantime with coil springs. There was no engineering reason; Land Rover was merely awaiting demand, reckoning that EAS air suspension could wait a while yet. Changes in March 1994 introduced the 300Tdi engine, on

which more efforts had been expended to make it quieter and meet new European emissions legislation, and the model carried on after the introduction of the second generation Range Rover later the same year as the Range Rover Classic. This remained in limited production until 1996 with a 25th anniversary special edition 3.9litre Vogue SE.

INTRODUCTION: November 1992
BODY: 5-door, 5-seat, 4525lb (2052kg)
ENGINE 4-cyl, in-line, front, 90.47mm x 97mm, 2495cc; compr 19.5:1, (MY 1993) 113bhp (84.26kW) @ 4000rpm; 195lbft (264.3Nm) @ 1800rpm.
ENGINE STRUCTURE 2 overhead valves per cylinder, belt-driven camshaft; aluminium cylinder head, cast iron block. Bosch fuel injection, Garrett turbocharger, air-air intercooler; 5-bearing crankshaft, water-cooled.
TRANSMISSION permanent four wheel drive.10.5in (26.7cm); Borg-Warner transfer box with Morse chain drive, bevel central differential with viscous coupling lock; 5-speed manual LT77S (MY 1994 R380), or (from 1994) ZF 4HP22 4-speed automatic with overdrive top lock-up; Rover front and rear banjo axles; hypoid bevel final drive, ratio 3.54:1, transfer box low ratio 3.244:1, high ratio 1.206:1
CHASSIS welded steel ladder frame; front and rear live axles with coil springs, telescopic dampers and anti-roll bars, located by radius arms and Panhard rod; rear located by radius arms, support rods and central A-frame with Boge Hydromat self-levelling strut; worm and roller PAS; 3.75 turns lock to lock; dual circuit, servo-assisted hydraulic brakes with ABS, 11.8in

(30cm) ventilated front discs, four-piston callipers, 11.42in (29.0cm) rear discs, 2-piston callipers, 10in (25.4cm) drum transmission parking brake; 18gal (81.8l) fuel tank; 16in 5-spoke alloy wheels with 7in rims; 205x16 Michelin XM+S tyres.
DIMENSIONS wheelbase 100in (254cm); track 58.5in (148cm); length 175in (444.7cm); width 72in (181.3cm); height 71in (179.2cm); ground clearance 7.5in (19cm); turning circle 41.75ft (12.7m).
EQUIPMENT: air conditioning; electric windows, and mirrors; 6-speaker stereo; raised load cover; 5-spoke alloy wheels, driving and fog lamps.
PERFORMANCE 0-60mph (96kph), 16.6sec; top speed, 94mph (150.89kph); 29.6mph (47.51kph) @ 1000rpm; fuel consumption 32.9mpg (8.58l/100km), 41mpg (6.89l/100km), 29.1mpg (9.7l/100km).
PRICE £39,995

Last hurrah of the old style Range Rover after 22 years. There were limits to what could be achieved by cosmetics on the old shape and by the last decade of the 20th century they had probably been reached.

1994 Range Rover

BMW came too late to have any influence on the 1994 Range Rover, although the Bavarians did solve Range Rover's diesel dilemma, with an engine deal concluded well ahead of the German acquisition of Rover. Some £300million was invested in a redesign hailed as a reinvention of the Range Rover, even though in some respects it turned out to be an interim model, laying the foundations of the one that would take the model into the next century. Buyers were offered a choice of two V8 petrol engines, and the BMW straight-6-cylinder diesel, for which scrutiny and negotiation had been conducted for around six years. Long-term planning indicated that to obtain a diesel comparable in smoothness to the petrol V8, six cylinders were needed. Sixes were inherently smoother than fours, the VM 4-cylinder was not the answer, so half a dozen alternatives were appraised including the VM in 6-cylinder 3.6litre form, but BMW's engine engineering was second to none, and the winner was an advanced 2.5litre designed in Munich made at the company's engine facility at Steyr in Austria. It had been under development for BMW cars and was adapted to enable it to run at pitch angles up to 45deg and roll of 35deg. In its car configuration it could provide 57bhp/l (42.5kW/l) but top-end power was surrendered for low-speed torque. There were high hopes for it in markets such as Italy, where although 2.5litres might appear feeble for such a heavy cars, bigger engines suffered fiscal penalties. For its part the V8 gained another increase in stroke, from 71mm to 82mm, making a new 4.6litre for which scarcely anything of the original Buick was now left. The new crankshaft had bigger main and big-end bearings, the cylinder block was strengthened to cope, pistons lightened, and individual connecting rods balanced to improve refinement. A polyvee belt drove the auxiliaries reducing engine length by 3in (7.6cm) and allowing it to be moved forward by 4.7in (12cm).

INTRODUCTION: September 1994
BODY: 5-door, 5-seat, 4.0, 4607.6lb (2090kg); 4.6, 4739.9lb (2150kg); DTi, 4552.7lb (2115kg)
ENGINES 4.0, 90deg V8 petrol, in-line; 94mm x 71.1mm, 3947cc; compression ratio 9.35:1; 185bhp (137.95kW) @ 4,750rpm; 46.9bhp/l (34.97kW/l); 235ftlb (316.5Nm) @ 3000rpm. 4.6, 94mm x 82mm, 4552cc; compression ratio 9.35:1; 225bhp (167.78kW) @ 4,750rpm; 49.4bhp/l (36.8kW/l); 277ftlb (371.4Nm) @ 3000rpm. DTi, 6-cylinders; 80mm x 82.8mm; 2497cc; compr 22:1; 134bhp (99.9kW) @ 4400rpm; 53.6bhp/l (40.01kW/l);199lbft (266.9Nm) @ 2300rpm, (from 1997 136bhp (101.41kW) and 197lbft).
ENGINE STRUCTURE: V8 pushrod ohv with hydraulic tappets; single central chain-driven camshaft; aluminium alloy LM25 block and cylinder heads, dry liners; Lucas GEMS engine management; 5-bearing crankshaft. DTi, ohv; toothed belt camshaft drive; indirect injection; iron block, aluminium head, turbocharged and intercooled.
TRANSMISSION permanent four wheel drive.10.5in (26.7cm); Borg-Warner transfer box with Morse chain drive, central differential with viscous coupling lock; 5-speed manual, or ZF 4HP22 4-speed automatic; Rover front and rear banjo axles; hypoid bevel final drive, ratio 3.54:1, transfer box low ratio 3.27:1, high ratio 1.22:1

CHASSIS welded steel ladder frame; front and rear live axles with Electronically Controlled Air Suspension (ECAS), telescopic dampers and anti-roll bars, located by radius arms and Panhard rod; rear located by radius arms, support rods and central A-frame; recirculating ball PAS; 3.2 turns lock to lock; dual circuit, servo-assisted hydraulic brakes with ABS, 11.7in (29.7cm) ventilated front discs, four-piston calliers, 12in (30.5cm) rear discs, 2-piston calliers, 10in (25.4cm) drum transmission parking brake; 22gal (100 l) fuel tank; 16in 5-spoke alloy wheels with 7in rims; 205x16 Michelin XM+S 244 tyres.
DIMENSIONS wheelbase 108.07in (274.5cm); front track 60.6in (154cm), rear 60.2in (153cm); length 185.6in (471.3cm); width 75.4in (181.7cm); height 71.6in (153cm); ground clearance 7.5in (19cm); turning circle 41.75ft (12.7m).
EQUIPMENT: HSE air conditioning; electric windows, and mirrors; 6-speaker stereo; raised load cover; 5-spoke alloy wheels, cruise control
PERFORMANCE 4.0, 0-60mph (96kph), 9.9sec manual, 10.4 automatic; top speed, 118mph (189.4kph); 26.7mph (42.9kph) @ 1000rpm; fuel consumption average 14.1mpg (20.03l/100km). 4.6 auto, 0-60, 9.3sec; top speed 118mph (189.42kph); fuel consumption Autocar overall 15.3mpg (18.46l/100km). DTi, 0-60, 14.3sec; top speed 105.9mph (170kph) fuel consumption 28.82mpg (9.8l/100km) PRICE 4.0 and DTi £31,950-£36,100; 4.2 HSE £43,500

Camshafts were reprofiled and an engine management system, known as Gems and developed with Lucas, was installed. The 3.9litre engine was henceforward known as the 4.0litre to show that it was not quite the same as hitherto. Land Rover by now working on metric dimensions fixed the new wheelbase at 274.5cm (108.07in) for a new chassis framed differently from the long wheelbase LSE of 1992, which had been stretched round rear seat legroom. The new chassis was somewhat subtler than before, with thin sections reflecting the need for reducing the weight, thick sections putting strength where it was needed, deformable places for impact crushability where it was required. Beam axles remained; it was still the view that they remained necessary for off-road performance and 29cm (11.4in) of bump and 33cm (12.99in) of rebound remained more than almost any independent system could provide while guaranteeing to retain traction all round. Air suspension was standard on all models, the front hubs and brake callipers were reconfigured to improve the feel of the steering, (53 per cent of the Range Rover's weight lay on the front wheels) and as a refinement to the ZF automatic transmission it now engaged with the engine management, to retard ignition timing and make gearshifts smoother.

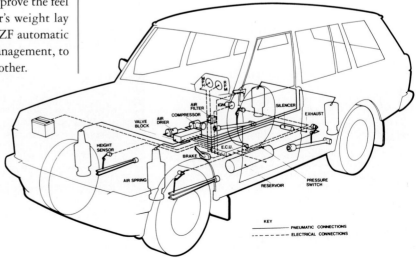

Pictured on the press launch at Cliveden the Range Rover was a technical tour de force. The first major new model under its new owners BMW, it was wider, taller and longer and felt more like a car. Test prototypes broke cover in the spring undergoing long-distance testing in Scotland before the new model, based on the best part of twenty-five years' experience, appeared in October. It ought to have been exemplary yet it remained to be seen if it was good enough. Drawing (below left) illustrates air suspension on introduction in 1992.

1999 Range Rover

The shape of the Range Rover was a matter of careful evolution. A number of radical designs were considered in the 1980s when proposals were being considered for a common platform for Land Rover and Range Rover. Multi Purpose Vehicle (MPV) designs were contemplated but by the time the project, code-named 38A after the building where the team worked, got into the third phase of designing the 1994 Range Rover, its proportions were still recognisably those arrived at by the logical mind of Spen King in the 1960s. Important detailing had been needed to freshen it up without losing its essential identity, which was fine until in 1998, when the competition became keener and revisions were necessary to keep the model going until it was due for a major revision for MY2002. Plans for BMW V8 and V12 engines were discarded, together with a tentative new super-expensive Range Rover, so the now venerable ex-Buick V8 received yet another makeover with a cast alloy structural sump, and engine mountings changed to transmit less noise and vibration to the occupants. As a further enhancement in refinement, there was a new engine management system, and an inlet manifold with characteristic curved branches to give power and pull at lower rpm. Separate ignition coils were installed for each bank of cylinders, long-life double platinum spark plugs, and silicon HT leads were all symptomatic of a new drive towards better build quality as justification of ever-rising prices. Together with the Series II Discovery Electronic Traction Control (ETC) was standardised. Trim was enhanced, new safety features introduced and affirming that diesel was by no means a down-market alternative the HSE specification was also applied to the 2.5DHSE. Among the subtler cosmetics were new headlight units, still rectangular, but with twin circular units behind the glass. Limited Editions had been a feature of Range Rover marketing for years and as though to emphasise its upper-crust pretensions between 1999 and 2001 several were introduced including the County SE, which offered trim and colour options, two sorts of Vogue SE with upholstery in walnut leather; the Linley limited to ten examples although only six were made named after David Linley the Queen's nephew and furniture designer and hand-finished in black. This had piano black veneer trim with stainless steel etching. The Holland & Holland connected the Range Rover with the celebrated gunsmith, and 300 were made for America, 100 for Europe with bridle leather providing the country pursuit feel. On a more practical note, the quality improvements made throughout the range enabled the replacement of the old one-year warranty with a three year or 60,000mile extended term.

INTRODUCTION: October 1998
BODY: 5-door, 5-seat, 4.0, 4607.6lb
(2090kg); 4.6, 4739.9lb (2150kg); DTi,
4552.7lb (2115kg).
ENGINES 4.0, 90deg V8 petrol, in-
line; 94mm x 71.1mm, 3947cc;
compression ratio 9.35:1; 185bhp
(137.95kW) @ 4,750rpm; 46.9bhp/l
(34.97kW/l); 235ftlb (316.5Nm) @
3000rpm. 4.6, 94mm x 82mm, 4552cc;
compression ratio 9.35:1; 225bhp
(167.78kW) @ 4,750rpm; 49.4bhp/l
(36.8kW/l); 277ftlb (371.4Nm) @
3000rpm. DTi, 6-cylinders; 80mm x
82.8mm; 2497cc; compr 22:1; 134bhp
(99.9kW) @ 4400rpm; 53.6bhp/l
(40.01kW/l);199lbft (266.9Nm) @
2300rpm, (from 1997 136bhp
(101.41kW) and 197lbft).
ENGINE STRUCTURE: V8 pushrod
ohv with hydraulic tappets; single
central chain-driven camshaft;

aluminium alloy LM25 block and
cylinder heads, dry liners; Bosch
Motronic engine management; 5-
bearing crankshaft. DTi, ohv; toothed
belt camshaft drive; indirect injection;
iron block, aluminium head,
turbocharged and intercooled.
TRANSMISSION permanent four wheel
drive.10.5in (26.7cm); Borg-Warner
transfer box with Morse chain drive,
central differential with viscous
coupling lock; 5-speed manual, or ZF
4HP22 4-speed automatic; Rover front
and rear banjo axles; hypoid bevel final
drive, ratio 3.54:1, transfer box low
ratio 3.27:1, high ratio 1.22:1.
CHASSIS welded steel ladder frame;
front and rear live axles with
Electronically Controlled Air Suspension
(ECAS), telescopic dampers and anti-roll
bars, located by radius arms and
Panhard rod; rear located by radius

arms, support rods and central A-frame;
recirculating ball PAS; 3.2 turns lock to
lock; dual circuit, servo-assisted
hydraulic brakes with ABS, 11.7in
(29.7cm) ventilated front discs, four-
piston callipers, 12in (30.5cm) rear
discs, 2-piston callipers, 10in (25.4cm)
drum transmission parking brake; 22gal
(100 l) fuel tank; 16in 5-spoke alloy
wheels with 7in rims; 205x16 Michelin
XM+S 244 tyres.
DIMENSIONS wheelbase 108.07in
(274.5cm); front track 60.6in (154cm),
rear 60.2in (153cm); length 185.6in
(471.3cm); width 75.4in (181.7cm);
height 71.6in (153cm); ground
clearance 7.5in (19cm); turning circle
41.75ft (12.7m).
EQUIPMENT: HSE air conditioning;
clcctric windows, and mirrors; 11
speaker stereo; raised load cover; 5-
spoke alloy wheels, cruise control; optional

Carin satellite navigation.
PERFORMANCE 4.0, 0-60mph
(96kph), 9.9sec manual, 10.4 automatic;
top speed, 118mph (189.4kph);
26.7mph (42.9kph) @ 1000rpm; fuel
consumption average 14.1mpg
(20.03l/100km). 4.6 auto, 0-60, 9.3sec;
top speed 118mph (189.42kph); fuel
consumption Autocar overall 15.3mpg
(18.46l/100km). DTi, 0-60, 14.3sec; top
speed 105.9mph (170kph) fuel
consumption 28.82mpg (9.8l/100km).
PRICE 4.0 and DTi £31,950-£36,100;
4.2 HSE £43,500. County SE £42,595;
Vogue SE £54,995; Linley £100,000;
Holland & Holland £63,495 plus
£5,000 for optional TV and video; 30th
Anniversary £57,500-£63,000;
Westminster £46,495; Bordeaux £38,995;
Braemar £42,995; 2002 Vogue SE.

2001 Range Rover

The third generation Range Rover arrived at the end of 2001, just in time for MY 2002, and it was new from end-to-end. Like the previous model it was conceived under one management and launched by another, BMW having invested heavily in it, arranging for it to be powered by a choice of their latest engines, yet it was launched only after Ford bought the business in 2000. In every way this was a no-compromise model, with a totally new structure, style and features. Larger, heavier, better equipped and altogether more capable than the one it replaced, it was fast, petrol engined versions were capable of speeds approaching 130mph (209kph), and it had all the modern chassis and equipment that could be expected of a class-leading luxury car. Although still a supreme off-road machine, and little could defeat its ability on the roughest terrain, its designers realised that for the most part it would rarely be used off the highway. As a result it gained a new emphasis on refinement, quietness, and luxurious equipment. It remained a 5-door estate, larger although subtly more rounded than before, and was based on what its new owner Ford called a body-on-frame structure. This was essentially a monocoque, but with massive members welded to the underside of the shell, so it had the strength and stiffness of an old-style chassis frame. In an effort to contain the weight of this addition, and also to stave off corrosion, much of the body shell was made in aluminium. The venerable ex-Buick V8 was at last relinquished, after more than 30 years' staunch service, and replaced by BMW engines, a choice of 4.4-litre V8 petrol, or 2.9-litre 6-cylinder turbo-diesel. Also for the first time, all cars were sold only with automatic or manual-automatic Steptronic transmission, and selectable high-range or low-range. This was also the first Range Rover to have independent suspension, at front and rear, incorporating the now well-proven air springs. These were self-levelling and height-adjustable, with wishbone linkage, and steering was power-assisted rack-and-pinion. Maintaining BMW's fondness for electronic features and it not only had ABS brakes, but also Brake Assist, Dynamic Stability Control, and Hill Descent Control. Nothing was spared to make this the world's most accomplished 4x4, and capable of dealing with approaching competition not only from traditional rivals from the far East including a new Lexus, but also from closer to home Volvo, Mercedes-Benz, Porsche, VW and in due course BMW itself. Land Rover engineers' major concern was its on-road ride, handling, and overall quality, to justify the claim that the new Range Rover was: " ...the world's most capable, with the greatest breadth of ability of any vehicle ever". This was a sweeping statement with which few unbiased engineers would disagree. *Autocar* confirmed that: "Solihull's engineers have had the courage to totally re-imagine the Range Rover, transforming its road manners without sacrificing its off-road ability." Although there was a big demand for both petrol and diesel in most territories, only the petrol-engined version was sold in North America, where the model was launched in January 2002. The standard specification included satellite navigation, air conditioning, traction control and leather trim, yet it was still easy to spend well over £60,000 on a new car. However there seemed no reluctance for customers to pay out cheerfully on whatever was available. The interior, particularly the fascia, instrument panel, and front seat area was as carefully and completely equipped as that of any high-grade car. Technically, the third-generation Range Rover was a well ahead of the older types, and quickly proved a commercial success.

2001 Range Rover continued

INTRODUCTION Winter 2001/2002
BODY estate, 5-doors, 5-seats; weight
5535lb (2510kg).
ENGINES V8-cylinder, petrol, front;
in-line; 92mm x 82.7mm, 4398cc;
compr 10.0:1; 282bhp (210kW) @
5400rpm; 64.1bhp/l (47.7kW/l);
325lbft (444Nm) @ 3600rpm; 6-
cylinder turbo-diesel, front, in-line,
84mm x 88mm, 2926cc, compr 18.0:1,
177bhp (130kW) @ 4000rpm;
60.5bhp/l (44.4kW/l); 287lbft
(392Nm) @ 2000rpm.
ENGINE STRUCTURE V8, BMW 32
valves; twin chain-driven overhead
camshafts; aluminium cylinder heads,
and block; Bosch Motronic electronic
fuel injection and engine management;
5-bearing crankshaft; 6-cylinder turbo-
diesel, BMW, twin overhead camshafts,
chain camshaft drive, aluminium
cylinder heads and block, Bosch DDE
electronic fuel injection and engine
management, KKK turbocharger,
intercooler, 7-bearing crankshaft.
TRANSMISSION four wheel drive;
five-speed ZF automatic transmission
(4.4-litre petrol) or GM (turbo-diesel);
final drive V8 petrol 3.73:1; 6-cylinder
turbo-diesel 4:1. Choice of high-ratio
and low-ratio transmission ratios (low
with a step-down of 2.7:1).

CHASSIS steel frame welded to steel
and aluminium-panelled body shell
monocoque; ifs by air springs,
Macpherson struts, telescopic dampers;
irs by air springs, wishbones, telescopic
dampers, hydraulic servo-assisted
brakes, front 13.5in (34.4cm) dia
ventilated disc, rear 13.9in (35.4cm) dia
discs, drum parking brake, ABS anti-
lock and Brake Assist; rack-and-pinion
PAS; 22.0gal (100l) fuel tank; 255/60-
18in. radial ply tyres on cast alloy wheel
rims; larger wheels/tyres optional.
DIMENSIONS wheelbase; 113.4in
(288cm) track front; 64.1in (162.9cm)
track rear; 64.0in (162.6cm) length;
194.9in (495.0cm) width; 86.2in
(219cm) height; 73.3in (186.3cm)
turning circle 38.0ft (11.6m)
PERFORMANCE
maximum speed; V8, 129mph
(207.5kph); 6-cyl diesel 111mph
(178.5kph); V8 30.0mph (48.3kph) @
1000rpm; diesel 29.1mph (46.8kph);
0-60mph (96kph) V8, 8.7sec; diesel
12.1sec; fuel consumption V8, 12.8mpg
(16.07l/100km); diesel 21.5mpg
(9.7l/100km).
PRICE; V8 from £52,995, 6-cyl diesel
from £45,995

The new Range Rover was subject
to intense testing overseas, over all
kinds of terrain and in extreme
temperatures. This test car still
carries remains of the 'camouflage'
tape on the headlights.

2005–2007 Range Rover

Three years after the introduction of the third generation Range Rover, a range of up-dates and improvements were introduced at the Detroit Motor Show in January. There were several minor, but important cosmetic changes, and the engine line-up was revised to include a supercharged premium model for the first time. Visually, the 5-door estate car was little changed, except for a revised, larger front grille with horizontal expanded metal bars that quickly earned the soubriquet of cheese-grater. The headlights were re-grouped and the bumper and apron re-shaped. Front screen pillars were made slimmer to do away with driver's-eye blindspots, rear light clusters revised, and there was the option of swivelling headlamps to illuminate bends in the road. The existing sumptuous fascia and instrument show were unchanged, using the display panel to include a screen for the optional reversing camera, a boon on a tall vehicle with indifferent rearwards visibility. Huge front brakes, Brembo on the supercharged model, and revised spring and damper rates were all part of the package. The major development was to discard the petrol BMW V8, in favour of Jaguar-based V8s from within the Ford Premier Automotive Group. One was a normally-aspirated 4.4-litre with 305bhp (225kW), the other a supremely-powerful supercharged 4.2-litre producing 400 SAE bhp (298kW), providing a top speed of well over 130mph (209kph). This was 42 per cent more power than the outgoing BMW V8, and both engines were modified for the Range Rover, with up to 29 per cent more torque. To match the new power plants came a new type of ZF 6-speed automatic transmission, bringing the Range Rover into line with the Discovery 3, which had gone on the market a year earlier. The BMW turbo-diesel, with its 5-speed GM automatic transmission carried on unchanged, although it was never one of BMW's quietest or smoothest diesels, and struggled slightly on inclines against faster opposition. The V8s' enhanced performance came at a premium price, but once again met the aspirations of a large and generally satisfied clientele. The V8 Supercharged Vogue SE cost £72,995, though the prices of the normally-aspirated Jaguar engined versions started at £22,000 less.

For Model Year 2007 Land Rover made a continuing commitment to the Defender with a series of upgrades to meet new legislation and continue production of the iconic model until 2010. Work was put in hand to stretch its manufacture ever further in view of consistent sales of 25,000 vehicles a year. Total Defender production now exceeded 1.8 million, of which two out of three remained in regular service.

Six Range Rovers in ten sold in the UK were now diesels. Over 118,000 had been sold since 2002 and for MY 2007 Range Rover gained a new TDV8 diesel, claimed to reduce its 0-60mph acceleration by over 4sec, with much the same fuel consumption as the outgoing 6-cylinder. The TDV8 gained 54 per cent more power and 64 per cent more torque. Other developments included an electronic parking brake, which at long last dispensed with the archaic drum brake in the transmission that had been a feature of almost every model of Land Rover for almost 60 years, and the fitment of Terrain Response and electronic rear 'e' differential.

Replacing the 2.9litre BMW turbo-diesel, the TDV8 shared technologies with the TDV6 already used on Discovery and Range Rover Sport, but with 90deg cylinder banks, instead of 60 deg. Driving through a ZF 6-speed automatic, which had a wider spread of ratios than before, it provided a 12 per cent lower first gear and a 28 per cent higher top. The TDV8 was built at Ford's diesel engine centre at Dagenham.

Changes between the 2005 and 2007 models were almost entirely internal. At long last the archaic drum brake in the transmission was replaced with an electronic parking brake.

INTRODUCTION Spring 2005/Spring 2007.
BODY estate, 5-doors, 5-seats; weight 5634lb (2555kg).TDV8 6003lb(2723kg)
ENGINES V8-cylinder, petrol, front, in-line, 88mm x 90.3mm, 4394cc; compr 10.75:1; 305bhp (225kW) @ 5750rpm; 69.4bhp/l (51.2kW/l); 322lbft (440Nm) @ 4000rpm. Supercharged V8-cylinder, petrol, front; in-line; 86mm x 90.3mm, 4197cc; compr 9.1:1; 396bhp (291kW) @ 5750rpm; 94.3bhp/l (69.3kW/l); 410lbft (560Nm) @ 3500rpm. 6-cylinder turbo-diesel, front, in-line, 84mm x 88mm, 2926cc, compr 18.0:1, 177bhp (130kW) @ 4000rpm; 60.5bhp/l (44.4kW/l); 287lbft (392nM) @ 2000rpm.TDV8-cylinders, front; 81mm x 88mm, 3630cc; compr 17.3:1; 272bhp (200kW) @ 4000rpm; 74.9bhp/l (55.85kW/l; 472lbft (640Nm).
ENGINE STRUCTURE V8, Jaguar 32 valves; twin chain-driven overhead camshafts; aluminium cylinder heads, and block; Denso electronic fuel injection and engine management: supercharger and intercooler on

supercharged model. 6-cylinder turbo-diesel, BMW, twin overhead camshafts, chain camshaft drive, aluminium cylinder heads and block, Bosch DDE electronic fuel injection and engine management, KKK turbocharger, intercooler, 7-bearing crankshaft. TDV8 32 valves; 2 ohc per bank; intake camshaft drive by chain, exhaust by gears; aluminium cylinder heads, compacted graphite iron block; twin variable nozzle turbochargers; common rail fuel injection; piezo injectors.
TRANSMISSION four wheel drive; with V8 engines six-speed ZF automatic transmission; final drive 3.73:1; choice of high-ratio or low-ratio transmission, step-down ratio 2.93:1. with 6-cylinder turbo-diesel 5-speed GM automatic, final drive ratio 4:1; choice of high-ratio or low-ratio transmission, step-down ratio 2.7:1.
CHASSIS steel frame welded to steel and aluminium-panelled body shell monocoque; ifs by air springs, Macpherson struts, telescopic dampers, irs by air springs, wishbones, telescopic dampers, hydraulic servo-assisted brakes, front (Supercharged) 14.2in (36.0cm)

dia, or 13.5in (34.4cm) dia ventilated disc, rear 13.9in (35.4cm) dia discs, drum parking brake, ABS anti-lock and Brake Assist; rack-and-pinion PAS; 22.0gal (100l) fuel tank; 255/60-18in. radial ply tyres on cast alloy wheel rims; larger wheels/tyres optional.
DIMENSIONS wheelbase, 113.4in (288cm); track front, 64.1in (162.9cm); track rear, 64.0in (162.6cm); length, 194.9in (495.0cm); width, 86.2in (219cm); height, 73.3in (186.3cm); turning circle 38.0ft (11.6m).
PERFORMANCE
maximum speed; V8 Supercharged 132mph (211.9kph), V8 125mph (200.6kph), turbo-diesel 111mph

(178.5kph)
V8, 33.4mph (53.6kph) @ 1000rpm in 6th; superch 32.95mph (52.9kph); diesel 28.22mph (45.3kph) in 5th 0-60mph (96kph) V8 superch 7.5sec, V8 8.7sec, turbo-diesel 13.6sec. fuel consumption Supercharged V8, 12.8mpg (16.07l/100km), V8 17.88mpg (15.8l/100km); diesel 21.5mpg (9.7l/100km).
TDV8 maximum speed 124mph (200kph); 0-60mph (96.3kph) 8.5sec; fuel consumption TDV8 25.1mpg (11.3l/100km).
PRICE; Diesel from £45,995), V8 from £50,995, Supercharged Vogue SE V8 £72,995

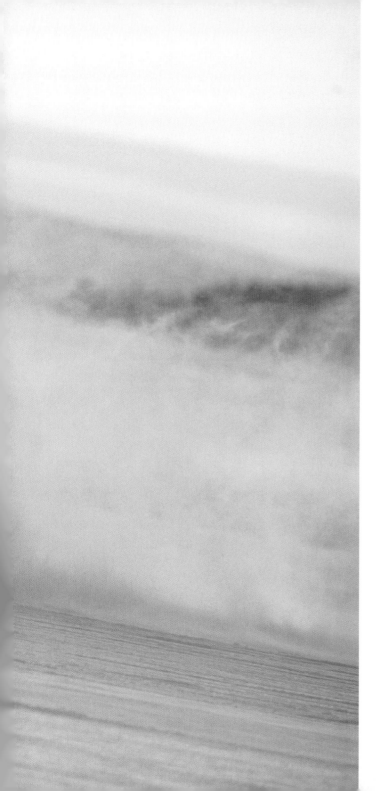

Range Rover Sport

Winter testing in disguise. Wearing
a false nose to confuse spy
photographers the new Range Rover
Sport underwent a rigorous test
programme before it went on sale.

2005 Range Rover Sport 4.4litre V8 4.2litre Supercharged V8 2.7litre V6 diesel

One problem with the fifth species of Land Rover was what to call it. Road Rover might have seemed an obvious choice, since the target was Range Rover customers who kept mostly to the road, preferring good handling and refinement to tackling mountain tracks. Like sports car drivers who never did 150mph, but could if they wanted to, Range Rover Sport drivers were not expected to venture much off-road. But if they ever did, Land Rover believed, they had the best equipment in the world with which to do it. In the 1950s Rover had called experimental prototypes Road Rovers, but the term was not deemed suitable for the new car, which filled a niche between the Discovery and the Range Rover.

Land Rover identified it, somewhat erratically as, "a new sports tourer Sports Utility Vehicle" and it competed with a formidable array including Porsche Cayenne and BMW X5. Following the Range Stormer, a 2004 concept car at the Detroit Motor Show, Range Rover Sport was different from but complementary to the regular Range Rover. It had a choice of supercharged or unsupercharged Jaguar-derived V8s and a V6 diesel, more electronics than ever before with Dynamic Response, and Terrain Response. Dynamic Response reduced roll through an active computer-controlled arrangement, which sensed cornering forces, and then acted on the air springs to reduce body lean. This was claimed to provide the nimble reactions of a much smaller vehicle, and was standard on the supercharged model, optional on others. Terrain Response, which made its production debut on the Discovery 3 was standard throughout, and provided a competent performance across landscapes ranging from slippery packed snow to obstructive boulders. It gave drivers a choice of five settings through a pop-up rotary control on the centre console, automatically selecting (or guided the driver to select) the most appropriate for the advanced electronic controls and traction aids, ride height, engine torque response, Hill Descent Control, Electronic Traction Control and transmission settings.

Chassis tuning was undertaken at the Nürburgring, where the supercharged version's race-bred four-piston Brembo front brakes came into their own. The integrated body-frame structure came from Discovery 3, with 6in (15.2cm) lopped off the wheelbase to provide agility, and fully independent, air-sprung suspension. Minimum body-roll and maximum driver feedback were priorities, so sports car-style double wishbone suspension was used front and rear. Range Rover Sport had the first Land Rover application of Adaptive Cruise Control. Audio systems were by Harman Kardon, and a twin-screen DVD rear seat entertainment, with high-resolution screens in the front seat headrests was available as an option. Described by Land Rover as aerodynamic and muscular, an effort was made to keep the Sport stylishly different yet still Range Roverish. The windscreen was more steeply raked, the roofline lower and sloped rearwards, the glass flush fitting, but the characteristic bonnet castellations were smoothed away and it sat lower. Roomy despite being shorter, there was space and comfort for five, with leather, wood and metallic finishes, and the single-piece aluminium tailgate had an opening glass. Unlike the Range Rover's split tailgate, the Range Rover Sport had a rounded rear, giving a compact tighter appearance. The so-called floating roof appearance was kept with blackened pillars.

Chunkier than the regular Range Rover, the Sport was instantly identifiable by the air vents by the front wheel arches and the extended roofline spoiler.

2005 Range Rover Sport 4.4litre V8 4.2litre Supercharged V8 2.7litre V6 diesel continued

"The interior is far more cocooning than the SUV norm," according to outgoing Land Rover MD Matthew Taylor. "Yet there is still the characteristic Land Rover Command driving position, which gives a superb view of the road ahead and the scenery around you. The Range Rover Sport will appeal to those who currently drive luxury executive cars as well as the more sporty SUVs, thanks to its overall refinement and unmatched breadth of capability."

The Jaguar-derived supercharged V8 provided an electronically limited top speed of 140mph (224.74kph), making it the fastest and swiftest-accelerating Land Rover ever. The V8's specially developed power and torque were fed full-time to all four wheels, through a ZF 6-speed intelligent shift automatic gearbox. The transmission had sport programming and Command Shift offered manual control of gear changes. Low range was electronically selectable on the move for tough off-roading. Other powertrain features were an electronically controlled centre differential. The turbodiesel V6 was not available in North America and some other markets.

Front and rear spoilers together with side skirts, not only increased the sporty character of the styling, but also aimed to improve high-speed stability and aerodynamic qualities. The Range Rover Sport was claimed to be one of the world's most aerodynamically efficient SUVs, with a drag coefficient of 0.37 (0.36 on some diesels).

The aerodynamic aids were designed with off-roading in mind. The front spoiler was made from rubber, to withstand knocks from rocks and ruts, the side skirts stopped mud splattering the sills, and prevented stone chips to the paintwork. A tail spoiler at the rear of the roof appeared to extend the roofline as well as prolonging the airflow to reduce wake turbulence. Smooth surfacing around the lights helped

clean up the aerodynamics. The nose strongly resembled the Range Stormer, which had demonstrated the need for efficient airflow round the engine, and a perforated mesh grille and one of the two side vents helped get air in and out of the engine space quickly. The other side vent was an intake for the engine induction system.

The headlight cluster continued the make's family look but was slimmer than those on the Range Rover and Discovery 3. It also featured adaptive headlights, swivelling to shine round corners. Rear lights were also distinctively styled and headlamp mouldings, front grille, vents, door handles and tailgate had Tungsten metal finish. The supercharged version was distinguished by brightwork for the perforated grille and side air apertures, black and silver Land Rover badges, 20-inch wheels and twin stainless steel exhausts.

INTRODUCTION Detroit Motor
Show, on sale spring 2005.
BODY Estate car; 5-doors, 5-seats;
weight 4.4 us/c 5720.93lb (2596kg);
4.2s/c 5787lb (2625kg); TDV6 5732lb
(2600kg).
ENGINE 4.4 AJ-V8-cylinders, in-line;
front; 88mm x 90.3mm, 4394cc; compr
10.75:1; 299bhp (222.6kW) @
5500rpm; 68bhp/l (50kW/l); 315lbft
(422Nm) @ 4000 rpm; 4.2s/c AJ-V8;
86mm x 90.3mm; 4197cc; compr 9.1:1;
390bhp (297kW) @ 5750rpm;
92.9bhp/l (68.4kW/l); 410lbft (550Nm)
@ 3500rpm; TDV6; V6; 81mm x
88mm; 2720cc; compr 18.1; 190bhp
(140kW) @ 4000rpm; 69.9bhp/l
(51.5kW/l); 325lbft (440Nm) @
4000rpm

ENGINE STRUCTURE AJ-V8 4.4, 4-
valves; 4 chain-driven overhead
camshafts; variable camshaft phasing;
continuously adaptable valve timing;
aluminium cylinder heads and block;
sequential multi-port fuel injection;
5-bearing crankshaft; Denso pan PAG
EMS engine management; sequential
multi-port fuel injection. 4.2s/c AJ-V8;
Eaton supercharger and twin
intercoolers; unique cam profiles.
TDV6, high-pressure common rail fuel
injection; compacted graphite iron
block; electronically controlled variable
nozzle turbocharger.
TRANSMISSION permanent four wheel
drive; 6-speed ZF automatic; electronic
traction control; 2-speed electronic
transfer gearbox, and locking centre
differential; low transfer ratio 2.93:1;
final drive s/c and TDV6, 3.54:1, us/c
3.73:1.

CHASSIS steel frame welded to steel
and aluminium-panelled body shell;
independent front and rear suspension
by wishbones, air springs, Terrain
Response, Dynamic Response; hydraulic
dual servo-assisted ventilated disc
brakes, front 12.48in (31.7cm), 13.26in
(33.7cm), 14.17in (36cm) rear 12.79in
(32.5cm), 35cm (13.77in); twin-piston
sliding callipers front, single pot rear;
s/c front 4-piston Brembo; Bosch 8
ABS; 8.3in (21cm) drum parking brake;
PAS ZF Servotronic rack-and-pinion;
19.35gal (88l) fuel tank; us/c 235/50R-
19in. radial ply tyres on cast alloy rims;
s/c 275/40R20.
DIMENSIONS wheelbase, 108in
(274.5cm); track front 63.2in 160.5cm),
rear 63.5in (161.2cm; length 188.5in
(479.8cm); width 85.4in (217cm);
height 71.5in (181.7cm); ground
clearance 6.8in (17.2cm) to 10in

(25.5cm); wading depth 27.6in (70cm)
turning circle 38.1ft (11.6m).
EQUIPMENT. Adaptive cruise control,
satellite navigation, Harman Kardon
audio standard; optional rear differential
lock.
PERFORMANCE
maximum speed us/c 130mph (209kph);
s/c 140mph (225kph); TDV6 120mph
(139kph); us/c 32.5mph (52.17kph) @
1000rpm; s/c 33.8mph
(54.26kph);TDV6 34.3mph (55.06kph);
0-100kph (62mph) us/c 8.9sec; s/c
7.6sec; TDV6 12.7sec
fuel consumption us/c 19.0mpg
(14.9l/100km); s/c 17.8mpg
(15.9l/100km); TDV6 8727.7mpg
(10.2l/100km).
PRICE 4.4 SE £45,454; 4.2 s/c HSE
£58,045; TDV6 SE £40,545.

Freelander

1993 Land Rover Freelander: early Pathfinder concepts and Honda-based buck

First thoughts on developing something smaller than the Discovery came in the late 1980s, even though there was not much investment money available to back up the foresight. So-called Lifestyle designs evolved modestly, around transversely positioned 4-cylinder Austin-Rover petrol and diesel engines, allied to four-wheel-drive versions of the PG1 gearbox from Rover cars of the period. By the early 1990s, Lifestyle became Pathfinder, and although some consideration was given to using a modified Rover Maestro or 800 car platform, it began to take shape around a new monocoque. In mock-up form it still looked somewhat utilitarian. Compact rival 4x4s like the Suzuki Vitara and the Daihatsu Fourtrak provided inspiration, and some management factions within Rover wanted it to be jointly developed, with one version (the Oden project) only having front-wheel-drive. Financial constraints soon killed off the Oden, which left Pathfinder as a definite four-wheel-drive Land Rover. Even at the clay model stage it was envisaged as a 3-door or 5-door. By the early 1990s, the Special Projects Group turned Pathfinder into Cyclone, producing a look/see/assess prototype on a much hacked-about Honda Civic Shuttle platform. One Land Rover insider admitted that something known as: "The Cut-and-Shuttle was used as proof of concept…" Project Director Dick Elsy insisted: "It became more and more obvious that there was a blank space in the Land Rover product plan …we set ourselves the target of plugging it with the definitive leisure 4WD vehicle …" Six months after Land Rover's directors had approved the project, it had turned into CB40, and soon after BMW took control in 1994, it allocated capital. Even so, it took another three years to bring it to market.

'Pathfinder' and 'Oden' mock-ups show how Land Rover's small car progressed in the early 1990s. *Above right*: 'Cyclone' was the project which followed 'Pathfinder', this prototype being based on a modified Honda Civic Shuttle platform.

1996 Land Rover Freelander Maestro van-based prototypes

While the style of the Pathfinder was being refined to that of the Freelander, testing continued with roughly constructed prototypes using existing components, which looked nothing like the final product. Even before the end of 1991, while commercial director Chris Woodwark was categorically denying to Richard Feast in *Autocar* that there would be a small Land Rover, "It's not what Land Rover is or what Land Rover customers expect it to be", the company was running prototypes based on converted Austin-Rover Maestro vans. In 1994/1995 a further series of similar development 'mules' went on the road. All had transversely-positioned engines, the first-ever such application in a Land Rover model. The original assessment was of the various potential power-units; Rover K-Series and T-Series, petrol and diesels, along with a new four-wheel-drive transmission, which had evolved from the Rover PG1 front-wheel-drive installation. No fewer than 22 Maestro Van-based mules eventually went on the road: except for their flared wheel arches, to accommodate larger-than-standard wheels and tyres, they looked almost normal, and had nondescript colour schemes. They were, however so much faster and more extrovert than the original Maestros that the engineers dubbed them the Mad Max series. It was important that development and endurance mileage should be gathered at an early stage, as the entire running gear/platform was still new, and un-proven. Much was gained before the very first true Freelander-shape vehicles were completed in 1995-1996, and by 1997 the roads and test tracks around Solihull were replete with disguised 3-door and 5-door prototypes. For sentimental reasons, Land Rover preserved a few of the Maestro-based mules, which seem likely to puzzle historians in future years. Woodwark also told Feast that Land Rover was spending £11million to ease some bottlenecks at Solihull as part of a £1million a week investment in new facilities and new models. "I think Land Rover's strengths are its marque image for reliability, robustness, ruggedness. It stands as the world's premier four-wheel drive. It's all-wheel drive, so it's permanent four-wheel drive. It stands for coil suspension and it stands for class leader in whatever sector it's in." It was about to enter a new sector.

To speed up development, early Freelander development work was carried out under disguised Austin-Rover Maestro vans. These were so fast that test drivers nicknamed them 'Mad Max'.

330

331

1997 Land Rover Freelander 3-door soft and hard back

Announced in September 1997, the Freelander was the first entirely new 4x4 from Solihull since 1948, and became the fourth 4x4 in the product range. Defender, Discovery and Range Rover types all continued. Not one component of the new model - body, chassis, engines or transmission - had ever before been seen on a previous Land Rover of any type. Although it was of a similar size to the old-type Defender, the Freelander was totally different, and a great deal more modern in its engineering. Aimed squarely at the sub-Discovery market, including cars like the Toyota RAV4, which were the obvious standard-setters in the class, the Freelander was sophisticated. It was smaller, lighter, more nimble, and sold at lower prices than the other Land Rover models. Even so, as evidence that cars of all types tended to become larger, the Freelander was almost as roomy as the Range Rover of 1970. Not only did it feature transversely-mounted engines, but it had independent front and rear suspension. Designed more of a stylish rather than a working 4x4, it was also the first Land Rover not to have a choice of High or Low range transmissions. All types were based on the same new unit-construction steel body/chassis platform and front-end, with long-travel coil spring/MacPherson strut independent suspension at front and rear, and all shared the same car-like interior, with 4 or 5-seat cabins. There were two basically different body styles, the entry-level models having just two passenger doors plus a tailgate, these being fitted with an extra rear-sloping pillar behind the doors. Behind the pillar on the 3-door, there could either be a rigid estate-car-like fitting, or a soft-back tilt, which allowed the Freelander to be used half-open. There were four individual seats, the rear pair being foldable to increase the stowage area, to align it against smaller Jeeps and competitors from Japan. Eight different derivatives - petrol, diesel, entry-level or fully-specified types,

soon became available. There was a choice of Rover engines, a fuel-injected 1.8-litre, which was a less-powerful version of the MGF unit, and an L-Series 2.0-litre turbo-diesel, another car power unit, which would soon be seen as four-fifths of the five cylinder Td5 engine in Defender and Discovery models. The transmission was evolved from an existing Rover front-wheel-drive type, and one quirk was that front and rear final drive ratios were very slightly different. A viscous coupling linked front to rear drives, along with Electronic Traction Control (ETC), which used the wheel-mounted ABS sensors to pick-up traction loss from any wheel. Although disc brakes and ABS anti-lock (optional on entry-level types, standard on others) were both as expected, the Hill Descent Control (HDC) feature was a real novelty. Using a yellow collar around the gear lever, the drive could engage HDC for steep down-hill descents, leaving the engine to idle in first gear, when sensors then restricted Freelander speeds to no more than 5 mph: this compensated for the lack of a mud-plugging low range in the transmission. Along with the 5-door estate car type, this soon became the fastest-selling Land Rover ever.

INTRODUCTION 1997, produced to 2000
BODY Estate/soft-back; 3-doors, 4-seats or 5-seats; weight from 3142lb (1425kg).
ENGINE 4-cylinders, in-line; front; transverse. Petrol 80.0mm x 89.3mm, 1796cc; compr 10.5:1; 118bhp (88kW) @ 5500rpm; 65.7bhp/l (49kW/l); 121lbft (164.1Nm) @ 2750rpm. Turbo-diesel 84.5mm x 88.9mm, 1994cc, comp 19.5:1, 96bhp (71.6kW) @ 2000rpm; 48.1bhp/l (35.9kW/l); 155lbft (210Nm) @ 2000rpm

ENGINE STRUCTURE (K-Series petrol) 4-valves per cylinder, twin cogged belt driven overhead camshafts; aluminium cylinder head and block; MEMS fuel injection and engine management, 5-bearing crankshaft; water-cooled. (L-Series turbo-diesel) 2-valves per cylinder, single overhead camshaft, chain camshaft drive, aluminium cylinder head, cast iron cylinder block; Bosch fuel injection and engine management; Garrett turbocharger; 5-bearing crankshaft; water-cooled.
TRANSMISSION permanent four-wheel drive; diaphragm spring clutch; manual gearbox, 5-speed all-synchromesh; transfer box ratio 1.46:1, final drive :4.20:1 (petrol) or 3.68:1 (diesel).

CHASSIS steel monocoque, with removable hardback or soft-back, ifs by coil springs, MacPherson struts, anti-roll bar; irs by coil springs, MacPherson struts, wishbones and links, anti roll bar; telescopic dampers; hydraulic servo-assisted brakes with ABS anti-lock, front 10.3in (26.16cm) dia ventilated discs, rear 10in (25.4cm) dia drums; rack-and-pinion PAS; 13gal (59l) fuel tank; 195/80-15in. radial ply tyres on steel or cast alloy rims.
DIMENSIONS wheelbase; 100.5in (255.5cm) track front; 60.4in (153.4cm), rear 60.8in (154.5cm) length; 172.5in (438.2cm) width; 71in (180.5cm) height; 69.2in (175.7cm) ground clearance; 7.9in (20cm) turning circle38ft (11.6m).

PERFORMANCE
maximum speed ; 1.8i, 103mph (165.35kph); 2.0 diesel, 93mph (149.29kph); 22.7mph (36.5kph) @ 1000rpm; 0-60mph (96kph) 1.8i, 10.8sec; 2.0 diesel, 15.1sec; fuel consumption 1.8i 23.9mpg (11.82l/100km); 2.0 diesel, 29.7mpg (9.5L/100km).
PRICE: 1.8i £15,995; 2.0 diesel £16,995

Three-door Freelanders were available as 'softback' (this type) or 'hardback' varieties, and were equipped with four individual seats.

1997 Land Rover Freelander Five-door station wagon

The 5-door station wagon version of the Freelander looked more conventional. It was more obviously related to larger Land Rovers than the 3-door, in particular the soft-back 3-door, but was still built on exactly the same pressed-steel platform, monocoque structure and engine/transmission/suspension. This 5-door estate car (station wagon was another description) was equipped much like a conventional car-based estate car, with the ability to fold down all or part of the rear seat, to enlarge the carrying space. The cabin had two separate front seats, and a rear bench seat with a 60/40 per cent fold-down feature. There were three-point inertia-reel safety belts for all five seats. From the beginning, there were 12 different sorts of Freelander, four 5-door wagons, two each petrol and diesel. XE types were more completely equipped than those at entry-level, with ABS anti-lock as standard, a passenger-side airbag, electronic traction control, and an electrically-actuated sun-roof. As with the 3-doors, there was a choice of high-revving petrol, or more torquey diesel engines, although no low range for the transmission, unlike Land Rovers and Range Rovers. Since Freelander was smaller, lighter and more aerodynamic than the Discovery, it was surprisingly fast and economical. Even with the conventional turbo-diesel engine, it could reach more than 90mph, and a carefully-driven diesel Freelander might record 30mpg (9.42l/100km), previously unheard-of with Land Rover 4x4s. Compared with the Discovery and the Defender, much was made of the character change that had been produced with the Freelander. When it was first promoted, there was much talk of life-style, leisure pursuits and fun-car potential. Yet with its good traction, sturdy construction, and ability to keep going in demanding conditions, it was still sure-footed off-road.

INTRODUCTION 1997, produced to 2000
BODY 5-door estate car, 5-seats; weight from 3142lb (1425kg).
ENGINE 4-cylinders, in-line; front; transverse. Petrol 80.0mm x 89.3mm, 1796cc; compr 10.5:1; 118bhp (88.0kW) @ 5500rpm; 65.7bhp/l (49kW/l); 121lbft (164.1Nm) @ 2750rpm : Turbo-diesel 84.5mm x 88.9mm, 1994cc, comp 19.5:1, 96bhp (71.6kW) @ 2000rpm; 48.1bhp/l (35.9kW/l); 155lbft (210Nm) @ 2000rpm.
ENGINE STRUCTURE K-Series petrol, 4-valves per cylinder; twin cogged belt-driven overhead camshafts; aluminium cylinder head and block; MEMS fuel injection and engine management, 5-bearing crankshaft; water-cooled: L-Series turbo-diesel, 2-valves per cylinder, single chain-driven overhead camshaft; aluminium cylinder head, cast iron block; Bosch fuel injection and engine management; Garrett turbocharger; 5-bearing crankshaft; water-cooled.
TRANSMISSION permanent four-wheel-drive; diaphragm spring clutch; manual gearbox, 5-speed all-synchromesh; transfer box-ratio 1.46:1, final drive 4.20:1 (petrol), 3.68:1 (diesel).

CHASSIS steel monocoque, ifs by coil springs, MacPherson struts, anti-roll bar; irs by coil springs, MacPherson struts, wishbones and links, anti roll bar; telescopic dampers; hydraulic servo-assisted brakes with ABS anti-lock, front 10.3in (26.16cm) dia ventilated discs, rear 10in (25.4cm) dia drums; rack-and-pinion PAS; 13gal (59l) fuel tank; 195/80-15in. radial ply tyres on steel or cast alloy rims.
DIMENSIONS wheelbase; 100.5in (255.5cm); track front 60.4in (153.4cm), rear 60.8in (154.5cm); length 172.5in (438.2cm); width 71in (180.5cm); height 69.2in (175.7cm); ground clearance 7.9in (20cm); turning circle 38ft (11.6m).
PERFORMANCE
maximum speed; 1.8i, 108mph (173.37kph); 2.0 diesel, 93mph (149.29kph); 19.7mph (31.62kph) @ 1000rpm; 0-60mph (96kph) 1.8i, 10.5sec; 2.0 diesel, 15.1sec; fuel consumption 1.8i, 24.6mpg (11.48l/100km); 2.0 diesel 29.7mpg (9.51l/100km).
PRICE; 1.8i £17,995; 2.0 diesel £18,995

The five-door Freelander station wagon soon became Land Rover's best-selling 4x4, with a choice of petrol or diesel engines.

1999 Land Rover Freelander Commercial

As with the Discovery Commercial, Land Rover developed a purely commercial derivative of the Freelander, which made its debut in 1999. Since a 3-door existed already, it was easy to evolve a Commercial type using the same front end, doors and screen/overhead panelling, along with a specially developed hardback, to complete the van bodywork. Land Rover's first monocoque structure, the sheet steel pressings of the Commercial aft of the B-post were the same as the passenger versions but without the window perforations. Mechanically the Freelander Commercial was always available with the 1.8-litre petrol or the 4-cylinder turbo-diesel engines. In line with the passenger types, the original diesel was the Rover L-Series type, but when the BMW Td4 type diesel was adopted instead, this change was also made on the Freelander Commercial. Previewed at Geneva in 2000 this was a thoroughly up-to-the-minute design, made at Steyr in Austria for the Rover 75 and BMW 3 and 3-series cars. It was lighter than the L-series, quieter, with more power and torque yet more economical. Some Commercials were also made, to very special order, with the later KV6, but these were extremely rare. Cleverly equipped as a working van, the Commercial had a convenient and commendable 1400-litre load space behind the two seats (there were, of course, no rear seats), and could carry a payload of up to 580kg (1281lb). There was heavy-duty floor covering, and a three-quarter mesh bulkhead behind the seats, while other useful fittings included lashing points to help tie down the cargo, along with an optional chequerplate floor, shelving and racking systems.

INTRODUCTION April 1999
BODY Van; 3-doors, 2-seats; weight from 3142lb (1425kg).
ENGINE 4-cylinders, in-line; front; transverse. Petrol 80.0mm x 89.3mm, 1796cc; compr 10.5:1; 118bhp (88kW) @ 5500rpm; 65.7bhp/l (49kW/l); 121lbft (164.1Nm) @ 2750rpm. Turbo-diesel 84.5mm x 88.9mm, 1994cc; compr 19.5:1; 96bhp (71.6kW) @ 2000rpm; 48.1bhp/l (35.9 kW/l); 155lbft (210Nm) @ 2000rpm. From 2001; 4-cylinder turbodiesel, in line, front, transverse; 84mm x 88mm, 1951cc, compr 18.0:1; 110bhp (82kW) @ 4000rpm; 56.4bhp/l (45.2kW/l); 192lbft (260Nm) @ 1750rpm.
ENGINE STRUCTURE (K-Series petrol) 4-valves per cylinder, twin-overhead camshafts, camshaft drive by cogged belt; aluminium cylinder head and block; MEMS fuel injection and engine management, 5-bearing crankshaft; water-cooled. (L-Series turbo-diesel) 2-valves per cylinder, single chain-driven overhead camshaft; aluminium cylinder head, cast iron block; Bosch fuel injection and engine management, Garrett turbocharger, 5-bearing crankshaft; water-cooled. 2001 turbo-diesel; camshaft drive by chain, aluminium cylinder heads and blocks; Bosch fuel injection and engine management.
TRANSMISSION permanent four-rear wheel drive; diaphragm spring clutch; manual gearbox, 5-speed all-synchromesh; transfer box ratio 1.46, final drive 4.20:1 (petrol) or 3.68:1.

CHASSIS steel monocoque structure, with special hardback three-door van bodywork, ifs by coil springs, MacPherson struts, anti-roll bar, irs; coil springs, MacPherson struts, wishbones and links, anti roll bar; telescopic dampers; hydraulic servo-assisted brakes with ABS anti-lock, front 10.3in (26.16cm) dia ventilated disc, rear 10in (25.4cm) dia rear drums; rack-and-pinion PAS; 13gal (59l) fuel tank; 195/80-15in. radial ply tyres, on steel rims.
DIMENSIONS wheelbase 100.5in (255.5cm); track front 60.4in (153.4cm), rear 60.8in (154.5cm); length 172.5in (438.2cm); width 71in (180.5cm); height 69.2in (175.7cm); ground clearance 7.9in (20cm); turning circle 38ft (11.6m).
PERFORMANCE maximum speed ; 1.8i, 103mph (165.34kph); 2.0 diesel 93mph (149.29kph); 22.7mph (36.5kph) @ 1000rpm; 0-60mph (96kph) 1.8i, 10.8sec; 2.0 diesel, 15.1sec fuel consumption. 1.8i 23.9mpg (11.82l/100km); 2.0 diesel, 29.7mpg (9.51l/100km).

Announced in 1999, the Freelander Commercial was a van conversion of the three-door type, with only two seats, a heavy-duty floor covering and a bulkhead behind the seats.

2000 Land Rover Freelander

The Freelander range was three years old before two engines that made it such an outstanding prospectarrived. These were a high-tech. diesel from BMW, and a smooth V6 petrol engine from Rover. These, together with the arrival of a new Jatco automatic transmission, made all the difference. Ironically, the BMW engine was adopted in the same year in which BMW sold the Land Rover brand to Ford. Previewed in March 2000, but on UK sale from August, the revised 3-door and 5-door Freelanders looked substantially the same as before, the only exterior style change was to provide a slightly lengthened nose to wrap around the bulky V6 engine. Improvements to the interior included new instruments, larger air bags on some models, plus air-conditioning and a multi-disc CD player on the top-of-the-range ES Types. As soon as BMW authorised the new Freelander, it laid plans to add its own-brand 4-cylinder diesel engine instead of the Rover L-Series, though this was used for a time at first. Slightly smaller than the Rover engine at 1951cc instead of 1994cc, the BMW had 110bhp instead of 96bhp, and 192lbft of torque instead of 155lbft. Closely related to engines used in BMW cars, very refined, with twin overhead camshafts, four valves per cylinder, and the latest type of high-tech common rail fuel injection, it was a formidable power unit. Such a Freelander, which could almost reach 100mph, and record up to 28mpg (10.09l/100km) in normal on-the-road use, instantly became the best-seller in the range. Not only that, but after the financial collapse of MG-Rover in 2005, it was the only engine that kept the Freelander going. The V6 Freelander, which was only available with automatic transmission, was the most sophisticated of the burgeoning range, and specifically intended for North America. Developed by Rover for its luxury 75 car, with a construction closely related to the clever K-Series 4-cylinder, the KV6 was compact, high-revving, and powerful. Even so, it was hardly an engine best suited to for low-speed mud-plugging, as peak torque was developed at a lofty 4,000rpm. As *Autocar* commented: "... the V6 has converted the Freelander into a high-speed motorway express." Yet ...."This ain't no sports car. It's an off-roader, even if it's not so seriously muddy as to require a low-range gearbox." Land Rover had to push the front bumper slightly forward to make space for the bigger engine, but its light-alloy construction meant the front/rear-balance was unaffected. This was a fast and stylish machine in which a 22 or 23mpg fuel consumption figure seemed absolutely reasonable especially when equipped with the new automatic box, with its adaptable BMW-style Steptronic control. Its relatively high UK price ensured that it would never be the best-seller in the range, but it had real style, and an engaging turn of speed.

From 2000, the 2.5-litre Rover KV6 engine became available, which meant that the front-end style had to be modified to accept its bulk.

INTRODUCTION 2000, produced to 2003

BODY 5-door estate or 3-door hardtop or softback, 4-seats or 5-seats; weight from 3,142lb (1,425kg).

ENGINE V6-cylinders, in 90 deg vee, front; transverse; 80.0mm x 82.8mm, 2497cc; compr 10.5:1; 177bhp (132kW) @ 6250rpm; 70.9bhp/l (52.9kW/l); 177lbft (240Nm) @ 4000rpm. 4-cylinder petrol, in-line, front, transverse; 80mm x 89.3mm, 1796cc; compr 10.5:1; 118bhp (88kW) @ 5500rpm; 65.7bhp/l (49 kW/l); 121lbft (164.1Nm) @ 2750rpm: 4-cylinder turbodiesel, in line, front, transverse; 84mm x 88mm, 1951cc, compr 18.0:1; 110bhp (82kW) @ 4000rpm; 56.4bhp/l (45.2kW/l); 192lbft (260Nm) @ 1750rpm.

ENGINE STRUCTURE (All types) 4-valves per cylinder, twin-overhead camshafts; Rover V6 and 4-cyl petrol camshaft drive by cogged belt; turbo-diesel camshaft drive by chain, aluminium cylinder heads and blocks; Bosch fuel injection and engine management; Rover V6, 4-bearing crankshaft; 4-cyl, 5-bearing crankshaft; water-cooled .

TRANSMISSION permanent four-wheel-drive; diaphragm spring clutch; manual gearbox 5-speed all-synchromesh, transfer box ratio 1.46:1 (not with V6 engine); Jatco automatic transmission (optional with turbo-diesel, standard with V6, not available with 4-cyl. petrol). Final drives: V6, 3.66:1; 4-cyl petrol, 4.20:1; 4-cyl turbo-diesel, 3.18:1.

CHASSIS steel monocoque structure, closed or with removable hardback, or soft-back, ifs by coil springs, MacPherson struts, anti-roll bar; irs by coil springs, MacPherson struts, wishbones and links, anti roll bar; telescopic dampers; hydraulic servo-assisted brakes with ABS anti-lock, front 10.9in (27.7cm) dia ventilated disc, rear 10in (25.4cm) dia drums; rack-and-pinion PAS; 13gal (59l) fuel tank; 195/80-15in. radial ply tyres on alloy rims.

DIMENSIONS wheelbase 100.5in (255.5cm); track front 60.4in (153.4cm), rear 60.8in (154.5cm); length 172.5in (438.2cm); V6, 175in (444.5cm); width 71in (180.5cm); height 69.2in (175.7cm); ground clearance 7.9in (20cm); turning circle 38ft (11.6m).

PERFORMANCE maximum speed; 1.8i 108mph (173.37kph); Td4 diesel, 99mph (158.92kph); V6, 113mph (181.39kph); 1.8i, 22.7mph (36.5kph); V6, 22.9mph (36.85kph); diesel, 26.6mph (42.8kph) @ 1000rpm; 0-60mph (96kph); 1.8i, 10.5sec; Td4 diesel, 14.6sec; V6 10.1sec; fuel consumption 1.8i, 24.6mpg (11.48l/100km); Td4, 27.7mpg (10.19L/100km); V6 22.7mpg (12.44l/100km).

PRICE; 1.8i from £15,995; Td4 diesel from £17,195; V6 from £21,595

2003 Land Rover Freelander

Revealed in September 2003, the revised Freelander had what the industry knew as a mid-term facelift. Mechanically, its engine, transmission and running gear was well-established, but a range of style and cosmetic changes freshened it up, to keep it going until the next-generation model arrived in 2006. The successful trio of engines, 4-cylinder and V6 Rover petrol, along with 4-cylinder BMW diesel, carried on as before, and the only significant chassis change was for a new Sport version, sitting 30mm (1.2in) closer to the ground, with suitably stiffened-up anti-roll bars to improve response on the road. The important innovations were to the front-end style and to the interior. The nose was reworked, to include twinned/interlinked headlamps, which re-used the theme adapted for modern-generation Discoverys and Range Rovers, with a more substantial three-dimensional bumper front panel moulding, while at the rear there were new tail lamps and a wrap-around bumper. Inside the facia/instrument panel was made even more car-like than ever, with a sturdy four-spoke steering wheel, new switchgear, new seats and a whole range of fresh fabrics. Subtly, but without losing any of its cross-country abilities, the Freelander was becoming more of a lifestyle machine than ever. Shortly after MG-Rover collapsed in April 2005, supplies of Rover 4-cylinder and V6 petrol engines began to dry up, even though Land Rover had been stockpiling them against such an emergency. Once it became obvious that no more would be forthcoming at the end of 2005 the Freelander was withdrawn temporarily from North America. Almost all 2006 models were built with BMW Td4 diesel engines. Finally, in the summer of 2006, the long-running first-generation Freelander gave way to a new-generation Ford-influenced model after well over 500,000 had been built.

INTRODUCTION September 2003, built to 2006.

BODY 5-door estate or 3-door hardtop or softback, 4-seats or 5-seats; weight from 3,142lb (1,425kg).

ENGINE V6-cylinders, in 90-degree vee, front, transverse, 80.0mm x 82.8mm, 2497cc; compr 10.5:1; 177bhp (132kW) @ 6250rpm; 70.9bhp/l (52.9kW/l); 177lbft (240Nm) @ 4000rpm. 4-cylinder petrol, in-line; front; transverse; 80mm x 89.3mm, 1796cc; compr 10.5:1; 118bhp (88kW) @ 5500rpm; 65.7bhp/l (49kW/l); 121lbft (164.1Nm) @ 2750rpm. 4-cylinder turbo-diesel, in-line, front, transverse; 84mm x 88mm, 1951cc, compr 18.0:1; 110bhp (82kW) @ 4000rpm; 56.4bhp/l (45.1 Kw/l); 192lbft (260Nm) @1750rpm.

ENGINE STRUCTURE (All types) 4-valves per cylinder, twin-overhead camshafts; Rover V6 and 4-cyl petrol camshaft drive by cogged belt; turbo-diesel camshaft drive by chain, aluminium cylinder heads and blocks; Bosch fuel injection and engine management; Rover V6, 4-bearing crankshaft; 4-cyl, 5-bearing crankshaft; water-cooled.

TRANSMISSION permanent four-wheel drive; diaphragm spring clutch, manual gearbox 5-speed all-synchromesh, transfer box ratio 1.46:1, final drive 3.188 (front), 3.214:1 (rear).

CHASSIS steel monocoque structure, closed, or with removable hardback or softback, ifs by coil springs, MacPherson struts, anti-roll bar; irs by coil springs, MacPherson struts, wishbones and links, anti roll bar; telescopic hydraulic dampers; hydraulic servo-assisted brakes with ABS anti-lock, front 10.3in (26.16cm) dia ventilated front discs, rear 10in (25.4cm) dia drums; rack-and-pinion PAS; 13gal (59l) fuel tank; 195/80-15in. radial ply tyres on cast alloy rims.

DIMENSIONS wheelbase; 100.7in (255.7cm); track front 60.4in (153.4cm); rear 60.8in (154.5cm); length; 175.5in (445.9cm); width; 71.2in (180.9cm); height; 67.6in (171.7cm); ground clearance; 8.66in (22cm); turning circle38ft (11.6m).

PERFORMANCE maximum speed; 1.8i, 108mph (173.37kph); Td4 diesel, 99mph (158.92kph); V6, 113mph (181.39kph) 1.8i, 22.7mph (36.5kph); V6, 22.9mph (36.85kph); Td4, 26.6mph (42.8kph) @ 1000rpm; 0-60mph (96kph); 1.8i, 10.5sec; Td4 diesel, 14.6sec; V6, 10.1sec; fuel consumption; 1.8i, 24.6mpg (11.48l/100km); Td4, 27.7mpg (10.19l/100km); V6, 22.7mpg (12.44l/100km).

PRICE; 1.8i from £16,995; Td4 diesel from £20,900; V6 from £23,595

From September 2003, the Freelander was given a new nose/headlamp front-end style.

2006 Land Rover Freelander 2

At the Geneva Motor Show in March 2006, Richard Parry-Jones vice-president of global product development, and chief technical officer Ford Motor Company, summed up one of the emerging techniques for making cars. Future Fords would be built like Lego Technics the mechanical version of the popular building blocks. "This gives us extreme flexibility. If you give an identical set of Legos to five kids they will each end up with five different technical creations." At Geneva the Ford Galaxy MPV and S-Max estate shared 85 per cent of their components with the Volvo S80. The time-honoured concept of building cars on different platforms was over. With Ford in the driving seat, Freelander could be more radical, drawing on the modular resources of Ford's C1 family that included Focus, Volvo S40 and V50, and Mazda 3. The design task was to bring Freelander up to date without losing the support that had made it Britain's and Europe's best-selling off-roader. In a good year it had sold 70,000, and with the prospect of increases in the United States where it was LR2 next to the Discovery's LR3, 100,000 became a possibility. In 2006 it moved up a notch in speed and style, it became slightly bigger and its appearance kept pace with fashion. At long last it abandoned the spare wheel hung outside the back door. An icon of the 4x4 since the long-gone days of the WW2 Jeep, the spare was now sensibly tucked under the boot floor, so although overall length was much the same as before, without the overhanging wheel there was a useful gain of 6in (15cm).

Even though it still lacked an ultra low off-road gear and suspension height adjustment, Freelander 2 was replete with every electronic or mechanical appliance, making certain it lived up to the off-road qualifications of every Land Rover since 1948. Almost 2 million man-hours were absorbed in developing what had been code-named L359. The welded-on chassis-like stiffeners under the monocoque were relinquished, and the structure was wider, longer, and taller than before so it was a little heavier. McPherson struts in front and a unique coil-sprung independent rear drove the Freelander up a growing market that was confidently expected to reach an annual 4.3 million by 2010. This premium small SUV segment, which the original Freelander effectively created in Europe, was expected to more than double in size.

Among Freelander 2's impressive array of advanced technologies was a driveline combining the intelligence of a torque-splitting Haldex centre coupling, with the proactive control of Land Rover's Terrain Response. This allowed the driver to select the best engine and transmission settings for different conditions. Another innovation Gradient Release Control gave confidence and control on steep and low friction surfaces.

Engine supply, which had proved so problematical in the closing months of the old model, was solved by two new power units. These were a specially engineered derivative of the PSA-Ford 2.2 litre 16-valve turbodiesel, and unusually for a transverse mounting, the 3.2litre Bridgend-built petrol straight-i6 similar to one used by Volvo. Known internally as SI6 for Short Inline 6, it measured a scant 23.64in (60.05cm) from the front of the engine to the rear face of the block, and to ensure stiffness even the cam cover was a structural member. While the diesel featured a double walled cylinder block and counter-rotating Lanchester-style balance shafts for low noise and vibration, the naturally smooth i6 petrol engine had clever cam-profile switching, variable valve timing (VVT), variable intake tracts and highly sensitive fuelling control for even sportier performance.

To obtain the diesel's lag-free torque it had intake port deactivation, common rail fuel injection, and a variable

geometry turbine. Each of the two inlet valves had its own tract from the manifold. One worked at low airflows to create swirl in the combustion chamber, best for lower speeds, while the other provided a lot of air at higher loads without creating in-cylinder turbulence. The low-flow helical port worked all the time, while the filling-port, which took the long way round over the top of the engine, was deactivated by a butterfly valve until called upon. Among the adjustments necessary for the engine installation in a 4x4 was a repositioning of components to suit off-road activities such as wading, and a relatively high bonnet-line to provide good pedestrian head-impact protection. Freelander was one of the first with a new type of fuel injector expected to allow European diesels to comply with US emission regulations and remove the requirement to fit NOx traps in the exhaust. The piezo injector was a smaller, lighter, and faster electronic injector also supplied by Robert Bosch to Mercedes-Benz and Audi. Piezo crystals changed shape when electrically charged (piezen is Greek meaning to apply pressure) and the injector crystalline discs enabled fuel to be added at higher pressure, and so quickly acting, that seven actions could be made inside the 6millisec of a piston stroke. A mechanical solenoid injector might manage two or three on a good day. The piezo gave smoother quieter cleaner running through simulating the smooth flame-front combustion petrol engines provide, rather than the sudden explosive force of a traditional diesel. Fuel economy was also enhanced.

The Freelander had no entry-level petrol and no V6. Transmissions were 6-speed manual on the diesel with the choice of a 6-speed, automatic, and automatic-only on the 6-cylinder. Audio units offered the convenience of i-Pod compatible input sockets, and extended to a 14 speaker Dolby-Prologic system with fibre-optic interconnects. User-

friendly satellite navigation had an intuitive, menu-driven touch screen, and optional tyre pressure warnings monitored the actual temperature-corrected pressure within each tyre, avoiding the shortcomings of wheel-revolution systems. Even the seat heating technology was better than the outgoing car, as Land Rover decided that existing heaters would not last Freelander 2's expected lifetime.

Other worthy details included a clamshell bonnet with commendable pedestrian head impact protection, and the sculpted front end that concealed the car's crash structure, developed to be less aggressive on other vehicles during an impact. Six separate frontal loadpaths were expected to dissipate collision impact forces. Rear passengers enjoyed good leg and shoulder room in Land Rover's unusual layout that raised the back seats 2in (5cm) above those in front.

INTRODUCTION Autumn 2006 BODY Estate car; 5-doors, 5-seats; weight petrol 4264lb (1934kg), diesel 4200lb (1905lb) diesel automatic 4239lb (1923kg). ENGINE i6 petrol 6-cylinders, in-line; front; transverse; 84mm x 96mm, 3192cc; compr 10.8:1; 236bhp (175kW) @ 6300rpm; 73.9bhp/l (55.1kW/l); 236lbft (320Nm) @ rpm. TD4 Diesel 4-cylinders, in-line; transverse; 84mm x 96mm; 2179cc; compr 16.6:1; 156bhp (115kW) @ 4000rpm; 71.59bhp/l (53.38kW/l); 280lbft (389Nm) @2000rpm. ENGINE STRUCTURE i6, 4-valves; twin inverted chain-driven overhead camshafts; cam profile switching (CPS), variable valve timing (VVT), variable intake system; aluminium block and head, block; Denso fuel injection, engine management; 7-bearing forged steel crankshaft; water-cooled. TD4 diesel, 4-valves with intake port deactivation; toothed belt exhaust camshaft drive; chain inlet camshaft drive; double-walled cast iron block, aluminium head; common rail 3, 1800bar fuel injection; piezoelectric injectors; Bosch fuel injection and engine management; Honeywell Garret variable nozzle turbocharger; balancer shafts; dual mass flywheel; 5-bearing crankshaft. TRANSMISSION four wheel drive; hydraulic clutch; 6-speed gearbox, manual diesel only, automatic diesel and petrol; Haldex centre coupling, electronic wet clutch with variable torque transfer; spiral bevel final drive 2.580:1.

CHASSIS steel monocoque; MacPherson ifs, anti-roll bar, coil springs 55mm twin-tube struts; irs by lateral and longit links, anti-roll bar, coil springs, 55mm twin-tube struts; rack and pinion PAS; reverse vented disc brakes front, diesel 11.89in (30.2cm), petrol 12.44in (31.6cm); rear vented discs 11.81in (30cm). Drum in disc parking brake; 14.5gal (66l) fuel tank; 215/75 x 16, 235/65 x 17, 235/60 x 18 ATS 235/45 x 19 ATS tyres, aluminium wheels. DIMENSIONS wheelbase 104.7in (265.93cm); track front 63in (160cm), rear 63.1in (160.27cm); length 177.1in (449.83cm); width 85.66in (217.6cm) including mirrors; height 68.46in (173.9cm); ground clearance; 8.3in (21cm); turning circle 36.75ft (11.2m).

EQUIPMENT Terrain Response (depending on trim level); Roll Stability Control (RSC); Hill Descent Control (HDC); Dynamic Stabity Control (DSC); Electronic Traction Control (ETC); anti-lock brakes (ABS); Emergency Brake Assist (EBA); Engine Drag Control (EDC); Electronic Brakeforce Distribution (EBD); Corner Brake Control (CBC) and Gradient Release Control (all standard). PERFORMANCE maximum speed 121mph (194.24kph); 109mph (174.97kph) diesel manual, 106mph (170.16kph) automatic; 0-60mph (96kph) 8.4sec, petrol auto; 10.9sec diesel manual, 11.8sec automatic.

SERIES I CHASSIS NUMBERS

The Land Rover Model-year

Land Rovers have always been dated by the model-year or season of their manufacture. This is not necessarily the same as the calendar year when they were built!

In Britain, the Motor Show was always held in the autumn. Manufacturers drew attention to their new models at the Show, and made them sound even newer by describing them as models for the next calendar-year. Thus, a new model introduced at the October 1950 Motor Show would be described as a 1951 model. Land Rover chassis numbers always reflected this "model-year."

Traditionally, the Solihull factory closed down during August, allowing the bulk of the workforce to take their annual holidays while specialist staff stayed behind to carry out production line changes needed to build the new models. The build dates for the Land Rover model-year therefore ran from the re-start of production in September to the annual closedown the following summer.

This explains how a 1951-model Land Rover might have been built between September and the end of December 1950, and not in 1951 at all!

80-inch 1.6-litre, basic models

1948	R86-0001 to R86-3000	
1949	R866-3001 to R866-7920	
1950	R0610-0001 to R0610-9999	
	R0611-0001 to R0611-5440	
	0710-0001 to 0710-0050 (2-litre prototypes)	

Notes: The R prefix stood for RHD and was replaced when appropriate by an L for LHD.

1951	1610-0001 to 1610-3971	Home market
	1613-0001 to 1613-7145*	LHD
	1616-0001 to 1616-3268	RHD export
	1663-0001 to 1663-0081	LHD, CKD
	1666-0001 to 1666-2320	RHD, CKD

* Surviving records finish at 6120, but several higher numbers have been documented. 1613-7145 was the highest known by early 2006.

80-inch Station Wagons

1949	R867-0001 to R867-0070	
1950	R0620-0001 to R0620-0480	
1951	1623-0001 to 1623-0080	LHD
	1626-0001 to 1620-0020	RHD export

80-inch 2-litre

1952	2610-0001 to 2610-5569	Home market
	2613-0001 to 2613-6424	LHD
	2616-0001 to 2613-3614	RHD export
	2663-0001 to 2663-1985	LHD, CKD
	2666-0001 to 2666-1092	RHD, CKD
1953	3610-0001 to 3610-4122	Home market
	3613-0001 to 3613-4613	LHD
	3616-0001 to 3616-4007	RHD export
	3663-0001 to 3663-7268	LHD, CKD
	3666-0001 to 3666-2122*	RHD, CKD

* No records exist for RHD CKD models, but the highest chassis number traced by early 2006 (in Australia) was 3666-2122.

Notes: The Minerva 80-inch models were built in batches within the 2663-series (1952 season) and 3663-series (1953 season). The Tempo 80-inch models were built in batches within the 3613-series.

80-inch Welders

1949	R868-0001 to R 868-0010	(L prefix for LHD)
1950	R0630-0001 to R0630-0030	(L prefix for LHD)
1951	1630-0001 to 1630-0004	Home market
	1633-0001 to 1633-0007	LHD
	1636-0001 to 1636-0009	RHD export
1952	2630-0001 to 2630-0014	Home market
	2633-0001 to 2633-0013	LHD
	2636-0001 to 2636-0004	RHD export
1953	3630-0001 to 3630-0008	Home market
	3633-0001 to 3633-0007	LHD
	3636-0001 to 3636-0007	RHD export

86-inch, all models

1954	4710-0001 to 4710-2861	Home market
	4713-0001 to 4713-5125	LHD
	4716-0001 to 4716-3434	RHD export
	4763-0001 to 4763-0564	LHD, CKD

Chassis Numbers

	4766-0001 to 4766-3096	RHD, CKD
1955	5710-0001 to 5710-8185	Home market
	5713-0001 to 5713-5760	LHD
	5716-0001 to 5713-3537	RHD export
	5763-0001 to 5763-0482	LHD, CKD
	5766-0001 to 5766-2250	RHD, CKD
1956	1706-00001 to 1706-04807	Home market
	1736-00001 to 1736-04433	LHD
	1746-00001 to 1746-01000	LHD, CKD
	1766-00001 to 1766-02441	RHD export
	1776-00001 to 1776-01367	RHD, CKD

Notes: The Minerva 86-inch models were built in batches within the 4763-series (1954 season), 5763-series (1955 season) and 1746-series (1956 season).

The Tempo 86-inch models were built in batches within the 4713-series (1954 season), 5713-series (1955 season) and 1736 series (1956 season). There were 12 1954 models, 46 1955 models, and 129 1956 models. It is possible that there were two further Tempos built from 1146-series chassis in 1956.

107-inch utilities

1954	4720-0001 to 4720-0441	Home market
	4723-0001 to 4723-1245	LHD
	4726-0001 to 4726-1674	RHD export
	4773-0001 to 4773-0114	LHD, CKD
	4776-0001 to 4776-0346	RHD, CKD
1955	5720-0001 to 5720-1205	Home market
	5723-0001 to 5723-2120	LHD
	5726-0001 to 5726-3863	RHD export
	5773-0001 to 5773-0066	LHD, CKD
	5776-0001 to 5776-1436	RHD, CKD
1956	2706-00001 to 2706-00948	Home market
	2736-00001 to 2736-02399	LHD
	2746-00001 to 2746-00246	LHD, CKD
	2766-00001 to 2766-03054	RHD export
	2776-00001 to 2776-01188	RHD, CKD

107-inch Station Wagons

1956	8706-00001 to 8706-00065	Home market
	8736-00001 to 8736-00632	LHD
	8746-00001 to 8746-00006	LHD, CKD

	8766-00001 to 8766-00550	RHD export
	8776-00001 to 8776-00012	RHD, CKD
1957	1317-00001 to 1317-00053	Home market
	1327-00001 to 1327-01024	RHD export
	1337-00001 to 1337-00024	RHD, CKD
	1347-00001 to 1347-01283	LHD
	1357-00001 to 1357-00036	LHD, CKD
1958	1318-00001 to 1318-00120	Home market
	1328-00001 to 1328-01541	RHD export
	1338-00001 to 1338-00036	RHD, CKD
	1348-00001 to 1347-01618	LHD

(There were no 1358-series CKD Station Wagons with LHD.)

88-inch, all models

1956	1116-04808 to 1116-05472	Home market
	1126-02442 to 1126-02800	RHD export
	1136-01368 to 1136-01488	RHD, CKD
	1146-04434 to 1146-05372	LHD
	1156-01001 to 1156-01186	LHD, CKD
	1166-00001 to 1166-00006	Diesel prototypes
1957	1117-00001 to 1117-03951	Home market, petrol
	1127-00001 to 1127-02957	RHD export, petrol
	1137-00001 to 1137-01798	RHD, CKD, petrol
	1147-00001 to 1147-04526	LHD, petrol
	1157-00001 to 1157-00745	LHD, CKD, petrol
	1167-00001 to 1167-00298	Home market, diesel
1958	1118-00001 to 1118-01912	Home market, petrol
	1128-00001 to 1128-01702	RHD export, petrol
	1138-00001 to 1138-01296	RHD, CKD, petrol
	1148-00001 to 1148-02230	LHD, petrol
	1158-00001 to 1158-00198	LHD, CKD, petrol
	1168-00001 to 1168-01488	Home market, diesel
	1178-00001 to 1178-00176	RHD export, diesel
	1188-00001 to 1188-00048	RHD, CKD, diesel
	1198-00001 to 1198-00283	LHD, diesel
	1208-00001 to 1208-00060	LHD, CKD, diesel

109-inch

1956	1216-04808 to 1216-01227	Home market
	1226-03055 (one only)	RHD export
	1236-01368 to 1236-01440	RHD, CKD

Chassis Numbers

	1246-04434 to 1246-03001	LHD
	1256-01001 to 1256-00264	LHD, CKD
	1266-00001 (one only)	Diesel prototype
1957	1217-00001 to 1217-00719	Home market, petrol
	1227-00001 to 1227-03850	RHD export, petrol
	1237-00001 to 1237-01281	RHD, CKD, petrol
	1247-00001 to 1247-02581	LHD, petrol
	1257-00001 to 1257-00044	LHD, CKD, petrol
	1267-00001 to 1267-00153	Home market, diesel
1958	1218-00001 to 1218-00435	Home market, petrol
	1228-00001 to 1228-02450	RHD export, petrol
	1238-00001 to 1238-01125	RHD, CKD, petrol
	1248-00001 to 1248-01371	LHD, petrol
	1258-00001 to 1258-00024	LHD, CKD, petrol
	1268-00001 to 1268-00457	Home market, diesel
	1278-00001 to 1268-00309	RHD export, diesel
	1288-00001 to 1268-00075	RHD, CKD, diesel
	1298-00001 to 1268-00093	LHD, diesel
	1308-00001 to 1308-00012	LHD, CKD, diesel

	1469-00001 to 1469-01761	Home market, diesel
	1479-00001 to 1479-00215	RHD export, diesel
	1489-00001 to 1489-00060	RHD, CKD, diesel
	1499-00001 to 1499-00355	LHD, diesel
	1509-00001 to 1509-00294	LHD, CKD, diesel
1960	1410-00001 to 1410-04545	Home market
	1420-00001 to 1420-02899	RHD export, petrol
	1430-00001 to 1430-01671	RHD, CKD, petrol
	1440-00001 to 1440-06518	LHD, petrol
	1450-00001 to 1450-00276	LHD, CKD, petrol
	1460-00001 to 1460-02192	Home market, diesel
	1470-00001 to 1470-00369	RHD export, diesel
	1480-00001 to 1480-00041	RHD, CKD, diesel
	1490-00001 to 1490-00494	LHD, diesel
	1500-00001 to 1500-00047	LHD, CKD, diesel
1961	1411-00001 to 1411-04450	Home market , petrol
	1421-00001 to 1421-02256	RHD export, petrol
	1431-00001 to 1431-02302	RHD, CKD, petrol
	1441-00001 to 1441-05602	LHD, petrol
	1451-00001 to 1451-00312	LHD, CKD, petrol
	1461-00001 to 1461-01282	Home market, diesel
	1471-00001 to 1471-00392	RHD export, diesel
	1481-00001 to 1481-00018	RHD, CKD, diesel
	1491-00001 to 1491-00704	LHD, diesel
	1501-00001 to 1501-00054	LHD, CKD, diesel

SERIES II CHASSIS NUMBERS

The Land Rover model year once again ran from September to August.

88-inch utilities

1958	1418-00001 to 1418-01703	Home market, petrol
	1428-00001 to 1428-01359	RHD export, petrol
	1438-00001 to 1438-00960	RHD, CKD, petrol
	1448-00001 to 1448-02288	LHD, petrol
	1458-00001 to 1458-00840	LHD, CKD, petrol
	1468-00001 to 1468-00587	Home market, diesel
	1478-00001 to 1478-00243	RHD export, diesel
	1488-00001 to 1488-00156	RHD, CKD, diesel
	1498-00001 to 1498-00239	LHD, diesel
	1508-00001 to 1508-00036	LHD, CKD, diesel
1959	1419-00001 to 1419-04072	Home market, petrol
	1429-00001 to 1429-01964	RHD export, petrol
	1439-00001 to 1439-01822	RHD, CKD, petrol
	1449-00001 to 1449-04010	LHD, petrol
	1459-00001 to 1459-01068	LHD, CKD, petrol

Station Wagons were numbered within the overall sequences used for the Series II 88-inch Land Rovers.

109-inch utilities

1958	1518-00001 to 1518-00360	Home market, petrol
	1528-00001 to 1528-01153	RHD export, petrol
	1538-00001 to 1538-00480	RHD, CKD, petrol
	1548-00001 to 1548-00903	LHD, petrol
	1558-00001 to 1558-00048	LHD, CKD, petrol
	1568-00001 to 1568-00261	Home market, diesel
	1578-00001 to 1578-00309	RHD export, diesel
	1588-00001 to 1588-00132	RHD, CKD, diesel
	1598-00001 to 1598-00083	LHD, diesel
	1608-00001 to 1608-00006	LHD, CKD, diesel
1959	1519-00001 to 1519-01137	Home market, petrol
	1529-00001 to 1529-03458	RHD export, petrol

Chassis Numbers

	1539-00001 to 1539-00481	RHD, CKD, petrol
	1549-00001 to 1549-01911	LHD, petrol
	1559-series (None built)	LHD, CKD, petrol
	1569-00001 to 1569-01089	Home market, diesel
	1579-00001 to 1579-00586	RHD export, diesel
	1589-00001 to 1589-00060	RHD, CKD, diesel
	1599-00001 to 1599-00362	LHD, diesel
	1609-00001 to 1609-00030	LHD, CKD, diesel
1960	1510-00001 to 1510-01587	Home market
	1520-00001 to 1520-04533	RHD export, petrol
	1530-00001 to 1530-01922	RHD, CKD, petrol
	1540-00001 to 1540-03116	LHD, petrol
	1550-00001 to 1550-00280	LHD, CKD, petrol
	1560-00001 to 1560-01310	Home market, diesel
	1570-00001 to 1570-00747	RHD export, diesel
	1580-00001 to 1580-00113	RHD, CKD, diesel
	1590-00001 to 1590-00565	LHD, diesel
	1600-00001 to 1600-00005	LHD, CKD, diesel
1961	1511-00001 to 1511-01500	Home market , petrol
	1521-00001 to 1521-04909	RHD export, petrol
	1531-00001 to 1531-02955	RHD, CKD, petrol
	1541-00001 to 1541-02832	LHD, petrol
	1551-00001 to 1551-00168	LHD, CKD, petrol
	1561-00001 to 1561-00911	Home market, diesel
	1571-00001 to 1571-00818	RHD export, diesel
	1581-00001 to 1581-00156	RHD, CKD, diesel
	1591-00001 to 1591-00756	LHD, diesel
	1601-series (None built)	LHD, CKD, diesel

109-inch Station Wagon

1959	1619-00001 to 1619-00106	Home market, petrol
	1629-00001 to 1629-00567	RHD export, petrol
	1639-00001 to 1639-00025	RHD, CKD, petrol
	1649-00001 to 1649-00962	LHD, petrol
	1659-series (None built)	LHD, CKD, petrol
	1669-series (None built)	Home market, diesel
	1679-00001 to 1679-00006	RHD export, diesel
	1689-series (None built)	RHD, CKD, diesel
	1699-00001 to 1699-00026	LHD, diesel
	1709-series (None built)	LHD, CKD, diesel
1960	1610-00001 to 1610-00101	Home market
	1620-00001 to 1620-01188	RHD export, petrol

	1630-00001 to 1630-00063	RHD, CKD, petrol
	1640-00001 to 1640-01267	LHD, petrol
	1650-00001 to 1650-00024	LHD, CKD, petrol
	1660-series (None built)	Home market, diesel
	1670-00001 to 1670-00020	RHD export, diesel
	1680-series (None built)	RHD, CKD, diesel
	1690-00001 to 1690-00073	LHD, diesel
	1700-series (None built)	LHD, CKD, diesel
1961	1611-00001 to 1611-00134	Home market , petrol
	1621-00001 to 1621-01314	RHD export, petrol
	1631-00001 to 1631-00180	RHD, CKD, petrol
	1641-00001 to 1641-01366	LHD, petrol
	1651-00001 to 1651-00006	LHD, CKD, petrol
	1661-00001 to 1661-00004	Home market, diesel
	1671-00001 to 1671-00080	RHD export, diesel
	1681-series (None built)	RHD, CKD, diesel
	1691-00001 to 1691-00067	LHD, diesel
	1701-series (None built)	LHD, CKD, diesel

SERIES IIA CHASSIS NUMBERS

The Land Rover model year once again ran from September to August.

88-inch utilities

1722-00001 to 1722-00003 prototype batch	RHD diesel, 1961
1772-00001 to 1772-00004 prototype batch	LHD diesel, 1961
241-00001A to 241-42494H	Home market, petrol
242-00001A to 242-13449H	RHD export, petrol
243-00001A to 243-08207H	RHD, CKD, petrol
244-00001A to 244-45282H	LHD, petrol
245-00001A to 245-02629H	LHD, CKD, petrol
271-00001A to 271-15263H	Home market, diesel
272-00001A to 272-02707H	RHD export, diesel
273-00001A to 273-00294H	RHD, CKD, diesel
274-00001A to 274-07561H	LHD, diesel
275-00001A to 275-00355H	LHD, CKD, diesel

Notes: Station Wagons were numbered in the main sequence until 1965, but had their own sequence thereafter.

Chassis Numbers

88-inch Station Wagons

315-00001B to 315-00782H	Home market, petrol
316-00001B to 316-01652H	RHD export, petrol
317-series (None built)	RHD CKD, petrol
318-00001B to 318-09216H	LHD, petrol
319-series (None built)	LHD CKD, Petrol
320-00001B to 320-00041H	Home market, diesel
321-00001B to 321-00228H	RHD export, diesel
322-series (None built)	RHD CKD, deisel
323-00001B to 323-01653H	LHD, diesel
324-series (None built)	LHD CKD, deisel

88-inch Half-Ton (Lightweight)

236-00001A to 236-01893H	RHD
239-00001A to 239-01096H	LHD

109-inch utilities

251-00001B to 251-22019H	Home market, four-cyl petrol
252-00001A to 252-34662H	RHD export, four-cyl petrol
253-00001A to 253-11218H	RHD, CKD, four-cyl petrol
254-00001A to 254-39150H	LHD, four-cyl petrol
255-00001A to 255-00541H	LHD, CKD, four-cyl petrol
276-00001A to 276-13140H	Home market, diesel
277-00001A to 277-07673H	RHD export, diesel
278-00001A to 278-01273H	RHD, CKD, diesel
279-00001A to 279-08620H	LHD, diesel
280-00001A to 280-00462H	LHD, CKD, diesel
345-00001D to 345-02100H	Home market, six-cyl petrol
346-00001D to 346-01232H	RHD export, six-cyl petrol
347-series (See below)	RHD, CKD, six-cyl petrol
348-00001D to 348-02149H	LHD, six-cyl petrol
349-series (No records)	LHD, CKD, six-cyl petrol

Note: Large numbers of the 347-series vehicles were shipped to Australia for local assembly, and the highest chassis number known by early 2006 was 347-07906G on a 1971 model. It is quite possible that there were no 349-series vehicles.

109-inch Station Wagon

261-00001A to 261-03542H	Home market, four-cyl petrol
262-00001A to 262-11569H	RHD export, four-cyl petrol
263-series (None built)	RHD CKD, four-cyl petrol
264-00001A to 264-18516H	LHD, four-cyl petrol
265-series (None built)	LHD CKD six-cyl petrol
281-00001A to 281-01453H	Home market, diesel
282-00001A to 282-01649H	RHD export, diesel
283-00001A to 283-00081H	RHD, CKD, diesel
284-00001A to 284-04326H	LHD, diesel
285-00001A to 285-00042H	LHD, CKD, diesel
350-00001D to 350-01625H	Home market, six-cyl petrol
351-00001D to 351-01133H	RHD export, six-cyl petrol
352-series (None built)	RHD CKD six-cyl petrol
353-00001D to 353-02191H	LHD, six-cyl petrol
354-series (None built)	LHD CKD six-cyl petrol

109-inch Airportable

310-00001A to 310-00028A

109-inch NADA Station Wagon

343-00001A to 343-00811A

109-inch One Ton

221-00001G to 221-00170H	Home market, six-cyl petrol
222-00001G to 222-00052H	RHD export, six-cyl petrol
223-00001G to 223-00064H	LHD, six-cyl petrol
231-00001G to 231-00022G	Home market, four-cyl petrol

Chassis Numbers

SERIES III CHASSIS NUMBERS (1971–1979) AND VIN CODES (1980–1985)

The Land Rover model year once again ran from September to August.

During 1975, the chassis numbering system changed. The type identifier prefixes in use since 1971 were retained, but there were now only two separate serial numbering series. One was for petrol-engined models and the other for diesel-engined types. In each case, utilities and Station Wagons were included together, but Lightweights were excluded.

From November 1, 1979, VIN codes were used, with a single serial numbering system which embraced 88, 88 Lightweight, and 109 models of all types. For an explanation of the VIN codes applicable to Series III models, see the table below.

It is not always possible to determine the suffix code on the final vehicle in a sequence. In such cases, the code is represented here by the symbol "x".

88-inch utilities

(1971-1975):
901-00001A to 901-11900x	Home market, basic, four-cyl petrol
902-00001A to 902-02640x	RHD export, basic, four-cyl petrol
903-00001A (No records)	RHD, CKD, basic, four-cyl petrol
904-00001A to 904-09283x	LHD, basic, four-cyl petrol
905-00001A (No records)	LHD, CKD, four-cyl petrol
906-00001A to 906-07270x	Home market, basic, diesel
907-00001A to 907-00964x	RHD export, basic, diesel
908-00001A (No records)	RHD, CKD, basic, diesel
909-00001A to 909-02807x	LHD, basic, diesel
910-00001A (No records)	LHD, CKD, diesel

(1975-1979):
The petrol series began at 12500x and ended at 57435x.
The diesel series began at 08000x and ended at 29522x.

88-inch Station Wagons

(1971-1975):
921-00001A to 921-00757x	Home market, four-cyl petrol

922-00001A to 922-00894x	RHD export, four-cyl petrol
923-00001A (No records)	RHD, CKD, four-cyl petrol
924-00001A to 924-04050x	LHD, four-cyl petrol
925-00001A (No records)	LHD, CKD, four-cyl petrol
926-00001A to 926-00046x	Home market, diesel
927-00001A to 926-00148x	RHD export, diesel
928-00001A (No records)	RHD, CKD, diesel
929-00001A to 929-01200x	LHD, diesel
930-00001A (No records)	LHD, CKD, diesel

Chassis numbers (1975-1979):
The petrol series began at 12500x and ended at 57435x.
The diesel series began at 08000x and ended at 29522x.

88-inch Federal De Luxe Hardtops
259-00001A to 259-03572x

88-inch Half-Tons (Lightweights)
(1972-1980):
895-00001A to 895-01909x	LHD export, diesel
951-00001A to 951-05805x	Home market, petrol
952-00001A to 952-00102x	RHD export, petrol
953 series (None built)	RHD CKD, petrol
954-00001A to 954-04518x	LHD, petrol
955 series (None built)	LHD CKD, petrol

109-inch utilities
(1971-1975):
911-00001A to 911-07289x	Home market, four-cyl petrol
912-00001A to 912-05039x	RHD export, four-cyl petrol
913-series (No records)	RHD, CKD, four-cyl petrol
914-00001A to 914-16091x	LHD, four-cyl petrol
915-series (No records)	LHD, CKD, four-cyl petrol
916-00001A to 916-05070x	Home market, diesel
917-00001A to 917-02026x	RHD export, diesel
918-series (No records)	RHD, CKD, diesel
919-00001A to 919-02991x	LHD, diesel
920-series (No records)	LHD, CKD, diesel

941-00001A to 941-02122x   Home market, six-cyl petrol
942-00001A to 942-00486x   RHD export, six-cyl petrol
943-series (No records)   RHD, CKD, six-cyl petrol
944-00001A to 944-01761x   LHD, six-cyl petrol

(1975-1979):

The four-cylinder petrol series began at 16000x and went up to 99999x; the sequence then began again at 00001x, finally ending at 16127x. Some serial numbers therefore duplicated those issued earlier, although their suffix letters differed.

The diesel series began at 06000x and ended at 34641x.

The six-cylinder petrol series began at 12000x and ended at 28641x.

109-inch Station Wagons

(1971-1975):

931-00001A to 931-01848x   Home market, four-cyl petrol
932-00001A to 932-02232x   RHD export, four-cyl petrol
933-series (No records)   RHD, CKD, four-cyl petrol
934-00001A to 934-08752x   LHD, four-cyl petrol
935-series (No records)   LHD, CKD, four-cyl petrol

936-00001A to 936-00782x   Home market, diesel
937-00001A to 937-00488x   RHD export, diesel
938-series (No records)   RHD, CKD, diesel
939-00001A to 939-02163x   LHD, diesel
940-series (No records)   LHD, CKD, diesel

946-00001A to 946-01378x   Home market, six-cyl petrol
947-00001A to 947-00693x   RHD export, six-cyl petrol
948-series (No records)   RHD, CKD, six-cyl petrol
949-00001A to 949-01785x   LHD, six-cyl petrol
950-series (No records)   LHD, CKD, six-cyl petrol

Chassis numbers (1975-1979):

The four-cylinder petrol series began at 16000x and went up to 99999x; the sequence then began again at 00001x, finally ending at 16127x. Some serial numbers therefore duplicated those issued earlier, although their suffix letters differed.

The diesel series began at 06000x and ended at 34641x.

The six-cylinder petrol series began at 12000x and ended at 28641x.

109-inch One Ton

266-00001A to 266-00238x   Home market, basic
267-00001A to 267-00064x   RHD, Export
268-series (No records)   RHD, CKD
269-00001A to 269-00148x   LHD
270-series (No records)   LHD, CKD

Stage 1 V8 109-inch

Chassis numbers :

All production Stage 1 V8 models had VIN-style chassis numbers, even though these were not introduced for other Land Rover models until later in 1979. A single serial numbering system embraced 109 models of all types, together with 88s and Half-Ton (Lightweight) models. For an explanation of the VIN codes applicable to the Stage 1 models, see the table on this page.

VIN codes for Series III models (1979-1985)

From November 1, 1979, the Land Rover chassis numbering system changed to conform to internationally-agreed VIN (Vehicle Identification Number) code standards. It is probable that some vehicles built in October 1979 also had these codes. Those used for the first year (i.e. 1980 model-year) had 14 characters. From November 1, 1980, three further characters (SAL) were added to the prefix, making 17 characters in all.

Example (later type):   SALLBAAG1AA-123456.

This breaks down as follows:

SAL   Manufacturer code (then British Leyland)
LB   Land Rover Series III
A   88-inch wheelbase
        C = 109-inch wheelbase
A   Utility body (soft top, truck cab or hardtop)
        B = 88in Station Wagon
        H = HCPU
        M = 109-inch Station Wagon
G   2.25-litre diesel engine
        H = 2.25-litre petrol engine
        P = 2.6-litre six-cylinder petrol engine
        V = 3.5-litre V8 petrol engine
1   RHD with 4-speed manual gearbox
        2 = LHD with 4-speed manual gearbox

	5 = RHD with 4-speed manual gearbox and overdrive
	6 = LHD with 4-speed manual gearbox and overdrive
A	88in or 109in
A	Assembled at Solihull
	F = Shipped as KD for overseas assembly
123456	Serial number

NINETY, ONE TEN AND ONE TWO SEVEN VIN CODES

A single serial numbering system embraced all RHD, LHD, and CKD variants. For an explanation of the VIN codes applicable to One Tens built in this period, see the table on this page.

VIN codes for One Tens (1983-1990)

The VIN codes used in this period consisted of 17 characters, made up of an 11-character prefix code and a six-digit serial number.
Example: SALLDHAB1BA-123456.
This breaks down as follows:

SAL	Manufacturer code (Austin Rover to 1986; Rover Group thereafter)
LD	Land Rover coil-sprung utility
H	110-inch wheelbase
	K = 127-inch wheelbase
	M = Australian Heavy-Duty 6x6
	S = 110-inch military model
	V = 92.9-inch wheelbase
A	Truck cab, soft-top or hardtop body
	E = Two-door crew cab (export only)
	F = Four-door crew cab (export only)
	H = HCPU
	M = Station Wagon
B	2.5-litre Diesel Turbo engine
	C = 2.5-litre diesel engine
	D = 2.5-litre petrol engine
	G = 2.3-litre diesel engine
	H = 2.3-litre diesel engine
	V = 3.5-litre petrol engine
	Z = 3.9-litre Isuzu diesel engine (Australia only)
1	RHD with 4-speed manual gearbox

	2 = LHD with 4-speed manual gearbox
	7 = RHD with 5-speed manual gearbox
	8 = LHD with 5-speed manual gearbox
B	Model-years 1985-1987
	A = 1983-1984
	E = 1988
	F = 1989
	G = 1990
A	Assembled at Solihull
	F = Shipped as KD for overseas assembly
	Y = Part-KD, part-Australian built (Heavy-Duty 6x6 only)
123456	Serial number

DEFENDER VIN CODES

VIN codes for Defender 90, 110 and 130, except Brazilian and NAS models
The 17-digit VIN codes break down as follows:

SAL	Manufacturer code (Rover Group)
LD	Defender
A	90 XD
	B = 110 XD
	C = 130 XD
	H = 110 (standard)
	K = 130 (standard)
	L = 147 (South Africa)
	R = 110 (standard)
	S = 110 (military models)
	V = 90 (standard)
A	Truck cab, hardtop or soft-top body
	B = Two-door Station Wagon (Defender 90)
	E = Two-door Crew Cab (Defender 110 and 130)
	F = Four-door Crew Cab (Defender 110 and 130)
	H = High-Capacity Pick-Up (Defender 110)
	J = Station Wagon (Defender 110)
	M = Station Wagon (Defender 110)
C	2.5-litre diesel engine
	D = 2.5-litre petrol engine

Chassis Numbers

F = 2.5-litre 200 Tdi diesel (later 300 Tdi), no EGR or catalyst
K = 2.5-litre 300 Tdi, with cooled EGR and/or catalyst
L = 3.5-litre V8 carburettor petrol engine
M = 4.0-litre injected petrol V8
Y = 2.0-litre four-cylinder petrol engine
1 = 2.5-litre Td5 to EU1 spec
5 = 2.5-litre Td5 to EU3 spec
6 = 2.5-litre 300 Tdi with EGR and/or catalyst
7 = 2.5-litre Td5 for Rest of World
8 = 2.5-litre Td5
3   RHD with four-speed automatic gearbox
    4 = LHD with four-speed automatic gearbox
    7 = RHD with five-speed manual gearbox
    8 = LHD with five-speed manual gearbox
H   Model-year 1991

J = 1992	M = 1995	W = 1998	1 = 2001	4 = 2004
K = 1993	T = 1996	X = 1999	2 = 2002	5 = 2005
L = 1994	V = 1997	Y = 2000	3 = 2003	6 = 2006

A   Assembled at Solihull
    C = Assembled in Zimbabwe
    F = Shipped as KD for overseas assembly
J = Assembled in Malaysia
    K = Assembled in Kenya
    N = Assembled in Morocco
    V = Assembled in South Africa
    W = Assembled in Turkey
123456 Serial number

VIN codes for Brazilian models

The 17-digit VIN code breaks down as follows:
93R Manufacturer code (Land Rover Brazil)
LD Defender
H   110
    K = 130
    V = 90
A   Standard body configuration
    B = Station Wagon (90)
    F = Crew cab with standard pick-up body
    H = Hi-Cap body with or without crew cab
    M = Station Wagon (110)
    N = Five-door, five-seater utility

8   2.5-litre Tdi without EGR or catalyst, built by Maxxion
8   LHD with 5-speed manual gearbox
    4 = LHD with 4-speed automatic gearbox
1   Model-year 2001
    2 = 2002   4 = 2004
    3 = 2003   5 = 2005
T   Assembled in Brazil
123456 Serial number

VIN codes for NAS models

The 17-digit VIN codes break down as follows:
SAL Manufacturer code (Land Rover)
D   Defender
H   110 model
    V = 90 model (except Californian specification)
    X = 90 model (Californian specification)
1   110 Station Wagon body
    2 = 90 open body
    3 = 90 Station Wagon
2   3.9-litre V8 petrol engine
    3 = 4.0-litre V8 petrol engine
8   LHD with 5-speed manual gearbox
4 = LHD with 4-speed automatic gearbox
0   Security check digit
    (0 to 9, or X)
P   Model-year 1993
    R = 1994   V = 1997
    S = 1995
A   Assembled at Solihull
123456 Serial number

Chassis Numbers

FORWARD CONTROL CHASSIS NUMBERS

The Land Rover model year once again ran from September to August.

Series IIA
109-inch Forward Control

286-00001A to 286-00353A	Home market, four-cyl petrol
287-00001A to 287-00940A	RHD export, four-cyl petrol
288-00001A to 288-00303A	RHD, CKD, four-cyl petrol
289-00001A to 289-00459A	LHD, four-cyl petrol
290-00001A to 290-00036A	LHD, CKD, four-cyl petrol

300-00001A (one only)	Home market, six-cyl petrol
301-00001A to 301-00361A	RHD export, six-cyl petrol
302-00001A to 302-00096A	RHD, CKD, six-cyl petrol
303-00001A to 303-00633A	LHD, six-cyl petrol
304-00001A to 304-00006A	LHD, CKD, six-cyl petrol

305-00001A to 305-00005A	Home market, diesel

Series IIB
110-inch Forward Control

325-00001A (one only)	Home market, four-cyl petrol
326-00001A to 326-00452A	RHD export, four-cyl petrol
327-series (None built)	RHD, CKD, four-cyl petrol
328-00001A to 328-00074A	LHD, four-cyl petrol
329-series (None built)	LHD, CKD, four-cyl petrol

330-00001A to 330-00360A	Home market, six-cyl petrol
331-00001A to 331-00524A	RHD export, six-cyl petrol
332-series (None built)	RHD, CKD, six-cyl petrol
333-00001A to 333-00370A	LHD, six-cyl petrol
334-series (None built)	LHD, CKD, six-cyl petrol

335-00001A to 335-00168A	Home market, diesel
336-00001A to 336-00176A	RHD export, diesel
337-series (None built)	RHD, CKD, diesel
338-00001A to 338-00180A	LHD, diesel
339-series (None built)	LHD, CKD, diesel

101-inch One-Tonne Forward Control

956-00001A to 956-01322A	Home market, 12v (1972-1978)
957-00001A to 956-00028A	RHD export, 12v (1976-1977)
959-00001A to 959-00583A	LHD, 12v (1972 and 1975-1977)
961-00001A to 961-00170A	Home market, 24v (1972-1973 and
	(1975-1977)
962-00001A to 962-00092A	RHD export, 24v (1977-1978)
964-00001A to 964-00474A	LHD, 24v (1972-1973 and 1975-1978)

FREELANDER VIN CODES

VIN codes (except Chinese, Mexican and NAS models)
The 17-digit VIN codes break down as follows:

SAL   Manufacturer code (Rover Group, later Land Rover UK)

LN   Freelander

A Standard trim
- B = Commercial trim
- F = Sport model

A Three-door body (Hardback or Softback)
- B = Five-door body (Station Wagon)

A 1.8-litre petrol engine (High octane, unleaded fuel)
- B = 2.0-litre L-series diesel engine
- C = 1.8-litre petrol engine (Low octane, unleaded fuel)
- D = 1.8-litre petrol engine (Low octane, leaded fuel)
- E = 2.0-litre Td4 diesel engine
- F = 1.8-litre petrol engine (High octane, leaded fuel)
- G = 2.5-litre V6 petrol engine (for unleaded fuel)
- H = 2.5-litre V6 petrol engine (for leaded fuel)
- J = 2.5-litre V6 petrol engine (for ethanol fuel)

1 RHD with 5-speed automatic gearbox
- 2 = LHD with 5-speed automatic gearbox
- 7 = RHD with 5-speed manual gearbox
- 8 = LHD with 5-speed manual gearbox

W Model-year 1998
- X = 1999   1 = 2001   3 = 2003   5 = 2005
- Y = 2000   2 = 2002   4 = 2004   6 = 2006

A Assembled at Solihull
- D = Assembled in Thailand
- J = Assembled in Malaysia

123456 Serial number

VIN codes for Chinese, Mexican and NAS models

The 17-digit VIN codes break down as follows:

SAL   Manufacturer code (Rover Group, later Land Rover UK)
N   Freelander
A   Standard trim (early NAS)
     C = Standard trim (2004 on)
     E = HSE trim (NAS)
     N = Chinese specification
     Y = SE trim (NAS)
1   Three-door body
     2 = Station Wagon
1   1.8-litre petrol engine
     2 = 2.5-litre V6 petrol engine
     4 = 2.0-litre Td4 diesel engine
2   5-speed Steptronic automatic gearbox
0   Security check digit
     (0 to 9, or X)
2   Model-year 2002
     3 = 2003   5 = 2005
     4 = 2004   6 = 2006
A   Assembled at Solihull
123456 Serial number

DISCOVERY CHASSIS NUMBERS

Discovery (Series I)
VIN codes (1989-1998), except North American models

The 17-digit VIN codes break down as follows:

SAL   Manufacturer code (Rover Group)
LJ Discovery
G   Standard (100-inch) wheelbase
     D = Honda Crossroad
B   Three-door body
     M = Five-door body
V   3.5-litre V8 carburettor petrol engine
     F = 2.5-litre 200 Tdi diesel engine (300 Tdi from 1994)
     L = 3.5-litre V8 injected petrol engine
     M = 3.9-litre V8 injected petrol engine
     Y = 2.0-litre four-cylinder petrol engine
3   RHD with automatic gearbox

4 = LHD, automatic
7 = RHD with 5-speed manual gearbox
8 = LHD with 5-speed manual gearbox
G   Model-year 1990
     H = 1991   L = 1994   V = 1997
     J = 1992   M = 1995   W = 1998
     K = 1993   T = 1996
A   Assembled at Solihull
     F = Shipped as KD for overseas assembly
123456 Serial number

VIN codes for NAS models, 1994-1998

The 17-digit VIN codes break down as follows:

SAL   Manufacturer code (Land Rover)
J   Discovery
     P = Range Rover 38A
A   108-inch wheelbase (Range Rover only)
G = 100-inch wheelbase (Discovery only)
1   Four-door body
J   4.6-litre V8 petrol engine
     3 = 4.0-litre V8 petrol engine
4   LHD with 4-speed automatic gearbox
8 = LHD with 5-speed manual gearbox (Discovery only)
1   Security check digit
     (0 to 9, or X)
R   Model-year 1994 (March to summer 1994)
     S = 1995   V = 1997
     T = 1996   W = 1998
A   Assembled at Solihull
123456 Serial number

Series II
VIN codes (except NAS models)

The 17-digit VIN codes break down as follows:

SAL   Manufacturer code (Rover Group, later Land Rover UK)
LT   Discovery Series II
A   Japanese specification
     G = All other markets
M   Standard body configuration
1   4.0-litre V8 for Australia
     2 = 4.0-litre V8 for EEC and Japan

3 = 4.0-litre V8 for other countries

7 = Td5 diesel for all countries except (8) and (9)

8 = Td5 diesel for UK

9 = Td5 diesel for Australia, EEC and Japan

3 RHD with 4-speed automatic gearbox

    4 = LHD with 4-speed automatic gearbox

X Model-year 1999

      Y = 2000   2 = 2002   4= 2004

      1 = 2001   3 = 2003

A Assembled at Solihull

      F = Shipped as KD for overseas assembly

123456 Serial number

VIN codes (NAS models)

The 17-digit VIN codes break down as follows:

SAL   Manufacturer code (Rover Group, later Land Rover UK)

TY   Discovery Series II (except California)

      TN = Discovery Series II for California

1   Standard specification

3   4.0-litre V8

      4 = 4.6-litre V8

2   LHD with automatic gearbox

0   Check digit (0 to 9, or X)

X   Model-year 1999

      Y = 2000   2 = 2002   4 = 2004

      1 = 2001   3 = 2003

A   Assembled at Solihull

123456 Serial number

Discovery 3
VIN codes (except Canada and USA)

The 17-digit VIN code breaks down as follows:

SAL   Manufacturer code (Land Rover UK)

LA   Discovery 3

A   Standard

      J = Japan

A Four-door

1   2.7-litre V6 turbodiesel

      4 = 4.0-litre V6 petrol

      5 = 4.4-litre V8 petrol

3 RHD with automatic gearbox

      4 = LHD with automatic gearbox

      7 = RHD with manual gearbox

      8 = LHD with automatic gearbox

1 Model-year 2005

      6 = 2006

A Assembled at Solihull

123456 Serial number

VIN codes for LR3 (Canada and USA)

The 17-digit VIN code breaks down as follows:

SAL   Manufacturer code (Land Rover UK)

A LR3

A Standard

      B = S trim with five seats

      C = S trim with seven seats

      D = SE trim with five seats

      E = SE trim with seven seats

      F = HSE trim with five seats

      G = HSE trim with seven seats

2 Four-door

4 4.0-litre V6 petrol

      5 = 4.4-litre V8 petrol

4 LHD with automatic gearbox

0 Check digit (0 to 9, or X)

5 Model-year 2005

      6 = 2006

A Assembled at Solihull

123456 Serial number

RANGE ROVER CHASSIS NUMBERS

(1970-1975)

It is not always possible to determine the suffix code on the final vehicle in a sequence. In such cases, the code is represented here by the symbol "x".

355-00001A to 355-11062D	Home market
356-00001A to 356-03292D	RHD export
357-00001A to 357-00432x	RHD, CKD

Chassis Numbers

358-00001A to 358-10556D   LHD
359-00001A to 359-02340x   LHD, CKD

From 1975-1979, the earlier three-digit type identifier prefixes were used with a single serial numbering system. The new series began at serial number 12024E and finished at 61821G.

VIN codes (1979-1996)

From November 1, 1979, VIN codes were used, with a single serial numbering system which embraced all RHD, LHD, and CKD variants. Those used for the first year (i.e. 1980 model-year) had 14 characters. From November 1, 1980, three further characters (SAL) were added to the prefix, making 17 characters in all.
The 17-digit codes break down as follows:

SAL   Manufacturer code (British Leyland)
LH   Range Rover
A   100-inch wheelbase
    B = Long (108-inch) wheelbase
B   Two-door body
    A = Two-door "van" body
M = Four-door body
    R = Monteverdi four-door conversion
V   3.5-litre carburettor V8 petrol engine
    E = 2.4-litre VM diesel engine
    F = 2.5-litre 200 Tdi diesel engine (300 Tdi from 1994)
L = 3.5-litre V8 injected petrol engine
    M = 3.9-litre V8 injected petrol engine
    N = 2.5-litre VM diesel engine
    3 = 4.2-litre V8 petrol engine
1   RHD with 4-speed manual gearbox
    2 = LHD with 4-speed manual gearbox
    3 = RHD, automatic
    4 = LHD, automatic
    7 = RHD with 5-speed manual gearbox
    8 = LHD with 5-speed manual gearbox
A   Model-code (all model-years to mid-1984)

B = 1985	F = 1989	K = 1993
C = 1986	G = 1990	L = 1994
D = 1987	H = 1991	M = 1995
E = 1988	J = 1992	N = 1996

A   Assembled at Solihull

F = Shipped as KD for overseas assembly
123456 Serial number

VIN codes for NAS models (1987-1995)

The 17-digit codes break down as follows:
SAL   Manufacturer code (British Leyland)
LH   Range Rover
A   100-inch wheelbase
    B = Long (108-inch) wheelbase
M   Four-door body
L   3.5-litre injected V8 petrol engine
    M = 3.9-litre V8 injected petrol engine
    3 = 4.2-litre V8 petrol engine
4   LHD, automatic
H   Model-year 1987

J = 1988	M = 1991	R = 1994
K = 1989	N = 1992	S = 1995
L = 1990	P = 1993	

A   Assembled at Solihull
    F = Shipped as KD for overseas assembly
123456 Serial number

Second-generation (38A) Range Rover

VIN codes (1994-2001), except North American models

The 17-digit VIN codes break down as follows:
SAL   Manufacturer code (Rover Group, later Land Rover UK)
LP   Range Rover 38A
A   Standard (108-inch) wheelbase
M   Four-door body
J   4.6-litre V8 petrol engine
    3 = 4.0-litre V8 petrol engine
    W = 2.5-litre six-cylinder diesel engine
3   RHD with automatic gearbox
    4 = LHD, automatic
    7 = RHD with 5-speed manual gearbox
    8 = LHD with 5-speed manual gearbox
M   Model-year 1995

T = 1996	Y = 2000
V = 1997	1 = 2001

Chassis Numbers

W = 1998   2 = 2002
X = 1999

A Assembled at Solihull
123456 Serial number

3 = 2003   5 = 2005
4 = 2004   6 = 2006

A Assembled at Solihull
123456 Serial number

VIN codes for North American models

The 17-digit VIN codes break down as follows:

SAL   Manufacturer code (Land Rover)
P Range Rover 38A
A Standard (108-inch wheelbase)
1 Four-door body
J 4.6-litre V8 petrol engine
     3 = 4.0-litre V8 petrol engine
4 LHD with 4-speed automatic gearbox
8 = LHD with 5-speed manual gearbox (Discovery only)
1 Security check digit
     (0 to 9, or X)
R Model-year 1994 (March to summer 1994)
     S = 1995   V = 1997   X = 1999   1 = 2001
     T = 1996   W = 1998   Y = 2000   2 = 2002
A Assembled at Solihull
123456 Serial number

Third-generation (L322) Range Rover

VIN codes (European and Rest of World models)

The 17-digit VIN codes break down as follows:

SAL   Manufacturer code (Land Rover UK)
LM Range Rover L322
A Standard specification
M Standard four-door body
A 4.4-litre BMW V8
     C = 3.0-litre Td6 turbodiesel
     4 = 4.2-litre supercharged Jaguar V8
     5 = 4.4-litre Jaguar V8
1 RHD with five-speed automatic gearbox
     2 = LHD with five-speed automatic gearbox
     3 = RHD with six-speed automatic gearbox
     4 = LHD with six-speed automatic gearbox
2 Model-year 2002

VIN codes (Canadian, Chinese, Mexican and US models)

The 17-digit VIN codes break down as shown below. Note that early models have an E or V after the model type code and before the trim code to indicate the level of emissions equipment fitted; on 2006 and later models, this is replaced by an additional digit between the trim specification and the engine type codes.

SAL   Manufacturer code (Land Rover UK)
M   Range Rover L322
E   Californian specification (pre-2006 models only)
     V = For other US States and Canada (pre-2006 models only)
A   S specification
     B = HSE without Luxury Pack
     C = HSE with Luxury Pack
     D = Limited edition
     E = HSE without Luxury Pack, with Logic 7 and Bi-Xenon
     F = HSE with Luxury Pack, Logic and Bi-Xenon
     G = SE trim
     H = Westminster
     N = Standard trim (China only)
6   Four-door Station Wagon (2006 on)
A   4.4-litre BMW V8
     5 = 4.4-litre Jaguar V8
2   LHD with five-speed automatic gearbox
     4 = LHD with six-speed automatic gearbox
0   Check digit (0 to 9, or X)
2   Model-year 2002
     3 = 2003   5 = 2005
     4 = 2004   6 = 2006
A   Assembled at Solihull
123456 Serial number

Bibliography

The Guide to Land Rover Expeditions (various editions) was available from Land Rover Ltd, Lode Lane, Solihull, West Midlands B92 8NW free of charge.

Rover Memories, Richard Hough, Michael Frostick; George Allen and Unwin, 1966

Military Wheeled Vehicles, Olyslager; Ward Lock 1972

British Cars series, Olyslager; Warne 1973

The Rover Story, Graham Robson; Patrick Stephens, 1977 and 1981

Illustrated Encyclopedia of Military Vehicles; Ian Hogg, John Weeks, Hamlyn 1980 A-Z 5vols 1920s-1980s, Sedgwick, Gillies, Robson, Baldwin, Lewis; Bay View

Classic Rovers 1934-1977, James Taylor; Motor Racing Publications 1983 and 1989

Land Rover 1948-1988, James Taylor; Motor Racing Publications 1984, 1988, 1990

Rover, The First Ninety Years, Eric Dymock, Dove Publishing 1993

World War Two Military Vehicles, G N Georgano; Osprey 1994

Range Rover Gold Portfolio, Brooklands Books 1995

Range Rover The First Generation, James Taylor, Nick Dimbleby 1995 and 2002

Land Rover 1948-1983, James Taylor; Motor Racing Publications 1996

Land Rover since 1983, James Taylor; Motor Racing Publications 1996

Cars in the UK, Vol 1 and Vol 2, Graham Robson; Motor Racing Publications 1997

Rover P5 and P5B, James Taylor; Crowood, 1997

Fifty Years of Selling Land Rover 1948-1998, James Taylor, Brooklands Books

Land Rover Simply the Best, Martin Hodder; Haynes 1998

Catalogue of British Cars, Culshaw & Horrobin; Veloce 1999

Land Rover Discovery 1989-1998, James Taylor; Motor Racing Publications 1999)

The Beaulieu Encyclopædia of the Automobile; The Stationery Office 2000

End of the Road, BMW & Rover, Chris Brady Andrew Lorenz; Financial Times 2001

Land Rover Series One to Freelander, Graham Robson, Crowood 2003

You and Your Land Rover Freelander, James Taylor; Haynes 2003

Range Rover The Second Generation, James Taylor; Crowood 2004

Among the sources used in research were the author's archive collections of the annuals *Automobil Revue/Revue Automobile* published by BTM AG Bern, *Automobile Year* published by Editions J-R Piccard, *The Motor Year Books*, Temple Press 1949-1957, Land Rover press books, statements, reprints, and other material, *Land Rover Enthusiast*, and also of *The Motor, The Autocar, Autosport, Automotive News Europe, Auto Express, Classic Car, Classic Car Profiles, Classic & Sportscar, The Automobile, On Four Wheels, Automobile Quarterly, What Car?* and *Veteran & Vintage*, to all of whose contributors and proprietors motoring historians owe continuing thanks.

Acknowledgements

The publishers thank Stuart Dyble, Vice President Communications and Public Affairs Premier Automotive Group, Andrew Roberts Director Global Brand and Product Communications Land Rover and their staff, in particular James Andrew and Mark Foster for their help and encouragement in making this book possible. Special thanks are due to Roger Crathorne for his generous support, often beyond the call of duty and going back many years before this book. Manager Technical Communications, Roger arranged many meetings and contacts as well as unearthing much rare material. Thanks also go to Randal Jackson for his help with Freelander 2, and Jane Roche for her invaluable help. The author and researchers thank generations of press officers for making Land Rovers of every sort available for test since the 1950s. The publisher and author express their gratitude to researchers Graham Robson and James Taylor, for providing their matchless experience on all things connected with Land Rover, to ensure accuracy and continuity. Our thanks also go to The British Motor Industry Heritage Trust, Gaydon for access to their archive of images, and documents relating to the Rover Company and to Land Rover; Brian and Phil Bashall of the Dunsfold Land Rover Collection for access to their archive of Land Rover-related documents, for permission to use their images and for their help and support; Kevin Shearman likewise for the opportunity to share his insight into the story of Land Rover's beginnings and for the use of his images; Andrew McRobb for the use of his extensive library; Ken Wheelwright for sharing the results of his work in restoring early Land Rovers; current and past Land Rover staff including Peter Armel, John Bilton, Alan Edis, Mike Gould, Geof Miller, Bill Morris, Bob Lees and the late Frank Shaw for sharing their knowledge and passion for the brand. Mike Gould also contributed to the history of Land Rover and to the section covering the 'Series 1' and Defender vehicles. Thanks are due to the Wilks family for the images of them using the Jeep and early Land Rovers in Anglesey, also to Blueprint of Witney for help in researching and providing images, DriveLine Creative Media of Abingdon for its work in scanning, retouching and digitising many of the images used in this book.

Land Rover is well documented, yet the quest for accuracy remained challenging. Specialists who spot any anomalies should let the publisher know. This applies to facts, and not matters of opinion, which remain our own. As with all Dove Publishing books, thanks are due to production consultant David Bann. Book and cover design by Janet McCallum. Publishing Director, Mike Roberts.

Index

Index

Index

Index

Index

Index

Index

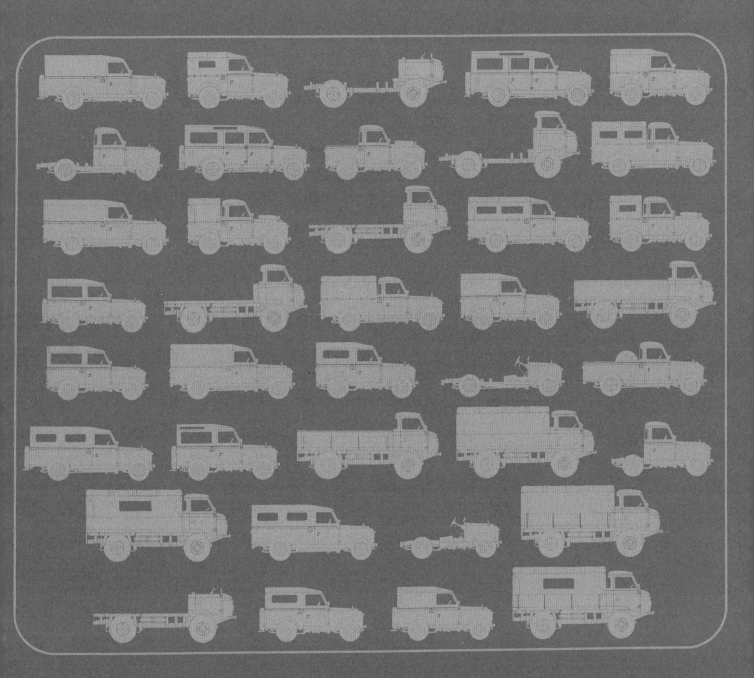

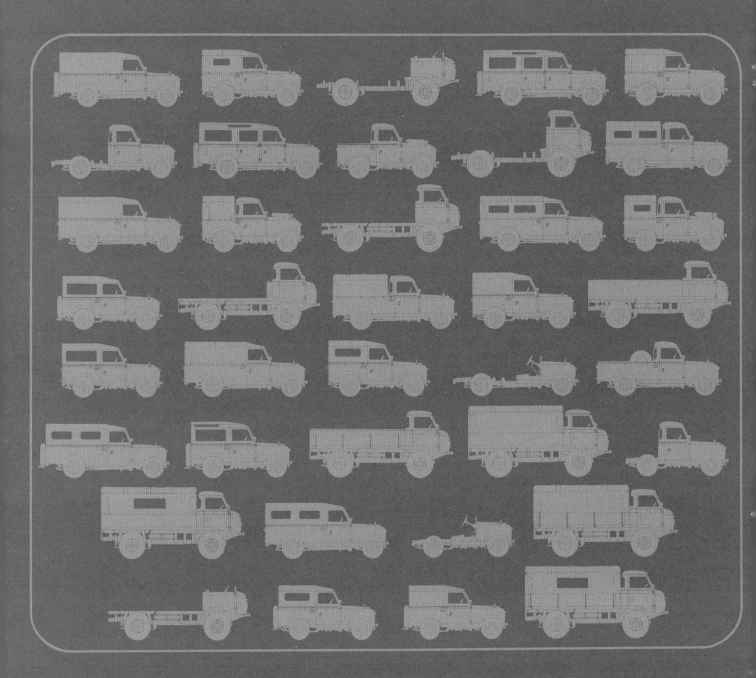